A Guide to Expert Systems

A Guide
to
Expert Systems

Donald A. Waterman
The Rand Corporation

Addison-Wesley Publishing Company

Reading, Massachusetts • Menlo Park, California
Don Mills, Ontario • Wokingham, England • Amsterdam
Sydney • Singapore • Tokyo • Mexico City • Bogotá
Santiago • San Juan

Figure 9.3 on page 101 is reprinted with permission from Mark Stefik, Daniel G. Bobrow, Sanjay Mittal, and Lynn Conway "Knowledge programming in loops," *AI Magazine*, Fall, 1983.

The trace of system output on pages 85–87 is reprinted with permission from Davis and Lenat *Knowledge-Based Systems in Artificial Intelligence*, © 1982, McGraw-Hill Book Company, New York.

Figure 21.1 on page 219 is reprinted with permission from Judith Bachant and John McDermott "R1 revisited: Four years in the trenches," *AI Magazine*, 5:3, 1984.

Library of Congress Cataloging in Publication Data

Waterman, D. A. (Donald Arthur).
  A guide to expert systems.

  Bibliography: p.
  Includes indexes.
  1. Expert systems. I. Title
QA76.9.E96W369 1985   001.53'5 85-6022
ISBN 0-201-08313-2

ABCDEFGHIJ-HA-898765

Series Foreword

In recent years, research in the field of artificial intelligence has had many important successes. Among the most significant of these has been the development of powerful new computer systems known as "expert" or "knowledge-based" systems. These programs are designed to represent and apply factual knowledge of specific areas of expertise to solve problems. For example, collaborative efforts by human experts and system developers have resulted in systems which diagnose diseases, configure computer systems, and prospect for minerals at performance levels equal to or surpassing human expertise. The potential power of systems which can replicate expensive or rare human knowledge has led to a worldwide effort to extend and apply this technology.

The Teknowledge Series in Knowledge Engineering is a collaborative effort by Teknowledge Inc., an editorial board of knowledge system engineers, and Addison-Wesley to aid in this effort through book publication. Through this series we hope to provide an effective channel for informing and educating people interested in understanding and implementing this technology. We will be defining needed works, encouraging their development, and editorially managing their publication. Our intended audience includes practicing knowledge engineers, students and scientists in related disciplines, and technical managers assessing the potential of these systems. Readers with criticisms or suggestions for needed books are urged to contact the managing editor or a member of the editorial board.

Over time, the knowledge engineering field will have an impact on all areas of human activity where knowledge provides the power for solving important problems. We can foresee two beneficial effects. The first and most obvious will be the development of knowledge systems that replicate and autonomously apply human expertise. For these systems, knowledge engineering will provide the technology for converting human knowledge into industrial power. The second benefit may be less obvious. As an inevitable side effect, knowledge engineering will catalyze a global effort to collect, codify, exchange, and exploit applicable forms of human knowledge. In this way, knowledge engineering will accelerate the development, clarification, and expansion of human knowledge itself. If this series contributes to these exciting developments we will have achieved our aims.

Contents

13 Choosing a Tool for Building Expert Systems 142

14 Acquiring Knowledge from the Experts 152

15 An Example of the Expert-System-Building Process 162

SECTION FOUR

Difficulties with Expert System Development 177

16 Difficulties in Developing an Expert System 179

17 Common Pitfalls in Planning an Expert System 186

18 Pitfalls in Dealing with the Domain Expert 192

19 Pitfalls During the Development Process 196

SECTION FIVE

Expert Systems in the Marketplace 201

20 Where Is Expert System Work Being Done? 203

26 Bibliography of Expert Systems 300

27 Index for Expert System Tools 336

28 Catalog of Expert System Tools 339

Preface

This book describes the purpose, structure, and applications of expert systems.

Expert systems are sophisticated computer programs that manipulate knowledge to solve problems efficiently and effectively in a narrow problem area. Like real human experts, these systems use symbolic logic and heuristics—rules of thumb—to find solutions. And like real experts, they make mistakes but have the capacity to learn from their errors. However, this artificial expertise has some advantages over human expertise: It is permanent, consistent, easy to transfer and document, and cheaper. In sum, by linking the power of computers to the richness of human experience, expert systems enhance the value of expert knowledge by making it readily and widely accessible.

The book is designed to meet the needs of a variety of audiences:

- Data processing managers responsible for evaluating or starting an expert system project
- Students with or without programming experience who want an introduction to the basic concepts in the expert systems area
- Professionals who wonder if expert systems can be useful in their fields
- Experienced systems programmers without experience in artificial intelligence who are given the task of building an expert system, and
- High-level managers who want to know what expert systems can do for their companies.

I have organized the discussion to mirror the interests and technical background of each audience. Section I provides a general introduction to expert systems and assumes no computer experience. Section II is especially relevant for readers who want a more detailed examination of the components of expert systems and the tools available to build them. Sections III and IV address the concerns of those charged with deciding whether and how to implement an expert system. Section V surveys expert system work today, makes some predictions for the future, and lists sources for readers who want more information. Section VI presents a catalog of expert systems and tools for those interested in a broad view of work in this area.

A number of people have contributed significantly to the development of this book. The assistance of these people is gratefully acknowledged: Mary Vaiana, for help with the reorganization and rewriting of the text; Jody Paul, for help with the compilation of the catalog sections; Janet DeLand, for editing and proofreading the text; Susan Pond for proofreading; and Dean Schlobohm and Diane Butera for their comments on early versions of the manuscript. Special thanks to Rick Hayes-Roth and Teknowledge for their comments on the final draft.

Santa Monica, California   D.W.

Introduction to Expert Systems

In this section, we provide an overview of expert systems. We define them by examining their basic structure, their uses, and their differences from conventional computer programs. We conclude our overview by looking in some detail at an expert system at work: PROSPECTOR, a system designed to aid exploration geologists.

1

What Are Expert Systems?

A Little History

The phase of the computer revolution that spawned expert systems actually started in the early seventies, in the guise of computer hardware advances destined to send the price of computers plummeting below even the most optimistic scientist's prediction. While computer hardware specialists were developing microchip technology, software specialists—the people who design and build the programs to control the computers—were laying the groundwork for a breakthrough in the software area. But this breakthrough wasn't the invention of a new way to encode information with laser beams or the development of a smaller, faster microchip. It was a conceptual breakthrough in a fledgling field of computer science known as *artificial intelligence*—AI.

The goal of AI scientists had always been to develop computer programs that could in some sense think, that is, solve problems in a way that would be considered intelligent if done by a human. Expert systems are the fruit of a 20-year quest to define the appropriate nature of such programs. Figure 1.1 puts expert systems in their historical context.

In the sixties, AI scientists tried to simulate the complicated process of thinking by finding general methods for solving broad classes of problems; they used these methods in general-purpose programs. However, despite some interesting progress, this strategy produced no breakthroughs. Developing general-purpose programs was too difficult and ultimately fruitless. The more classes of problems a single program could handle, the more poorly it seemed to do on any individual problem.

3

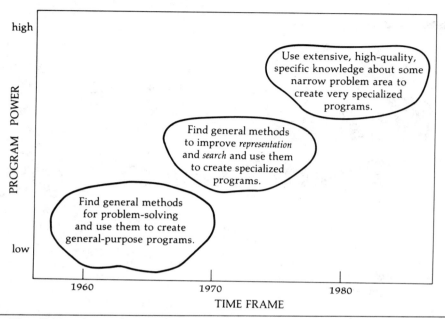

FIGURE 1.1 The shifting focus of AI research.

AI scientists decided there must be another way to make a computer program intelligent. If it was too difficult to make the entire program general purpose, they would concentrate instead on developing general methods or techniques to use in more specialized programs. So during the seventies they concentrated on techniques like *representation*—how to formulate the problem so it would be easy to solve—and *search*—how to cleverly control the search for a solution so it wouldn't take too long or use too much of the computer's memory capacity. Again the strategy produced some successes but no breakthroughs.

It wasn't until the late 1970s that AI scientists began to realize something quite important: The problem-solving power of a program comes from the knowledge it possesses, not just from the formalisms and inference schemes it employs. The conceptual breakthrough was made and can be quite simply stated.

To make a program intelligent, provide it with lots of high-quality, specific knowledge about some problem area.

This realization led to the development of special-purpose computer programs, systems that were expert in some narrow problem area. These programs were called *expert systems*, and a new field began.

At first, designing and building an expert system was considered more an artistic endeavor than a scientific enterprise. Now, however, the process is better understood and more clearly defined, due in part to the efforts of more than 40 AI scientists who collaborated on the seminal volume *Building Expert Systems*, a book that organizes the technical state of the art and describes the use of different expert-system-building techniques on a common problem [HAY83a].

The process of building an expert system is often called *knowledge engineering*. It typically involves a special form of interaction between the expert-system builder, called the *knowledge engineer*, and one or more human experts in some problem area. The knowledge engineer "extracts" from the human experts their procedures, strategies, and rules of thumb for problem solving, and builds this knowledge into the expert system, as shown in Figure 1.2.

The result is a computer program that solves problems in much the same manner as the human experts. The following quote by Paul E. Johnson [JOH83a], a scientist who has spent many years studying the behavior of human experts, quite accurately describes what we mean by the term *expert*.

> An expert is a person who, because of training and experience, is able to do things the rest of us cannot; experts are not only proficient but also smooth and efficient in the actions they take. Experts know a great many things and have tricks and caveats for applying what they know to problems and tasks; they are also good at plowing through irrelevant information in order to get at basic issues, and they are good at recognizing problems they face as instances of types with which they are familiar. Underlying the behavior of experts is the body of operative knowledge we have termed expertise. It is reasonable to suppose, therefore, that experts are the ones to ask when we wish to represent the expertise that makes their behavior possible.

FIGURE 1.2 Knowledge engineering: transferring knowledge from an expert to a computer program.

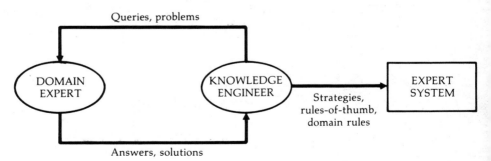

Knowledge engineering relies heavily on the study of human experts in order to develop intelligent, skilled programs. As Hayes-Roth and others point out in the book *Building Expert Systems* [HAY83a]:

> The central notion of intelligent problem-solving is that a system must construct its solution selectively and efficiently from a space of alternatives. When resource-limited, the expert needs to search this space selectively, with as little unfruitful activity as possible. An expert's knowledge helps spot useful data early, suggests promising ways to exploit them, and helps avoid low-payoff efforts by pruning blind alleys as early as possible. *An expert system achieves high performance by using knowledge to make the best use of its time.* [Italics added.]

Features of an Expert System

Let's examine the characteristics of expert systems in more detail.

The heart of an expert system is the powerful *corpus of knowledge* that accumulates during system building. The knowledge is explicit and or-

FIGURE 1.3 General features of an expert system.

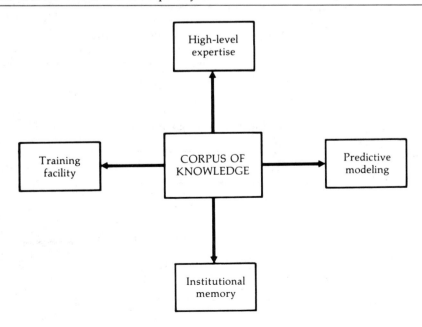

ganized to simplify decision making. The importance of this feature of expert systems cannot be overemphasized:

The accumulation and codification of knowledge is one of the most important aspects of an expert system.

This has implications that go beyond the mere construction of a program to perform some class of tasks. This is because the knowledge that fuels the expert system is *explicit* and *accessible*, unlike most conventional programs. It has the value that any large body of knowledge has and can be widely disseminated via books and lectures.

The most useful feature of an expert system is the *high-level expertise* it provides to aid in problem solving. This expertise can represent the best thinking of the top experts in the field, leading to problem solutions that are imaginative, accurate, and efficient. It's the high-level expertise together with skill at applying it that makes the system cost-effective, able to earn its own way in the commercial marketplace. The system's flexibility also helps here. It can grow incrementally to meet the needs of the business or institution. This means that one can start with a relatively modest investment and expand over time as the need arises.

Another useful feature of an expert system is its *predictive modeling power*. The system can act as an information processing theory or model of problem solving in the given domain, providing the desired answers for a given problem situation and showing how they would change for new situations. The expert system can explain in detail how the new situation led to the change. This lets the user evaluate the potential effect of new facts or data and understand their relationship to the solution. Similarly the user can evaluate the effect of new strategies or procedures on the solution by adding new rules or modifying existing ones.

The corpus of knowledge that defines the proficiency of an expert system can also provide an additional feature, an *institutional memory*. If the knowledge base was developed through interactions with key personnel in an office, department, or billet, it represents the current policy or operating procedures of that group. This compilation of knowledge becomes a consensus of high-level opinion and is a permanent record of the best strategies and methods used by the staff. When key people leave, their expertise is retained. This is important in business and especially critical in military and government with their rapid turnovers and frequent personnel shifts.

A final feature of an expert system is its ability to provide a *training facility* for key personnel and important staff members. Expert systems can be designed to provide such training, since they already contain the necessary knowledge and the ability to explain their reasoning processes. Software must be added to provide a smooth, friendly interface between the trainee and the expert system, and knowledge about teaching methods and user modeling must be included. As a training device the expert system provides new staff members with a vast reservoir of experience and strategies from which to learn about recommended policies and methods. The system can also be adapted to train novices in specific tasks, such as claims adjusting or financial planning.

Who Is Involved in Expert System Building?

The main players in the expert system game are the *expert system*, the *domain expert*, the *knowledge engineer*, the *expert-system-building tool*, and the *user*. Their basic roles and their relationship to each other are summarized in Figure 1.4.

The expert system is the collection of programs or computer software that solves problems in the domain of interest. It's called a system rather than just a program because it contains both a problem-solving component and a support component. This *support environment* helps the user interact with the main program and may include sophisticated debugging aids to help the expert-system builder test

FIGURE 1.4 The players in the expert system game.

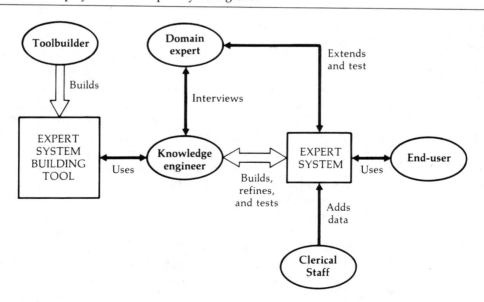

and evaluate the program's code, friendly editing facilities to help the experts modify knowledge and data in the expert system, and advanced graphic devices to help the user input and read information as the system is running.

The domain or area expert is an articulate, knowledgeable person with a reputation for producing good solutions to problems in a particular field. The expert uses tricks and shortcuts to make the search for a solution more efficient, and the expert system models these problem-solving strategies. Although an expert system usually models one or more experts, it may also contain expertise from other sources such as books and journal articles.

The knowledge engineer is a human, usually with a background in computer science and AI, who knows how to build expert systems. The knowledge engineer interviews the experts, organizes the knowledge, decides how it should be represented in the expert system, and may help programmers to write the code.

The expert-system-building tool is the programming language used by the knowledge engineer or programmer to build the expert system. These tools differ from conventional programming languages in that they provide convenient ways to represent complex, high-level concepts (see Chapters 3 and 4). In AI jargon, the term *tool* usually refers both to the programming language and to the support environment used to build the expert system.

The user is the human who uses the expert system once it is developed. The user may be a scientist using the system to help discover new mineral deposits, a lawyer using it to help settle a case, or a student using it to learn more about organic chemistry. The term *user* is a bit ambiguous. It normally refers to the *end-user*, the person for whom the expert system was developed. However, in this book it will refer to anyone who uses the expert system. As Figure 1.4 suggests, the user may be a *tool builder* debugging the expert-system-building language, a *knowledge engineer* refining the existing knowledge in the system, a *domain expert* adding new knowledge to the system, an *end-user* relying on the system for advice, or a member of the *clerical staff* adding data to the system.

It is important to distinguish between the tool used to build the expert system and the expert system itself. The expert-system-building tool includes both the language used to represent and access the knowledge contained in the system and the support environment—programs that help the users to interact with the problem-solving component of the expert system. Even computer scientists may blur these distinctions. The support environment is, by definition, also part of the completed expert system. Since the user interacts with the expert system through

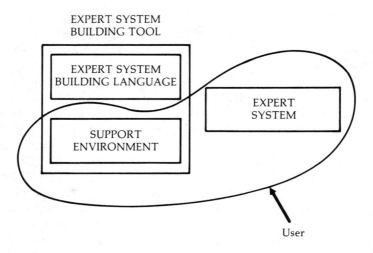

FIGURE 1.5 The expert-system-building tool is not the expert system.

the support environment, it is easy to see how the confusion can arise. Figure 1.5 illustrates the distinction.

The most important terms discussed in this chapter are summarized in Table 1.1. For a more complete description of these concepts, see the glossary of expert system terms at the end of the book.

TABLE 1.1 Basic expert system terminology.

Term	Meaning
Artificial intelligence	The part of computer science concerned with developing intelligent computer programs.
Domain expert	A person who through years of training and experience has become extremely proficient at problem solving in a particular domain.
End-user	The person who uses the finished expert system; the person for whom the system was developed.

Continued

TABLE 1.1 Continued

Term	Meaning
Expert system	A computer program using expert knowledge to attain high levels of performance in a narrow problem area.
Expert-system-building tool	The programming language and support package used to build the expert system.
Knowledge engineering	The process of building expert systems.
Knowledge engineer	The person who designs and builds the expert system.
Representation	The process of formulating or viewing a problem so it will be easy to solve.
Search	The process of skillfully looking through the set of possible solutions to a problem so as to efficiently find an acceptable solution.
Support environment	Facilities associated with an expert-system-building tool that help the user interact with the expert system. These may include sophisticated debugging aids, friendly editing programs, and advanced graphic devices.
Tool	A shorthand notation for expert-system-building tool.
Tool builder	The person who designs and builds the expert-system-building tool.
User	A person who uses an expert system, such as an end-user, a domain expert, a knowledge engineer, a tool builder, or a clerical staff member.

2

What Good Are Expert Systems?

Why Not Use Real Experts?

Let's ask the obvious question: Why develop expert systems rather than rely on human expertise as we have done in the past?

There are some excellent reasons for using artificial expertise to augment human reasoning [KAP84]. Some of these advantages are summarized in Table 2.1.

One advantage of artificial expertise is its permanence. Human expertise can quickly fade, regardless of whether it involves mental or physical activity. An expert must constantly practice and rehearse to maintain proficiency in some problem area. Any significant period of disuse can seriously affect the expert's performance. The adage "use it

TABLE 2.1 Comparing human and artificial expertise: the good news.

The Good News	
Human Expertise	Artificial Expertise
Perishable	Permanent
Difficult to transfer	Easy to transfer
Difficult to document	Easy to document
Unpredictable	Consistent
Expensive	Affordable

or lose it" certainly applies here. However, the adage does not apply to artificial expertise. Once it is acquired, it is around forever, barring catastrophic accidents related to memory storage. Its permanence is not related to its use.

Another advantage of artificial expertise is the ease with which it can be transferred or reproduced. Transferring knowledge from one human to another is the laborious, lengthy, and expensive process called education (or in some cases, knowledge engineering). Transferring artificial expertise is the trivial process of copying or cloning a program or data file.

Artificial expertise is also much easier to document. Documenting human expertise is extremely difficult and time-consuming, as any experienced knowledge engineer will verify. Documenting artificial expertise is relatively easy. There is a straightforward mapping between the way in which the expertise is represented in the system and the natural language description of that representation.

Artificial expertise produces more consistent, reproducible results than does human expertise. A human expert may make different decisions in identical situations because of emotional factors. For example, a human may forget to use an important rule in a crisis situation because of time pressures or stress. An expert system is not susceptible to these distractions.

A final advantage of artificial expertise is its low cost. Human experts, especially the top-notch ones, are very scarce, and hence very expensive. They demand large salaries and get them. Expert systems, by contrast, are relatively inexpensive. They are costly to develop but cheap to operate. Their operating cost is just the nominal computer cost of running the program. Their high development cost (years of effort by high-priced knowledge engineers and domain experts) is offset by their low operating cost and the ease with which new copies of the system can be made.

Why Keep a Human in the Loop?

If artificial expertise is so much better than human expertise, why not eliminate human experts, replacing them with expert systems? The most highly skilled expert can perhaps be eliminated, but in many situations a moderately skilled expert should be kept in the loop. The expert system can then be used to augment and enhance this user's skills.

There are some very good reasons for not entirely eliminating the human from the loop.

TABLE 2.2 Comparing human and artificial expertise: the bad news.

The Bad News	
Human Expertise	Artificial Expertise
Creative	Uninspired
Adaptive	Needs to be told
Sensory experience	Symbolic input
Broad focus	Narrow focus
Commonsense knowledge	Technical knowledge

Although expert systems tend to perform well, there are important areas in which human expertise is clearly superior to the artificial kind. This doesn't reflect a fundamental limitation of AI, just the current state of the art.

One such area is creativity. People are much more creative and innovative than even the smartest programs. A human expert can reorganize information and use it to synthesize new knowledge, while an expert system tends to behave in a somewhat uninspired, routine manner. Human experts handle unexpected events by using imaginative and novel approaches to problem solving, including drawing analogies to situations in completely different problem domains. Programs have had little success doing this.

Another area where human expertise excels is learning. Human experts adapt to changing conditions; they adjust their strategies to conform to new situations. Expert systems are not particularly adept at learning new concepts or rules, probably because this is a very difficult task that has always been somewhat of a stumbling block for AI. Progress has been made in developing programs that learn, but these programs tend to work in extremely simple domains and don't do well when confronted with the complexity and detail of real-world problems.

Human experts can make direct use of complex sensory input, whether it be visual, auditory, tactile, or olfactory. But expert systems manipulate symbols that represent ideas and concepts, so sensory data must be transformed into symbols that can be understood by the system. Quite a bit of information may be lost in the translation, especially when visual scenes are mapped into sets of objects and the relations between them. The old saying "a picture is worth a thousand words" turns out to be an understatement in this case.

Human experts can look at the big picture—examine all aspects of a problem and see how they relate to the central issue. Expert systems, on the other hand, tend to focus on the problem itself, ignoring issues relevant to, but separate from, the basic problem. This happens because it takes a huge amount of expertise just to handle the basic problem, and it would take almost as much expertise to handle each of the hundreds of tangential problems that could arise. Although they might affect the basic problem, they're not likely to occur, making it less than cost-effective to acquire the knowledge needed to handle them. In the future, when faster and cheaper techniques for acquiring expert knowledge are developed, this situation may change.

Finally, human experts and nonexperts alike have what we might call *commonsense knowledge*. This is a very broad spectrum of general knowledge about the world and how it works, knowledge that virtually everyone has and uses. Because of the enormous quantity of commonsense knowledge, there is no easy way to build it into an intelligent program, particularly a specialist like an expert system.

As an example of commonsense knowledge, suppose you are given a medical history that refers to a patient's weight as 14 pounds and age as 110 years. You would immediately suspect an error in the data, not because a person couldn't weigh 14 pounds or be 110 years old, but because the combination of the two is virtually impossible. In fact, you might suspect that the two entries had accidentally been reversed. An expert system designed to perform medical decision making would probably not catch this type of error unless it had been given tables of likely age/weight ratios to check against the data.

Commonsense knowledge includes knowing what you don't know as well as what you do know. For example, if you were asked to recall the phone number of your previous residence, you would search your memory, trying to retrieve the information. If you were asked to give the phone number of England's prime minister, you would know immediately that you didn't know the answer and not even try a retrieval. If you were asked the phone number of Shakespeare, you would know at once that no answer exists, since telephones weren't around in Shakespeare's time. When an expert system is given questions it can't answer or for which no answer exists, it doesn't have the common sense to give up. Instead, it may waste much time searching through its data and rules for the solution. Even worse, when the solution isn't found, it may think it's because its knowledge is incomplete and ask for additional information to complete the knowledge base.

For these reasons and others relating to the public acceptance of artificial expertise, expert systems are often used in an advisory capacity—as a consultant or aid to either an expert or novice user in some problem area.

3

How Are Expert Systems Organized?

We have stressed that the heart of an expert system is its corpus of knowledge, structured to support decision making. How is that knowledge organized and represented?

Organizing Knowledge

When AI scientists use the term *knowledge,* they mean the information a computer program needs before it can behave intelligently. This information can take the form of facts or rules like those shown below.

> **FACTS:** Tank #23 contains sulfuric acid.
> The plaintiff was injured by a portable power saw.
> **RULES:** If the sulfate ion test is positive,
> the spill material is sulfuric acid.
> If the plaintiff was negligent in the use of the product,
> the theory of contributory negligence applies.

Facts and rules in an expert system aren't always either true or false; sometimes there is a degree of uncertainty about the validity of a fact or the accuracy of a rule. When this doubt is made explicit, it's called a *certainty factor.* The use of certainty factors is illustrated below.

> **FACTS:** Building 3047 contains tank #23 with certainty 1.0.
> The power saw was defective with certainty 0.8.
> **RULES:** If the spill material is sulfuric acid with certainty 1.0,
> the source of the spill is building 3047 with certainty 0.9.
> If the product was defective with certainty >0.5,
> the theory of strict liability applies with certainty 1.0.

Many of the rules in expert systems are *heuristics*—rules of thumb or simplifications that effectively limit the search for solutions. Expert systems use heuristics because the tasks these systems undertake, such as finding new mineral deposits or settling a lawsuit, are typically difficult and poorly understood. They tend to resist rigorous mathematical analysis or algorithmic solutions. An algorithmic method guarantees to produce the correct or optimal solution to a problem, while a heuristic method produces an acceptable solution most of the time.

Figure 3.1 illustrates the difference between algorithmic and heuristic methods. Here we compare an algorithm to prevent the skyjacking of commercial airliners with a heuristic to accomplish the same thing.

The algorithm given here would certainly stop skyjackings since it virtually guarantees that no one could board the plane with a weapon. Unfortunately, it would be too time-consuming, expensive, and—most of all—unpopular to be of any practical value. The heuristic presented here would also stop most skyjackings but could not guarantee that they wouldn't occur. The use of heuristic rules makes the search for solutions much easier and more practical.

FIGURE 3.1 Algorithmic versus heuristic methods.

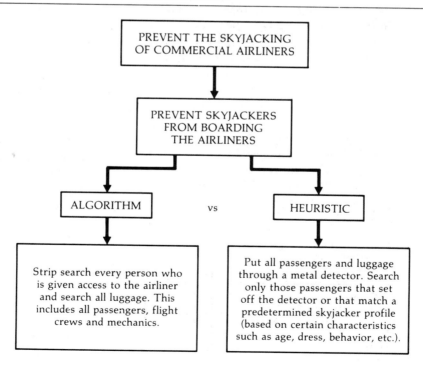

The knowledge in an expert system is *organized* in a way that separates the knowledge about the problem domain from the system's other knowledge, such as general knowledge about how to solve problems or knowledge about how to interact with the user—for example, how to print characters at the user's terminal or modify lines of data in response to the user's commands. This collection of domain knowledge is called the *knowledge base*, while the general problem-solving knowledge is called the *inference engine*. A program with knowledge organized this way is called a *knowledge-based system*.

As Figure 3.2 indicates, virtually all expert systems are knowledge-based systems, while the converse is not necessarily true. An AI program to play tic-tac-toe would not be considered an expert system, even if the domain knowledge was separated from the rest of the program.

The knowledge base in an expert system contains facts (data) and rules (or other representations) that use those facts as the basis for decision making. The inference engine contains an interpreter that decides how to apply the rules to infer new knowledge and a scheduler that decides the order in which the rules should be applied. This organization is shown in Figure 3.3.

Having the domain knowledge separate makes it easier for the knowledge engineer to design procedures for manipulating this knowledge. How the system uses its knowledge is of the utmost importance because an expert system must have both *the appropriate knowledge* and *the means to use the knowledge effectively* to be considered *skilled* at some task. Thus to be skilled, an expert system must have a knowledge base containing lots of high-powered knowledge about the problem domain

FIGURE 3.2 Expert systems are knowledge-based systems.

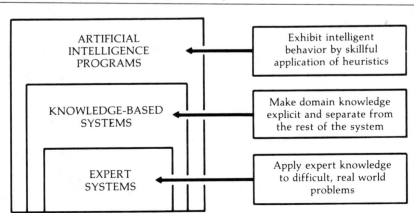

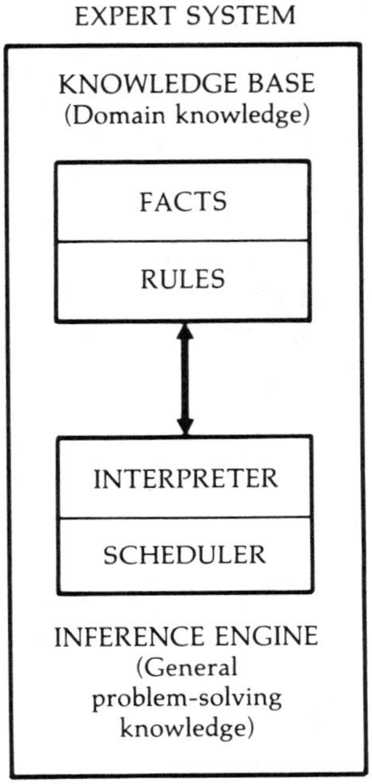

EXPERT SYSTEM

```
┌─────────────────────────────────────┐
│        KNOWLEDGE BASE                │
│        (Domain knowledge)            │
│   ┌─────────────────────────────┐   │
│   │           FACTS             │   │
│   ├─────────────────────────────┤   │
│   │           RULES             │   │
│   └─────────────────────────────┘   │
│                 ↕                    │
│   ┌─────────────────────────────┐   │
│   │        INTERPRETER          │   │
│   ├─────────────────────────────┤   │
│   │         SCHEDULER           │   │
│   └─────────────────────────────┘   │
│       INFERENCE ENGINE              │
│          (General                   │
│       problem-solving               │
│         knowledge)                  │
└─────────────────────────────────────┘
```

FIGURE 3.3 The structure of an expert system.

and an inference engine containing knowledge about how to make effective use of the domain knowledge.

The concept of the *inference engine* often causes some confusion among newcomers to the expert systems area. It's usually fairly clear how domain expertise can be written as facts and rules but not so clear how to construct and use the so-called "inference engine." This confusion occurs because there is no simple, general way to characterize an inference engine. How it should be structured depends on both the nature of the problem domain and the way in which knowledge is represented and organized in the expert system. Many high-level expert-system-building languages, e.g., EMYCIN [MEL81], have the inference engine, in some sense, built in as part of the language. Other lower-level languages, e.g., LISP [SIK76], require the expert-system builder to design and implement the inference engine.

Both approaches have their advantages and disadvantages. A high-level language with the inference engine built in means less work for the expert-system builder. However, the builder also has fewer options regarding how knowledge can be organized and accessed and must look very carefully at the question of whether or not this prefabricated control scheme is really appropriate for the problem domain being considered. A lower-level language with no inference engine requires a greater development effort, but it provides some basic building blocks so that the system developer can tailor the control scheme to the needs of the problem domain.

The inference engine is not an all-or-none proposition. Some expert-system-building tools, e.g., HEARSAY-III, have a set of inference mechanisms built in but allow the builder to augment or redefine these mechanisms to fit the problem domain. (Expert-system-building tools are discussed in more detail in Section II.)

Representing Knowledge

Finally, let's consider how knowledge is structured in a program—*knowledge representation*. There are a standard set of knowledge representation techniques, any of which can be used alone or in conjunction with others to build expert systems. Each technique provides the program with certain benefits, such as making it more efficient, more easily understood, or more easily modified. An excellent summary of the most important techniques can be found in the *Handbook of Artificial Intelligence* [BAR81]. The three most widely used in current expert systems are rules (the most popular), semantic nets, and frames. We describe them here briefly and discuss them in more detail in Chapter 7.

Rule-based Methods

Rule-based knowledge representation centers on the use of IF *condition* THEN *action* statements. For example,

> **[1]** If the patient was an insulator before 1965,
> then the patient directly handled asbestos.
> **[2]** If the patient directly handled asbestos and
> the patient was exposed in confined spaces,
> then the patient had a severe exposure.

When the current problem situation satisfies or matches the IF part of a rule, the action specified by the THEN part of the rule is performed. This action may affect the outside world (e.g., cause text to be printed at the user's terminal), may direct program control (e.g., cause a particular set of rules to be tested and fired), or may instruct the system to reach a conclusion (e.g., add a new fact or hypothesis to the database).

This matching of rule IF portions to the facts can produce what are called *inference chains*. The inference chain formed from successive exe-

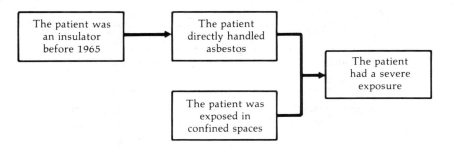

FIGURE 3.4 Inference chain for inferring the severity of asbestos exposure.

cution of rules **1** and **2** is shown in Figure 3.4. This inference chain indicates how the system used the rules to infer the severity of the patient's exposure to asbestos.

Rules provide a natural way for describing processes driven by a complex and rapidly changing environment. A set of rules can specify how the program should react to the changing data without requiring detailed advance knowledge about the flow of control. In a conventional program, the flow of control and use of data are predetermined by the program's code. Processing takes place in sequential steps, and branching occurs only at selected choice points. This works fine for problems with algorithmic solutions and slowly changing data such as solving a set of simultaneous linear equations. This doesn't work very well for problems driven by the data, where branching is the norm rather than the exception. For problems like these, rules offer the opportunity to examine the state of the world at each step and react appropriately. The use of rules also simplifies the job of explaining what the program did or how it reached a particular conclusion (see Chapter 8).

Frame-based Methods

We consider both frame and semantic nets to be frame-based representation methods. Frame-based knowledge representation uses a network of nodes connected by relations and organized into a hierarchy. Each node represents a concept that may be described by attributes and values associated with the node. Nodes low in the hierarchy automatically inherit properties of higher-level nodes. These methods provide a natural, efficient way to categorize and structure a taxonomy, such as ore deposits or medical diseases.

This chapter's most important terms are summarized in Table 3.1. For a more complete description of these concepts, see the glossary of expert system terms at the end of the book.

TABLE 3.1 More expert-system terminology.

Term	Meaning
Algorithm	A formal procedure guaranteed to produce correct or optimal solutions.
Certainty factor	A number that measures the certainty or confidence one has that a fact or rule is valid.
Domain knowledge	Knowledge about the problem domain; e.g., knowledge about geology in an expert system for finding mineral deposits.
Frame	A knowledge representation method that associates features with nodes representing concepts or objects. The features are described in terms of attributes (called *slots*) and their values.
Heuristic	A rule of thumb or simplification that limits the search for solutions in domains that are difficult and poorly understood. (also Heuristic Rule)
Inference engine	That part of a knowledge-based system or expert system that contains the general problem-solving knowledge.
Interpreter	The part of the inference engine that decides how to apply the domain knowledge.
Knowledge	The information a computer program must have to behave intelligently.
Knowledge representation	The process of structuring knowledge about a problem in a way that makes the problem easier to solve.

Continued

TABLE 3.1 Continued

Term	Meaning
Knowledge-based system	A program in which the domain knowledge is explicit and separate from the program's other knowledge.
Knowledge base	The portion of a knowledge-based system or expert system that contains the domain knowledge.
Rule	A formal way of specifying a recommendation, directive, or strategy, expressed as IF *premise* THEN *conclusion* or IF *condition* THEN *action*.
Scheduler	The part of the inference engine that decides when and in what order to apply different pieces of domain knowledge.
Semantic net	A knowledge representation method consisting of a network of nodes, standing for concepts or objects, connected by arcs describing the relations between the nodes.

4

How Do Expert Systems Differ from Conventional Programs?

Another way to define expert systems is to compare them with ordinary programs. The most basic difference is that expert systems manipulate *knowledge* while conventional programs manipulate *data*. Teknowledge, a company devoted to engineering commercial expert systems, characterizes the differences as shown in Table 4.1.

In Chapter 3, we discussed how expert systems use heuristics and inferential processes and considered some of the common ways in which their knowledge base is represented.

TABLE 4.1 Comparison of data processing and knowledge engineering.

Data Processing	Knowledge Engineering
Representations and use of data	Representation and use of knowledge
Algorithmic	Heuristic
Repetitive process	Inferential process
Effective manipulation of large data bases	Effective manipulation of large knowledge bases

Basic Characteristics of an Expert System

AI researchers have a somewhat more restricted (and more complex) view of an expert system [BRA83]. An expert system is defined as a computer program that has the properties shown in Figure 4.1.

Let's consider each of these characteristics in more detail.

Expertise

An expert system must perform well, that is, achieve the same levels of performance in the domain of interest that human experts can achieve. But simply producing good solutions is not enough. Real experts not only produce good solutions but often find them quickly, while novices tend to take much longer to find the same solutions. Thus an expert system must be *skillful*—apply its knowledge to produce solutions both efficiently and effectively, using the shortcuts or tricks that human experts use to eliminate wasteful or unnecessary calculations. To truly mimic a human expert, an expert system must also have *robustness*. This means having not only depth in a subject, but breadth as well. This can be achieved by using general knowledge and problem-solving methods to reason from first principles when given incorrect data or incomplete rules. This is one of the least developed techniques in current expert systems, but one that human experts do easily.

FIGURE 4.1 Characteristics of an expert system that distinguish it from a conventional program.

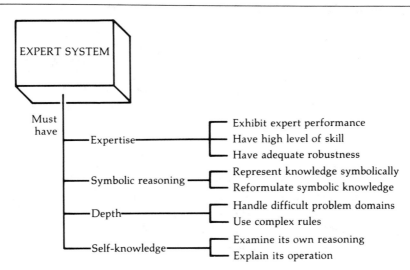

Symbolic Reasoning

When human experts solve problems, particularly the type we consider appropriate for expert system work, they don't do it by solving sets of equations or performing other laborious mathematical computations. Instead they choose symbols to represent the problem concepts and apply various strategies and heuristics to manipulate these concepts. An expert system also represents knowledge symbolically, as sets of symbols that stand for problem concepts. In AI jargon a *symbol* is a string of characters that stands for some real-world concept [STE83a]. Examples of symbols are shown below.

    product
    defendant
    0.8

These symbols can be combined to express relationships between them. When these relationships are represented in an AI program they are called *symbol structures*. The following are examples of symbol structures:

    (DEFECTIVE product)
    (LEASED-BY product defendant)
    (EQUAL (LIABILITY defendant) 0.8)

These structures can be interpreted to mean "the product is defective," "the product is leased by the defendant," and "the liability of the defendant is 0.8."

To solve a problem, an expert system manipulates these symbols rather than performing standard mathematical computations. This is not to say that expert systems don't do math; rather the emphasis is on manipulating symbols. The consequence of this approach is that *knowledge representation*—the choice, form, and interpretation of the symbols used—becomes very important. Also, experts can take a problem stated in some arbitrary manner and convert it to a form that lends itself to a fast or efficient solution. This *problem reformulation* capability is something expert systems need to make their skill level closer to that of human experts. Unfortunately, most current expert systems do not have this capability.

Depth

An expert system has depth; that is, it operates effectively in a narrow domain containing difficult, challenging problems. Thus the rules in an expert system are necessarily complicated, either through their individual complexity or their sheer number. Expert systems typically work in real-world problem domains, rather than what AI scientists call *toy do-*

mains. In a real-world domain, the problem solver applies actual data to a practical problem and produces solutions that are useful in some cost-effective way. In a toy domain, the problem is usually a gross simplification or unrealistic adaptation of some complex real-world problem. The problem solver handles artificial data that are simplified to make the problem easier and produces solutions that are of theoretical interest only.

The distinction between real-world and toy domains is important to understand because, as we will see in Chapter 11, defining an appropriate problem scope for an expert system is absolutely crucial to its success. We now illustrate this distinction.

A real-world domain is case settlement in product liability law [WAT81]. The data would include the facts of the case, such as medical reports, eyewitness reports, correspondence between attorneys, and other documents relating to the litigation. The problem would be to determine a fair and equitable settlement amount for the case. The solution might be an estimate of case worth and a recommendation of a settlement amount.

A toy domain is *the blocks world*, as it's known in AI circles. It consists of a set of children's blocks on a clear flat board. The data are representations of the block configurations and relationships to one another. The problem is to devise a plan for manipulating the blocks in some way, such as stacking them in a pile or clearing them off some object. The solution might be a plan stating how to go about stacking them all in a pile with the largest on the bottom. A program that produced plans of this sort, however accurate, would not be considered an expert system.

AI researchers working in the expert systems area tend to avoid toy domains completely. They do this to steer clear of a classic problem in artificial intelligence, the *scaling problem*, illustrated in Figure 4.2.

When gross simplifying assumptions are made about a complex problem and its data, the resulting solution may not scale up to the point where it's applicable to the real problem. The methods needed for representing and organizing knowledge and for applying problem-solving techniques to that knowledge are often tied to the size and complexity of the *search space*, the set of possible intermediate and final solutions to the problem. When the problem is oversimplified or unrealistic, the search space is likely to be reduced and issues of speed and efficiency don't have to be faced. This problem arises so naturally and subtly that even researchers with extensive experience in AI can fall victim to it.

Self-Knowledge

An expert system has knowledge that lets it reason about its own operation plus a structure that simplifies this reasoning process. For example,

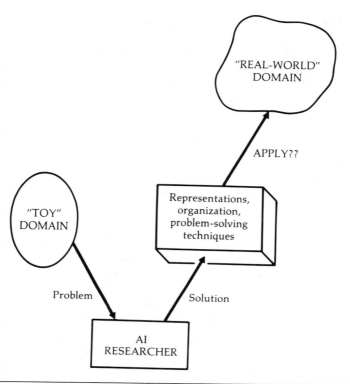

FIGURE 4.2 The scaling problem in AI.

if an expert system is organized as sets of rules, then it can easily look at the inference chains it produces to reach a conclusion. If it's given special rules that tell it what to do with these inference chains, it can use them to check the accuracy, consistency, and plausibility of its conclusions and can even devise arguments that justify or explain its reasoning. This knowledge the system has about how it reasons is called *metaknowledge*, which just means knowledge about knowledge.

Most current expert systems have what is called an *explanation facility*. This is knowledge for explaining how the system arrived at its answers. Most of these explanations involve displaying the inference chains and explaining the rationale behind each rule used in the chain. The ability to examine their reasoning processes and explain their operation is one of the most innovative and important qualities of expert systems. Why is it so important?

Self-knowledge is important in an expert system because:

- Users tend to have more faith in the results, more confidence in the system.
- System development is faster since the system is easier to debug.
- The assumptions underlying the system's operation are made explicit rather than being implicit.
- It's easier to predict and test the effect of a change on the system operation.

Explanation is just one small aspect of self-knowledge. In the future, self-knowledge will allow expert systems to do even more. They will be able to create the rationale behind individual rules by reasoning from first principles. They will tailor their explanations to fit the requirements of their audience. And they will be able to change their own internal structure through rule correction, knowledge-base reorganization, and system reconfiguration [LEN83].

A first step in this direction is to make the expert system's metaknowledge separate and explicit, just as the domain knowledge is now made separate and explicit. An example of metaknowledge, knowledge about how to use the domain knowledge, is shown below.

> **IF:** More than one rule applies to the situation,
> **THEN:** Use rules supplied by experts before rules supplied by novices.

This metarule tells the expert system how to select the domain rules to execute. AI researchers are just beginning to experiment with the form and organization of metaknowledge in expert systems.

Expert Systems Make Mistakes

There is another important way in which expert systems differ from conventional programs. While conventional programs are designed to produce the correct answer every time, expert systems are designed to behave like experts, usually producing correct answers but sometimes producing incorrect ones. John McDermott, describing the development of an expert system for configuring VAX-11 computer systems for the Digital Equipment Corporation [MCD81], neatly summarizes the problem:

> . . . I have hammered on the theme that a knowledge-based program must pass through a relatively lengthy apprenticeship stage and that even after it has become an expert, it will, like all experts, occasionally make mistakes. The first part of this message got through, but I suspect

that the second has not. My concern, then, is whether, as this characteristic of expert systems is recognized, Digital (or any large corporation) will be emotionally prepared to give a significant amount of responsibility to programs that are known to be fallible.

At first glance it would seem that conventional programs have a distinct advantage over expert systems in this regard. However, the advantage is an illusion. Conventional programs for performing complex tasks, like those suitable for expert systems, will also make mistakes. *But their mistakes will be very difficult to remedy since the strategies, heuristics, and basic assumptions upon which these programs are based will not be explicitly stated in the program code.* Thus they cannot be easily identified and corrected. Expert systems, like their human counterparts, will make mistakes. But, unlike conventional programs, they have the potential to learn from their errors. With the help of skillful users, expert systems can be made to improve their problem-solving abilities on the job.

The most important terms discussed in this chapter are summarized in Table 4.2. For a more complete description of these concepts, see the glossary of expert system terms at the end of the book.

TABLE 4.2 More expert system terminology.

Term	Meaning
Explanation facility	That part of an expert system that explains how solutions were reached and justifies the steps used to reach them.
Metaknowledge	Knowledge in an expert system about how the system operates or reasons. More generally, knowledge about knowledge.
Problem reformulation	Converting a problem stated in some arbitrary way to a form that lends itself to a fast, efficient solution.
Real-world problem	A complex, practical problem whose solution is useful in some cost-effective way.
Robustness	That quality of a problem solver that permits a gradual degradation in performance when it is pushed to the limits

Continued

TABLE 4.2 Continued

Term	*Meaning*
	of its scope of expertise or is given faulty, inconsistent, or incomplete data or rules.
Scaling problem	The difficulty associated with trying to apply problem-solving techniques developed for a simplified version of a problem to the actual problem itself.
Search space	The set of all possible solutions to a problem.
Skill	The efficient and effective application of knowledge to produce solutions in some problem domain.
Symbol	A string of characters that stands for some real-world concept.
Symbolic reasoning	Problem solving based on the application of strategies and heuristics to manipulate symbols standing for problem concepts.
Toy problem	An artificial problem, such as a game or an unrealistic adaptation of a complex problem.

5

What Have Expert Systems Been Used For?

We can broaden our understanding of expert systems by reviewing some of their most characteristic uses. In this chapter, we'll describe these uses from two perspectives: the basic activities of expert systems and the areas in which they solve problems. Together, these perspectives provide a vision of the breadth of application, the diversity of data, and the variety of knowledge representation forms found in expert systems currently in use.

Basic Activities of Expert Systems

Expert systems have been built to solve many different types of problems, but their basic activities can be grouped into the categories shown in Table 5.1.[1] Below we define each of these activities, describe the kinds of data typically involved, and give examples of how knowledge is represented in expert systems currently performing these activities.

Expert systems that perform *interpretation* typically use sensor data to infer situation descriptions. An example is interpreting gauge readings in a chemical process plant to infer the status of the process. Interpretation systems deal directly with real data rather than with clean symbolic representations of the problem situation. They face difficulties that many other types of systems avoid because they may have to handle data that are noisy, sparse, incomplete, unreliable, or erroneous.

[1]Adapted from *Building Expert Systems* [HAY83b].

TABLE 5.1 Generic categories of expert system applications.

Category	Problem Addressed
Interpretation	Inferring situation descriptions from sensor data
Prediction	Inferring likely consequences of given situations
Diagnosis	Inferring system malfunctions from observables
Design	Configuring objects under constraints
Planning	Designing actions
Monitoring	Comparing observations to expected outcomes
Debugging	Prescribing remedies for malfunctions
Repair	Executing plans to administer prescribed remedies
Instruction	Diagnosing, debugging, and repairing student behavior
Control	Governing overall system behavior.

They need special techniques for extracting features from continuous data streams, waveforms, or pictures, and methods for representing them symbolically.

A typical rule from an interpretation system is shown below. The system, SPE [WEI84], interprets waveforms from a scanning densitometer to distinguish between different causes of inflammatory conditions in medical patients.

> **IF:** The tracing pattern is "asymmetric gamma"
> and the gamma quantity is normal (correlated with age)
> **THEN:** The concentration of gammaglobulin is within
> the normal range.

Interpretation systems may process many different kinds of data. For example, both vision and speech understanding systems use natural input—visual images in one case, audio signals in the other—to infer features and meaning. Chemical interpretation systems use X-ray diffraction data or mass spectral and nuclear magnetic response data to infer the structure of compounds. Geological interpretation systems use dipmeter logs—measurements of rock conductivity in and around holes bored in the earth—to determine subsurface geological structure. Medical interpretation systems use measurements from patient monitoring systems (e.g., heart rate, blood pressure) to diagnose and treat illnesses. Finally, military interpretation systems use signals from radar, radio, and sonar devices to perform situation assessment and target identification.

Expert systems that perform *prediction* infer the likely consequences of given situations. Examples are predicting the damage to crops from some type of insect, estimating global oil demand from the current geopolitical world situation, and predicting where armed conflict will next occur based on intelligence reports. Prediction systems sometimes use simulation models, programs that mirror real-world activity, to generate situations or scenarios that could occur from particular input data. These potential situations, together with knowledge about the processes that originated them, form the basis for the predictions. AI researchers have developed relatively few prediction systems to date, possibly because of the difficulty in creating and interfacing with simulation models.

An example of a rule from a prediction system is given below. The system, PLANT/cd [BOU83], predicts Black Cutworm damage to corn using a simulation model to perform needed computations.

> **IF:**   1) The Black Cutworm vs. leafstage table has been computed,
> 2) Whether there are greater than 4 weeds/foot of row is known,
> 3) The corn variety is known, and
> 4) The soil moisture in the field is known
>
> **THEN:**   Compute the corn yield without insecticide treatment and assign it the variable YIELD1.

Expert systems that perform *diagnosis* use situation descriptions, behavior characteristics, or knowledge about component design to infer probable causes of system malfunctions. Examples are determining the causes of diseases from symptoms observed in patients, locating faults in electrical circuits, and finding defective components in the coolant systems of nuclear reactors. Diagnosis systems are often consultants that not only diagnose the problem but also assist with *debugging*. They may interact with the user to help find the faults and then suggest courses of action to correct them. The medical domain seems quite a natural one for diagnosis applications, and indeed, more diagnosis systems have been developed for medicine than for any other single problem area. However, many diagnosis systems are now being built for engineering and computer systems applications.

An example of a rule from a diagnosis system is given below. The system, called MYCIN [SHO76], diagnoses bacterial infections in hospital patients.

> **IF:** 1) The stain of the organism is grampos, and
> 2) The morphology of the organism is coccus, and
> 3) The growth conformation of the organism is chains
>
> **THEN:** There is suggestive evidence (0.7) that the
> identity of the organism is streptococcus.

Expert systems that perform *design* develop configurations of objects based on a set of problem constraints. Examples are gene cloning, designing integrated circuit layouts, and creating complex organic molecules. Design systems often use synthesis to construct partial designs and simulation to verify or test design ideas. Because design is so closely coupled with *planning*, many design systems provide mechanisms for developing and refining plans to achieve the desired design. The design system can save much unnecessary search by creating plans for producing the wanted configuration and evaluating them in the context of the problem constraints. The two most popular application areas for design systems seem to be molecular biology and microelectronics. This may be due to the current interest of venture capitalists rather than to any fundamental properties of those problem domains.

An example of a rule from a design system is shown below. The system, called XCON (also referred to as R1) [MCD82], configures VAX computer systems. This rule helps assign power supplies to the SBI, a high-speed synchronous bus that interconnects the VAX computer components.

> **IF:** The most current active context is assigning a power supply
> and an SBI module of any type has been put in a cabinet
> and the position it occupies in the cabinet (its nexus) is known
> and there is space available in the cabinet for a power supply
>   for that nexus
> and there is an available power supply
>
> **THEN:** put the power supply in the cabinet in the available space.

Expert systems that perform *planning* design actions; they decide on an entire course of action before acting. Examples are creating a plan for applying a series of chemical reactions to groups of atoms in order to synthesize a complex organic compound, and creating an air strike plan, projected over several days, for reducing a particular military capability of enemy forces. Planning systems often must backtrack, that is, reject a particular line of reasoning or portion of the plan because it violates problem constraints, and fall back to an earlier point or situation from which the analysis must start anew. Backtracking can be costly, so some planning systems factor the planning task into subproblems and try to order them so as to avoid replanning from failed choice points. The most common application areas for planning systems are chemistry, electronics, and the military.

An example of a rule from a planning system is shown below. The system, called TATR [CAL84], plans air strikes against enemy airfields. This rule helps evaluate the desirability of attacking targets on an enemy airfield.

> **IF:** The airfield does have exposed aircraft
> and the number of aircraft in the open at the airfield is greater
> than 0.25 × the total number of aircraft at that airfield,
> **THEN:** Let EXCELLENT be the rating for aircraft at that airfield.

Expert systems that perform *monitoring* compare actual system behavior to expected behavior. Examples are monitoring instrument readings in a nuclear reactor to detect accident conditions and assisting patients in an intensive care unit by analyzing data from the ICU monitoring equipment. Monitoring systems look for observed behavior that confirms their expectations about normal behavior or their assumptions about possible deviant behavior. Monitoring systems, by their very nature, deal with *time* and must make both a context and time-dependent interpretation of the behavior they observe. This may mean remembering all the values that a parameter in the system (e.g., pulse rate) has acquired at various time intervals, since the rate and direction of change may be just as important as the actual parameter value at any point in time.

An example of a rule from a monitoring system is given below. The system, called REACTOR [NEL82], monitors instrument readings in a nuclear reactor, looking for signs of an accident.

> **IF:** The heat transfer from the primary coolant system to the
> secondary coolant system is inadequate
> and the feedwater flow is low
> **THEN:** The accident is loss of feedwater.

Expert systems that perform *debugging* find remedies for malfunctions. Examples are suggesting how to tune a computer system to reduce a particular type of performance problem, selecting the type of maintenance needed to correct faulty telephone cables, and choosing a repair procedure to fix a known malfunction in a locomotive. Many current debugging systems rely on simple tables of associations between types of malfunctions and particular remedies, but the general problem of debugging is quite difficult and requires *designing* remedies and evaluating them by *predicting* their effectiveness. Debugging systems often incorporate a diagnosis component to uncover the cause of the malfunction. This is particularly common in medical expert systems where the system diagnoses the disorder and then *debugs* it by prescribing a treatment to remedy it.

An example of a rule from a debugging system is given below. This system, called ONCOCIN [TSU83], helps treat cancer patients undergoing chemotherapy.

For patients with any lymphomas undergoing CHOP chemotherapy using Adriamycin:

> **IF:** 1) The patient has received chemotherapy, and
> 2) The blood counts do warrant dose attenuation
>
> **THEN:** Conclude that the current attenuated dose is the previous dose attenuated by the minimum of the dose attenuation due to low WBC and the dose attenuation due to low platelets.

Expert systems that perform *repair* follow a plan to administer some prescribed remedy. An example is tuning a mass spectrometer, i.e., setting the instrument's operating controls to achieve optimum sensitivity consistent with correct peak ratios and shapes. Very few repair systems have been developed to date, partially because the act of executing an actual repair on a real-world object adds an extra dimension of complexity to the problem. Also, repair systems usually require diagnosis, debugging, and planning capabilities to set up the repair context.

An example of a rule from a repair system is given below. The system, called TQMSTUNE [WON83], tunes a triple-quadrupole mass spectrometer.

> **IF:** The detector output voltage is maximized after varying the LENS1-Q1 voltage, and
> The detector output voltage is maximized after varying the LENS2-Q1 voltage, and
>
> The detector output voltage is maximized after varying the Q1 bias-voltage, and
> The detector output voltage is maximized after varying the Q3 bias-voltage
>
> **THEN:** The detector unit is coarse-tuned.

Expert systems that perform *instruction* diagnose, debug, and repair student behavior. Examples are teaching students to troubleshoot electrical circuits, instructing Navy personnel in the operation of a steam propulsion plant, and educating medical students in the area of antimicrobial therapy selection. Instruction systems develop a *model* of what the student knows and how that knowledge is applied to solve problems. They diagnose and debug student deficiencies by analyzing the model and devising plans for correcting the deficiencies. They repair the student behavior by executing these plans via direct interaction with the student.

An example of a rule from an instruction system is shown below. The system, called GUIDON [CLA79], teaches medical students rules for selecting antimicrobial therapy for patients with bacterial infections. The rule shown below reasons about the medical rules (domain rules) the student may have learned and adjusts the system's belief that the student did learn them.

> **IF:** You believe the student considered a particular domain rule, and
> that rule concludes a value present in the student's conclusions, and
> no other rule that mentions this value is believed to have been considered by the student,
>
> **THEN:** Increase the cumulative belief that the student considered this rule by 0.40.

Expert systems that perform *control* adaptively govern overall system behavior. Examples are managing the manufacturing and distribution of computer systems and controlling the treatment of patients in an intensive care unit. Control systems must include a *monitoring* component to track system behavior over time, but they also may require components to perform any or all of the other types of tasks just discussed: interpretation, prediction, diagnosis, design, planning, debugging, repair, and instruction. A likely combination of tasks for a control system is monitoring, diagnosis, debugging, planning, and prediction.

Two examples of rules from a control system are given below. The system, called VM [SHO82], controls the treatment of postsurgical patients in an intensive care unit.

> **1** APPLIES to patients on VOLUME, CMV, ASSIST, and T-PIECE types of ventilation therapies.
>
> **IF:**
> HEART RATE is ACCEPTABLE
> PULSE RATE does NOT CHANGE by 20 beats/minute in 15 minutes
> MEAN ARTERIAL PRESSURE is ACCEPTABLE
> MEAN ARTERIAL PRESSURE does NOT CHANGE by 15 torr in 15 minutes
> SYSTOLIC BLOOD PRESSURE is ACCEPTABLE
>
> **THEN:** The HEMODYNAMICS are STABLE.

2 APPLIES to all patients on controlled mandatory ventilation (CMV) therapy.

IF: ONE OF:
   PATIENT TRANSITIONED FROM VOLUME TO CMV
   PATIENT TRANSITIONED FROM ASSIST TO CMV

THEN: EXPECT THE FOLLOWING:

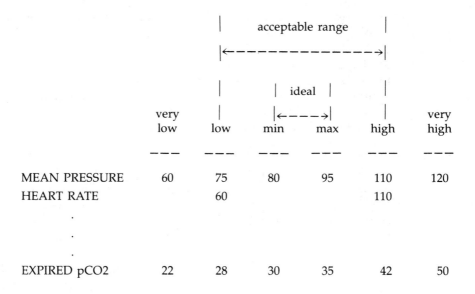

	very low	low	min	max	high	very high
			ideal			
			acceptable range			
MEAN PRESSURE	60	75	80	95	110	120
HEART RATE		60			110	
.						
.						
.						
EXPIRED pCO2	22	28	30	35	42	50

Rule **1** illustrates how the control system monitors the patient's condition over time, using terms which vary with the clinical context, like *acceptable*. Rule **2** shows how the system uses its expectations within a context to precisely define terms like *acceptable* mean arterial pressure.

The Types of Problems That Expert Systems Solve

Although the basic activities of expert systems shown in Table 5.1 are easy to describe, it is misleading to use them to categorize existing expert systems because many expert systems perform more than just one activity. For example, diagnosis often occurs with debugging, monitoring with control, and planning with design. Consequently, AI researchers find it useful to categorize expert systems by the types of problems they solve. Table 5.2 shows some of the problem domains in which expert systems are now working. Of these areas, the medical domain seems the most popular; more expert systems have been developed for medicine than for any other single problem area, although chemistry is a close second and closing fast.

In the next seven figures, we briefly describe selected expert systems in the seven most active areas of Table 5.2—chemistry, computer systems, electronics, engineering, geology, medicine, and the military—and show how they relate to the basic expert system activities shown in Table 5.1. All of these expert systems are described in more detail in Chapter 25.

Expert system work in *chemistry* started with DENDRAL, an innovative research project begun at Stanford University in the mid-1960s and dedicated to developing AI methods for determining the topological structure of organic compounds. Current expert system work in chemistry includes inferring molecular structure, synthesizing organic molecules, and planning experiments in molecular biology.

Expert system work in *computer systems* is typified by XCON, one of the first and most successful systems of this type. Begun by Digital Equipment Corporation and Carnegie-Mellon University in the late 1970s as a research project, XCON evolved into a commercial system for configuring computers. Current expert system work in computer systems includes fault diagnosis, computer configuration, and manufacturing control.

Expert system work in *electronics* is dominated by research and development efforts involving equipment fault diagnosis and integrated circuit design. ACE, developed by Bell Laboratories in the early 1980s, typifies fault diagnosis systems in this area. It is being used by AT&T to locate and identify trouble spots in telephone networks. Current expert system work in electronics also includes the development of instruc-

TABLE 5.2 Application areas for expert systems.

Agriculture	Manufacturing
Chemistry	Mathematics
Computer Systems	Medicine
Electronics	Meteorology
Engineering	Military Science
Geology	Physics
Information Management	Process Control
Law	Space Technology

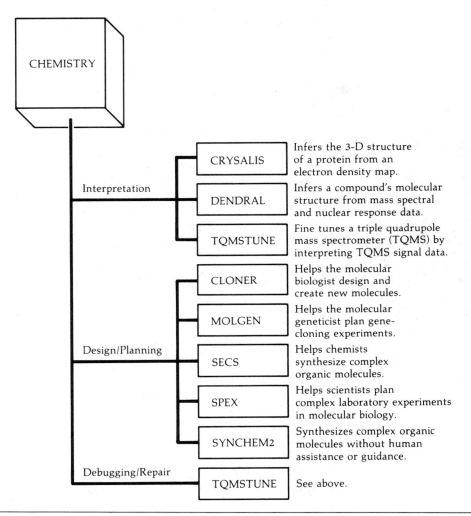

FIGURE 5.1 Selected expert systems in chemistry.

tional systems for electrical troubleshooting and digital circuit design.

Expert system work in *engineering* is typified by DELTA, a fault diagnosis system developed by General Electric in the mid-1980s. General Electric plans to use DELTA on a commercial basis to help maintenance personnel find malfunctions in diesel electric locomotives. Current expert system work in engineering includes other fault diagnosis efforts and instruction in the operation of complex process control systems.

FIGURE 5.2 Selected expert systems in the computer systems domain.

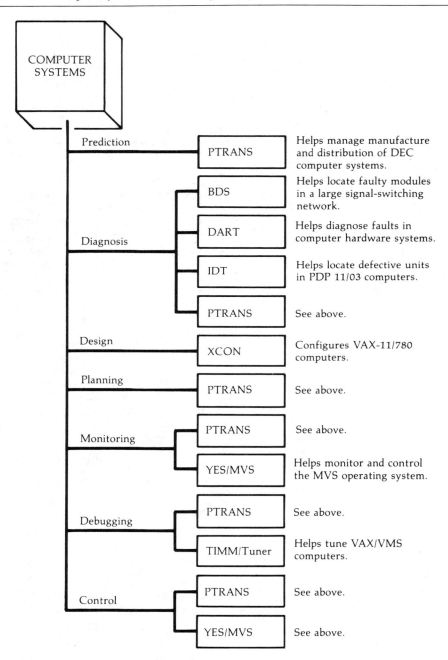

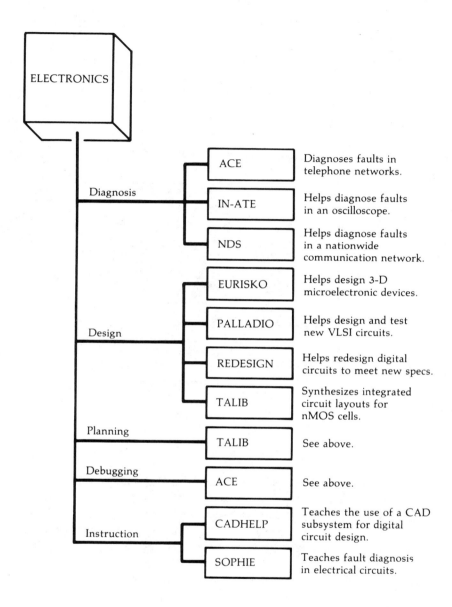

FIGURE 5.3 Selected expert systems in electronics.

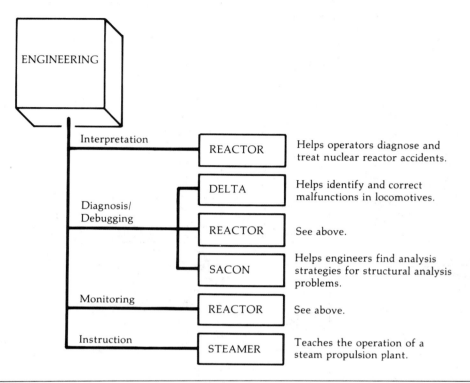

FIGURE 5.4 Selected expert systems in engineering.

Expert system work in *geology* began with PROSPECTOR, a system developed by Stanford Research Institute in the mid-1970s. PROSPECTOR was designed to help geologists locate ore deposits and accurately predicted the existence of a multimillion dollar molybdenum deposit in 1980 (see Chapter 6). Current expert system work in geology includes well log analysis and fault diagnosis related to drilling operations.

Expert system work in *medicine* began with MYCIN, one of the earliest and best known expert systems. Developed at Stanford University in the mid-1970s, MYCIN helps a physician diagnose and treat infectious blood diseases and is now being used for research and medical teaching. Current expert system work in medicine includes interpretation of medical test data, disease diagnosis, disease treatment, and instruction in medical diagnosis and management techniques.

Expert system work in *the military* has focused on interpretation, prediction, and planning. One of the first military expert systems was

HASP/SIAP, developed jointly by Stanford University and Systems Control Technology in the early 1970s. This system indentifies ship types by interpreting data from hydrophone arrays that monitor regions of the ocean. Current expert system work in the military includes interpretation of sensor data, prediction of combat results, and tactical planning.

This survey of expert system applications has given us a very broad view of what expert systems do and what kinds of problems they solve. In the next chapter, we use a different kind of lens and examine a particular application in great detail.

FIGURE 5.5 Selected expert systems in geology.

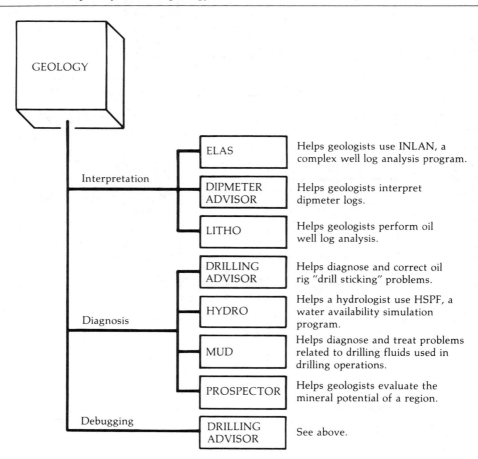

FIGURE 5.6 Selected expert systems in medicine.

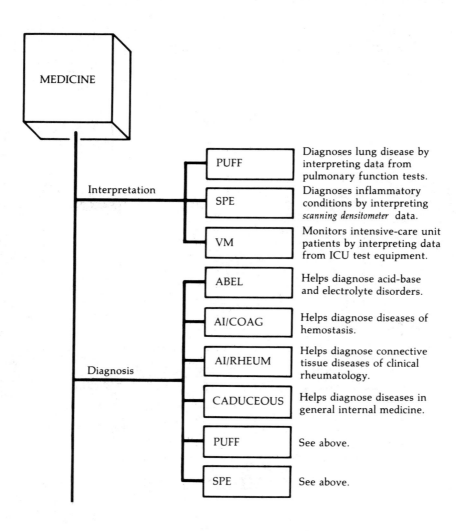

FIGURE 5.6 Continued

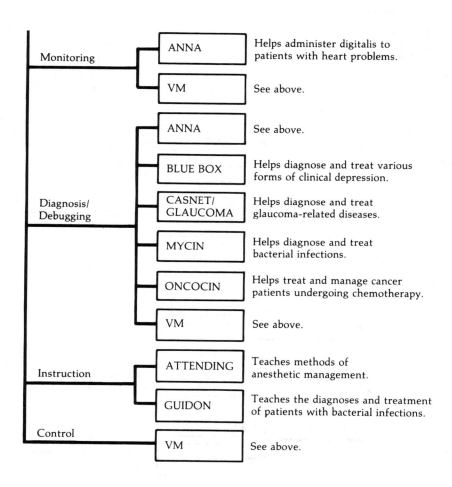

FIGURE 5.7 Selected expert systems in military science.

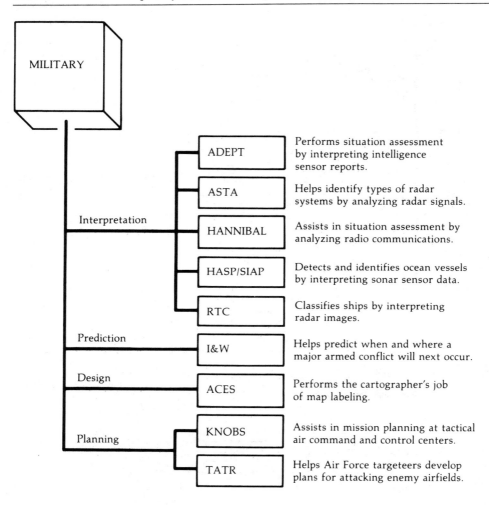

ADEPT	Performs situation assessment by interpreting intelligence sensor reports.
ASTA	Helps identify types of radar systems by analyzing radar signals.
HANNIBAL	Assists in situation assessment by analyzing radio communications.
HASP/SIAP	Detects and identifies ocean vessels by interpreting sonar sensor data.
RTC	Classifies ships by interpreting radar images.
I&W	Helps predict when and where a major armed conflict will next occur.
ACES	Performs the cartographer's job of map labeling.
KNOBS	Assists in mission planning at tactical air command and control centers.
TATR	Helps Air Force targeteers develop plans for attacking enemy airfields.

6

PROSPECTOR: An Expert System at Work

What is PROSPECTOR?

This chapter describes an actual expert system, called PROSPECTOR, developed by the Stanford Research Institute (SRI) to aid exploration geologists in their search for ore deposits [DUD78]. PROSPECTOR has the distinction of being the first computer system built to assist geologists in mineral exploration.

Work on PROSPECTOR started at SRI in 1974 and continued until 1983. Over the course of the project, nine different mineral experts contributed their skills and expertise, working with several knowledge engineers and programmers. It took more than 30 person-years of effort to produce the current PROSPECTOR system including the field testing and evaluation. System development required extensive effort for several reasons: 1) PROSPECTOR was implemented directly in INTERLISP, a powerful but relatively low-level language as far as expert-system-building tools go, 2) a sophisticated support package was developed for PROSPECTOR that included both explanation and knowledge acquisition facilities, and 3) the system needed extensive domain knowledge. PROSPECTOR is not small; it contains over 1,000 rules and uses a taxonomy of geological terms containing more than 1,000 entries.

Richard Duda, a major contributor to PROSPECTOR, describes the operation of the system as follows:

> An exploration geologist starts by telling the program the characteristics of a particular prospect of interest—the geologic setting, structural controls, and kinds of rocks, minerals, and alteration products present or suspected. The program compares these observations with models of

various kinds of ore deposits, noting the similarities, differences, and missing information. The program then engages the geologist in a dialog to obtain additional relevant information and uses that information to make an assessment of the mineral potential of the prospect. Our goal here is to provide the geologist with a service comparable to giving him telephone access to authorities on many different kinds of ore deposits.

One version of PROSPECTOR has a knowledge base with information about three different classes of ore deposits. This information is organized into three *models* of geological knowledge: one for describing a type of sulfide deposit, one for a type of lead/zinc deposit, and one for a type of copper deposit. Each model contains rules combined with semantic nets, as described later in the chapter.

PROSPECTOR at Work

The easiest way to describe PROSPECTOR is to provide examples of its operation. Below are portions of a transcript showing a user-PROSPEC-TOR interaction followed by samples of rules that PROSPECTOR uses [DUD77,REB81]. Most of the ideas illustrated by the transcript and rules could have been presented in a simpler context—for example, an artificially small expert system that solved a very simple problem. However, this strategy would have prevented the reader from learning a simple but very important truth: *expert systems are expert because they contain complex, specialized knowledge.* This point can be driven home only by seeing a real expert system at work.

Readers unfamiliar with geology will not understand all the terminology used in the examples or even be able to decide whether or not a rule used by the system was reasonable. But this isn't necessary to attain a general understanding of what the system does and how it does it. The things to watch for are shown in Figure 6.1. A partial taxonomy of terms used in the transcript is given in Figure 6.2.

The portions of transcript presented below illustrate how PROS-PECTOR interacts with a user to classify a given geographical region. The user's input is shown in bold type and comments are shown in italics.

First, the user volunteers information about the region. This can be done at any point during the session and as often as desired. PROSPECTOR restates the input and supplies a certainty measure based on the user's confidence about the input. In line 3 it

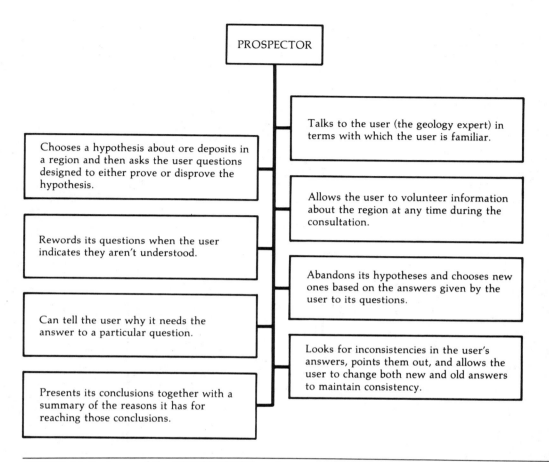

FIGURE 6.1 Features of the PROSPECTOR system.

substituted a synonym for the term
syenodiorite, *telling the user this was the preferred form.*

1: **THERE ARE DIKES**
(Dike) (5)

2: **THERE ARE CRETACEOUS DIORITES**
(Cretaceous diorites) (5)

3: **THERE IS PROBABLY SYENODIORITE**
(Monzonite) (3)

4: **THERE MIGHT BE SOME QUARTZ MONZONITE**
(Quartz-monzonite) (2)

. . . . .
. . . . .
. . . . .

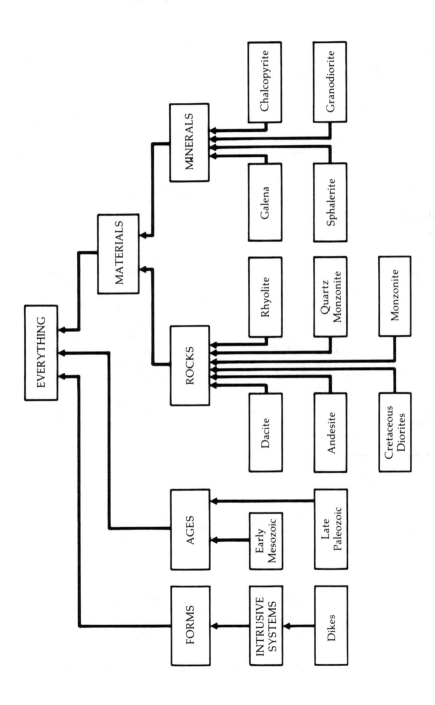

FIGURE 6.2 A partial taxonomy of PROSPECTOR terms.

13: **DONE**
> *This completes the volunteering phase.*
> *PROSPECTOR now hypothesizes a massive*
> *sulfide deposit in the region and begins*
> *to test the hypothesis.*

I am considering the possibility of a (*Kuroko-type massive sulfide deposit—MSD) in the target area.

14: To what degree do you believe that:
(*Volcanic province and major fault zone)? **?**
> *By responding with ''?'' the user asks for a rephrasing of the question.*

*While faulting is important, note that it may well be present but difficult to notice. Thus, do not let absence of observed faulting influence your answer too strongly. With this in mind, to what degree do you believe that the prospect is in a volcanic province and that it lies in a major fault zone? **−2**

. . . . .

. . . . .

. . . . .

16: To what degree do you believe that:
(*Galena, sphalerite, or chalcopyrite filled cracks in rhyolite or dacite or andesite)? **−5**
> *This negative answer causes PROSPECTOR to abandon the sulfide deposit hypothesis and instead hypothesize the presence of porphyry copper deposits. It now asks questions to test this new hypothesis.*

I am considering the possibility of a (*Type-A porphyry copper deposit—PCDA) in the target area.

. . . . .

. . . . .

. . . . .

28: To what degree do you believe that:
(*There are volcanic rocks in the region contemporaneous with the intrusive system, i.e., coeval volcanic rocks)? **WHY**
> *Here the user wants to know PROSPECTOR's purpose in asking the question.*

I am trying to establish the depth environment in your area. The presence of coeval volcanic rocks is good evidence for the right level of exposure. The target (PCDA) would in general lie below the level of (at a greater depth than) a coeval volcanic pile.

28: To what degree do you believe that:
(*There are volcanic rocks in the region contemporaneous with the intrusive system, i.e., coeval volcanic rocks)? **3**

. . . . .
. . . . .
. . . . .

32:   To what degree do you believe that:
(*There is quartz monzonite in the intrusive system)? **4**
**This answer seems inconsistent with your previous answers to the
following questions:

4:   (QUARTZ-MONZONITE) (2)
Do you want to change your answer to Question 32? **NO**
New answer to Question 4 = ? **4**

> *Here PROSPECTOR notices an inconsistency in the user's
> input, since the information volunteered in line 4 should agree
> with the answer to question 32. The user decides to revise his
> or her earlier statement.*

33:   To what degree do you believe that:
(*There is granodiorite in the intrusive system)? **3**

. . . . .
. . . . .
. . . . .

> *After asking 44 more questions PROSPECTOR decides it has
> enough information to make a conclusion about the hypothesis
> that the region contains porphyry copper deposits of type-A.
> This hypothesis is abbreviated (PCDA).*

On a scale from −5 to 5,
my certainty in (PCDA) is now: 1.683.
In summary, the following have been observed:
The major favorable conclusions were
   Right regional environment (3.576)
   Right petro-tectonic setting (3.333)
   Right PCDA intrusive system. (1.683)
The first four encouraging observations were
   There is a granite intrusive system
   in the region (5.0)
   The continental margin mobile belt
   contains granitic intrusives (5.0)
   The belt contains metamorphosed late
   Paleozoic to early Mesozoic eugeosynclinal
   volcanic and sedimentary rocks (5.0)
   There are altered looking rocks. (5.0)
There were many other encouraging observations;
   do you want to see more? **NO**
I cannot do any more with this hypothesis;
   do you want to pursue another one? **QUIT**

How Does PROSPECTOR Do It?

The PROSPECTOR system contains rules linking observed evidence (E) of particular geological findings with hypotheses (H), implied by the evidence. A rule has the form:

> IF E THEN H (to degree) LS, LN.

This means that evidence E suggests the hypothesis H to a degree specified by the certainty factors LS and LN. The number LS indicates how encouraging it is to our belief in the hypothesis to find the evidence present, while LN indicates how discouraging it is to find the evidence absent. LS and LN aren't the only certainty factors in PROSPECTOR. Each piece of evidence and each hypothesis in the system has its own certainty factor P, standing for the probability that the evidence is present or the hypothesis is valid.

The evidence in PROSPECTOR can be any logical combination of pieces of evidence, for example,

> $E1$ and $E2$ and $E3$,
> $E1$ or $E2$,
> $E1$ and ($E2$ or $E3$).

The hypothesis (H) is always a single concept, e.g., $H2$, and can be used in the IF portion of a rule to suggest or imply other hypotheses, as shown below.

> $H2 \longrightarrow H1$ ($LS2$, $LN2$)

The rules in PROSPECTOR form a large *inference net*, which indicates all the connections between evidence and hypotheses and hence all the possible inference chains that could be generated from the rules. The inference net for three simple rules is shown in Figure 6.3.

Each of the three models in PROSPECTOR is a collection of hundreds of rules that forms an inference net. The values for the certainty factors LS and LN were defined when the model was built and remain unchanged during system operation. The values of P, the certainty factors for the evidence and hypotheses, were also built into the model, but they change as new information is presented by the user. For example, suppose the user volunteers the following information about evidence $E1$ in Figure 6.3:

> $E1$ might be present in the region.

PROSPECTOR maps this subjective expression of certainty about $E1$ onto a scale that ranges from -5 (certain it's absent) to $+5$ (certain it's present). In this case the number chosen might be 2 (somewhat certain

RULES: E1 and E2 ⟶ H2 (LS1, LN1)
                H2 ⟶ H1 (LS2, LN2)
                E3 ⟶ H1 (LS3, LN3)

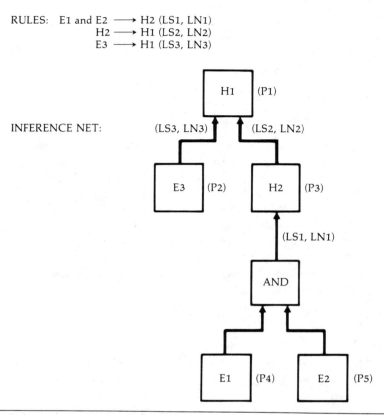

INFERENCE NET:

FIGURE 6.3 Inference net in PROSPECTOR.

it's present). The system then uses the number 2 to adjust the probability $P4$ that was already associated with evidence $E1$. Since 2 is greater than 0, $P4$ would be adjusted upward. But the adjusting doesn't stop there. As soon as $P4$, the probability of $E1$ occurring, changes, $P3$, the probability of $H2$ being valid, also changes. The change in $P3$ is calculated by applying a generalization of Bayes rule in mathematics [KON79] using the values of $LS1$ and $LN1$.

Changing the probability of $E1$ causes a change in the probability of $H2$, which in turn causes a change in the probability of $H1$. This *probability propagation* occurs automatically in PROSPECTOR whenever the user inputs new information. The propagation continues all the way to the top nodes, changing the probabilities of the goal hypotheses, e.g., that the region contains a particular type of sulfide, lead/zinc, or copper deposit. If the probability of the current active goal hypothesis falls below the probability of either of the other two goals as a result of probability propagation, PROSPECTOR switches goals, picking the new one with the highest probability. Line 16 of the transcript illustrates this: The system abandons the goal of showing sulfide deposits are likely in the region, trying instead to show that copper deposits are likely.

The part of the system that actually propagates the probabilities forward (or upward) through the inference net is what would be termed PROSPECTOR's *inference engine*. Since the rules are being processed by starting with the IF portions and proceeding to the THEN portions, this is considered a type of *forward chaining*. This concept is discussed in more detail in Chapter 7.

Probability propagation can't begin until the user supplies a new piece of information to the system. So PROSPECTOR's inference engine must also decide what questions to ask the user. It does this by examining the rules that support the current goal hypothesis and asking the best question it can about the evidence in those rules. The best question is one that, when answered, will most affect the probability of the goal node.

In Figure 6.3, if $H1$ were the current goal, the system would examine rules "$E3 \longrightarrow H1$" and "$H2 \longrightarrow H1$" to determine whether knowing $E3$ or $H2$ would most affect the probability of $H1$. If $E3$ would have more effect, the system would ask the user about $E3$. If $H2$ would have more effect, the system would use this same procedure to find the question, that when answered, would most affect the probability of $H2$. This backward search through the rules continues until a question is finally chosen. Since the rules are being accessed from THEN to IF portions, this is considered a form of *backward chaining* (see Chapter 7).

Rules in PROSPECTOR tend to have a simple structure with only a few pieces of evidence (often only one) in the IF portion of each rule. Figure 6.4 shows a set of seven typical rules from the PROSPECTOR system. The inference net corresponding to these rules is illustrated in Figure 6.5.

What Has PROSPECTOR Accomplished?

PROSPECTOR is both an interesting and successful expert system— interesting from an AI perspective because of the way it combines rule-based and semantic net knowledge representation, successful from a scientific viewpoint because of the skill demonstrated by the system during performance evaluation. PROSPECTOR's initial testing, which involved the analysis of prospecting information from known mineral

[1] IF: The igneous rocks in the region
have a fine to medium grain size

THEN: They have a porphyritic texture (0,5).

[2] IF: The igneous rocks in the region
have a fine to medium grain size

THEN: They have a texture suggestive of
a hypabyssal regional environment (2,0.000001).

[3] IF: The igneous rocks in the region
have a fine to medium grain size
and they have a porphyritic texture

THEN: They have a texture suggestive of
a hypabyssal regional environment (100,0.000001).

[4] IF: The igneous rocks in the region have a texture
suggestive of a hypabyssal regional environment

THEN: The region is a hypabyssal regional environment (65,0.01).

[5] IF: The igneous rocks in the region have a morphology
suggestive of a hypabyssal regional environment

THEN: The region is a hypabyssal regional environment (300,0.0001).

[6] IF: The region is a hypabyssal regional environment

THEN: The region has a favorable level of erosion (200,0.0002).

[7] IF: Coeval volcanic rocks are present in the region

THEN: The region has a favorable level of erosion (800,1).

FIGURE 6.4 PROSPECTOR rules.

discoveries, showed that the system could indeed accurately predict the location of mineral deposits.

Although the system designers were satisfied with these post hoc analyses, they felt that the real test would be to have the system select geologically favorable sites in an unexplored area and then test its predictions through actual exploration drilling. This was done in 1980 using a test site near Mount Tolman in eastern Washington that had been only partially explored. PROSPECTOR analyzed the geological, geophysical, and geochemical data describing the region and predicted the existence of molybdenum in a particular location [CAM82]. Subsequent drilling by a mining company confirmed the prediction as to both where ore-grade molybdenum mineralization would be found and where it would not be found. One could hardly ask for a better confirmation of the system's expertise.

FIGURE 6.5 Inference net for rules of Figure 6.4.

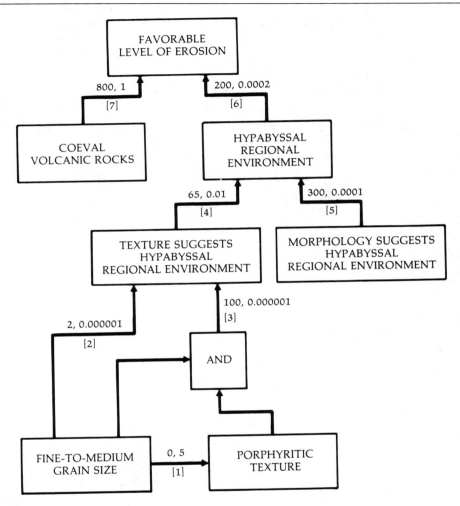

The most important terms discussed in this chapter are summarized in Table 6.1. For a more complete description of these concepts, see the glossary of expert system terms at the end of the book.

TABLE 6.1 More expert system terminology.

Term	Meaning
Inference net	All possible inference chains that can be generated from the rules in a rule-based system.
Probability propagation	The adjusting of probabilities at the nodes in an inference net to account for the effect of new information about the probability at a particular node.

Expert System Tools

In Section I, we examined the basic structure, components, and uses of expert systems. In this section, we will adopt a more technical perspective. We will look closely at how knowledge is represented in expert systems, examine the range of tools available for building them, and describe four popular knowledge engineering languages in detail.

7

Knowledge Representation in Expert Systems

In Chapter 3, we briefly described the three most common ways to represent knowledge in expert systems: rules, frames, and semantic nets. In this chapter, we will consider each of these methods in more detail.

Knowledge Representation Using Rules

In expert systems jargon the term *rule* has a much narrower meaning than it does in ordinary language. It refers to the most popular type of knowledge representation technique, the rule-based representation [WAT78a]. *Rules* provide a formal way of representing recommendations, directives, or strategies; they are often appropriate when the domain knowledge results from empirical associations developed through years of experience solving problems in an area. Rules are expressed as IF-THEN statements, as shown below.

[1] If a flammable liquid was spilled,
call the fire department.

[2] If the pH of the spill is less than 6,
the spill material is an acid.

[3] If the spill material is an acid,
and the spill smells like vinegar,
the spill material is acetic acid.

These are rules that might exist in a crisis management expert system for containing oil and chemical spills [WAT83]. Rules are sometimes written with arrows (⎯⎯→) to indicate the IF and THEN portions of the rules.

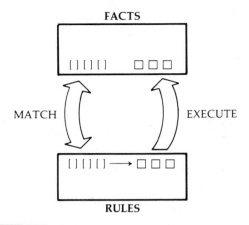

FACTS

MATCH   EXECUTE

RULES

FIGURE 7.1 The rule interpreter cycles through a match-execute sequence.

Rule **2** in this notation would look like:

[2] if the PH of the spill ⟶ the spill material
    is less than 6   is an acid.

In a rule-based expert system, the domain knowledge is represented as sets of rules that are checked against a collection of facts or knowledge about the current situation. When the IF portion of a rule is satisfied by the facts, the action specified by the THEN portion is performed. When this happens the rule is said to *fire* or *execute*. A rule interpreter compares the IF portions of rules with the facts and executes the rule whose IF portion matches the facts, as shown in Figure 7.1. The rule's action may

FIGURE 7.2 Rule execution can modify the facts in the knowledge base.

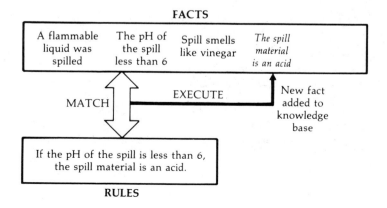

FACTS

A flammable liquid was spilled | The pH of the spill less than 6 | Spill smells like vinegar | *The spill material is an acid*

MATCH   EXECUTE   New fact added to knowledge base

If the pH of the spill is less than 6, the spill material is an acid.

RULES

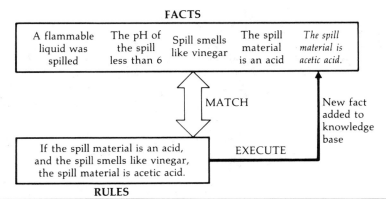

FIGURE 7.3 Facts added by rules can match rules.

modify the set of facts in the knowledge base, for example, by adding a new fact, as shown in Figure 7.2. The new facts added to the knowledge base can themselves be used to form matches with the IF portion of rules as illustrated in Figure 7.3. The action taken when the rule fires may directly affect the real world, as shown in Figure 7.4.

This matching of rule IF portions to the facts can produce what are called *inference chains*. The inference chain formed from successive execution of rules **2** and **3** is shown in Figure 7.5. This inference chain

FIGURE 7.4 Rule execution can affect the real world.

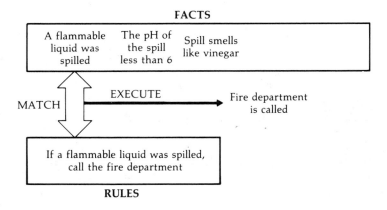

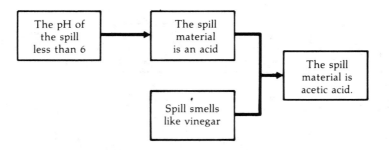

FIGURE 7.5 Inference chain for inferring the spill material.

indicates how the system used the rules to infer the identity of the spill material. An expert systems's inference chains can be displayed to the user to help explain how the system reached its conclusions. We saw an example of this explanation process in the PROSPECTOR dialogue shown in Chapter 6.

There are two important ways in which rules can be used in a rule-based system; one is called *forward chaining* and the other *backward chaining* [WAT78b]. The spill material example just presented used forward chaining. Figure 7.6 shows in more detail how forward chaining works for a simple set of rules.

FIGURE 7.6 An example of forward chaining.

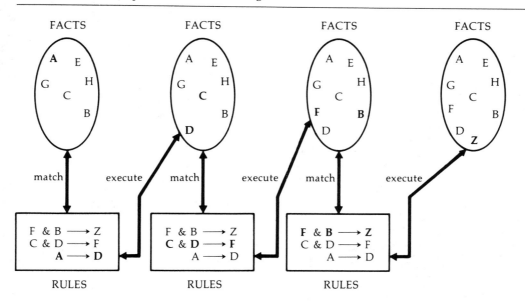

The rules in this example use letters to stand for situations or concepts.

F & B ⟶ Z

means

IF: both situation F
and situation B exist,

THEN: situation Z also exists.

The known set of facts we will call the *data base.*

Let's consider how these rules work. We'll assume that each time the set of rules is tested against the data base, only the first (topmost) rule that matches is executed. That's why, in Figure 7.6, the rule A → D is only executed once even though it always matches the data base.

The first rule that fires is A → D because A is already in the data base. As a consequence of that rule, the existence of D is inferred and D is placed in the data base. That causes the second rule C & D → F to fire, and as a consequence F is inferred and placed in the data base. This in turn causes the third rule F & B → Z to fire, placing Z in the data base.

This technique is called forward chaining because the search for new information seems to be proceeding in the direction of the arrows separating the left- and right-hand sides of the rules. The system uses information on the left-hand side to derive information on the right. The inference chain produced by the example in Figure 7.6 is shown in Figure 7.7. Situation Z was inferred to exist as well as situations F and D.

Suppose you had used this system with the express goal of determining whether or not situation Z existed. You might think that it worked quite well, zeroing in quickly on the fact that Z did exist. Unfortunately, this is just an artifact of the example. A real expert system wouldn't have just three rules; it would have hundreds or even thousands of them. If you used a system that large just to find out about Z, many rules would be executed that had nothing to do with Z. A large number of inference chains and situations could be derived that were valid but unrelated to Z. So if your goal is to infer one particular fact, like Z, forward chaining could waste both time and money.

FIGURE 7.7 Inference chain produced by the example in Figure 7.6.

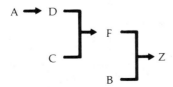

In such a situation *backward chaining* might be more cost-effective. With this *inference method* the system starts with what it wants to prove, e.g., that situation Z exists, and only executes rules that are relevant to establishing it. Figure 7.8 shows how backward chaining would work using the rules from the forward chaining example.

In step 1 the system is told to establish (if it can) that situation Z exists. It first checks the data base for Z, and when that fails, searches for rules that conclude Z, i.e., have Z on the right side of the arrow. It finds the rule F & B → Z, and decides that it must establish F and B in order to conclude Z.

In step 2 the system tries to establish F, first checking the data base and then finding a rule that concludes F. From this rule, C & D → F, the system decides it must establish C and D to conclude F.

In steps 3 through 5 the system finds C in the data base but decides it must establish A before it can conclude D. It then finds A in the data base.

In steps 6 through 8 the system executes the third rule to establish D, then executes the second rule to establish F, and finally executes the first rule to establish the original goal, Z. The inference chain created here is identical to the one created by forward chaining. The difference in the two approaches hinges on the method in which data and rules are searched.

FIGURE 7.8 An example of backward chaining.

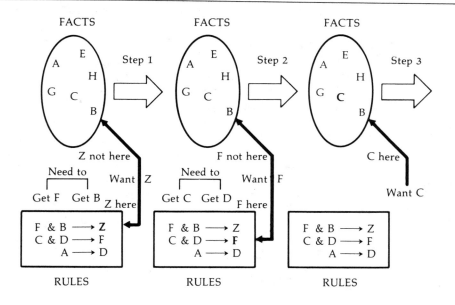

FIGURE 7.8 *Continued*

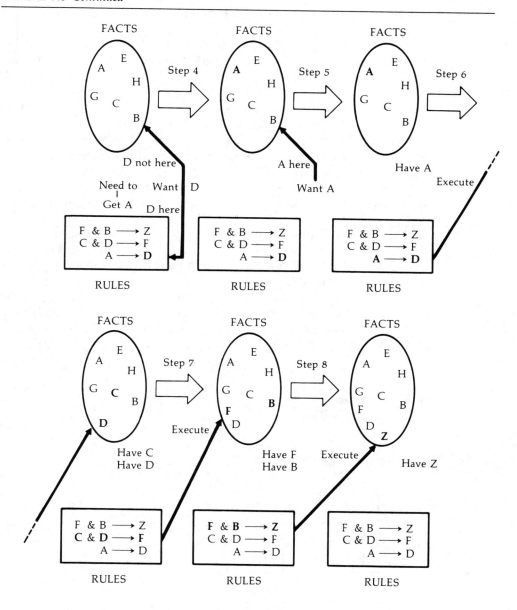

Knowledge Representation Using Semantic Nets

The term *semantic net*[1] is used to describe a knowledge representation method based on a network structure. Semantic nets were originally developed for use as psychological models of human memory but are now a standard representation method for AI and expert systems [BRA79]. A semantic net consists of points called *nodes* connected by links called *arcs* describing the relations between the nodes. The nodes in a semantic net stand for objects, concepts, or events. Arcs can be defined in a variety of ways, depending on the kind of knowledge being represented. Common arcs used for representing hierarchies include *isa* and *has-part*. Semantic nets used to describe natural languages use arcs such as *agent, object,* and *recipient.* Figure 7.9 shows the structure of a semantic net.

As a simple example, consider the statements "The Queen Mary is an ocean liner" and "Every ocean liner is a ship." These can be represented in semantic net form as shown in Figure 7.10. This example uses an important type of arc: *isa.*

Because we know about the properties of the relations linking the nodes (e.g., the *isa* relation is transitive), we can infer a third statement from the net, that "The Queen Mary is a ship," even though it wasn't explicitly stated. The *isa* relation and others (like the *has-part* relation)

[1] Also called a *semantic network.*

FIGURE 7.9 Structure of a semantic net.

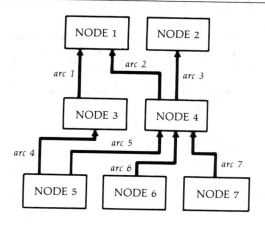

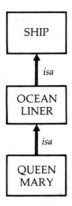

FIGURE 7.10 A simple semantic net using the *isa* relation.

establish a property *inheritance hierarchy* in the net. This means that items lower in the net can inherit properties from items higher up in the net. This saves space since information about similar nodes doesn't have to be repeated at each node. Instead it can be stored in one central location, as shown in Figure 7.11.

For example, in the ship semantic net the parts of a ship, such as the engine, hull, and boiler, are stored once at the ship level, rather than repeatedly at lower levels like ship type or particular ship. This can save

FIGURE 7.11 A simple semantic net for the concept of a ship.

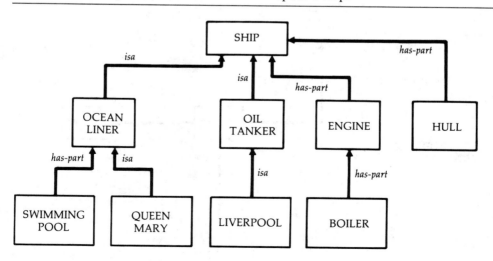

huge amounts of space, even when dealing with only hundreds of ships and ship parts. The net can then be searched, using knowledge about the meaning of the relations in the arcs, to establish facts like "The Queen Mary has a boiler." Semantic nets are a useful way to represent knowledge in domains that use well-established taxonomies to simplify problem solving.

Semantic nets have also been used successfully in *natural language* research to represent complex sentences expressed in English. One example of this is Norman and Rumelhart's work [NOR75] illustrated in Figure 7.12.

Note that here the arcs define the relations between the predicate (GIVE) and the concepts (such as JUDY and GIFT) associated with that predicate. The same technique can be used to represent the more complicated sentence shown in Figure 7.13.

The semantic net representation is useful because it provides a standard way of analyzing the meaning of a sentence. Also, it points out the similarities in the meanings of sentences that are closely related but have different structures. Although the sentences in Figures 7.12 and

FIGURE 7.12 A semantic net representation of an English sentence.

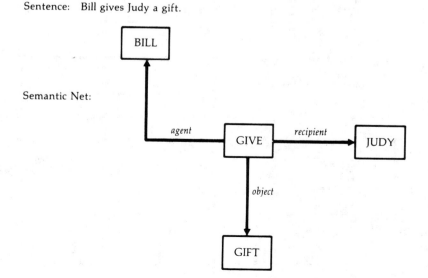

Sentence: Bill gives Judy a gift.

Semantic Net:

Sentence: Bill told Laura that he gave Judy a gift.

Semantic Net:

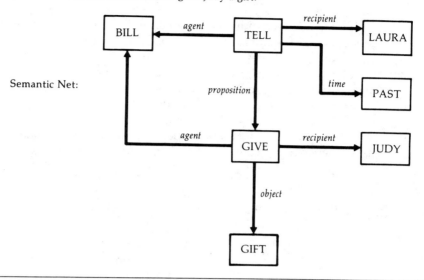

FIGURE 7.13 A semantic net representation of a complex English sentence.

7.13 look very different, the semantic nets representing the meanings of those sentences look similar. In fact, the semantic net of Figure 7.12 is completely contained in the net of Figure 7.13.

Knowledge Representation Using Frames

In the field of artificial intelligence, the term *frame* refers to a special way of representing common concepts and situations. Marvin Minsky [MIN75], who originated the frame idea, describes it as follows:

> A *frame* is a data-structure for representing a stereotyped situation, like being in a certain kind of living room, or going to a child's birthday party. Attached to each frame are several kinds of information. Some of this information is about how to use the frame. Some is about what one can expect to happen next. Some is about what to do if these expectations are not confirmed.

A frame is organized much like a semantic net. (In fact, we consider both semantic nets and frames to be frame-based systems.) A frame is a network of nodes and relations organized in a hierarchy, where the topmost nodes represent general concepts and the lower nodes more specific instances of those concepts. In a frame system, the concept of a written report could be organized as shown in Figure 7.14.

So far this looks just like a semantic net. But in a frame system the concept at each node is defined by a collection of attributes (e.g., name, color, size) and values of those attributes (e.g., Smith, red, small), where the attributes are called *slots*. Each slot can have procedures (arbitrary pieces of computer code) attached to it which are executed when the information in the slot (the values of the attribute) is changed. A typical node is organized as shown in Figure 7.15.

Each slot can have any number of procedures attached to it. Three useful types of procedures often attached to slots are listed below:

1. If-added Procedure: Executes when new information is placed in the slot.

2. If-removed Procedure: Executes when information is deleted from the slot.

3. If-needed Procedure: Executes when information is needed from the slot, but the slot is empty.

These attached procedures can monitor the assignment of information to the node, making sure that appropriate action is taken when values change. As their structure suggests, frame systems are useful for prob-

---

FIGURE 7.14 The concept of a written report.

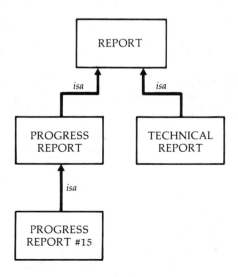

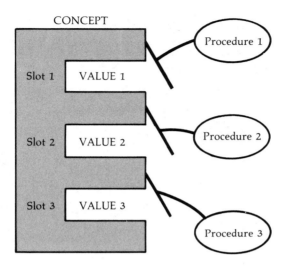

CONCEPT

FIGURE 7.15 A node in a frame system.

lem domains where expectations about the form and content of the data play an important role in problem solving, such as interpreting visual scenes or understanding speech.

To illustrate how a frame system operates, the report hierarchy shown in Figure 7.15 is presented in Figure 7.16, this time with slots, values, and procedures included. We assume, for simplicity, that some slots have default values; e.g., unless given information to the contrary, the author of a progress report is the project leader.

How would someone use knowledge organized in this way? Suppose a large corporation's program manager accesses this frame system using a desktop computer terminal. Let's assume the program manager connects to the frame system via an interface program that lets requests be stated quite naturally. The program manager types, "I need a progress report on the Biological Gasification Project." The interface program analyzes this and inserts *Biological Gasification Project* into the topic slot of the next empty progress report node, in this case #15. Now things start happening automatically.

1. The if-added procedure attached to the topic slot executes because a value was inserted into the slot. This procedure searches a data base associated with the system to find the project leader for Biological

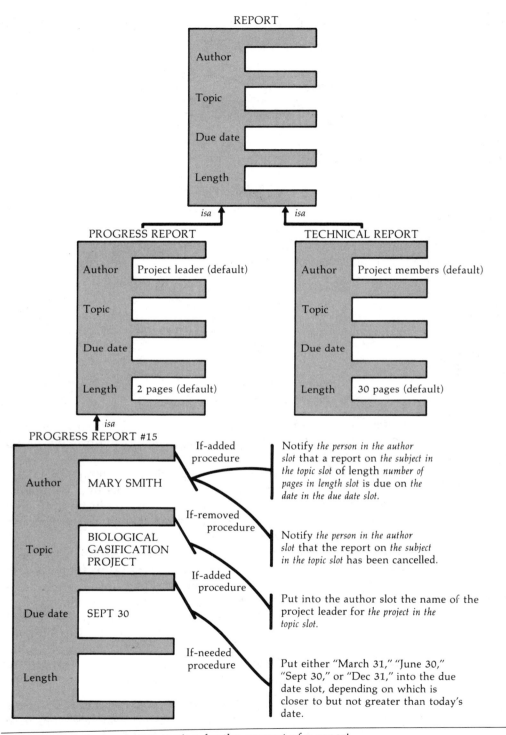

FIGURE 7.16 A frame representation for the concept of a report.

Gasification. Assume the project leader's name is Mary Smith. The procedure then inserts *Mary Smith* into the author slot of progress report #15.

2. The if-added procedure attached to the author slot executes because a value was just inserted. This procedure starts to compose a message to send to Mary Smith, but finds that a value it needs, the due date, isn't there.

3. The if-added procedure, having looked in the due date slot and having found nothing, activates the if-needed procedure attached to that slot. The if-needed procedure then finds today's date by using a calendar in the data base and decides that September 30 is closest to it. The procedure then inserts *Sept 30* into the due date slot.

4. Now the if-added procedure attached to the author slot finds that another value it needs to compose its message, the report length, is missing. The length slot has no attached procedures to help supply the missing value. But in the node above #15, the one for the general concept of progress report, there is a value for length. The procedure uses this value and composes the following message:

Mary Smith: please complete a progress report on the Biological Gasification project by Sept 30. The suggested length is two pages.

If at any time Mary Smith's name is removed from the author slot, the system will automatically send her a message telling her the report is canceled (because of the if-removed procedure).

The most important new terms introduced in this chapter are summarized in Table 7.1. For a more complete description of these concepts, see the glossary of expert system terms at the end of the book.

TABLE 7.1 More expert system terminology.

Term	Meaning
Backward chaining	An inference method where the system starts with what it wants to prove, e.g., Z, and tries to establish the facts it needs to prove Z.
Data base	The set of facts, assertions, and conclusions used to match against the rules in a rule-

Continued

TABLE 7.1 Continued

Term	Meaning
	based system (often has a broader meaning).
Forward chaining	An inference method where rules are matched against facts to establish new facts.
Frame	A knowledge representation method that associates features with nodes representing concepts or objects. The features are described in terms of attributes (called *slots*) and their values.
Inference chain	The sequence of steps or rule applications used by a rule-based system to reach a conclusion.
Inference method	The technique used by the inference engine to access and apply the domain knowledge, e.g., forward chaining and backward chaining.
Inheritance hierarchy	A structure in a semantic net or frame system that permits items lower in the net to inherit properties from items higher up in the net.
Natural language	The standard method of exchanging information between people, such as English (to be contrasted with artificial languages, such as programming languages).
Rule	A formal way of specifying a recommendation, directive, or strategy expressed as IF *premise* THEN *conclusion* or IF *condition* THEN *action*.
Semantic net	A knowledge representation method consisting of a network of nodes standing for concepts or objects connected by arcs describing the relations between the nodes.

Continued

TABLE 7.1 Continued

Slot	An attribute associated with a node in a frame system. The node may stand for an object, concept, or event; e.g., a node representing the object *employee* might have a slot for the attribute *name* and one for the attribute *address*. These slots would then be filled with the employee's actual name and address.

8

The Nature of Expert System Tools

Expert system tools are programming systems that simplify the job of constructing an expert system. They range from very high-level programming languages to low-level support facilities. We divide expert system tools into four major categories as shown in Figure 8.1. In this chapter, we'll describe these tools and explain briefly how they are used.

For the purposes of this discussion, we distinguish between programming languages that have been used for expert system development and knowledge engineering languages expressly designed for expert system development.

A *programming language* is an artificial (as opposed to natural) language developed to control and direct the operation of a computer. One class of programming languages is known as *knowledge engineering languages*. They are expressly designed for constructing and debugging expert systems. Knowledge engineering languages provide special facilities for constructing expert systems but are often less flexible than ordinary programming languages with regard to how knowledge can be represented and manipulated.

Programming Languages for Expert System Applications

The programming languages used for expert system applications are generally either *problem-oriented languages,* such as FORTRAN and PASCAL, or *symbol-manipulation languages,* such as LISP and PROLOG. Problem-oriented languages are designed for particular classes of problems; e.g., FORTRAN has convenient features for performing algebraic calcu-

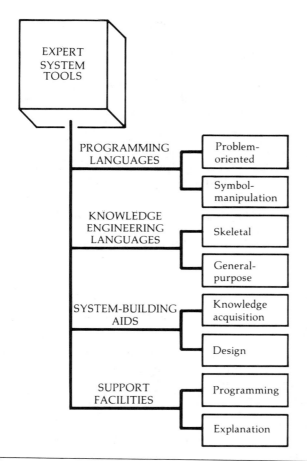

FIGURE 8.1 Types of tools available for expert system building.

lations and is most applicable to scientific, mathematical, and statistical problem areas. Symbol-manipulation languages are designed for artificial intelligence applications; e.g., LISP has mechanisms for manipulating symbols in the form of *list structures*. A list is simply a collection of items enclosed by parentheses, where each item can be either a symbol or another list. List structures are useful building blocks for representing complex concepts.

The most popular and widely used programming language for expert system applications is LISP, although PROLOG seems to be steadily gaining in popularity. Symbol-manipulation languages like these are more suitable for work in artificial intelligence, although a few expert

systems have been written in problem-oriented languages like FOR-
TRAN and PASCAL.

LISP's popularity stems from several features: easy and flexible symbol manipulation, automatic memory management, sophisticated editing and debugging aids, and the uniform treatment of program code
and data, which means a LISP program can modify its own code as
easily as its data. This last feature lends itself to writing programs that
learn new rules or modify existing ones in the knowledge base.

In addition, LISP is available in a number of dialects which run on a
variety of computers, including special-purpose LISP machines designed to execute LISP code quickly and efficiently. The two most common LISP dialects, INTERLISP and MACLISP, have somewhat different
support environments (editing and debugging aids) but a similar syntax.

In LISP, relations between objects are often characterized as lists
containing a relation followed by the objects the relation links. For example, "the oil spill is in building 5523" could be written in a LISP-like
notation as shown below.

English	*LISP*
The oil spill is	
in building 5523.	(LOCATION (SPILL OIL)(BUILDING 5523))

The term *LOCATION* acts as a relation that indicates that its first argument is located in its second argument. Using this same scheme we can
write "if the spill is in a building, call the fire department" in a LISP-like
notation, as shown below.

English	*LISP*
If the spill is in	(IF (LOCATION SPILL BUILDING)
a building, call	THEN (CALL FIRE-DEPARTMENT))
the fire department.	

Now we could write an inference engine to match rule expressions like
(LOCATION SPILL BUILDING) against data expressions like (LOCA-
TION (SPILL OIL)(BUILDING 5523)), and our effort to develop an ex-
pert system for oil spill crisis management would be underway.

The LISP notation shown above is not the correct or best way of
representing this information; it's simply one of many ways. This is both
a blessing and a burden. Knowledge engineers can tailor LISP programs
to their exact needs, if they can only figure out what their exact needs
are and which of the many ways of representing and accessing information in LISP best meets these needs.

Programming languages, like LISP, offer the greatest flexibility to
the expert-system builder but fail to provide guidance on how to represent knowledge or mechanisms for accessing the knowledge base. On
the other hand, knowledge engineering languages, like KAS, offer little
flexibility since the system builder must use the control scheme defined

by the ready-made inference engine. They do, however, provide representation guidelines and ready-made inference engines for controlling the use of the knowledge base.

Knowledge Engineering Languages

A knowledge engineering language is a sophisticated tool for developing expert systems, consisting of an expert system building language integrated into an extensive support environment. Knowledge engineering languages can be categorized as either *skeletal systems* or *general-purpose systems*. AI researchers developed these languages expressly for building expert systems. A skeletal knowledge engineering language is simply a stripped-down expert system—that is, an expert system with its domain-specific knowledge removed, leaving only the inference engine and support facilities. The designers of PROSPECTOR (Chapter 6) stripped it of knowledge about geology to turn it into KAS, a skeletal system for diagnosis and classification. Similarly, the MYCIN system for diagnosing and treating bacterial infections became the skeletal system EMYCIN (Empty MYCIN; see Figure 10.1 in Chapter 10), and the CASNET consultation system for glaucoma became the skeletal system EXPERT. Skeletal systems provide structure and built-in facilities that make system development easy and fast. But they lack generality and flexibility; they only apply to a restricted class of problems and greatly reduce the expert-system builder's design options.

A general-purpose knowledge engineering language can handle many different problem areas and types. It provides more control over data access and search than does a skeletal system but may be more difficult to use. These general-purpose languages vary a great deal in the extent of their generality and flexibility.

The skeletal and general-purpose languages just mentioned all fall under the category of research systems. However, a few AI companies now sell commercial versions of knowledge engineering languages. These languages lie somewhere between skeletal systems and general-purpose ones; many evolved from skeletal systems through enhancements aimed at increasing usability and generality.

System-Building Aids

The system-building aids consist of programs that help acquire and represent the domain expert's knowledge and programs that help design the expert system under construction. These programs address very difficult tasks; many are research tools just beginning to evolve into practical and useful aids, although a few are offered as full-blown commercial systems.

Compared with programming and knowledge engineering languages, relatively few system-building aids have been developed. Those that exist fall into two major categories: design aids and knowledge acquisition aids. The AGE system exemplifies design aids, while TEIRESIAS provides a nice example of a knowledge acquisition aid. We now briefly discuss these two systems. Descriptions of other system-building aids (ROGET—knowledge acquisition; TIMM and EXPERT-EASE—system construction; and SEEK—knowledge refinement) can be found in Chapter 9 and in Chapter 28, the catalog of expert system tools.

AGE

This software tool helps the knowledge engineer design and build an expert system. AGE provides the user with a set of components which, like building blocks, can be assembled to form portions of an expert system. Each component, a collection of INTERLISP functions, supports an expert system framework, such as forward chaining, backward chaining, or a *blackboard architecture*. The term *blackboard* refers to a central data base used by systems with this architecture to coordinate and control the operation of independent groups of rules called *knowledge sources*. The knowledge sources communicate by writing messages on the blackboard and reading messages from other knowledge sources. This architecture was first used in HEARSAY-II, a speech understanding system developed in the mid-1970s, and led to HEARSAY-III, a knowledge engineering language for controlling multiple knowledge sources.

Knowledge engineers have used AGE to design and build HANNI-BAL, an expert system that performs situation assessment by interpreting enemy radio communication data. The system uses information about the location and signal characteristics of the data to identify enemy organizational units and their communications order of battle. AGE has reached the stage of a *research system* and is designed for use by an experienced knowledge engineer with a solid background in INTER-LISP programming.

TEIRESIAS

This system-building aid helps transfer knowledge from a domain expert to a knowledge base. The system acquires new rules about the problem domain through an interaction that allows users to state rules in a restricted subset of English. The system analyzes the rules, makes suggestions regarding their completeness and consistency, and helps the user debug them. The following trace shows TEIRESIAS [DAV76] helping a domain expert add a new rule to MYCIN. Bold type indicates user input while italics indicate explanatory comments.

> *The domain expert indicates that a new rule should be created.*

The new rule will be called RULE383

IF: 1 - **THE PATIENT'S INFECTION IS PRIMARY-BACTEREMIA**
      and 2 - **THE SITE IS ONE OF THE STERILE SITES**
      and 3 -
THEN: 1 - **THERE IS EVIDENCE (0.8) THAT THE CATEGORY IS ENTEROBACTERIACEAE**
      and 2 -

This may take a few moments . . .

> *TEIRESIAS analyzes each input clause on a word-by-word basis to decide which of its known concepts the domain expert was trying to express.*

This is my understanding of your rule:
RULE383

———————

IF: 1 - Primary-bacteremia is an associated infection for which therapy should cover, and
     2 - The infection with the organism was acquired while the patient was hospitalized, and
     3 - The culture was taken from a sterile source, and
     4 - The organism is not normally found at this site
THEN: There is strongly suggestive evidence (0.8) that the category of the organism is enterobacteriaceae.

> *TEIRESIAS recognizes the word* primary-bacteremia *from the first input clause and selects one of several meanings it has stored for this term. It then displays the English text associated with that meaning in clause 1 above. Similarly, it uses the word* infection *from the first input clause to generate clause 2,* sterile *from the second input clause to generate clause 3, and* sites *from the second input clause to generate clause 4.*

Ok? (Yes or no)
+ + ** **N**

> *The expert indicates there is a problem with the way TEIRESIAS interpreted the rule.*

Change premise?
+ + ** **Y**

What clause should be changed in premise? (Type HELP for list of commands.)
+ + ** **CHANGE 1**

> *TEIRESIAS selects the second most likely meaning for primary-bacteremia, the word that led to the generation of clause 1.*

Suppose (1) were changed to read:
>1   the infection is primary-bacteremia

Would that be ok?
+ + ** **Y**

> *TEIRESIAS realizes that the new clause 1 is inconsistent with clause 2 and indicates this to the expert.*

Then you'll probably want to delete:
>2   The infection with the organism was acquired while the patient was hospitalized.

Correct?
+ + ** **Y**

Anything else?
+ + ** **D 4**

Clause(s) 4 deleted

Anything else?
+ + ** **C 3**

Suppose (3) were changed to read:
>3   The site of the culture is one of: those sites that are normally sterile

Would that be ok?
+ + ** **Y**

Anything else?
+ + ** **?**

> *The expert asks the system to display the revised rule.*
> 1 - The infection is primary-bacteremia
and 2 - (deleted)
and 3 - The site of the culture is one of: those sites that are normally sterile
and 4 - (deleted)

+ + ** **OK**

> *The expert indicates that the rule's conditions are now correct, and its action does not need to be modified.*

Change action?
+ + ** **N**

This is my understanding of your rule:
RULE383

```
IF:  1)      The infection is primary-bacteremia, and
     2)      The site of the culture is one of: those sites that are
             normally sterile
THEN:  There is strongly suggestive evidence (0.8) that the
       category of the organism is enterobacteriaceae
```

Okay? (Yes or no)
++**Y

> *TEIRESIAS has interpreted the expert's text, turned it into*
> *a LISP rule, and then translated it back into English for*
> *final approval. Now that the expert is through with the rule,*
> *TEIRESIAS checks it to see if it meets TEIRESIAS's*
> *expectations about rules of that type.*

I hate to criticize, Dr. Davis, but did you know that most rules
about what the category of a organism might be, that mentioned
                        the site of a culture
                        the infection

ALSO mention-
        [A]-the portal of entry of a organism
Shall I try to write a clause to account for [A]?
++**Y

How about-
        [A] The portal of entry of the organism is gi
Ok?
++**Y

Also, most rules about what the category of a organism might be ALSO
conclude about-
        [A]-the identity of a organism
Shall I try to write a clause to account for [A]?
++**N

> *The domain expert always has the last word.*

The rule now reads:
RULE383

```
IF:  1)      The infection is primary-bacteremia, and
     2)      The site of the culture is one of: those sites that are
             normally sterile, and
     3)      The portal of entry of the organism is gi
THEN:  There is strongly suggestive evidence (0.8) that the category of
       the organism is enterobacteriaceae.
```

TEIRESIAS was developed in the mid-1970s as a vehicle for exploring new ideas in knowledge acquisition and data base maintenance
rather than as a tool for building expert systems. This interesting program reached the stage of a research system.

Support Facilities

The support facilities consist of tools for helping with programming, such as debugging aids and knowledge base editors, and tools that enhance the capabilities of the finished system, such as built-in input/output and explanation mechanisms. These facilities usually come as part of a knowledge engineering language and are designed to work specifically with that language.

The tool support environment is simply the extra software packages that come with the tool to make it easier to use, friendlier, and more efficient. Figure 8.2 shows four typical components of an expert system support environment: *debugging aids, input/output (I/O) facilities, explanation facilities,* and *knowledge base editors.* We now briefly discuss these components. Although few expert system tools support all the facilities illustrated here, they all support some of them.

FIGURE 8.2 Components of a support environment for expert system tools.

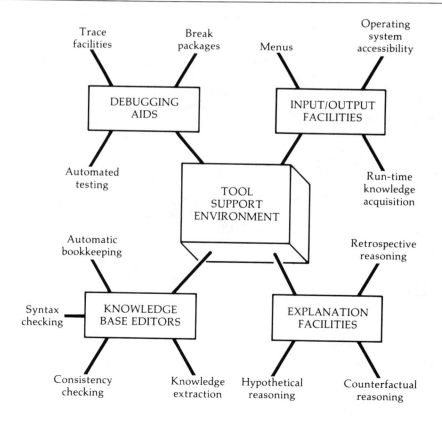

Debugging Aids

Most programming and knowledge engineering languages contain *tracing facilities* and *break packages*. Tracing provides the user with a trace or display of system operation usually by listing the names (or numbers) of all rules fired or showing the names of all subroutines called. A break package lets the user tell the program, in advance, where to stop so the user can stop program execution just before some reoccurring error and examine the current values in the data base. All expert system tools should have these basic aids.

A few expert system tools incorporate *automated testing*, a somewhat more exotic debugging aid then trace facilities or break packages. This aid lets the user automatically test a program on a large number of benchmark problems to uncover errors or inconsistencies in the solutions. For example, EXPERT can store and index thousands of test cases together with their correct solutions and use them to automatically test the rules in a knowledge base. Users find this facility particularly useful when making revisions or extensions to a debugged expert system, because they can quickly test the revised system to see if the changes introduced errors.

I/O Facilities

Different tools deal with input/output in different ways. Some provide *run-time knowledge acquisition* where mechanisms in the tool itself let the user converse with the running expert system. For example, EMYCIN programs ask the user for needed information whenever they can't find it in the knowledge base. EXPERT programs not only ask for such information, but also provide *menus* for the user to select from when inputting the requested information. They also allow the user to input volunteered information as the expert system runs. Since a knowledge engineer building a system in EMYCIN or EXPERT doesn't have to write code for run-time knowledge acquisition, system development is easier, but flexibility is reduced. I/O must be handled the way the tool designer decrees.

The following trace illustrates the type of I/O automatically generated by an expert system written in EMYCIN. This trace comes from BLUE BOX, a system for treating patients hospitalized with depression [MUL84]. Bold type indicates user input while italics indicate explanatory comments.

> *The program has already asked questions about the type and severity of depression and now tries to assess the suicidal risk.*

(24)   Is Mr. Blue suicidal? (If you answer U for unknown,

I will try to assess the suicidal risk myself.)
**U

(25)   Does Mr. Blue have access to firearms?
**UNKNOWN

(26)   Please grade the quality of the family
support of Mr. Blue:
**POOR

. . . .

(31)   Has Mr. Blue accepted to make a No-Suicide decision?
**?

> *When the user types a ? the system asks a more explicit
> question, possibly with a literature reference.*
>
> The No-suicide decision (as defined by Robert C. Drye et al.
> in *Am. J. Psychiatry* 130:2 February 3) consists of having the
> patient pronounce the sentence: No matter what happens, I
> will not kill myself accidentally or on purpose, at any time.

Expected responses are: YES or NO
Enter HELP for a list of user options
**UNKNOWN

Expert system tools may also handle I/O by providing a set of powerful commands or procedures that make writing I/O routines easy. For
example, ROSIE has special commands that let a ROSIE expert system
talk to the local operating system just as if it were a user on the system.
This feature of *operating system accessibility* allows the expert system to
monitor and control other jobs while it is running; e.g., it can run a
simulation program written in another language to obtain needed information.

Explanation Facilities

Almost all expert systems can explain to users how they reach particular
conclusions, but not all provide the same degree of software support for
explanation. Some, like EMYCIN, have a complete explanation mechanism built into the tool itself, so that any expert system written in that
language can automatically access the mechanism. Others have no built-
in explanation mechanism, thus forcing the knowledge engineer to
write one when building the expert system.

The most common type of explanation mechanism deals with *retro-
spective reasoning;* it explains how the system reached a particular state.
For example, the user may wish to know why the system needed the
answer to the question it just asked or how the system arrived at a
certain conclusion. Here the system may describe the rule that led to the
question or display part of the *chain* or sequence of rules that led to the

conclusion. Explanation mechanisms may also handle *hypothetical reasoning,* where the system explains what would have happened differently if a particular fact or rule had been different, and *counterfactual reasoning,* where the system explains why an expected conclusion was not reached.

The following trace illustrates one kind of explanation that an expert system written in EMYCIN can produce automatically. This trace comes from BLUE BOX and continues the trace just presented to illustrate I/O capabilities. Again, bold type indicates user input while italics indicate explanatory comments.

The system has just finished assessing the suicidal risk for the patient and, using its estimate of depression type and suicidal risk, has chosen one or more categories of treatment (e.g., electro-convulsive therapy, psychotherapy . . .). It now asks questions to discriminate more accurately among these categories.

(32)   You mentioned that a patient's relative has had a depression. Please single out a drug that has been successful in treating this depression.
       **UNKNOWN

(33)   You said earlier that Mr. Blue presents some anxiety. Please characterize the degree of anxiety:
       **MILD

(34)   Is the treatment of the patient planned in California?
       **WHY

       The user asks "why is the program asking this particular question at this particular time?"

(i.e., WHY is it important to determine whether the treatment of the patient is planned in California?)

(1.0)   This will aid in determining the types of treatment recommended. It has already been established that

(1.1)   ECT is one of the types of treatment under consideration. Therefore, if

(1.2)   there is evidence that the treatment of the patient is not planned in California, and

(1.3)   Mr. Blue has given his consent for electro-convulsive therapy, then

        it is definite (1.0) that ECT is one of the types of treatment recommended (RULE 087)

        (back to question 34 . . .)
        **YES

        The system hesitates to recommend ECT (electro-convulsive therapy) if treatment is planned in California because of the difficulty in prescribing an ECT in that state.

Knowledge Base Editors

Most expert system tools provide a mechanism for editing the knowledge base. In the simplest case, this is just a standard text editor for modifying rules and data by hand. But many tools include other facilities in their support environment. For example, EMYCIN uses *automatic bookkeeping*. The EMYCIN editor monitors the changes made by the user and records pertinent information about the event. If the user adds or changes a rule, the editor automatically stores the modification date and user name with the rule for later reference. Knowledge engineers find this particularly useful when a number of different experts modify or refine the knowledge base.

Another common facility in knowledge base editors is *syntax checking*, where the editor uses knowledge about the grammatical structure of the expert system language to help the user input rules with the correct spelling and format. When the user enters an ungrammatical rule or command, the editor catches it and explains what is wrong. Correcting mistakes of this sort during editing rather than during system testing can significantly reduce development time.

An extremely useful but generally unavailable facility for knowledge base editors is *consistency checking* where the system checks the semantics or meanings of the rules and data being entered to see if they conflict with existing knowledge in the system. When a conflict occurs, the editor helps the user resolve the conflict by explaining what caused it and describing ways to remove it. AI researchers have had difficulty with consistency checking, although some research system-building aids (e.g., TEIRESIAS) and some commercial system-building aids (e.g., TIMM) have addressed the problem. To perform consistency checking in more than just a superficial way, the editor must understand what the various forms of rules and data actually mean. For example, suppose the knowledge base had in it the fact:

| acid is stored in tank 23,

and the user added a new fact that stated:

| hydraulic oil is stored in tank 23.

The editor would have to know something about the storage of liquids in tanks to realize that since two liquids are seldom stored in the same container at the same time, this new fact conflicts with one already in the knowledge base. Even if the editor recognized the inconsistency, it couldn't easily correct it. There are at least three possibilities:

1) Acid used to be stored in the tank but it was replaced with hydraulic oil.

2) The hydraulic oil is actually stored in some other tank, perhaps tank 32 (a typographical error).

3) An accident occurred, violating normal operating procedures, and somehow both liquids ended up in the tank at the same time.

Since the editor would have difficulty choosing between the alternatives, it would probably have to ask the user for help.

Another potentially useful but generally unavailable facility for knowledge base editors is *knowledge extraction* where the editor helps the user enter new knowledge into the system. It combines syntax and consistency checking with sophisticated prompting and explanation to let even naive users add or modify rules. A knowledge extraction facility in the editor would shorten system development time and training time for new system users. Some system-building aids (e.g., TEIRESIAS, TIMM, and EXPERT-EASE) use knowledge extraction mechanisms.

The most important terms discussed in this chapter are summarized in Table 8.1. For a more complete description of these concepts, see the glossary of expert system terms at the end of the book.

TABLE 8.1 More expert system terminology.

Term	*Meaning*
Blackboard architecture	A way of representing and controlling knowledge based on using independent groups of rules called *knowledge sources* that communicate through a central data base called a *blackboard*.
Break package	A mechanism in a programming or knowledge engineering language for telling the program where to stop so the programmer can examine the values of variables at that point.
General-purpose knowledge engineering language	A computer language designed for building expert systems and incorporating features that make it applicable to different problem areas and types.
List structure	A collection of items enclosed by parentheses where each item can be either a symbol or another list, e.g., (BALL SHOE (Y5 BILL) 23 (CAT 7)).
Problem-oriented language	A computer language designed for a particular class of problems, e.g., FORTRAN designed for efficiently performing algebraic

Continued

TABLE 8.1 Continued

Term	Meaning
	computations, COBOL with features for business record keeping.
Programming language	An artificial language developed to control and direct the operation of a computer.
Skeletal knowledge engineering language	A computer language designed for building expert systems and derived by removing all domain-specific knowledge from an existing expert system.
Symbol-manipulation language	A computer language designed expressly for representing and manipulating complex concepts. Examples are LISP and PROLOG.
Tools for knowledge engineering	Programming systems that simplify expert system development. They include languages, programs, and facilities that assist the knowledge engineer.
Tracing facility	A mechanism in a programming or knowledge engineering language that can display the rules or subroutines executed, including the values of variables used.

9

Stages in the Development of Expert System Tools

An expert system tool evolves over a period of time. In this chapter, we'll survey expert system tools in various stages of development.

Expert system tools often start in a research environment as an *experimental system* created for a specific task (see Figure 9.1). The developer applies it to that task but seldom tests it on other problems in any exhaustive or systematic way. Tools that never evolve past this initial stage tend to be slow and inefficient and use more computer time and memory than necessary. Users of experimental systems should never count on the developer's help when something goes wrong with the tool; the developer seldom supports the use of an experimental system.

The expert system tool may reach the next stage of development and emerge as a *research system*. Such a tool will have been extensively tested and may be supported by the developer; however, it may still be relatively slow and inefficient. Developers like to try out new ideas, and research systems often include esoteric and exotic features known only to a few and used by almost none. This can lead to slow, inefficient operation. Still, not all research systems are slow and bulky.

Only a few expert system tools have reached the stage of a *commercial system*. These tools are usually polished, streamlined, well-supported, and fast. They are engineered to meet the user's needs and ease the user-machine interaction problem. However, not all tools that get commercial application are equally polished. Current commercial programming languages have emerged as large complex systems with sophisticated features, but the commercial knowledge engineering languages and system-building aids now available seem somewhat conservative and limited by comparison.

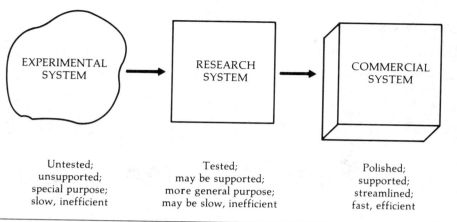

Untested;	Tested;	Polished;
unsupported;	may be supported;	supported;
special purpose;	more general purpose;	streamlined;
slow, inefficient	may be slow, inefficient	fast, efficient

FIGURE 9.1 Evolution of expert system tools.

What Representation and Programming Methods Do the Tools Support?

An expert system tool may support one or more methods for representing knowledge and organizing programs. We can group these methods into the six categories shown in Table 9.1.

Although many tools support only a single method, some support quite a few. For example, EMYCIN supports rule-based methods while LOOPS supports object-oriented, procedure-oriented, rule-based, and access-oriented ones.

Rules, Semantic Nets, and Frames

We have already discussed the three most common methods for knowledge representation: rules, semantic nets, and frames (see Chapter 7). Tool builders have had a fair amount of success combining frame-based and rule-based methods. The prime example is KAS, a knowledge engineering language derived from PROSPECTOR. KAS was created by removing all knowledge of geology from PROSPECTOR, leaving only the inference engine and rule syntax.[1]

---

[1] KAS has much in common with EMYCIN, as EMYCIN was derived from MYCIN by removing all domain-specific knowledge. KAS uses a semantic net to organize rule premises and streamline the process of matching rule conditions against the data. Chapter 6 describes PROSPECTOR and illustrates the PROSPECTOR/KAS control scheme.

TABLE 9.1 Representation and programming methods supported by expert system tools.

Method	Description	Tool
Rule-based	Uses IF-THEN rules to perform forward or backward chaining.	EMYCIN
Frame-based	Uses frame hierarchies for inheritance and procedural attachment.	SRL
Procedure-oriented	Uses nested subroutines to organize and control program execution.	LISP
Object-oriented	Uses items called *objects* that communicate with one another via messages.	SMALL-TALK
Logic-based	Uses predicate calculus to structure the program and guide execution.	PROLOG
Access-oriented	Uses probes that trigger new computations when data are changed or read.	LOOPS

Procedure-oriented Methods

These methods rely on the use of subroutines, a standard way of packaging code that increases efficiency by reducing duplication in the code. Nested procedures (procedures that call procedures that call procedures . . .) provide a convenient way for the programmer to organize the program. The programmer can define a set of high-level procedures that serve as a highly specialized language for describing actions the program should take, and then write the program in a clear, concise way using those procedures. Procedures provide great flexibility; the programmer can arrange them in a variety of ways. But this has an unfortunate side effect—it makes explanation more difficult. Programs organized in a standardized, restrictive fashion (e.g., in sets of rules) can more easily understand and explain their own operation.

Because rules and procedures each provide useful capabilities that the other lacks, it would seem natural to combine them in an expert system tool. The ROSIE knowledge engineering language does just that. It lets the programmer define procedures called *rule sets*, each containing rules that may call other rule sets. This means the programmer can organize a ROSIE program in much the same way as a LISP program, as a set of nested subroutines. ROSIE is discussed in more detail in Chapter 10.

Object-oriented Methods

These methods use a special organization consisting of objects (often called *actors*) that represent entities capable of exhibiting behavior. For example, in an object-oriented air battle simulation system called SWIRL, the objects are penetrators (offensive aircraft), AWACS (airborne radars), ground radars, missile installations, missiles, filter centers (that interpret radar reports), fighters (defensive aircraft), fighter bases, command centers, and targets. Each object has distinct properties associated with it and is situated in a network hierarchy that lets it inherit properties of higher-level objects, much as properties are inherited in semantic nets and frames. For example, in SWIRL the objects *penetrator, fighter, missile,* and *AWACS* all link to the higher-level object called *moving object.* In addition *AWACS* links to the higher-level object called *radar.* This means that each particular AWACS need have stored with it only those properties, such as current location, that distinguish it from the other AWACS. It can inherit the known properties of moving objects and radars.

So far, this doesn't seem much different from standard frame-based representation methods. However, object-oriented representations are unique in that all objects communicate with one another by sending and receiving *messages,* as indicated in Figure 9.2. When an object receives a message, it consults its data base and rules to decide what action to take. The rules may be stored directly with the object or in a higher-level object somewhere in the network hierarchy. In most cases the action involves sending new messages to other objects in the system.

For example, a particular AWACS might broadcast a message to all filter centers that it had detected a penetrator at a certain location. A particular filter center that had received other confirming reports might then send a message to a command center warning of the penetration. The command center could then decide which fighters to use to intercept the penetrators and send messages specifying this to the appropriate fighter bases.

The objects in an object-oriented system don't have to represent entities that normally send and receive messages, such as a fighter or an AWACS. They can just as easily represent less animate entities. For example, an object-oriented program to simulate the flow of traffic through a city might include objects representing automobiles, traffic lights, city blocks, and intersections, all of which would send and receive messages.

Like rules, objects and message passing provide a natural way for handling processes where the wealth and variety of data configurations determine the reasoning paths. Objects and message passing also provide a way to specify concurrent, asynchronous operations; it's possible to *simulate* many unrelated processes occurring at the same time. For example, in SWIRL, command centers can send locate-and-destroy messages to air force bases while ground radars are communicating with filter centers about the latest targets detected.

Logic-based Methods

These methods are based on a programming style developed by Kowalski [KOW79a,KOW79b] that uses predicate logic to control the analysis of a set of declarative clauses. Each clause has the form:

    consequent :- antecedent-1, antecedent-2, . . . antecedent-n

where the antecedents are predicates that can be tested for their truth value and the consequent is a predicate that is true if its antecedents can be proved true [COH82]. A logic program takes a *goal* and compares it with the consequents of the stored clauses. When it finds a match, it tries to prove the goal by considering the antecedents of the matched consequent as subgoals; when all the subgoals are shown to be true, the goal itself is proved.

This search through the antecedents to prove the consequent looks much like the *backward chaining* control scheme of rule-based languages.

FIGURE 9.2 Message passing in object-oriented programs.

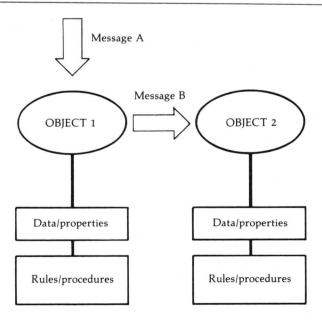

In logic-based programming languages, such as PROLOG, the search is rigidly controlled by the *interpreter,* the mechanism that analyzes and processes the clauses. Supporters of LISP, the natural rival to PROLOG, point out that this limited control over program operation encourages the development of very inefficient, time-consuming programs, since it's difficult to predict the extent of the required computations from the PROLOG statements themselves. Even when this can be predicted, there may be no way to limit the combinatorial explosion inherent in real-world search problems. PROLOG's adherents admit that programmers can write inefficient code, but they argue this is true to some extent for every programming language. They believe that PROLOG's advantages—sophisticated pattern-matching, built-in relational data base facilities, and efficient compilers—outweigh any disadvantages.

Access-oriented Methods

These methods use *demons,* procedures invoked when data are changed or read, to monitor programs or external devices. The demons act like probes connected to particular values of variables in a program. When computations or external events change these values, the probes trigger additional computations that may be used to drive graphical displays of gauges showing the values of the variables [STE83b]. Access-oriented methods make it easy to construct sophisticated visual displays for monitoring variables in a program. The LOOPS programming language provides access-oriented methods in the form of graphical gauges, as shown in Figure 9.3.

Gauges in LOOPS are defined as classes and driven by *active values,* the LOOPS terminology for probes connected to the variables of a LOOPS program. The box at the bottom of Figure 9.3 illustrates the relationships between the classes of gauges. From this we see that the DigiMeter is a combination of a Meter and an LCD. The graphical display of gauges has been used quite effectively in STEAMER, an expert system for tutoring engineering students in the operation of a steam propulsion plant (see Chapter 25).

Experimental Systems

Many experimental systems exist as knowledge engineering languages and system-building aids. We now briefly describe ROGET and SEEK, two experimental system-building aids that help to construct and refine expert systems.

ROGET helps a domain expert design a knowledge base for a diag-

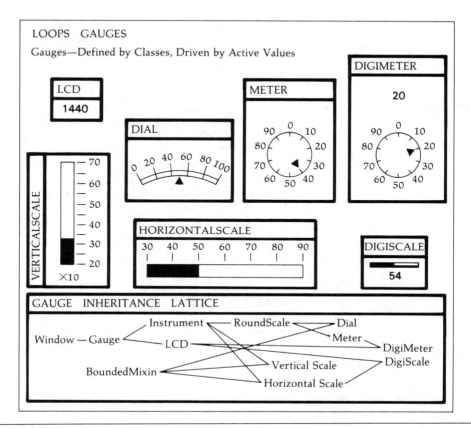

FIGURE 9.3 LOOPS gauges.

nosis-type expert system [BEN83]. It queries the domain expert, asking questions that identify types of subproblems that the expert system must solve, the results or solutions the system must produce, the evidence or data required to solve the problem, and the relationships between the data or facts of a case and its solution. Since these questions uncover the basic concepts or conceptual structure of the expert system, ROGET can be said to assist in the conceptualization phase of expert system development (see Chapter 12).

ROGET does not acquire rules of expertise during its interaction with the domain expert; instead, it helps the expert to define and organize the rule building blocks, the primitive concepts or pieces of knowledge to be used in rule formation. We next present portions of a transcript illustrating how ROGET interacts with a user to acquire the conceptual structure needed for diagnosing infectious diseases. The user's input is shown in bold type and comments are shown in italics.

10)   What are the primary kinds of supporting inferences,
      evidence, and data that would be used to determine
      THE INFECTIOUS DISEASES OF PATIENT ARE PRESENT?

** **LABORATORY-TESTS**

**

Let's discuss the LABORATORY TESTS that will be used to support the
inference of THE INFECTIOUS DISEASES OF THE PATIENT ARE
PRESENT:

---

11)   What are the names of the laboratory tests that can
      be used to determine THE INFECTIOUS DISEASES OF THE
      PATIENT ARE PRESENT?

** **MICROBIOLOGICAL CULTURES**

**

Let's discuss MICROBIOLOGICAL CULTURES, a laboratory test:

12)   Who performs the test:

** **AN INFECTIOUS DISEASE FELLOW**

13)   Do the descriptive factors of microbiological cultures
      measure things about specific PARTS of PATIENT or about
      some particular ACTIVITIES that PATIENT engages in?

** **PARTS**

14)   What parts are measured?

** **ARTERY**

** **BLOOD**

** **BURN-SITE**

** **CSF**

** **SPUTUM**

** **URINE**

**

15)   What procedures are done or what pieces of equipment
      are used to collect the measurements for THE DESCRIPTIVE
      FACTORS OF MICROBIOLOGICAL CULTURES during the
      consultation?

** **CLEAN-CATCH**

** **FOLEY CATHETER**

** **NEEDLE**

** **SWAB**

**

> *ROGET continues until it acquires a general description of the
> test and what sort of thing it measures. It then determines
> how the actual measurements are made, as shown below.*

19) What are THE OBSERVATIONS FROM MICROBIOLOGICAL CULTURES?

** **THE LABORATORY-REPORTED IDENTITY OF THE ORGANISMS FOUND ON THE CULTURE**

** **THE GRAM STAIN OF THE ORGANISM**

** **THE MORPHOLOGY OF THE ORGANISM**

** **WHETHER PENICILLASE WAS ADDED TO THE CULTURE**

**

20) What KIND of values will you expect for THE LABORATORY-REPORTED IDENTITY OF THE ORGANISM FOUND ON THE CULTURE?

** **TERMS**

21) What is the list of expected values for THE LABORATORY-REPORTED IDENTITY OF THE ORGANISMS FOUND ON THE CULTURE?

** **E. COLI**

** **PROTEUS-MIRABILIS**

** **PSEUDOMONAS**

**

In this example ROGET uncovers some of the concepts required for developing the MYCIN program, an expert system that helps physicians to select an antimicrobial therapy. For a more complete example of this interaction, see [BEN83].

The SEEK system helps the domain expert or knowledge engineer to refine rules during the development of a diagnostic-type expert system. These rules are represented in the EXPERT language but expressed in a tabular format that divides the findings associated with a conclusion into two categories—major and minor—and the levels of confidence associated with a conclusion into three categories—definite, probable, and possible [POL84].

A list of major and minor findings are defined for each conclusion that the system can reach. For example, major findings for connective tissue disease, one of the rheumatic diseases, include swollen hands and severe myositis, while examples of minor findings include anemia and mild myositis.

Figure 9.4 shows the conventional format for three rules for diagnosing connective tissue disease. Figure 9.5 shows the same three rules in tabular form.

SEEK suggests possible ways to generalize or specialize rules by looking for regularities in the rules' performance on a body of stored cases with known conclusions. The system suggests the type of change (generalization or specialization) and what components to change, but it

> **IF:** 1) The patient has 4 or more major findings for mixed connective tissue disease, and
> 2) RNP antibody is positive, and
> 3) SM antibody is NOT positive,
>
> **THEN:** Conclude DEFINITE mixed connective tissue disease.
>
> **IF:** 1) The patient has 2 or more major findings and 2 or more minor findings for mixed connective tissue disease, and
> 2) RNP antibody is positive,
>
> **THEN:** Conclude PROBABLE mixed connective tissue disease.
>
> **IF:** 1) The patient has 3 or more major findings for mixed connective tissue disease,
>
> **THEN:** Conclude POSSIBLE mixed connective tissue disease.

FIGURE 9.4 Conventional form for rules diagnosing connective tissue disease.

lets the user decide exactly how to generalize or specialize those components. SEEK makes these suggestions based on its use of *metarules*, rules about rules. Figure 9.6 illustrates a typical SEEK metarule.

This refinement method works best when the expert's knowledge is fairly accurate and small changes in the knowledge base may lead to significant improvement in the performance of the expert system. SEEK was developed and tested using the AI/RHEUM expert system, a clinical consulting model for rheumatology written in the EXPERT language.

Research Systems

Table 9.2 shows selected knowledge engineering languages that are available as research systems. Four widely used systems—EMYCIN,

FIGURE 9.5 Tabular form of the rules shown in Figure 9.4.

	DEFINITE	PROBABLE	POSSIBLE
FINDINGS	4 majors	2 majors 2 minors	3 majors
REQUIREMENTS	Positive RNP antibody	Positive RNP antibody	None
EXCLUSIONS	Positive SM antibody	None	None

IF:	1)	The number of test cases suggesting the rule should be generalized exceeds the number of test cases suggesting rule should be specialized, and
	2)	The rule most frequently fails to match test cases because it requires too many major findings to be present,
THEN:		Decrease the number of major findings required by by the rule.

FIGURE 9.6 A SEEK metarule for deciding how to refine domain rules.

EXPERT, OPS5, and ROSIE—will be described more fully in Chapter 10. One of these, OPS5, is also available from Digital Equipment Corporation as a commercial system (see Table 9.3). The other research systems shown in Table 9.2—AL/X, LOOPS, MRS, and SRL—although used less extensively, have generated considerable interest in the AI community. We will now briefly describe these systems.

TABLE 9.2 Selected knowledge engineering languages available as research systems.

Research Systems			
Tool	Description	Implementation Language	Developer
AL/X	Rule-based Frame-based	PASCAL	Intelligent Terminals Ltd.
EMYCIN	Rule-based	INTERLISP	Stanford University
EXPERT	Rule-based	FORTRAN	Rutgers University
LOOPS	Rule-based Procedure-oriented Object-oriented Access-oriented	INTERLISP-D	Xerox PARC
MRS	Rule-based Logic-oriented	INTERLISP	Stanford University
OPS5	Rule-based	BLISS MACLISP FRANZ LISP	Carnegie-Mellon University
ROSIE	Rule-based Procedure-oriented English-like	INTERLISP	The Rand Corporation
SRL	Frame-based	FRANZ LISP	Carnegie-Mellon University

AL/X closely resembles the KAS system [BAR83], that is, PROSPEC-TOR stripped of its knowledge about geology (see Chapter 6). Like KAS, it uses a rule-based representation combined with a semantic net that links rule components. The system makes inferences based on a combination backward and forward chaining control scheme and includes facilities for certainty handling, explanation, and automatic user querying. AL/X has been used by Intelligent Terminals Ltd. to explore the problem of diagnosing causes of automatic shutdowns on oil production lines [REI80].

The LOOPS system, developed at the Xerox Palo Alto Research Center, was intended to create an expert assistant for designers of integrated digital circuits. The language is based on an object-oriented representation scheme but also supports rule-based, procedure-oriented, and access-oriented representation methods. These four programming schemes provide the user with a great deal of flexibility. For example, rules and rule sets are considered LOOPS objects and can communicate by object-oriented message passing or by standard subroutine calls. Procedures can be either LISP functions or rule sets and can be used with *active values* to display gauges (see Figure 9.3). Applications involving LOOPS include PALLADIO, a system to help engineers create and refine design specifications for VLSI circuits, and ACES, a system that performs the cartographer's job of map labeling.

The motivation for the development of MRS was to design a language that could easily represent *metaknowledge*, that is, knowledge about how an expert system reasons with its domain knowledge. An expert system needs metalevel knowledge to help explain and control its operation. MRS facilitates this type of representation. For example, MRS permits the user to write statements about MRS subroutines just as easily as statements about geology or medicine. Although MRS is a knowledge engineering language for rule-based representation, it also supports logic-based representation methods. It incorporates a flexible control scheme utilizing forward and backward chaining and resolution theorem proving. MRS applications include DART, a system that assists in diagnosing faults in computer hardware systems, and AI/MM, a system that uses knowledge of anatomy and first principles of physiology to analyze the behavior of a renal physiological system.

SRL is a frame-based knowledge engineering language developed for exploring issues of inheritance in frame systems. It provides the user with much flexibility in defining a representation system. For example, in SRL the user can define new relations and their inheritance semantics, new slots, and new search specifications. Also, each SRL frame or *schema* may have metalevel knowledge associated with it. Applications involving SRL include ISIS, a system to help schedule jobs in a steam turbine blade plant, and PDS, a system for on-line, real-time diagnosis of malfunctions in machine processes.

Commercial Systems

We can divide the available commercial systems into three categories: programming languages, system-building aids, and knowledge engineering languages.

Programming Languages

Quite a few commercial versions of LISP are available, many packaged as workstations containing hardware and support software designed especially to accommodate LISP in a stand-alone environment. For example, LISP Machine, Inc. has developed a machine that runs a version of LISP derived from MIT's MACLISP. Symbolics, Inc. has developed the 3600 family of processors which run ZETALISP, another variant of MACLISP. The Symbolics 3600 machines support FLAVORS, an object-oriented programming environment embedded in ZETALISP, and MACSYMA, a commercial expert system for algebraic computation. Xerox Corporation produces LISP machines that run INTERLISP. The Xerox 1100 system, like many of the other workstations, has a sophisticated user interface based on a high-resolution display, multiple overlapping windows, a mouse pointing device, and pop-up menus for selection of operations. A few commercial versions of PROLOG also exist, such as the one offered by Quintus Computer Systems. Table 9.3 summarizes the systems just described.

TABLE 9.3 Selected commercial systems.

		Commercial Systems			
Category	*Tool*	*Use*	*Description*	*Hardware*	*Developer*
	INTER- LISP-D	General- purpose	Procedure- oriented	Xerox 1100	Xerox Corporation
	LISP	General- purpose	Procedure- oriented	Lambda machines	LISP Machine Inc.
Programming Languages	PROLOG	General- purpose	Logic-based Procedure- oriented	DEC 10 system DEC 20 system	Quintus Computer Systems, Inc.
	SMALLTALK −80	General- purpose	Object- oriented	Tektronix 4404	Xerox Corporation
	ZETALISP	General- purpose	Procedure- oriented	Symbolics 3600	Symbolics Inc.

Continued

TABLE 9.3 Continued

Commercial Systems				
Category	*Tool*	*Use*	*Description*	*Hardware*	*Developer*
---	---	---	---	---	---

Category	*Tool*	*Use*	*Description*	*Hardware*	*Developer*
System-Building Aids	EXPERT-EASE	Knowledge acquisition	Infers a decision tree from examples	IBM PC IBM-XT Victor 9000 DEC Rainbow	Export Software International
	PLUME	Natural language interface development	Software tool for building interfaces	Symbolics 3600 VAX-11 systems	Carnegie Group, Inc.
	RULE-MASTER	Knowledge acquisition	Infers a decision tree from examples	VAX-11 systems Apollo system Sun system	Radian Corporation
	TIMM	Knowledge acquisition	Infers rules from examples	VAX 11/780 Prime 400	General Research Corporation
Knowledge Engineering Languages	ART	General-purpose	Rule-based Frame-based Procedure-oriented	CADR machines Symbolics 3600	Inference Corporation
	DUCK	General-purpose	Logic-based Rule-based	Symbolics 3600 DEC VAX systems	Smart Systems Technology
	KEE	General-purpose	Rule-based Frame-based Procedure-oriented Object-oriented	Xerox 1100 Symbolics 3600	Intellicorp
	KES	General-purpose	Rule-based Frame-based	DEC VAX systems operating under UNIX or VMS	Software Architecture & Engineering Inc.
	M.1	General-purpose	Rule-based English-like syntax	IBM PC	Teknowledge
	OPS5	General-purpose	Rule-based	VAX-11 systems	Digital Equipment Corporation
	OPS5e	General-purpose	Rule-based	Symbolics 3600	Verac Corporation

Continued

TABLE 9.3 Continued

		Commercial Systems			
Category	*Tool*	*Use*	*Description*	*Hardware*	*Developer*
	OPS83	General-purpose	Rule-based Procedure-oriented	VAX-11 systems	Production Systems Technologies Inc.
	PERSONAL CONSULTANT	Diagnosis	Rule-based	TI Professional Computer	Texas Instruments
	S.1	General-purpose	Rule-based Frame-based Procedure-oriented	Xerox 1100 Xerox 1108	Teknowledge
	SeRIS	Diagnosis	Rule-based	IBM PC	SRI-International
	SRL+	General-purpose	Frame-based	Symbolics 3600 VAX-11 systems	Carnegie Group, Inc.

System-building Aids

Only a few commercial expert-system-building aids are now on the market. Table 9.3 shows three of these tools, TIMM, RULEMASTER, and EXPERT-EASE, each designed to assist in knowledge acquisition. The systems are quite similar—the user defines the problem in terms of all possible decisions that can be made and the names and values of factors to consider in arriving at a decision. The system then queries the user for examples describing conditions leading to each decision. From the examples, the system infers a procedure for solving the problem. In RULEMASTER and EXPERT-EASE, this procedure is a decision tree; in TIMM, it's a set of IF-THEN rules incorporating certainty factors. Versions of all three systems have been developed to operate on an IBM Personal Computer.

Knowledge Engineering Languages

The commercial knowledge engineering languages are complete tools for expert system development, combining powerful languages with sophisticated support environments. Many of these knowledge engineering languages use rules as their primary representation method. The ART, KES, M.1, OPS5, OPS5e, PERSONAL CONSULTANT, and S.1 languages shown in Table 9.3 fall into this category, although most of them support other representation methods also. KEE, on the other hand, supports frames and objects as its primary representation method, with rule- and procedure-oriented methods playing a secondary role. For more information on the knowledge engineering languages listed in Table 9.3, see the catalog of expert system tools (Chapter 27).

The most important terms discussed in this chapter are summarized in Table 9.4. For a more complete description of these concepts, see the glossary of expert system terms at the end of the book.

TABLE 9.4 More expert system terminology.

Term	*Meaning*
Active value	A procedure invoked when program data are changed or read, often used to drive graphical displays of gauges that show the values of the program variables.
Access-oriented methods	Programming methods based on the use of probes that trigger new computations when data are changed or read.
Demon	A procedure activated by the changing or accessing of values in a data base.
Frame-based methods	Programming methods using frame hierarchies for inheritance and procedural attachment.
Interpreter	That part of a programming system that analyzes the code to decide what actions to take next.
Logic-based methods	Programming methods that use predicate calculus to structure the program and guide execution.
Metaknowledge	Knowledge about the use and control of domain knowledge in an expert system.
Metarule	A rule that describes how other rules should be used or modified.

Continued

TABLE 9.4 Continued

Term	Meaning
Object-oriented methods	Programming methods based on the use of items called *objects* that communicate with one another via messages.
Predicate calculus	A formal language of classical logic that uses functions and predicates to describe relations between individual entities.
Procedure-oriented methods	Programming methods using nested subroutines to organize and control program execution.
Rule-based methods	Programming methods using IF-THEN rules to perform forward or backward chaining.
Schema	A frame-like representation formalism in a knowledge engineering language (e.g., SRL).
Units	A frame-like representation formalism employing slots with values and procedures attached to them.

10

Examples of Knowledge Engineering Languages

Knowledge engineering languages come in many sizes and shapes with differing features and degrees of sophistication and development. But most have one thing in common—a predefined inference engine ready to process a knowledge base constructed according to the specifications of the language. This gives them a bit of an edge over programming languages. When knowledge engineers develop an expert system in a programming language (e.g., LISP), they tend to use it as a building block for constructing high-level knowledge representations and an inference engine to access the knowledge. This means the system can be tailored to fit the problem, but the tailoring involves much time and effort. With a knowledge engineering language, the tailoring is already done; the difficulty is finding a language suited to your problem. In Chapter 13, we discuss this difficulty and present guidelines for selecting appropriate system building tools.

Four knowledge engineering languages merit our special attention because they are so widely used. The languages are EMYCIN, EXPERT, OPS5, and ROSIE. Table 10.1 lists their basic features. In this chapter, we'll consider these languages in some detail, paying particular attention to the ways in which they represent domain knowledge and the kinds of applications for which they have been used.

EMYCIN

This skeletal knowledge engineering language is essentially MYCIN with the domain knowledge removed, as illustrated in Figure 10.1.

TABLE 10.1 Knowledge engineering languages for building expert systems.

Tool	Type	Features	Implementation Language	Developer
EMYCIN	Skeletal system	Rule-based Backward chaining Certainty handling Explanation Acquisition	INTERLISP	Stanford University
EXPERT	Skeletal system	Rule-based Forward chaining Certainty handling Explanation Acquisition Consistency checking	FORTRAN	Rutgers University
OPS5	General-purpose system	Rule-based Forward chaining Flexible control Flexible representation	FRANZ LISP	Carnegie-Mellon University
ROSIE	General-purpose system	Rule-based Forward chaining Procedure-oriented English-like syntax	INTERLISP	The Rand Corporation

EMYCIN uses a rule-based knowledge representation scheme with a rigid backward chaining control mechanism that limits its application to diagnosis and classification-type problems. However, the system provides sophisticated explanation and acquisition facilities that clearly speed expert system development.

EMYCIN has been used to build diagnosis-type expert systems in medicine, geology, engineering, agriculture, and other areas. Figure 10.2 shows some of these EMYCIN applications.

An EMYCIN rule has the form IF **antecedent** THEN **consequent**, where the antecedent is a collection of true/false expressions and the consequent is a conclusion that follows from the antecedent. A context tree organizes EMYCIN objects in a simple hierarchy and provides some of the inheritance characteristics of a frame system. EMYCIN associates a certainty value ranging from -1 (false) to $+1$ (true) with every expression in an antecedent. The IF portion of a rule is considered to be true if its certainty is greater than some threshold (say 0.2) and false if below some other threshold (say -0.2). EMYCIN uses special evidence-com-

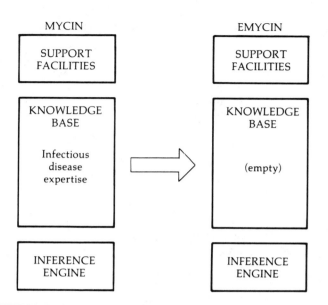

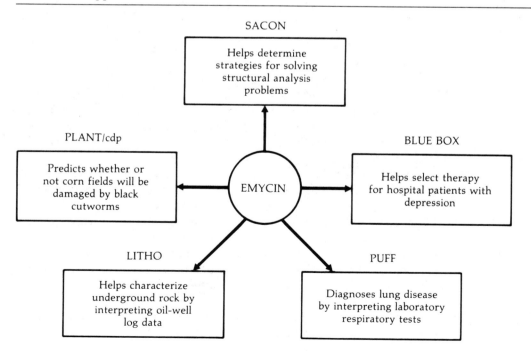

FIGURE 10.1 The creation of a skeletal system: MYCIN to EMYCIN.

FIGURE 10.2 Applications of EMYCIN.

IF: 1) The material composing the substructure is
         one of: the metals, and
      2) The analysis error (in percent) that is tolerable is
         between 5 and 30, and
      3) The nondimensional stress of the substructure is
         greater than 0.9, and
      4) The number of cycles the loading is to be applied is
         between 1000 and 10000

THEN: It is definite (1.0) that fatigue is one of the
         stress behavior phenomena in the substructure.

} English translation of the EMYCIN rule shown below.

PREMISE: ($AND (SAME CNTXT MATERIAL (LISTOF METALS))
                 (BETWEEN* CNTXT ERROR 5 30)
                 (GREATERP* CNTXT NO-STRESS 0.9)
                 (BETWEEN* CNTXT CYCLE 1000 10000))
ACTION: (CONCLUDE CNTXT SS-STRESS FATIGUE TALLY 1.0)

} Actual EMYCIN rule.

FIGURE 10.3 An EMYCIN rule from the SACON expert system.

bining formulas [SHO75] to decide how to combine the certainties in the antecedent and update the certainty of the consequent.

This description becomes clearer when we look at actual rules written in EMYCIN. Figure 10.3 shows a rule from SACON, a consultation system that provides advice to a structural engineer regarding the use of a structural analysis program called MARC [MAR76]. MARC uses mathematical analysis techniques to simulate the mechanical behavior of objects.

Figure 10.4 shows a rule from PUFF, an expert system that interprets measurements from respiratory tests administered to patients in the pulmonary function laboratory at Pacific Medical Center in San Francisco. PUFF uses the measurements to produce a set of interpretation statements and a diagnosis for the patient.

The EMCYIN rules in Figures 10.3 and 10.4 are the strange-looking PREMISE-ACTION expressions at the bottom of each figure. EMCYIN stores and executes this LISP-like code, and the expert-system builder must be able to read and write it. Life is less bleak for the system user, since EMYCIN prints an English version of each rule, as shown at the top of each figure, whenever the user asks to see rules or wants explanations involving rules.

```
    IF:   1) A: The mmf/mmf-predicted ratio is between 35 and 45, and
             B: The fvc/fvc-predicted ratio is greater than 80, or      }  English
          2) A: The mmf/mmf-predicted ratio is between 25 and 35, and      translation
             B: The fvc/fvc-predicted ratio is less than 80               of the
  THEN:   1)    There is suggestive evidence (0.5) that the degree of      EMYCIN
                obstructive airways disease as indicated by the mmf       } rule
                is moderate, and                                           shown
          2)    It is definite (1.0) that the following is one of the      below.
                findings about the diagnosis of obstruction airways
                disease: Reduced mid-expiratory flow indicates
                moderate airway obstruction.

PREMISE:      [$AND ($OR ($AND (BETWEEN* (VAL1 CNTXT MMF) 35 45)
                         (GREATERP* (VAL1 CNTXT FVC) 80))
                    ($AND (BETWEEN* (VAL1 CNTXT MMF) 25 35)         }  Actual
                         (LESSP* (VALI CNTXT FVC) 80]                  EMYCIN
  ACTION:  (DO-ALL (CONCLUDE CNTXT DEG-MMF MODERATE TALLY 500)        rule.
                  (CONCLUDE TEXT CNTXT FINDINGS-OAD
                         (TEXT $MMF/FVC2) TALLY 1000))
```

FIGURE 10.4 An EMYCIN rule from the PUFF expert system.

EXPERT

This skeletal knowledge engineering language uses a rule-based knowledge representation scheme and has a limited forward chaining control mechanism that makes it suitable for diagnosis and classification-type problems. EXPERT has built-in explanation, knowledge acquisition, and consistency checking facilities to speed system development. The consistency checking module works by storing a data base of representative cases with known conclusions and using it to test the expert system after the knowledge engineer adds new rules. If a case doesn't produce correct conclusions, EXPERT displays the reasoning for that case so that the knowledge engineer can understand how the new rules led to the unexpected results.

EXPERT has been used to build diagnosis programs in medicine, geology, and other areas. Figure 10.5 shows some of these applications.

Since EXPERT was designed to handle consultation problems in medicine, it structures knowledge to facilitate medical interpretation. Rules in EXPERT distinguish between findings and hypotheses. Findings are observations like a patient's age or blood pressure, while hy-

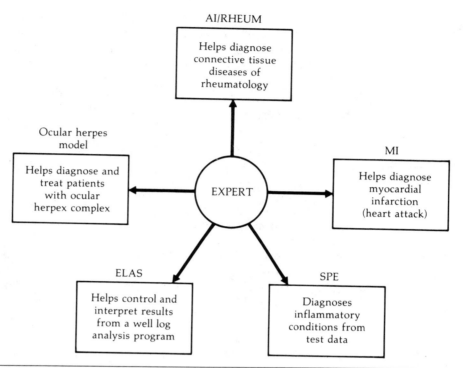

FIGURE 10.5 Applications of EXPERT.

potheses are conclusions inferred from findings or other hypotheses. In EXPERT, findings have the form f(*finding-name, truth-value*), while hypotheses have the form h(*hypothesis-name, certainty-interval*). The truth value is *t* if the finding is true and *f* if false. The certainty interval represents the confidence the expert has in the hypothesis, e.g., h(matrl, 0.2:1) means conclude hypothesis *matrl* with a confidence of 0.2 to 1. Confidence values range from −1 (complete denial) to 1 (complete confirmation).

Figure 10.6 shows an EXPERT rule from AI/RHEUM, a consultation system that diagnoses connective tissue diseases in rheumatology. These diseases include some found to be particularly difficult for physicians other than rheumatologist physicians to diagnose, such as rheumatoid arthritis and systemic sclerosis.

Figure 10.7 shows an EXPERT rule from an experimental spill-management system for the discovery and containment of hazardous chemical and oil spills [BAR83]. When a spill occurs, the system recommends spill notification and containment procedures, locates the spill source, and identifies the spill material.

As the figures show, the actual EXPERT rules use a concise short-hand notation, which, although easy to learn, is not so easy to read without lists defining the meanings of all terms. However, at any point during an EXPERT consultation, the user can ask for an interpretive analysis, and EXPERT will give an English description of what it has done and what remains to be done, including any intermediate or final conclusions reached.

OPS5

This general-purpose knowledge engineering language uses a rule-based representation scheme that works via forward chaining. The system's generality supports diverse data representation and control structures within a single program. OPS5 has a powerful pattern-matcher and an efficient interpreter for matching rules against the data but lacks a sophisticated support environment. It has no built-in explanation or acquisition mechanisms and only minimal facilities for program editing

FIGURE 10.6 An EXPERT rule from the AI/RHEUM expert system.

```
** hypotheses
    CNS   The patient has a central nervous
          system disease
** findings
    SEIZ    seizures occur
   PSYCH    psychosis exists
   OBSYN    organic brain syndrome is present
    COMA    coma exists
** rules
    IF:   One of the following is true:           ⎫
          seizures, psychosis, organic brain      ⎪
          syndrome, or coma,                      ⎬ Translation of
  THEN:   Conclude serious central nervous        ⎪ the EXPERT
          system disease                          ⎪ rule shown
          at a confidence level of 1.0.           ⎭ below.

          [1:f(seiz,t), f(psych,t),               ⎫ Actual
              f(obsyn,t), f(coma,t)] → h(cns,1.0)  ⎬ EXPERT
                                                   ⎭ rule.
```

```
**hypotheses
MATRL   the spill material has been identified
HELTH   a potential health hazard exists
  HAZ   a complete hazard analysis is required
**rules
   IF:   The spill material has been identified
         with a confidence of 0.2 to 1, and
         a potential health hazard exists
         with a confidence of 0.1 to 1
 THEN:   Conclude a complete hazard analysis is
         required at a confidence level of 1.0.

         h(matrl,0.2:1) & h(helth,0.1:1) → h(haz,1.0)
```

Translation of the EXPERT rule shown below.

Actual EXPERT rule.

FIGURE 10.7 An EXPERT rule from a spill-management expert system.

and debugging. OPS5 is the latest in a succession of similar rule-based languages (e.g., OPS, OPS4) that evolved from work at Carnegie-Mellon University in developing programming languages for modeling human cognition and memory.

OPS5 and the earlier languages in the OPS series have been used for many cognitive psychology, AI, and expert system applications. Figure 10.8 shows some of these applications.

An OPS5 rule has the form **antecedent** → **consequent**, where the antecedent describes data elements and the consequent specifies the actions to take if the antecedent matches the data base. Data elements in OPS5 are objects described by a set of attribute-value pairs. They look a bit like LISP expressions, as illustrated below.

	English		*OPS5*
The tall woman is 23 years old.	→	(WOMAN ↑ HEIGHT TALL ↑ AGE 23)
The Job Entry System (JES) queue space is critically low.	→	(JES-Q ↑ MODE PANIC)

The object (e.g., WOMAN, JES-Q) comes first followed by the attribute-value pairs. Attributes are marked with a caret (↑) to distinguish them from values. One thing that makes OPS5 (and LISP) so difficult to read is the use of one-word terms to stand for complex concepts. In the JES example shown above, the OPS5 code literally says: "The mode of the job entry system queue = panic." Only the programmer would ever know this means space in the queue is critically low.

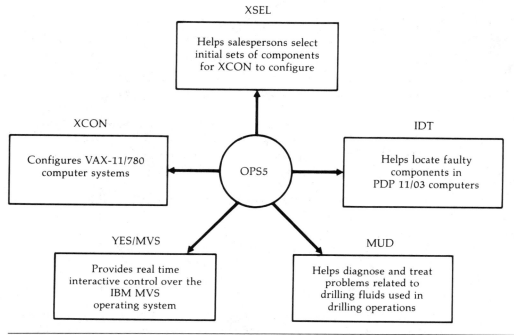

FIGURE 10.8 Applications of OPS5.

Figure 10.9 shows an actual OPS5 rule from the Yorktown Expert System for MVS Operators (YES/MVS). This system helps computer operators monitor and control Multiple Virtual Storage (MVS) operating systems, the most widely used operating system on large IBM mainframe computers. Its tasks include ensuring that the job entry system (JES) has enough available memory (queue space) to handle all the new jobs being sent to the computer.

FIGURE 10.9 An OPS5 rule from the YES/MVS expert system.

IF: The current task is to maintain the job entry system queue space, and the queue space is critically low, and there is a link to the computer that is actively receiving messages **THEN:** Send a command to cut the link and mark the link's reception status as "about to be no."	English translation of the OPS5 rule shown below.

Continued

FIGURE 10.9 Continued

```
(P STOP-RECEPTION
(TASK  ↑ TASK-ID JES-Q-SPACE)
(JES-Q  ↑ MODE PANIC)
   (<THE-LINK >  (LINK  ↑ ID < L-ID >
                        ↑ STATUS < <ACTIVE I/O-ACTIVE > >
                        ↑ RECEIVE YES))

  ──────▶

   (CALL REMOTE-MAKE
        LINK-COMMAND  ↑ ID < L-ID >
                      ↑ RECEIVE NO
                      ↑ RM-TO: MCCF)
   (MODIFY < THE-LINK >  ↑ RECEIVE TO-BE-NO))
```

Actual
OPS5
rule.

As Figure 10.9 indicates, OPS5 rules can be somewhat verbose and unintelligible. Even worse, the OPS5 language has no provision for displaying English versions of the rules to the user the way EMYCIN does. Despite this, OPS5 is one of the most widely used knowledge engineering languages available, and it has been used in many commercial expert system development efforts. Its widespread use is due partly to its execution efficiency and partly to its ready availability.

ROSIE

This general-purpose knowledge engineering language combines a rule-based representation scheme with a procedure-oriented language design (see Table 9.1 in Chapter 9). Thus ROSIE programs are typically nested procedures and functions, each defined as a set of rules. ROSIE has an English-like syntax that makes its code quite readable, powerful pattern-matching routines for matching the rule premises against the data, and control over remote jobs via an interface to the local operating system. ROSIE's support environment includes editing and debugging tools but no built-in explanation or acquisition facilities.

ROSIE has been used to build expert systems in a variety of problem domains, including law, crisis management, and the military. Figure 10.10 shows some of these ROSIE applications.

It is possible to represent five basic types of English relationships in ROSIE:

Relationship	ROSIE code
1) Class membership	The defendant is a corporation.
	The product is a champagne bottle.

2) Predication

    The plaintiff is young.
    The champagne bottle was defective.

3) Intransitive verbs

    The product did explode.
    Strict liability does apply.

4) Transitive verbs

    The product did injure the plaintiff.
    The corporation does manufacture the bottle.

5) Predicate complements

    The plaintiff is partially responsible.
    The injury was nearly avoided.

These relationships can be extended by using prepositional phrases:

6) Prepositional phrases

    The product did explode in the kitchen
    of the restaurant.

These five forms can be combined to express complex concepts in a direct way:

1,3,4 The exploding champagne bottle did injure the plaintiff.

  2,5 The young plaintiff is partially responsible for the injury.

  1,4 The defendant is a corporation that does manufacture the bottle.

FIGURE 10.10 Applications of ROSIE.

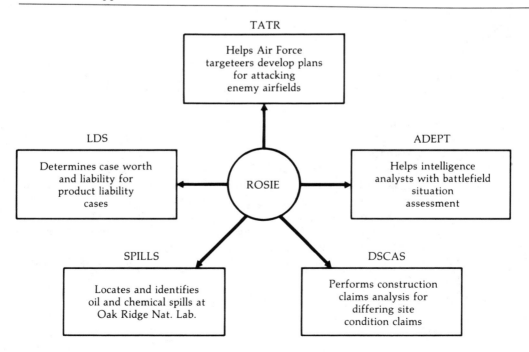

ROSIE programs take the form of rule sets, each defined to be either a procedure, a generator, or a predicate. A procedure is like a subroutine: It performs some task and then returns control to the portion of the program that called it. A generator is like a function: It returns a value or set of values. For example, a generator for determining medical costs would return a specific dollar amount when given the name of an injured party. A predicate is a function that always returns either *true* or *false*. For example, LDS has a predicate that decides whether or not the product is defective.

Figure 10.11 shows an actual ROSIE rule from LDS, an expert system for analyzing product liability cases. The system uses the facts of the case, together with rules based on formal legal principles and attorneys' informal procedures and strategies, to calculate defendant liability, case worth, and an equitable settlement amount.

The two ROSIE rules in Figure 10.11 represent executable code, not English translations of that code. ROSIE's expressiveness and readability speed expert system development, especially in domains where the rules are naturally complex and detailed.

FIGURE 10.11 Two ROSIE rules from LDS expert system.

```
If there is a test for product inspection and
    that test is recognized by experts as good and sound and    Actual
    that test is used for possible discovery of defects and      ROSIE
    the defendant did not perform that test,                     rule.
Assert the product was defective for failure to test and inspect.

If the product was dangerous to a substantial number of people and
    the plaintiff was injured by the product and
    the product is represented by the defendant and             Actual
    (the defendant did not warn of the danger or                ROSIE
    the warning was not complete or                             rule.
    the warning was insufficient) and
    the normal use of the product was both intended and foreseeable,
Assert the product was defective for failure to warn.
```

Building an Expert System

We've discussed the basic components of expert systems, looked at the ways in which they structure expertise, and surveyed the areas in which they are currently being used. It's time to turn our attention to the central concerns of anyone who is contemplating expert system development: "Is an expert system really what I need, and if so, what will the development process be like?" In this section, we suggest the kind of issues to consider when answering these questions and illustrate the development process with an example.

11

Will Expert Systems Work for My Problem?

AI scientists find it difficult to describe in general terms the characteristics that make a problem appropriate for expert system development. They are much better at taking the description of a specific problem and either rating its potential or revising its scope and focus to make it appropriate. Often the right question is not "will expert systems work for my problem area?" but rather "what aspect of my problem area lends itself to expert system development?" Thus we can't just make a list of suitable and unsuitable problem areas. For example, as a problem domain, medicine is no more or less appropriate than chemistry or geology for expert system development. But the particular problem of diagnosing glaucoma and prescribing therapy could indeed be more or less appropriate than the problem of discovering patterns in the primary sequences of functionally related proteins in order to obtain structure-activity correlations down to the gene level.

However, an organization that is thinking about developing an expert system has a rather different perspective. For obvious reasons, the organization's first question is "will the expert systems approach work for my particular problem?" Although we can't offer a simple, general answer to this important question, we can present some guidelines for considering the issue. These guidelines can be summarized as follows:

Consider expert systems only if expert system development is possible, justified, and appropriate.

Let's consider what we mean by "possible, justified, and appropriate."

When Is Expert System Development Possible?

Figure 11.1 summarizes the problem domain characteristics required to make expert system development possible.

One of the most important requirements is that genuine experts exist. These are people generally acknowledged to have an extremely high level of expertise in the problem area; they are significantly better than novices at solving problems in the domain. Without a source of extensive, powerful knowledge to draw on, the development effort will fail to produce a truly skillful program.

Having bona fide experts isn't enough. They must also generally agree about the choice and accuracy of solutions in the problem domain. Otherwise, validating the expert system's performance would be a near impossible task. The experts must also be able to articulate and explain the methods that they use to solve domain problems. If they can't do this, the knowledge engineers will have little success "extracting" knowledge from them and embedding it in a program.

The other requirements for expert system development deal with the characteristics of the problem that the expert system will solve—the task it will perform. The task must require cognitive, not physical, skills. If the task consists of physical manipulations that can only be learned through practice, the traditional expert systems approach won't work. However, this doesn't mean that every problem with a physical component must be ruled out. If the task requires a combination of cognitive and physical skills, such as monitoring and controlling the use of robot arms on an assembly line, the cognitive portion can be handled by knowledge engineering techniques and the physical portion by more conventional methods.

Another required characteristic is that the task not be extremely difficult. If an expert cannot teach the process to a novice because expertise can only be developed through on-the-job experience, the process may be too difficult to capture in an expert system. Or if any expert takes days or weeks rather than hours to solve the problem, there's a good chance that it's too difficult or too complex for a knowledge engineering approach. However, if a task that requires days or weeks of concentrated effort can be segmented into smaller, shorter, relatively independent subtasks, each subtask might be a candidate for expert system development.

Task difficulty also relates in certain ways to how well the experts understand the problem domain—that is, the degree to which problem-solving knowledge is precise and well-structured. If the task is so new or so poorly understood that it requires basic research to find solutions,

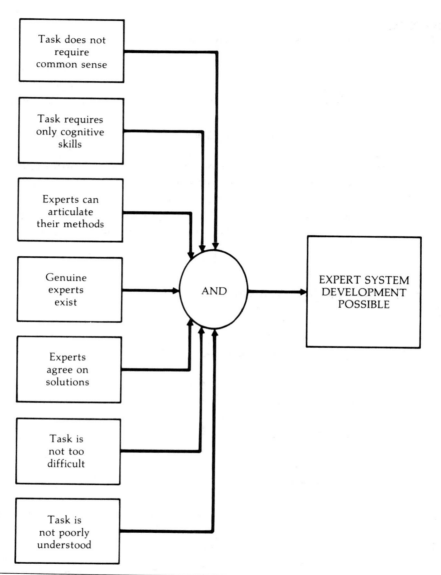

FIGURE 11.1 Necessary requirements for expert system development.

knowledge engineering will not work. It will also not work if the task requires a significant amount of common sense. As we pointed out in Chapter 2, AI programs stumble badly when faced with tasks that require commonsense reasoning.

When Is Expert System Development Justified?

Just because it's possible to develop an expert system for a particular task doesn't mean that it's desirable to do so. There are many ways to justify an expert system development effort; Figure 11.2 illustrates a few of these.

A company can justify expert system development when the task solution has a very high payoff. For example, an expert system for mineral exploration could uncover a rich ore deposit worth millions of dollars. If there is a reasonable possibility of a high payoff, development seems like a good idea.

Expert system development is justified when human experts are unavailable or unable to do the job. Often human experts are scarce,

FIGURE 11.2 Justification for expert system development.

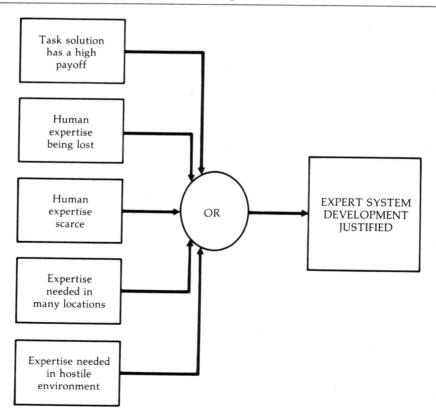

very much in demand—and thus expensive. The problem is compounded when the company needs similar expertise at many different physical locations, such as process control expertise for each distillation column owned by a petrochemical company. This generates a need for multiple versions of the expert, something that can be done easily and at virtually no cost when the expert is a computer program. In this sort of situation an expert system is a cheap, effective way to handle the problem. Indeed, it may be the only cost-effective alternative.

Expert systems are justified when significant expertise is being lost to an organization through personnel changes. Retirement, job transfer, and military duty reassignment often cause disruption and even havoc because of the vital expertise that experienced personnel take with them when they leave. The institutional memory aspect of an expert system can minimize or even eliminate this problem.

Finally, expert system development is justified when the expert decision making must take place in an unfriendly or hostile environment, such as a nuclear power plant, space station, or alien planet. It would be either too expensive or dangerous to try to maintain a human expert in such an environment. Of course, the expertise could be administered remotely by a human expert via electronic communication channels. The possibility of communication delays and jamming by military foes makes this solution less attractive than having self-contained, on-site expertise available.

When Is Expert System Development Appropriate?

The key factors in determining when it is appropriate to develop an expert system are the nature, complexity, and scope of the problem to be solved. Figure 11.3 illustrates these factors and their relationship to characteristics that make a problem appropriate for expert system work.

Nature

To be appropriate for expert system work, a problem must have certain intrinsic qualities. It must be a problem that can be solved quite naturally by manipulating symbols and symbol structures. As discussed in Chapter 4, the ability to perform symbolic reasoning is one thing that sets expert systems apart from conventional programs. Most real-world problems require symbolic reasoning. Exceptions are those that have tractable mathematical solutions. Thus mathematically-oriented problems, such as solving differential equations with numerical analysis techniques, are usually not appropriate for expert system development.

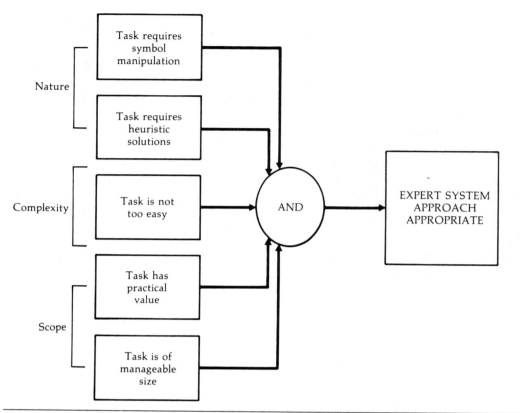

FIGURE 11.3 Characteristics that make the use of expert systems appropriate.

However, some mathematical problems, such as algebraic simplification, lend themselves quite readily to symbolic reasoning.

Most problems that are appropriate for expert system work are *heuristic* in nature; that is, they require the use of rules of thumb to achieve acceptable solutions. Problems that can be solved with algorithms—formal procedures that guarantee the correct solution every time—are not good candidates for expert system development. For example, there are many different algorithms for sorting lists, and it would be more cost-effective to solve this problem with a conventional program rather than with an expert system. In some sense, the expert systems approach is the last resort. If the problem can be solved mathematically or with clever algorithms, then those methods should be used. If it's too difficult for these conventional techniques, expert systems may be appropriate.

Complexity

The problem must *not be too easy*. It should be a formidable, serious problem, in a domain in which it takes a human years of study or practice to achieve the status of an expert. Thus the sorting problem just mentioned would not be appropriate for a second reason: It's not complex or difficult enough to justify the cost and effort of expert system development.

Scope

Finally, the problem should have the proper scope. It should be sufficiently narrow to make the problem manageable and sufficiently broad to ensure that the problem has some practical interest. Unfortunately, the definitions of *manageable* and *practical* depend on the particular problem domain. And to make matters worse, choosing the proper scope is crucial to the success of the expert system endeavor. Indeed, one of the most dangerous pitfalls in expert system building is choosing a problem that is too broad or general to be handled adequately.

The following example will help to clarify the scope issue. Suppose the problem is to build an expert system to help attorneys settle cases. We can divide the problem into two main subproblems, negotiation and evaluation, as illustrated in Figure 11.4.

To keep the scope from being far too broad, we must limit the type of case to a single category, such as product liability, construction claims, or automobile accident. But even within a single category, the scope is too broad. We could correct this by limiting the task to the negotiation process—how to interact with the other side to maximize (or minimize) the settlement amount. This involves considering both defense and plaintiff negotiations. Here we might limit the scope even further to just defense or just plaintiff negotiation.

Another possibility would be to consider case evaluation—determining the dollar value of the case. Case evaluation includes a number of steps, such as 1) setting an initial dollar value on the plaintiff's loss, 2) determining the defendant's degree of liability and its influence on the dollar amount, 3) estimating the proportion of responsibility that should be assessed to the plaintiff for his own carelessness and its effect on case value, 4) analyzing subjective considerations that affect case value, such as the personalities of the litigants and the skill of their attorneys, and 5) making adjustments to case value for matters of strategy, timing, and type of claim. The range of these considerations makes case evaluation a bit too broad in scope.

We could restrict the scope either by 1) only considering a specific

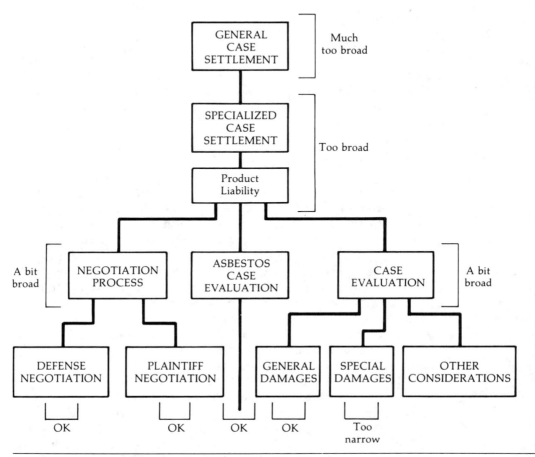

FIGURE 11.4 Ways to limit the scope of an expert system for case settlement.

type of case, e.g., asbestos cases, or 2) only considering a specific component of case value—for example, general damages, the amount the plaintiff should receive because of bodily injury. But if the component of case value considered were restricted to special damages—primarily adding up the medical expenses, lost income, and property damage—the task would probably be too narrow to have sufficient practical interest or use.

12

Building an Expert System

Suppose that your problem meets all the criteria discussed in Chapter 11. What would the process of building an expert system be like?

Expert system builders don't have a series of well-defined steps that they follow when constructing a system. The inherent complexity of the system building process precludes laying out all the steps in advance. As a result, system builders have found that an evolutionary development is the most effective way to proceed.

The evolution of an expert system normally proceeds from simple to hard tasks by incrementally improving the organization and representation of the system's knowledge. This incremental approach to development means that the system itself can assist in the development effort. As soon as builders acquire enough knowledge to construct even a very simple system, they do so and use feedback from the running model to direct and focus the effort. The incremental approach also means that the system builders can profit from what they learn in implementing the initial aspects of the system.

One common result of incremental development is what has been called a *paradigm shift* [HAY83b], as illustrated in Figure 12.1. At some point during development, the knowledge base may reach an unmanageable size; control becomes unwieldy and slow, and the system may resemble a patchwork of routines and unintegrated constructs. At this juncture, it may be wise to consider redesigning and reimplementing the system. The knowledge engineer and domain expert should reexamine the problem and reassess their initial representation scheme. This could lead to a more suitable architecture for the problem and even a different system-building tool. Long-term development efforts will be more likely to involve major paradigm shifts than will short-term efforts.

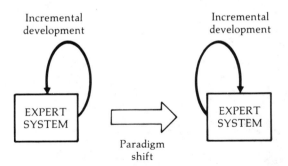

FIGURE 12.1 Expert system development may involve major redesign and reimplementation.

Even though we cannot specify the exact steps to follow in building an expert system, we can describe the stages of system development and the types of activities performed at each stage.

Tasks in Building Expert Systems

Expert system development can be viewed as five highly interdependent and overlapping phases: identification, conceptualization, formalization, implementation, and testing [BUC83]. Figure 12.2 illustrates how these phases interact.

Although we distinguish between these phases of expert system building, there is no simple way to describe the order in which they take place. Identification does happen first and testing last, but at any time during system development the knowledge engineer may engage in any of the processes. The arrows pointing from testing back to the earlier phases indicate how this might happen. In fact, to make the figure more accurate, we should draw arrows pointing from every phase to every other phase.

During *identification*, the knowledge engineer and expert determine the important features of the problem. This includes identifying the problem itself (e.g., type and scope), the participants in the development process (e.g., additional experts), the required resources (e.g., time and computing facilities), and the goals or objectives of building the expert system (e.g., improve performance or distribute scarce expertise). Of these activities, identifying the problem and its scope gives developers the most trouble. Often the problem first considered is too large or complex and must be scaled down to a manageable size. The knowledge engineer may obtain a quick measure of this complexity by focusing on a small but interesting subproblem and implementing routines to solve it.

During *conceptualization*, the knowledge engineer and expert decide what concepts, relations, and control mechanisms are needed to describe problem solving in the domain. Subtasks, strategies, and constraints related to the problem-solving activity are also explored. At this time the issue of *granularity* is usually addressed. This just means considering at what level of detail the knowledge should be represented. The knowledge engineer will normally pick the most abstract level of detail (coarsest grain) that still provides adequate discrimination between key concepts. A word of warning—the developers must avoid trying to produce a complete problem analysis before beginning program implementation. They will learn much from the first implementation that will shape and direct the conceptualization process.

Formalization involves expressing the key concepts and relations in some formal way, usually within a framework suggested by an expert system building language. Thus the knowledge engineer should have

FIGURE 12.2 Development phases for expert system building.

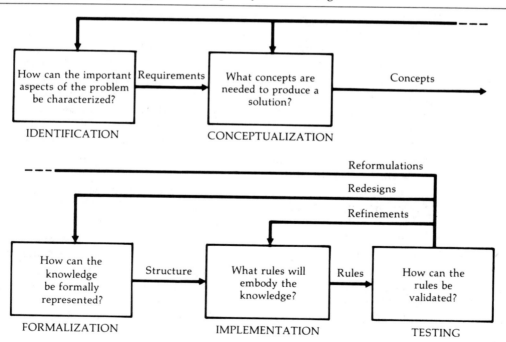

some ideas about appropriate tools for the problem by the time formalization begins. For example, if the problem seems amenable to a rule-based approach, the knowledge engineer might select ROSIE as the system-building language and gather expertise in the form of IF-THEN rules. If a frame-based approach seems more appropriate, the knowledge engineer might instead select SRL and work with the expert to express domain knowledge as a large network.

During *implementation,* the knowledge engineer turns the formalized knowledge into a working computer program. Constructing a program requires content, form, and integration. The content comes from the domain knowledge made explicit during formalization, that is, the data structures, inference rules, and control strategies necessary for problem solving. The form is specified by the language chosen for system development. Integration involves combining and reorganizing various pieces of knowledge to eliminate global mismatches between data structures and rule or control specifications. Implemetation should proceed rapidly because one of the reasons for implementing the initial prototype is to check the effectiveness of the design decisions made during the earlier phases of development. This means that there is a high probability that the initial code will be revised or discarded during development.

Finally, *testing* involves evaluating the performance and utility of the prototype program and revising it as necessary. The domain expert typically evaluates the prototype and helps the knowledge engineer to revise it. As soon as the prototype runs on a few examples, it should be tested on many problems to evaluate its performance and utility. This evaluation may uncover problems with the representational scheme, such as missing concepts and relations, knowledge represented at the wrong level of detail, or unwieldy control mechanisms. Such problems may force the developers to recycle through the various development phases, reformulating the concepts, refining the inference rules, and revising the control flow.

Evaluating the prototype system's performance means asking the following kinds of questions. Does the system make decisions that experts generally agree are appropriate? Are the inference rules correct, consistent, and complete? Does the control strategy allow the system to consider items in the natural order the expert prefers? (Querying the user in an unnatural or stupid-looking way quickly reduces the user's confidence in the system.) Are the system's explanations adequate for describing how and why conclusions are being reached? Do the test problems cover the domain, handling prototypical cases and probing the boundaries of expected hard cases?

In evaluating the system's utility, a different set of questions arises. For example, does the solution of the problem help the user in some significant way? Are the system's conclusions appropriately organized and ordered and presented at the right level of detail? Is the system fast enough to satisfy the user? Is the interface friendly enough?

The expert system must be refined and tested in a laboratory environment before it can be released for field testing. However, when it is tested by the user community on real problems, new complications will arise which may take some time to correct. Users in the field demand more than just high-quality performance; they want a system to be fast, reliable, easy to use, easy to understand, and very forgiving when they make mistakes. Thus the expert system needs extensive field testing before it will be ready for commercial use.

Stages of Expert System Development

In terms of sophistication and utility, expert systems evolve in much the same way as expert system tools (see Chapter 9). In Table 12.1, we classify current systems along these dimensions.

Most expert systems begin as a *demonstration prototype*, that is, a small, demonstration program that handles a portion of the problem that will eventually be addressed. This type of program is often used in two ways: first, to convince potential sources of funding that AI and expert systems technology can effectively be applied to the problem in question; and second, to test ideas about problem definition, scoping, and representation for the domain. A typical rule-based demonstration prototype might contain 50 to 100 rules, perform adequately on one or two test cases, and take one to three months to develop.

Most current expert systems have evolved to the stage of *research prototype*, a medium-sized program capable of displaying credible performance on a number of test cases. These systems tend to be fragile; they may fail completely when given problems that fall near the boundary separating problems they can handle from those they cannot. Because they lack sufficient testing, they may also fail on some problems well within their scope. A typical rule-based research prototype might contain 200 to 500 rules, perform well on a large number of test cases, and take one to two years to develop.

Some expert systems have evolved past the research prototype to the stage of *field prototype*. These systems are medium- to large-sized programs that have been revised through testing on real problems in the user community. They are moderately reliable, contain smooth, friendly interfaces, and address the needs of the end-user. A typical rule-based field prototype might contain 500 to 1000 rules, perform very well on many test cases, and take two to three years to develop.

TABLE 12.1 Evolution of expert systems.

Development Stage	Description
Demonstration prototype	The system solves a portion of the problem undertaken, suggesting that the approach is viable and system development is achievable.
Research prototype	The system displays credible performance on the entire problem but may be fragile due to incomplete testing and revision.
Field prototype	The system displays good performance with adequate reliability and has been revised based on extensive testing in the user environment.
Production model	The system exhibits high quality, reliable, fast, and efficient performance in the user environment.
Commercial system	The system is a production model being used on a regular commercial basis.

A few expert systems have reached the stage of *production prototype*. These systems are large programs that have been extensively field-tested and are likely to have been reimplemented in a more efficient language to increase speed and to reduce computer storage requirements. A typical rule-based production prototype might contain 500 to 1500 rules, provide accurate, fast, and efficient decision making, and take two to four years to develop.

Only a very few expert systems have reached the stage of *commercial system*. These systems are production prototypes used on a regular commercial basis. XCON, one of the best known examples of a commercial expert system, contains well over 3000 rules, reaches correct conclusions 90 to 95 percent of the time, and took six years to develop.

The catalog of expert systems in Chapter 25 categorizes a number of expert systems according to the five stages just described.

The most important terms discussed in this chapter are summarized in Table 12.2. For a more complete description of these concepts, see the glossary of expert system terms at the end of the book.

TABLE 12.2 More expert system terminology.

Term	Meaning
Granularity	The level of detail in a chunk of information.

13

Choosing a Tool for Building Expert Systems

Choosing the correct problem scope and picking the right tool for building the expert system are two of the most difficult decisions to make in expert system development. We have already discussed the issue of problem scope in Chapter 11. In this chapter, we turn to the challenge of selecting an expert-system-building tool.

Selecting a tool is difficult because most tools weren't developed to handle a particular class of problems. Many of the earlier research tools evolved from specific expert systems by stripping the systems of their domain knowledge (e.g., EMYCIN and KAS). Some of the recent commercial tools incorporate what AI researchers consider to be the most promising new ways of representing knowledge in hopes that this will make the tools appropriate for more types of problems. The difficulty is that AI researchers aren't really sure what tool features are required by specific classes of problems. This situation leads to what could be called Davis' law:[1]

For every tool there is a task perfectly suited to it.

Unfortunately, the converse isn't true. In fact, for any given task, there may be a number of tools that will perform equally well. It is also true that none of the tools will be perfectly suited to it.

Further compounding the selection problem is the fact that in the past many expert-system-building tools were chosen for the wrong reasons. Most of the existing expert systems were built with tools chosen because 1) the knowledge engineer was already very familiar with the

---

[1] Randall Davis, AAAI Expert System Tutorial Lectures.

tool, 2) the tool was the most efficient one available that ran on the developer's hardware, or 3) the tool was developed and then applications were found to test it—the solution in search of a problem paradigm.

Despite the fact that there are no easy answers, we can suggest some basic guidelines for deciding what tool is appropriate for a specific problem task. It is useful to think of this decision in two parts: initially selecting the tool and then evaluating it. We'll discuss each of these and then consider whether the tool that is best for developing the expert system is also best to use in the finished product.

Questions to Ask When Selecting a Tool

There are six basic questions to ask when choosing an expert system tool:

- Does the tool provide the development team with the power and sophistication they need?
- Are the tool's support facilities adequate considering the time frame for development?
- Is the tool reliable?
- Is the tool maintained?
- Does the tool have the features suggested by the needs of the problem?
- Does the tool have the features suggested by the needs of the application?

Development Constraints

Expert system development requires time, money, personnel, and hardware—all of which influence the choice of a tool. In particular, these factors influence the decision about what *type* of tool to select: a programming language (e.g., LISP) or a knowledge engineering language (e.g., KEE). As Chapter 8 points out, programming languages offer more flexibility, but they usually require the developer to design the knowledge base and implement the inference engine that accesses that knowledge. Development often takes longer with a programming language, but the result may more closely fit the needs of the problem domain. On the other hand, knowledge engineering languages offer less flexibility but more guidelines and mechanisms for how to represent and access the system's knowledge. Development should be easier, faster, and thus cheaper with a knowledge engineering language, but it may not result in a system that is as effective or efficient as one written in a programming language. The guideline here is *pick a tool that complements the strength of the knowledge engineering team*. A weak, inexperienced team would do better with a more powerful but less flexible tool, such as a knowledge engineering language.

Support Facilities

Support facilities speed development and thus save time and money. The more extensive the support facilities, the more attractive the tool becomes as a development vehicle. Chapter 8 discusses the kinds of support facilities now available in expert-system-building tools, including debugging aids, knowledge base editors, I/O facilities, and explanation mechanisms. The guideline here is *pick a tool with adequate support facilities*.

Reliability

Development will be seriously impaired if the tool isn't reliable. An experimental or research tool can cause problems because of incomplete testing, obsolete documentation, and fluctuating language specifications. The tool is more likely to be reliable if it has a large user community and a reputation for being robust and well-debugged. When considering a tool, check to see what expert systems have been built with it and how the builders feel about the tool and its utility packages. The guideline here is *don't build an expert system with a tool still under development*.

Maintainability

Users of a tool seldom want to get sidetracked with maintenance problems, so there should be someone available to maintain the tool's performance and clarify its use. Normally, this will be the tool's developer. A very old tool can be a problem since the developer may no longer have an interest in maintaining it or providing adequate documentation. The guideline here is *pick a tool you will not have to maintain yourself during expert system development*.

Task Characteristics

As Figure 13.1 suggests, the task characteristics typically influence the choice of an expert-system-building tool. Features of the problem will suggest types of solutions, which in turn suggest particular tool features. Similarly, features of the application will suggest features needed by the expert system itself, which will also suggest particular tool fea-

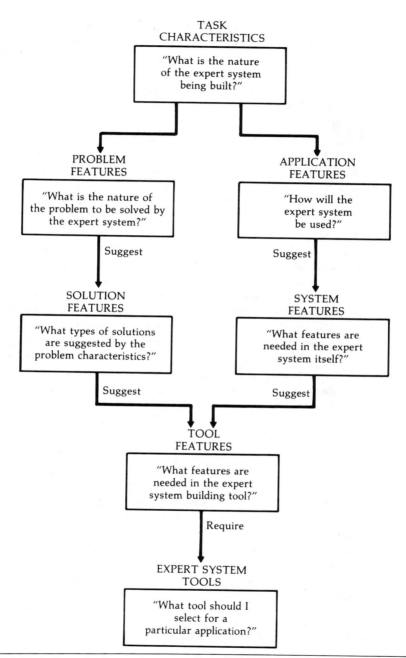

FIGURE 13.1 Basis for selecting an expert system tool.

tures. Once the needed tool features are determined, the choice of an expert-system-building tool can be narrowed by considering only those tools that provide the most important of the desired features. The guideline here is *pick a tool with features suggested by the problem and its application*.

Figure 13.2 shows how task characteristics can help to determine tool features.

Suppose that an important problem feature is that the problem solver must handle diverse types of knowledge, while an important application feature is that the user must be taught about the problem domain. The fact that knowledge about the same objects or events occurs in many different forms suggests the solution feature of cooperating knowledge sources, i.e., specialized subsystems each designed to analyze a particular type of knowledge and then communicate relevant findings to the other subsystems. This in turn suggests the need in the tool for a blackboard architecture where knowledge sources communicate via a central, structured data base called a *blackboard*.

The requirement that the system must function as a training device suggests the system feature of self-modification, since to be effective a trainer must build a model of the student's knowledge. This model normally includes rules that describe how the user or student tries to solve problems in the domain. The system would have to infer these rules from the user's responses and then add them to its knowledge base. This suggests the need for mechanisms in the tool that will permit rule and control modification.

AI research has not yet progressed to the point where we can list in the abstract all possible features suggested by Figure 13.1 and show how they map onto or suggest problem and application features. However, AI researchers can use this approach in analyzing a specific problem. When this mapping process is better understood, perhaps we will see tools that fit problem classes more naturally and effectively.

We will not attempt to provide a detailed description of problem, solution, application, and system features commonly found in expert system development efforts. Instead, we will provide some additional examples to make the discussion more concrete. However, more information is available on the subject of matching tasks to tools [CHA84, STE83a, STE83c].

Examples of Problem Features

Problem features include characteristics of the data and knowledge used by the expert system, characteristics of the search space, and the structure of the problem. For example, the data for a particular problem could vary over time, have a high acquisition cost, be of a spatial nature, be

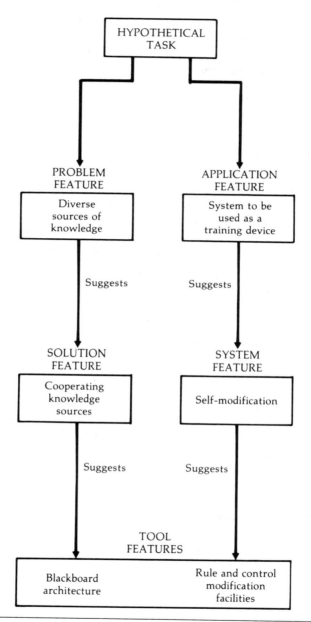

FIGURE 13.2 An example of determining tool features from task characteristics.

inconsistent, and be full of errors. The search space could be large or small, but if it's large, the problem is much more difficult. The problem structure could permit segmenting the problem into subproblems and solving them independently. On the other hand, the subproblems could interact, making the solution to one depend on the solutions to the others.

Examples of Application Features

Possible features of an expert system application include problem solving, training, and predictive modeling. Other features include the way the system will interact with users and the type of end-users expected. For example, will the system be an assistant that interacts with the user to solve the problem, or will it be autonomous? Will it handle only sophisticated, computer-oriented users, or will it have to deal with more naive users?

Examples of Solution Features

The solution features are the representation and search techniques used by the system to solve the problem. These are methods used to organize the system's knowledge and search for a solution. For example, *pruning via generate and test* is a search technique that can be effective even if the problem has a large number of possible solutions. However, it requires a method for *generating* possible solutions and *testing* their acceptability. Also, there must be ways to *prune* or drastically limit the possible solutions that are generated so that all possible solutions won't have to be tested. An alternative search technique uses *multiple lines of reasoning*. Here the search involves developing, in parallel, a limited number of possibly independent approaches to solving the problem. This method is appropriate when the rules controlling pruning of possible solutions are too restrictive and sometimes throw out good solutions before they can be tested.

Examples of System Features

System features include ways of interfacing with and handling the users and ways of adding new knowledge and data to the system. For example, the system could provide extensive graphics, help, or explanation capabilities. It could require that new knowledge be added through reprogramming, or it could allow it to be added via direct interaction with the domain expert. Even better, it might be self-modifying, able to extend itself by formulating new rules based on its experience and adding them when approved by the user.

Examples of Tool Features

The tool features are simply the features one might expect to find in various expert system building languages. They include such things as rule handling, rule modification, inheritance via frames, semantic nets, built-in explanation mechanisms, blackboard architectures, and certainty combining.

Of course, some tool features are always desirable, regardless of the task, because they speed system development. For example, an expert-system-building tool with a high-level and readable language will be easier to use than one without those features. Thus ROSIE is easier to use than OPS5 (see Chapter 10). Also, an expert-system-building tool should permit sequential processing, because there will be some sequential knowledge required for almost every application. Some rule-based systems, like EMYCIN, don't provide this, while others, like ROSIE, make sequential processing easy, even permitting nested procedures and cyclic rule evaluation.

Evaluating the System-Building Tool

Once you select a tool, consider implementing a prototype system with it in four to six weeks to test its effectiveness. This involves using the tool to solve a small, representative problem in the domain of interest. This step coincides with the need to implement a prototype quickly to verify that the problem scope and basic representation scheme are sound. We have discussed other advantages of this incremental development approach in Chapter 12.

During prototype testing, pay particular attention to the execution speed of the system. If it takes hours or minutes, rather than seconds, to obtain answers from the partially built system, then testing and refinement will be slow and the development impaired.

Davis points out that one indication of a good tool choice for an application is gradual degradation.[2] That is, as the problem becomes harder, the performance of the tool degrades gracefully rather than catastrophically, as illustrated in Figure 13.3.

[2] Randall Davis, AAAI Expert System Tutorial Lectures.

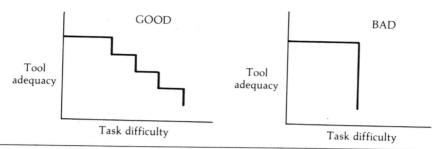

FIGURE 13.3 Gradual degradation of performance is one indication of tool adequacy.

The degradation-of-performance criterion provides one measure of a tool's adequacy but only after the tool has been used extensively in the problem domain.

Is the Best Development Tool the Best Production Tool?

In Chapter 12, we mentioned the possibility of a paradigm shift in developing an expert system. The tool best for developing the expert system may not be best for producing the system's final version. The development environment should have an abundance of support tools (e.g., debugging, editing), must provide the computing power to sustain a long-term development effort, and must be flexible enough to allow experimentation with different types of representation and control techniques. On the other hand, the delivery environment must have good interfacing to the user (e.g., natural language or graphics), and must be both fast and efficient.

The PUFF expert system for interpreting pulmonary function data provides one example of the shift between development and delivery vehicles. PUFF was developed in an INTERLISP-based EMYCIN on the DEC KI-10 and then later rewritten in BASIC, a production version designed to run on the Pacific Medical Center's own minicomputer.

The most important terms discussed in this chapter are summarized in Table 13.1. For a more complete description of these concepts, see the glossary of expert system terms at the end of the book.

TABLE 13.1 More expert system terminology.

Term	Meaning
Cooperating knowledge sources	Specialized modules in an expert system that independently analyze the data and communicate via a central, structured data base called a *blackboard*.
Exhaustive search	A problem-solving technique in which the problem solver systematically tries all possible solutions in some "brute-force" manner until it finds an acceptable one.
Generate and test	A problem-solving technique involving a generator that produces possible solutions and an evaluator that tests the acceptability of those solutions
Multiple lines of reasoning	A problem-solving technique in which a limited number of possibly independent approaches to solving the problem are developed in parallel.
Pruning	Reducing or narrowing the alternatives, normally used in the context of reducing possibilities in a branching *tree structure*.

14

Acquiring Knowledge from the Experts

Acquiring the knowledge needed to power an expert system and structuring that knowledge into a usable form is one of the primary bottlenecks in expert system development. At present, no automatic methods exist for doing this, with the exception of some very simple system-building aids capable of constructing rules from examples (see Chapter 9). Since it will be some time before these aids can even begin to replace the knowledge engineer, we'll devote this chapter to discussing how the knowledge engineer typically acquires expert knowledge.

The Knowledge Acquisition Process

Knowledge in an expert system may originate from many sources, such as textbooks, reports, data bases, case studies, empirical data, and personal experience. However, the dominant source of knowledge in today's expert systems is the domain expert. A knowledge engineer usually obtains this knowledge through direct interaction with the expert, as shown in Figure 14.1.

This interaction consists of a prolonged series of intense, systematic interviews, usually extending over a period of many months. During the interviews, the knowledge engineer presents the expert with realistic problems to solve that are the type of problems the expert system is being designed to handle.

For example, consider the problem of building an expert system that assists attorneys in the settlement of product liability cases. The knowledge engineer might provide the expert with descriptions of actual

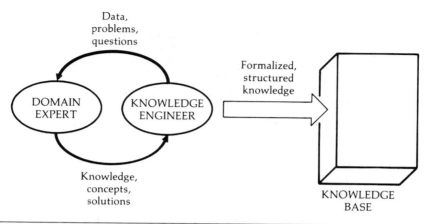

FIGURE 14.1 Typical knowledge acquisition process for building an expert system.

cases, including statements by witnesses and investigators, medical reports, and pertinent photographs and documents. After the expert has a chance to study the material, the knowledge engineer questions the expert in detail about how he or she would evaluate and attempt to settle the cases. The knowledge engineer can explore a range of issues within each case by varying case facts and noting how the expert adjusts to the changing conditions.

The knowledge engineer must work with the expert in the context of solving particular problems. It is seldom effective to ask the expert directly about his or her rule or methods for solving a particular type of problem in the domain. Domain experts usually have great difficulty expressing such rules. One reason for this is summarized below [WAT79].

> "Experts", it appears, have a tendency to state their conclusions and the reasoning behind them in general terms that are too broad for effective machine analysis. It is advantageous to have the machine work at a more basic level, dealing with clearly defined pieces of basic information that it can build into more complex judgments. In contrast, the expert seldom operates at a basic level. He makes complex judgments rapidly, without laboriously reexamining and restating each step in his reasoning process. The pieces of basic knowledge are assumed and are combined so quickly that it is difficult for him to describe the process. When he examines a problem, he cannot easily articulate each step and may even be unaware of the individual steps taken to reach a solution. He may ascribe to intuition or label a hunch that which is the result of a very complex reasoning process based upon a large amount of remembered

data and experience. In subsequently explaining his conclusion or hunch he will repeat only the major steps, often leaving out most of the smaller ones, which may have seemed obvious to him at the time. Knowing what to consider basic and relevant and not requiring further reevaluation is what makes a person an "expert."

This aspect of the expert's nature is somewhat unusual. In fact, it has been called the *paradox of expertise* [JOH83a]. In the context of expert system development we will call it the *knowledge engineering paradox.*

The more competent domain experts become, the less able they are to describe the knowledge they use to solve problems!

Even worse, studies have shown that when experts attempt to explain how they reached a conclusion, they often construct plausible lines of reasoning that bear little resemblance to their actual problem-solving activity [JOH83a]. This effect has at least two important implications for the building of expert systems: First, it suggests that domain experts need outside help to clarify and explicate their thinking and problem solving. This can be translated into the following rule of thumb:

Don't be your own expert!

If you are building an expert system and are a domain expert, have a knowledge engineer help you understand and formalize your problem-solving methods. If you are a knowledge engineer who has studied the domain extensively (and think you are an expert), work with a real expert anyway. If you are, in fact, a bona fide domain expert and an experienced knowledge engineer (a rare combination), play the role of knowledge engineer and find someone else to act as the domain expert. Good domain experts are more plentiful than experienced knowledge engineers.

The knowledge engineering paradox also suggests a second rule of thumb, directed toward the knowledge engineer:

Don't believe everything experts say!

Experienced knowledge engineers will develop working hypotheses based on what the experts say and will test the hypotheses for validity and consistency by having the experts solve new problems requiring the hypothesized knowledge. The knowledge engineer believes he or she has a legitimate rule of expertise not just because the expert *vouches* for the rule's accuracy, but because the expert *demonstrates* the use of the rule during problem solving.

Sometimes the behavior of experts appears more intuitive than intelligent. Larkin [LAR80] agrees with this idea (paraphrased):

Considerable knowledge has been found to be an essential prerequisite to expert skill. However, the expert is not merely an unindexed compendium of facts. Large numbers of patterns serve as an index to guide the expert in a fraction of a second to relevant parts of the knowledge store. This capacity to use patterns to guide a problem's interpretation and solution is probably a large part of what we call physical intuition.

An expert's knowledge seems compiled, that is, collapsed and reduced to a minimal and efficient form, which makes it more difficult to extract. When experts solve problems in their area of expertise, they recognize new situations as instances of things with which they are already familiar. This is the process shown at the top of Figure 14.2. However, when experts are faced with new or novel situations, they behave more like intelligent novices. They tend to apply general principles and deductive steps that provide causal links between various stages of a problem-solving sequence. The bottom half of Figure 14.2 illustrates this behavior.

FIGURE 14.2 Types of expert problem solving.

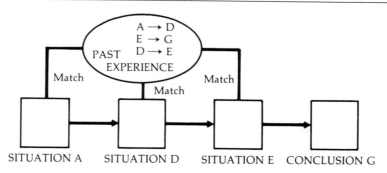

(a) Problem-solving by an expert in a familiar situation

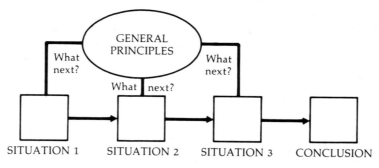

(b) Problem-solving by an expert in a novel situation

These differences in problem-solving strategies suggest some techniques for decompiling an expert's knowledge. One possibility is to present novel situations (perhaps suggested by other experts) and note the process he or she performs to solve the problem. An alternative is to present an intelligent novice with a standard problem (it will appear novel to him or her) to gain insight into the actual problem-solving activity.

Knowledge engineers at Schlumberger have confirmed this idea of compiled expert knowledge while building the DIPMETER ADVISOR, an expert system for well-log interpretation. They found that their domain expert seemed to use compiled knowledge until faced with a novel problem [SMI83]:

> When working with familiar examples our expert does indeed appear to apply forward-chained empirical rules—kind of compiled inferences. Recently, however, we have participated in experiments with a number of experts (and examples) from around the world. During these experiments we noted that our expert resorted to a different mode of operation when faced with completely unfamiliar examples. He appeared to reason from underlying geological and geometric models— abandoning the rules.

We would certainly like to have expert systems reason from first principles when confronted with novel problems, but we don't quite know how to make this happen yet. We are relying on AI researchers to advance the state of the art enough to make this possible.

Interviewing the Expert

Psychologists and management scientists have studied experts and their problem-solving techniques, using both observational and intuitive methods to measure performance and uncover expertise [LAR80, JOH83b]. The observational method relies on watching the expert solve realistic problems in the domain, being careful not to say or do anything that might influence the expert's problem-solving approach. The following quote neatly summarizes this method [JOH83b].

> A common approach is to use "thinking aloud" protocols to probe the problem solving mechanisms being used by experts. Such protocols can provide information about the organization of an expert's knowledge base, the actual knowledge it contains, and the control structures used to selectively apply that knowledge. Observational methods are sometimes followed by a refinement phase in which experts comment on preliminary models developed to describe their behavior.

Investigators applying the observational method don't interrupt the expert with questions or comments during problem solving. Instead, they analyze a transcript of the session after the fact, possibly with the expert's help. AI researchers have used this approach to study problem solving by nonexperts, calling it *protocol analysis* [WAT71]. Here the subject talks while solving a simple problem or puzzle, the verbalizations are transcribed, and the underlying problem-solving processes are inferred from the resulting trace.

The intuitive method relies on introspection by the expert or someone knowledgeable about the subject area. The following quote summarizes the intuitive approach [JOH83b].

> In one case an investigator of expertise (a knowledge engineer in the jargon of the expert systems field) studies and interacts with both experts and the literature of a field in order to become familiar with its major problem solving methods (he becomes a pseudo-expert). Acting in this capacity, the investigator develops a representation of expertise which is then checked against the opinion of other experts and eventually incorporated into a computer program. A second intuitive method of assessment occurs when an authentic or true expert acts as a builder of theories about his own behavior. Here the individual, through introspection, attempts to identify the basis for his or her own knowledge and skill and then incorporates this directly into a computer system.

Both approaches bring with them serious practical difficulties. With the observational method, the expert solves a problem while describing aloud what is being done. Although the act of thinking aloud may alter the expert's technique a bit, the real problem arises from huge gaps which often occur in the description of the process, especially when the expert accesses compiled knowledge. The investigator has great difficulty filling in these gaps, even if he or she interviews the expert after the session has ended, a transcript of the protocol in hand. If the expert is pushed to be more explicit, either during or after the problem-solving session, the expert may construct a line of plausible reasoning to explain his or her behavior. This line may or may not reflect the actual problem-solving techniques used.

The intuitive method has different kinds of problems. Since the expert uses introspection, he or she has trouble putting a finger on the actual techniques used to solve the problems. The knowledge is so well compiled through experience and overpractice that the expert accesses and manipulates it without thinking. As with the observational method, the expert may construct lines of plausible reasoning that don't truly reflect his or her behavior.

The knowledge engineer may use the two approaches just described, but relies primarily on an interview technique that combines the approaches. For example, the expert will introspect while solving a problem for the knowledge engineer and talk aloud about how he or she is solving it. The knowledge engineer jumps in whenever it seems appropriate, asking relevant questions to stimulate and probe the expert. The knowledge engineer plays an active rather than passive role, asking questions, suggesting possible rationales, and hypothesizing concepts and rules. We summarize some of the techniques for extracting knowledge from an expert in Table 14.1 [CLA81].

On-site Observation

The knowledge engineer observes the expert solving real problems on the job rather than contrived but realistic problems in a laboratory setting. Here the knowledge engineer doesn't interfere but rather acts as a

TABLE 14.1 Techniques for extracting knowledge from a domain expert.

Method	Description
On-site observation	Watch the expert solving real problems on the job.
Problem discussion	Explore the kinds of data, knowledge, and procedures needed to solve specific problems.
Problem description	Have the expert describe a prototypical problem for each category of answer in the domain.
Problem analysis	Present the expert with a series of realistic problems to solve aloud, probing for the rationale behind the reasoning steps.
System refinement	Have the expert give you a series of problems to solve using the rules acquired from the interviews.
System examination	Have the expert examine and critique the prototype system's rules and control structure.
System validation	Present the cases solved by the expert and prototype system to other outside experts.

passive observer. This approach gives the knowledge engineer some insight into the complexity of the problem and the type of interface facility needed by the expert to use the finished system in the field. However, this technique will not be practical or useful for some problem domains, usually because of time or privacy considerations.

Problem Discussion

The knowledge engineer picks a set of representative problems and informally discusses them with the expert. The goal is to determine how the expert organizes knowledge about each problem, represents concepts and hypotheses, and handles inconsistent, inaccurate, or imprecise knowledge and data relating to the problem. Questions that may arise include:

- How does the problem differ from prototypical problems in the domain?
- What kinds of data does the problem require?
- What kinds of solutions are adequate for the problem?
- Can the problem be reduced to noninteracting subproblems?
- What kinds of knowledge are needed to solve the problem?
- What constitutes an adequate explanation or justification of a problem solution?

During this discussion, the expert may introduce new terms, concepts, and relations. When this happens, the knowledge engineer asks the expert to define these new constructs and relate them to the existing body of concepts and relations. This may require redefining or combining existing concepts in the evolving knowledge base.

Problem Description

The knowledge engineer has the expert describe a typical problem for each main category of answer that could arise. This helps the knowledge engineer define a prototypical problem for each category of answer—a construct that the expert system can use to help it select a strategy or basic approach to solving a given problem. This exercise may also suggest ways to organize knowledge hierarchically in the expert system. This approach works particularly well for diagnostic-type problems, such as medical diagnosis or electronic troubleshooting.

Problem Analysis

The knowledge engineer asks the expert to solve a series of problems, probing the expert's reasoning as the problems are solved. As the expert solves each problem, the knowledge engineer provides any additional information or data requested by the expert. The expert must solve realistic problems, describing the solution process aloud and giving as many intermediate steps as possible. The knowledge engineer questions each step to determine the rationale behind it, including hypotheses being entertained, strategies being used to generate hypotheses, and goals being pursued which guide strategy selection.

The knowledge engineer may engage in a "depth-first probe" of the expert's reasoning. That is, ask the expert how a particular conclusion C was reached, then how the conclusions upon which C was based were reached, and so on, until the expert runs out of explanations or the knowledge engineer believes the discussion has gone too far astray. The trick here is to maintain focus, avoiding long paths or chains of reasoning that are somewhat tangential to the conclusion being explored.

Once the knowledge engineer has formulated some specialized rules relating to particular problems, he or she may revise the rules to make them as general as possible without destroying their ability to contribute to a solution in the context of the original problems. The expert's assistance may be needed for this process.

System Refinement

The expert gives the knowledge engineer problems to solve, ranging from very easy to fairly difficult. Before the expert system is operational, the knowledge engineer solves them on paper using the concepts, formalisms, and rules acquired to date from the expert. This provides a quick check of the consistency and completeness of the knowledge being extracted from the expert. As soon as the expert system can operate, in even a limited capacity, the knowledge engineer should use it to solve the problems supplied by the expert.

System Examination

The expert examines and critiques each rule in the prototype system and evaluates the control strategies used to select the rules. This includes verifying the accuracy of each rule and establishing a justification for each that the system can later use to explain its operation. The expert should compare the control strategies in the prototype with his or her method of handling problems in the domain.

System Validation

The knowledge engineer presents the cases solved by the expert and the prototype system to other experts. This provides a way to compare strategies of different experts and find essential points of disagreement.

A skilled knowledge engineer can decompile the expert's knowledge using the techniques just described. The more skilled the knowledge engineer, the more the final system will reflect the expert's actual heuristics and operating procedures.

15

An Example of the Expert-System-Building Process

In order to make our discussion of the expert-system-building process as concrete as possible, we now present a hypothetical scenario illustrating some of the steps that a knowledge engineer might take to develop an expert system. The problem domain for this scenario is the *evaluation of personal injury claims related to product liability*. Keep in mind that the scenario is somewhat idealized. Real experts are not as cooperative, understanding, explicit, or organized as the hypothetical expert described here—nor are real knowledge engineers so unfailingly insightful and accurate. If they were, building an expert system would take much less time than it actually does.

The Problem

The vice president of Acme Insurance has a problem. The volume of claims the company has received has risen dramatically during the last few years while the number of experienced claims adjusters working for the company has decreased. The company's costs have been unusually high, and many product liability cases have been settled for large amounts of money. There is concern that cases like these are being settled for amounts substantially higher than necessary. The vice president must find a way to help the 20 to 30 claims adjusters in each of the 28 branch offices of Acme Insurance evaluate cases more accurately.

The vice president assigns the job of solving this problem to the senior claims manager, who has just finished an evening course in computer programming. The claims manager, having heard about expert systems during the course, decides that perhaps an expert computer system could assist the claims adjusters by acting as an expert advisor and possibly even a tutor. After a long struggle to convince the vice president that this approach has merit, the project is finally approved. The claims manager now searches for and finds an experienced knowledge engineer willing to take on the job of building an expert system in this domain. The knowledge engineer, Mr. Jones, is hired as a full-time consultant, and work begins.

Characterizing the Problem

Knowledge engineer Jones now begins the first phase of expert system building, *identification*, where the task is to *identify the participants, resources, goals, and problem characteristics*. As a first step, he becomes familiar with the problem by reading books, studying product liability case histories, and talking to claims adjusters and attorneys about how they evaluate cases. During this time he characterizes the types of reasoning tasks the expert system is likely to perform and decides that determining case settlement value is probably a primary task, while estimating general damages is probably a secondary task.

During his two weeks of informal study, the knowledge engineer talks to the senior claims manager about a domain expert for the project. The claims manager suggests Ms. Smith because she is generally acknowledged to be one of the best claims adjusters.

Knowledge engineer Jones meets Ms. Smith and finds her articulate and knowledgeable about computers and their applications. Jones, aware that he has found an ideal expert, arranges to have her collaborate with him in building the expert system.

Knowledge engineer Jones decides to implement a small working system or demonstration prototype as quickly as possible to test ideas about problem scoping and representation. He further decides that the only *participants* necessary to build this small initial system are domain expert Smith and himself.

During his two weeks of informal study, Jones also considers various options regarding *resources* needed to build the expert system. He obtains a commitment from expert Smith to devote half of her time or more on the project and to be available for daily meetings throughout the first three months of the project. In addition, Jones evaluates the available computing resources and notes that Acme has an in-house VAX running UNIX 4BSD. He tentatively picks this as the hardware for prototype development. He can't make a final decision about hardware until the expert-system-building tool is selected, since the tool must run on the hardware.

To begin the task of identifying the *goals* and *problem characteristics*, knowledge engineer Jones schedules a series of initial meetings with expert Smith. During these meetings, Jones gives Smith closed claim files and informally discusses them with her. He listens carefully to her analyses of the claims, trying to understand how she characterizes the problems and decomposes them into important subproblems. Jones also focuses on expert Smith's way of characterizing the data and the problem solutions. Based on these meetings, Jones creates the problem description shown in Table 15.1.

Knowledge engineer Jones realizes that the problem description is far from complete; however, it gives him an initial understanding of the problem, the data, and the types of solutions that could arise.

What Concepts Are Needed to Produce a Solution?

Now that knowledge engineer Jones better understands the problem and its scope, he enters the next phase of expert system building, *conceptualization*. Here he *makes explicit the key concepts and relations needed to solve problems in the domain.* Jones spends a great deal of time with expert Smith, presenting sample cases and noting how she analyzes them.

One of the first results of this series of interactions is a more precise definition of the terms and concepts used by the expert. For example, Jones finds that special damages refer to specific economic losses resulting from an injury, such as medical expenses and lost income, while general damages include other effects of an injury, such as the trauma of the injury or the fear of losing a faculty, such as sight or hearing.

Another result of these interactions is an understanding of the relationships between the value of the case and the key concepts uncovered during the identification process. Jones notes that the expert combines the plaintiff's loss, defendant's liability, plaintiff's responsibility, case characteristics, and case context in the following way to estimate the case value:

$$\text{VALUE} = \text{LOSS} \times \text{LIABILITY} \times (1 - \text{RESPONSIBILITY}) \times \text{CHARACTERISTICS} \times \text{CONTEXT},$$

where the loss is the sum of special and general damages. Jones isn't sure at this point exactly what the characteristics and context encompass, but he knows they have a value greater than one when the case

TABLE 15.1 Initial problem description for product liability domain.

Category	Description
Project goal:	Help claims adjusters more accurately evaluate product liability cases.
Main problem:	Determine settlement value for product liability claims.
Subproblems:	Calculating special damages. Calculating general damages. Determining defendant's liability.
Problem characteristics:	Incomplete data. Case value depends on both objective and subjective considerations.
Data:	The severity of the plaintiff's loss (e.g., medical reports, photographs). The circumstances of the loss (e.g., witness reports, other evidence). Legal statutes. Product characteristics (e.g., expert testimony, witness reports). Participants' characteristics (e.g., case histories, personal observation).
Important concepts:	The extent of the plaintiff's loss. The degree of the defendant's liability. The plaintiff's responsibility for the loss. Subjective characteristics (e.g., litigants, lawyers, judges, jurisdictions). Case context (e.g., strategy, timing, claim type).
Solution:	The defendant's liability (a numerical estimate between 0 and 1). The plaintiff's loss (a numerical estimate in dollars). The settlement value (a numerical estimate in dollars).

characteristics are more favorable to the plaintiff than the defendant and a value less than one in the opposite situation.

Now Jones decides to explore the idea of the plaintiff's loss in more detail, concentrating on the rather difficult concept of general damages. Jones gives expert Smith a case from the closed claim files of Acme Insurance, including actual medical reports, correspondence between attorneys, and other relevant material. He also provides Smith with the following summary of the case.

> On December 18, 1980, claimant was opening a bottle of champagne bottled by the insured, Oxnard Vintners. Claimant had never opened a champagne bottle before. He rarely drank and the bottle had been brought to him by a guest. Claimant had partially loosened the wire cage when the cork forcefully shot out of the bottle, striking claimant in the right eye. The blow produced great pain and immediate blindness in the eye. Claimant was holding the cork toward his face when he was loosening the wire cage.
>
> Claimant was taken to the nearest emergency room and then transferred to the eye clinic at the local university hospital. He had suffered a detached retina. Doctors surgically repaired the eye, but for four days doctors did not know whether he would regain vision in the eye. Claimant's condition is now stable. He has slightly impaired visual acuity in the eye and must now wear glasses at all times. Claimant is a 30-year-old male and prior to this time did not wear glasses. Because of the injury, claimant has a five to ten percent chance of suffering glaucoma.
>
> Claimant's special damages total $4,500.

Jones now begins to explore the concept of general damages with the expert.

> KNOWLEDGE ENGINEER: Now let's consider the champagne bottle case. We know the special damages, which are medical expenses and lost income, are $4,500, so we can concentrate on what I guess is called general damages. What do you think the general damages would be in a case like this?
>
> EXPERT: Well, (pause), they would probably be about $50,000—uh, no, make that $60,000.
>
> KNOWLEDGE ENGINEER: How did you arrive at that figure?
>
> EXPERT: I've had many years of experience analyzing cases like this. I don't use any fixed rules like: "pain and suffering equals three times the medical expenses." I just look at the facts of the case and estimate the value.

Jones realizes that most experts have difficulty expressing the rules they use and often believe that they reason strictly by intuition developed through their extensive experience. He probes further to uncover the rules and concepts that Smith used to arrive at the answer.

> KNOWLEDGE ENGINEER: What factor seemed the most important in deciding general damages for this case?

EXPERT: Well, uh, probably the most important factor here was, uh, it was an eye injury. This can have a debilitating effect on the plaintiff. He deserves some compensation for suffering the indignity of being injured this way.

KNOWLEDGE ENGINEER: $60,000?

EXPERT: No, the injury itself was only worth about $18,000.

KNOWLEDGE ENGINEER: I see. You're saying the plaintiff should be compensated for the fact that he suffered an injury, kind of like the notion of being paid for pain and suffering.

EXPERT: Yes, that's right.

KNOWLEDGE ENGINEER: And the pain and suffering was worth $18,000.

EXPERT: Well, not exactly. I think the trauma of the injury itself was worth only about $10,000.

KNOWLEDGE ENGINEER: But you mentioned a figure of $18,000.

EXPERT: Yes, the other $8,000 was because the plaintiff spent four days blind in one eye. The doctors didn't know whether he would regain sight in that eye. Something like that would be rather frightening.

KNOWLEDGE ENGINEER: So you're saying that $10,000 should go to the plaintiff for the trauma of the injury itself and another $8,000 for the fear suffered. Then the $8,000 kind of represents the inconvenience the plaintiff went through while the $10,000 represents the actual pain and shock of the injury.

EXPERT: That's right, except that I wouldn't call his fear of being blind an inconvenience. The fact that he had to wear glasses after the injury although he never wore them before is an example of an inconvenience caused by the injury.

KNOWLEDGE ENGINEER: Would that add to general damages?

EXPERT: Yes, I'd say that was worth about $2,500.

KNOWLEDGE ENGINEER: So the plaintiff should be compensated $2,500 for having to wear glasses.

EXPERT: Not exactly. He should get $2,500 for the inconvenience of having to wear glasses. He should also get another $2,500 because of his partial faculty loss. His visual acuity was slightly reduced by the injury.

Knowledge engineer Jones now sees a pattern emerging—expert Smith seems to be assigning values to various aspects of the injury, such as the trauma, fear, inconvenience, and faculty loss suffered by the plaintiff, and then adding them together to obtain a final value. Jones is quite interested in these concepts and the way the expert uses them. He has been listening not only for basic domain concepts, but also for basic strategies the expert used when solving the problem. Jones also wants to know how Smith justifies her use of terms and strategies, since the expert system will need this type of information to provide adequate explanations about its operation. In an attempt to make her justify her position about inconvenience and faculty loss, Jones continues the dialogue as follows.

KNOWLEDGE ENGINEER: Five thousand dollars seems like a lot of money just for having to wear glasses.

EXPERT: Not really. It would have been more if the plaintiff's appearance had been particularly important for his job, like a movie star or TV personality.

KNOWLEDGE ENGINEER: Just a second—(looking through a stack of papers) it says here that the plaintiff is a broadcaster for a local radio station, but that prior to his injury he had interviewed for a job as a local television sportscaster. He claims he later didn't get the job because of his need to wear glasses.

EXPERT: Yes, that's what I'm talking about. His appearance is worth money. That should increase general damages by $5,000 more.

KNOWLEDGE ENGINEER: If the injury had caused a scar on his face, would that have been the same sort of thing?

EXPERT: Well, that would be worth considerably more, but it does fall into the same category of disfigurement.

KNOWLEDGE ENGINEER: Let's see now: $10,000 for the injury trauma, $8,000 for fear, $2,500 for inconvenience, $2,500 for faculty loss, and $5,000 for disfigurement. Are there any other factors you're considering that we haven't hit on yet?

EXPERT: I recall that the medical report mentioned the possibility of glaucoma as a result of the injury. A 10 percent chance, I believe.

KNOWLEDGE ENGINEER: Yes, that's what it said. Would this affect general damages?

EXPERT: It would have significant effect; should be worth about $30,000 because of the possibility the plaintiff will contract glaucoma. This is a serious illness.

KNOWLEDGE ENGINEER: So a possibility of a future trauma should always be taken into account?

EXPERT: Absolutely.

KNOWLEDGE ENGINEER: Adding in the future trauma factor, the sum comes to $58,000. That's almost exactly what you predicted initially.

EXPERT: Yes, $58,000 is a good approximation of general damages for this case.

At this point Jones ends the interview and begins to organize the concepts uncovered during the dialogue. The result is a set of initial concepts that the knowledge engineer believes is relevant to determining injury value.

- Task: Determination of value of injury.
- Attributes of injury:

  Type of injury: Eye

  Value of injury: Some dollar amount

  Extent of injury: One eye

  Result of injury: Visual acuity slightly reduced

                                 Temporary blindness in one eye

                                 Duration of blindness four days

                                 Uncertainty about permanence of blindness

                                 10 percent chance of contracting glaucoma

                                 Must wear glasses.
- Attributes of plaintiff:

  Did he wear glasses originally?

  Is his appearance important for work?
- Attributes of glaucoma:

  Type: Illness

  Degree: Serious
- Factors contributing to value of injury:

  Injury trauma factor

  Fear factor

  Inconvenience factor

  Faculty loss factor

  Disfigurement factor

  Future trauma factor

The knowledge engineer realizes that these concepts represent only a fraction of those used by the expert during problem solving in the domain. However, he decides that it will be useful to try to formalize them even at this early stage of development. He knows that he can always go back and continue with the conceptualization process at any time during the expert system development.

How Can the Knowledge Be Formally Represented?

Knowledge engineer Jones now enters the next phase of expert system building, *formalization,* where *the key concepts, subproblems, and control features are mapped into a more formal representation suggested by an expert-system-building tool.* He decides to test the appropriateness of the expert system building language, ROSIE, by using it to represent the concepts and ideas just extracted from the expert. Figure 15.1 shows the result of this analysis. Although this may look like prose, it's actually ROSIE code, capable of being executed by a computer.

Jones now goes back through his notes trying to find relations between the various concepts shown in Figure 15.1. Once he establishes them he feels ready to jump ahead to the implementation phase. Jones realizes that he will be returning to the formalization phase many times, but he wants to see how easily the relations between the concepts can be represented in ROSIE.

FIGURE 15.1 A formal representation of concepts from the champagne-bottle
case.

Assert the plaintiff did receive an eye injury.

Assert the plaintiff's injury does involve just one eye.

Assert the plaintiff's visual acuity is slightly reduced by the injury.

Assert the plaintiff's injury did cause (a temporary blindness in one eye)
and let the duration of that blindness be 4 days.

Assert the plaintiff's doctors were not certain about the blindness being
temporary.

Assert the plaintiff does have (a chance of contracting glaucoma)
and that chance was caused by the plaintiff's injury
and let the value of that chance be 10%.

Assert the plaintiff's injury does require (the plaintiff to wear glasses).

Assert the plaintiff did not wear glasses before the injury.

Assert the plaintiff's appearance is important for work.

Assert glaucoma is a serious illness.

Assert each of injury trauma, fear, inconvenience, faculty loss,
disfigurement and future trauma is a factor that does contribute to
the value of the injury.

Implementing a Prototype System

Knowledge engineer Jones now enters the *implementation* phase in which he *turns the concepts and relations between them into a working computer program*. These few tentative ROSIE rules are the first step toward the implementation of a prototype expert system.

[1]   If the plaintiff did receive an eye injury
        and the plaintiff's visual acuity is slightly reduced by the injury,
      increase the injury trauma factor by $10000.

[2]   If the plaintiff's injury did cause (a temporary blindness in one eye)
        and the plaintiff's doctors were not certain about (the temporary
              nature of that blindness),
      increase the fear factor by $8000.

[3]   If the plaintiff does have (a chance of contracting_glaucoma)
        and that chance was caused by the plaintiff's injury
        and the value of that chance = 10%,
      increase the future trauma factor by $30000.

[4]   If the plaintiff did receive an eye injury
        and the plaintiff's injury does involve just one eye
        and the plaintiff's visual acuity is slightly reduced by the injury,
      increase the faculty loss factor by $2500.

[5]   If the plaintiff's injury does require (the plaintiff to wear glasses)
        and the plaintiff did not wear glasses before the injury,
      increase the inconvenience factor by $2500.

[6]   If the plaintiff's injury does require (the plaintiff to wear glasses)
        and the plaintiff's appearance is important for work
        and the plaintiff did not wear glasses before the injury,
      increase the disfigurement factor by $5000.

[7]   For each factor that does contribute to the value of the injury,
      add that factor to the general_damages.

The rules look good to Jones, and they seem to predict the answer Smith gave during the last interview session. Jones now decides that he must have the expert help him test the rules.

Validating the Rules

Jones now enters the *testing* phase. He attempts to *validate the rules that have been formulated*. In a more fully developed system Jones would run the program on a few cases and ask Smith how well it predicted the value of general damages. However, with this small preliminary set of rules, Jones believes it will suffice simply to show the rules to the expert and ask for her opinion of them. At this stage the knowledge engineer expects the rules to be overly specific and hopes to uncover some basic high-level principles the expert is using that are exemplified by these low-level rules.

During the next interview session, Jones shows the expert one of the rules he generated and asks for her opinion of its accuracy.

KNOWLEDGE ENGINEER: Here is a rule I wrote to capture the idea that the possibility of a future trauma could add to the value of the injury. (Jones hands Smith a piece of paper with the following rule on it.)

> [3] If the plaintiff does have (a chance of contracting glaucoma)
>   and that chance was caused by the plaintiff's injury
>   and the value of that chance = 10%,
>   increase the future trauma factor by $30000.

EXPERT: That rule looks fine to me.

KNOWLEDGE ENGINEER: How does glaucoma compare with those injuries?

EXPERT: That depends on the severity of the potential injury. A catastrophic injury like paraplegia would be worth more than a moderate injury like a shortened limb.

KNOWLEDGE ENGINEER: How does glaucoma compare with those injuries?

EXPERT: It's somewhere in between. I'd rate glaucoma as a serious illness rather than catastrophic or moderate. It's in the same category as epilepsy and heart disease.

KNOWLEDGE ENGINEER: Would all of these serious illnesses or injuries be worth $30,000 if there was a 10 percent chance of their occurrence in the future?

EXPERT: Yes, $30,000 is about right.

KNOWLEDGE ENGINEER: What if there were a 20 percent chance of occurrence?

EXPERT: Well, then it would be worth more. It would be worth about $30,000 if there was anywhere from a 5 to 15 percent chance of occurrence.

KNOWLEDGE ENGINEER: What would it have been worth if the injury had definitely caused glaucoma rather than just presenting the possibility of causing it?

EXPERT: Glaucoma would be worth about $100,000. But since there was only a 5 to 15 percent chance of it, the plaintiff should only be compensated for 30 percent of that amount, $30,000.

Jones now revises the rule, making it more general and thus more useful to the expert system. To do this he introduces two new concepts: 1) a class of illnesses rated as serious, and 2) the value of contracting an illness. The new concepts and revised rule are shown below.

> Assert each of glaucoma, epilepsy, and heart disease is a serious illness.
> Let the value of glaucoma be $100000.
>
> **[3]** If the plaintiff does have (a chance of contracting_an_illness)
> and that chance was caused by the plaintiff's injury
> and the value of that chance > 5%
> and that value <=15%
> and the potential illness of the plaintiff is a serious illness,
> increase the future trauma factor by 30% of (the value of the plaintiff's potential illness).

In a similar manner the knowledge engineer queries Smith further about rule 2 to make it more general. He finds that she arrived at the figure $8000 by multiplying the number of days during which the plaintiff was partially blind (four days) by $2000. He adds this to the rule and introduces the concept of a disability of an important function. The new concept and rule are shown below.

> Assert each of blindness in_one_eye, severe dizziness,
> paralysis of_one_limb, and loss of_one_limb
> is a disability of an important function.
>
> **[2]** If the plaintiff's injury did cause (a temporary disability of an important function)
> and the plaintiff's doctors were not certain about (the temporary nature of that disability),
> increase the fear factor by ($2000 × the duration of that disability).

Now knowledge engineer Jones has a set of rules that seem to satisfy the expert, at least on an individual basis. He further tests the rules by devising hypothetical problems, presenting them to the expert, and comparing her answers with the ones that the rules would produce. During this refinement process, he finds that some rules are too general and must have additional conditions added to reduce their generality. For example, Smith indicates, among other things, that the disfigurement factor also depends on the plaintiff's age and that the injury trauma factor also depends on whether or not the plaintiff required surgery. Jones takes these refinements into account and produces a new set of rules.

[1] If the plaintiff did receive an eye injury
  and that injury did require surgery
  and the plaintiff's visual acuity is slightly reduced by that injury
  and the recovery from that injury is almost complete
  and the plaintiff's condition is fixed,
increase the injury trauma factor by $10000.

[2] If the plaintiff's injury did cause (a temporary disability of an
    important function)
  and the plaintiff's doctors were not certain about (the temporary
    nature of that disability)
  and the recovery from that injury is almost complete
  and the plaintiff's condition is fixed,
increase the fear factor by ($2000 × the duration of that disability).

[3] If the plaintiff does have (a chance of contracting_an_illness)
  and that chance was caused by the plaintiff's injury
  and the value of that chance > 5%
  and that value < =15%
  and the potential illness of the plaintiff is a serious illness,
increase the future trauma factor by 30% of (the value of the
    plaintiff's potential illness).

[4] If the plaintiff did receive an eye injury
  and the plaintiff's injury does involve just one eye
  and the plaintiff's visual acuity is slightly reduced by the injury,
increase the faculty loss factor by $2500.

[5] If the plaintiff's injury does require (the plaintiff to wear glasses)
  and the plaintiff did not wear glasses before the injury,
increase the inconvenience factor by $2500.

[6] If the plaintiff's injury does require (the plaintiff to wear glasses)
  and the plaintiff's appearance is important for work
  and the age (of the plaintiff) at (the time of the injury) > 25
  and the plaintiff did not wear glasses before the injury,
increase the disfigurement factor by $5000.

[7] For each factor that does contribute to the value of the injury,
add that factor to the general_damages.

Jones continues these interview sessions with Smith to uncover the concepts, rules, and problem-solving strategies she uses. In addition, Jones tries to understand how Smith *justifies* the rules and strategies, i.e., produces compelling arguments to convince her peers that her approach is valid. He decides that one of his goals is to build as much of this justification knowledge into the program as possible.

At the end of two months, Jones decides that ROSIE is an appropriate tool for the problem and begins to turn the feasibility demonstration into a full-fledged research prototype system. A year (and many interviews) later, the knowledge base reaches a significant size (many hundreds of rules and data objects). Jones now concentrates on testing and refining the research prototype by 1) bringing in additional experts to help validate the system's accuracy, and 2) using test cases not encountered by the system during its previous development.

But now something different happens. The research prototype has become so unwieldy, because of all the patches and changes made, that Jones decides to reimplement it from the ground up. Retaining the domain knowledge from the original prototype, Jones quickly designs and builds a better organized and more efficient expert system. He then spends a year refining and testing this new system in the field. Now the field prototype is given to a team of support programmers who reprogram it in a lower-level, more efficient language. The expert system is now ready to be introduced into the actual work environment at Acme Insurance.

So ends our hypothetical excursion into the life of a knowledge engineer. Please remember that this scenario is designed to illustrate the phases of expert system building. It does so in a rather oversimplified way, making no attempt to convey the actual complexity of the process.

Difficulties with Expert System Development

Building an expert system requires a major investment of time, money, energy, and faith. If the problem is appropriate, and if adequate resources are committed, the investment will be repaid many times over. But even the smoothest development effort will have rough spots. Some of them cannot be avoided: They stem from the fact that AI is still a very young field. But other potential stumbling blocks can be avoided if individuals or companies are aware of them. And in every case, a realistic vision of potential problems and appropriate solutions will help newcomers in the expert system field to make realistic development plans.

In the next four chapters, we will examine some of the more common pitfalls in the development process and suggest ways to avoid them.

16

Difficulties in Developing an Expert System

Companies encounter several types of difficulties when trying to apply expert system technology to their problems. Scarce resources make putting together a competent development team an arduous task. Inherent limitations of AI technology introduce severe restrictions on the expert-system-building process. Finally, expert systems take a long time to build. Being aware of these difficulties can help companies to accommodate them in their planning process. Let's examine each of these potential stumbling blocks.

Lack of Resources

Figure 16.1 summarizes the challenge that companies entering the expert system arena may face in gathering the resources needed for the job. Personnel competent to design and develop the systems are scarce, and few of the high-level support tools and languages are fully developed or reliable. In fact, many of them are new and untested.

There are two reasons for this lack of resources. First, expert systems, like its parent field AI, is new and unfamiliar to most computer specialists, and therefore somewhat difficult for them to understand and apply. Second, the crush of companies entering the AI arena has created

179

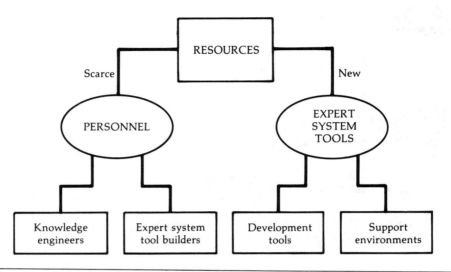

FIGURE 16.1 Lack of resources hampers expert system development efforts.

many more openings for experienced AI and expert systems people than can be filled with existing personnel. New openings occur faster than the universities can turn out PhDs in AI. To beat this problem, many companies now train their own personnel in expert system technology by sending them to school, enrolling them in apprenticeship training sessions at university AI centers, or providing short tutorial courses offered by commercial AI groups.

On the software side, things seem brighter. Although many of the high-level development tools created by universities and research institutions remain research vehicles—untested and unpolished—they have spawned simpler commercial versions now produced by AI companies (see Chapter 9). This fact, combined with the plummeting prices of hardware to run the tools, would seem to promise low-cost, reliable tools for system development in the near future.

Lack of sympathetic and knowledgeable management poses a different kind of problem in development efforts. Management can be skeptical and impatient because the field is new and because building an expert system requires very large amounts of money and time (two to five years). Recent media attention to AI has compounded this problem; their exaggeration and inaccuracies have caused unrealistic expectations that could lead to disappointment or disillusionment with AI and expert systems.

Inherent Limitations of Expert Systems

Some development difficulties are unavoidable at this stage of AI development. Current expert systems and expert system tools have limitations, many of which will gradually disappear as AI researchers advance the state of the art. But for development efforts in the near future, they are a fact of life. A few of the current major limitations of expert systems are shown in Figure 16.2.

Expert systems are not very good at representing temporal or spatial knowledge. Representations of this type can require huge amounts of memory to keep track of the state of things at various points in time or to record the spatial relations between different groups of objects. Clever representation and search techniques are needed to overcome efficiency problems in these areas.

We have already discussed the problems that expert systems have

FIGURE 16.2 Limitations of expert systems.

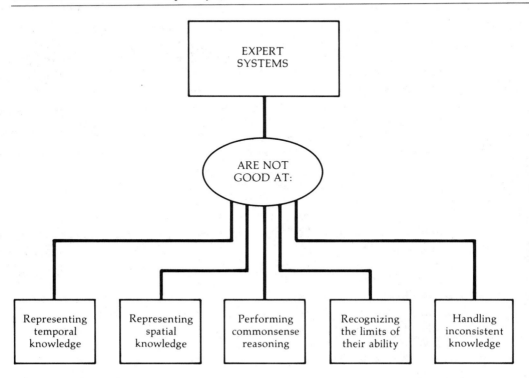

using common sense or general knowledge about the world. If this type of knowledge is crucial to solving a problem, the knowledge engineering approach will most likely fail.

Expert systems have a very narrow domain of expertise and hence their operation is not as robust as the users might want. Because of this, expert systems have difficulty recognizing the limits of their ability. When pushed beyond their limits or given problems different from those for which they were designed, expert systems can fail in surprising ways. To put it another way, expert systems exhibit rather fragile behavior at their boundaries. Further progress in AI will eventually suggest ways to help systems know their limitations. Then instead of attempting a problem beyond their scope of expertise, they would simply recommend experts (human or artificial) that could solve the problem.

Expert systems also have difficulty dealing with erroneous or inconsistent knowledge. This is because most expert systems rely on a body of rules that represent abstracted knowledge of the domain and aren't able to reason from basic principles to recognize incorrect knowledge or reason about inconsistencies.

Expert-system-building tools also have certain limitations that affect system design and development. Figure 16.3 illustrates some of the more important ones.

The most serious limitation of expert-system-building tools is their inability to perform knowledge acquisition. Knowledge acquisition is the major bottleneck in expert system development; it's tedious and time-consuming to extract knowledge from an expert and incorporate it into a large knowledge base. Despite research aimed at designing tools for automatically acquiring the knowledge from the expert, the bottleneck still exists and results in project development times that seem unnecessarily long. Chapter 8 discusses knowledge acquisition and describes features of expert system support environments that address the problem.

A closely related limitation of the current crop of tools is their inadequacy in helping to refine and correct the expert system's knowledge base. It may take a large effort to get a small improvement in performance. For example, PUFF, an expert system that interprets data from pulmonary function tests, had to have its number of rules increased from 100 to 400 just to get a 10 percent increase in performance. Many expert system tools include knowledge base editors, and they do help with this problem, but they aren't able to identify and remove inconsistencies from the system's knowledge base. No general technique for logically analyzing the system's completeness and consistency has been developed yet. Knowledge engineers typically use only one or two experts to create the system's initial knowledge base, thus reducing the chances of introducing inconsistencies into the knowledge base. How-

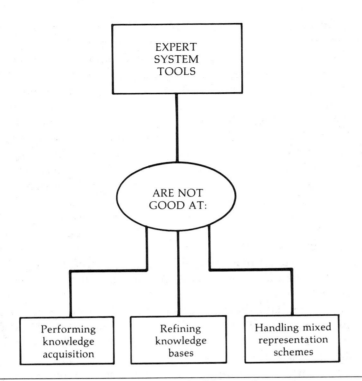

FIGURE 16.3 Limitations of expert-system-building tools.

ever, using a single expert can lead to evaluation problems in those domains where experts often disagree.

Languages for building expert systems are not as flexible and general as the knowledge engineer might want. Often, particular types of knowledge (e.g., temporal or spatial) cannot be represented easily, or different representational schemes (e.g., rules and frames) cannot be represented naturally and efficiently in the same language. Also, many languages do not provide mechanisms for building adequate user interfaces. The knowledge engineer needs sophisticated graphics and reliable natural language capabilities to make the user-system interaction smooth and efficient.

Expert Systems Take a Long Time to Build

Expert systems cannot be built quickly. With the currently available technology, it takes from five to ten person-years to build an expert system to solve a moderately complex problem. PUFF, the system that interprets lung function test data, required about five person-years of effort; XCON, a system that configures computers, took about eight person-years to reach reasonable performance configuring VAX 11/780 computers. Earlier systems, such as MACSYMA and DENDRAL, each took over 30 person-years of effort to build. This large effort was required partly because of the difficult nature of the tasks and partly because at the time of development the available knowledge engineering tools were not as sophisticated and refined as they are today.

The level of effort, in person-years, doesn't give a very accurate picture of the human resources needed or the time required to build the system. It implies that one could put 20 people on the project for six months to achieve 10 person-years of effort or use one person for 10 years. Neither extreme will work. Doubling personnel will not cut the development time in half because development is a succession of steps all closely related via massive feedback. It is, therefore, very difficult to structure independent subprojects so that some steps can be performed in parallel. At the other extreme, projects that have fewer than two full-time people have difficulty gathering and sustaining momentum. If more than six full-time people are involved, it may be hard to coordinate activities to avoid "dead time" where personnel must wait for items produced by others before they can proceed.

The actual time required to build the system depends on problem complexity and the number of full-time professionals assigned to the effort. A moderately difficult task might take between six months and one and one-half years at a two- to four-person level. A difficult task might take between one and one-half and three years at a three- to five-person level. A very difficult task could take from three to five years at a four- to six-person level. These estimates are summarized in Figure 16.4. The cross-hatching illustrates the range of effort that could be required for a task in each category.

A typical expert-system-building project for a moderately difficult problem domain would have the following characteristics:

PROBLEM:	Moderately difficult	
EFFORT:	6 person-years	
TIME:	2 years	
STAFF:	Senior knowledge engineer	.25
	Junior knowledge engineer	1.00
	AI programmer	1.00
	Domain expert	.75
	Total full-time professionals	3.00

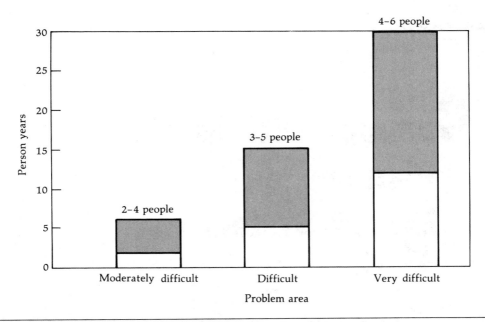

FIGURE 16.4 Person-years required to develop an expert system.

A company can reduce its development time by insuring the *accessibility* and *availability* of the domain expert(s). The experts must be nearby and able to devote up to three quarters of their time to the effort during the first six months and up to half of their time thereafter. When more advanced tools are developed for knowledge acquisition, the effort required to build a moderately complex expert system will be significantly reduced.

17

Common Pitfalls in Planning an Expert System

Many believe that expert system building is still more of an art than a science. To a certain extent, this is true. However, we can help the novice system builder by providing some planning guidelines. In the next three chapters, we attempt to do this by describing the major pitfalls at each stage of the development process and suggesting ways to avoid them. In this chapter, we discuss the pitfalls that may present themselves during the planning process. In Chapters 18 and 19, we turn our attention to problems during the knowledge acquisition and development processes.

In these discussions, we refer to the *development team*. By this we mean the knowledge engineers, support programmers, and domain experts required to build the system.

Choosing an Appropriate Problem

I. *Pitfall* • The expert system development effort is addressing a problem so difficult that it can't be solved within the constraints set by the available resources.

How to Avoid It • Have an experienced knowledge engineer develop a small prototype system. Evaluate the results of this effort to decide whether or not to proceed with full-scale development. If you decide to proceed, pay attention to the knowledge engineer's recommendations concerning required resources, problem scope, and appropriate tools.

Some problems are clearly appropriate for expert system development (e.g., certain types of medical diagnosis) while others seem quite inappropriate (e.g., certain scene analysis problems). Unfortunately, most problems fall somewhere between these extremes, and it's usually not immediately apparent how well they lend themselves to expert system development. For example, after hearing a two-hour description of a problem, an experienced knowledge engineer can't predict with certainty whether or not the problem is feasible for expert system work. Usually more analysis is required. This analysis is important because it helps the development team to avoid problems that are inappropriate for the expert system approach—particularly those that are too difficult.

II.   *Pitfall* • The problem that the expert system is designed to solve will not significantly alleviate the difficulty that motivated the development effort.

   How to Avoid It • First, consider carefully the relationship between the *basic difficulty* and the *target problems*—the problems to be solved by the expert system. Ask yourself: If the expert system works perfectly, will it have the long-term effect I desire? Second, after determining a reasonable problem scope, reassess the effectiveness of the expert system within the new problem scope.

Often an expert system will be designed to alleviate a specific difficulty for a commercial enterprise. This difficulty may be clearly understood; e.g., an insurance company may have a history of handling cases unwisely. Once the difficulty is recognized, the development team must 1) decide what problem solutions will significantly reduce or remove the difficulty, then 2) assess the feasibility of building an expert system to solve these problems. The result of this assessment may be a more constrained set of feasible problems. If so, the team must reconsider whether the problems that the expert system can solve will actually reduce the basic difficulty. Without this reassessment, the expert system may end up solving only a subset of the problems that need to be solved.

The difficulty that motivated the development effort will usually be related to the needs of the *funders*, the persons paying for the system development. When defining the problem to solve, the development team should consider the needs of both the funders and the end-users. If their needs differ or clash, strategies should be found to reconcile them.

III.   *Pitfall* • The problem that the expert system addresses is so general or complex that an excessive number of rules and data base objects are needed to describe the expertise adequately. Either it will take too long to accumulate all the rules, or the resulting system will run too slowly.

How to Avoid It • If the expert system will require more than a few thousand medium-sized or large rules,[1] reexamine the problem scope to see if it can be constrained.

A common mistake in expert system building is failure to choose the proper scope for the problem. When the development team does not satisfactorily constrain the problem to one feasible with current AI hardware and software technology, the development effort is in serious trouble. The novice knowledge engineer is more likely to tackle a problem that's too general rather than one that's too constrained.

A serious problem is estimating the number of rules (frames, objects, or other representational formalisms) required by the expert system. The best way to develop a reasonable estimate is to build a small prototype system during the feasibility study, one that will solve a simple subproblem in the domain. The size of this system will provide an experienced knowledge engineer with some idea of the size of the full-blown system.

Resources for Building the System

IV.   *Pitfall* • Only a limited amount of time exists in which to build the expert system. Therefore it is decided to provide the personnel necessary to build it in the alloted time period.

How to Avoid It • Don't gear the development effort timetable to production deadlines. Use the recommendations of an experienced knowledge engineer, preferably one who has performed a feasibility analysis, to determine the timetable for development.

You cannot hurry expert system development by increasing personnel. The interactive nature of the development process imposes limits on how fast development can take place. A knowledge engineer who has

---

[1] It's almost as difficult to define rule size as it is to define expert system size. We will define a large rule as one that covers one third of a page or more when expressed in English or a very high level knowledge engineering language such as ROSIE.

conducted some preliminary analysis is in the best position to provide a realistic estimate of development time.

V.   *Pitfall* • Management believes that an expert system is just a computer program to perform some task. Therefore, any experienced programming staff can build one. All the staff needs is the problem specifications and the right programming environment.

      How to Avoid It • Have the system development performed by an experienced knowledge engineer or knowledge engineering team. Either bring this talent in from the outside or train in-house personnel in AI and expert system techniques. In the latter case, use an experienced knowledge engineer as a consultant to monitor the work and keep it on track.

As Chapter 4 points out, expert systems differ from conventional programs in a number of ways, including how information is organized and represented. Many problems can arise from trying to build an expert system with personnel who lack expertise in knowledge engineering. For example, the system may require an unnecessarily long development time, may be difficult to extend or refine, and may not be able to explain its operation. Chapter 23 lists some firms that provide formal training in building expert systems.

Choosing the Expert-System-Building Tool

VI.   *Pitfall* • Using the chosen tool, the development team finds it difficult to represent the domain concepts and control structures needed to solve the problem.

      How to Avoid It • Carefully consider which expert-system-building tool to use. Pick a tool whose characteristics match the solution and system features suggested by the problem domain. If development reveals that the tool is inappropriate for the problem, immediately switch to a different tool.

As we have already mentioned in Chapter 13, the choice of an appropriate tool for building the system is a difficult one. Since this choice depends on characteristics of the problem solution, the development team may not be able to evaluate the chosen tool until a small prototype system has been implemented. If the chosen tool appears ineffective for the problem domain, don't hesitate to switch languages. Reimplementing the system in the more appropriate language will likely be the most efficient way to proceed.

VII. *Pitfall* • The knowledge engineer picks the most familiar tool even though other tools are better suited to the problem domain. If the tool is obviously ill-suited, the knowledge engineer reworks the problem so that it fits the capabilities of the chosen tool.

How to Avoid It • This pitfall is not easily avoided, because most knowledge engineers have strong preferences for specific tools. If you are the project manager, consult more than one knowledge engineer to develop a consensus (a costly and not entirely satisfactory solution). If you are the knowledge engineer, be aware of this trap and reexamine the justifications for choosing your favorite tool when you do so.

The knowledge engineer is the obvious person to pick the tool, but difficulty can arise when that person is much more deeply involved with one knowledge engineering language than with the others—if, for example, he or she helped design and develop such a language. In this situation the knowledge engineer's background may bias his or her choice.

If the knowledge engineer redefines the problem scope to fit the chosen tool, be sure the resulting expert system will still solve a broad enough range of problems to be of some practical use.

VIII. *Pitfall* • It is decided to develop the expert system in FORTRAN, PASCAL, C, or some other general-purpose programming language because the resulting system will be smaller, faster, and more portable. Unfortunately, this increases the development time to some unacceptable length.

How to Avoid It • Implement, test, and refine the system in a high-level expert system building language. Choose a tool as specialized as possible while still being appropriate for the problem area. If the system reaches a point where it performs satisfactorily except for slow execution speed, consider reimplementing the system in a more efficient language.

Knowledge engineering languages such as ROSIE, EMYCIN, and AL/X were designed to speed system development. They provide special features to ease the representation problem and often include many support facilities that facilitate rule acquisition and editing (see Chapter 8). Consequently, an expert system can usually be built much faster in one of these languages than it can in a conventional programming language. The drawback is that the expert system will often execute rather slowly in these complex knowledge engineering languages compared to its execution speed in conventional languages.

The time-consuming part of expert system development is extracting the knowledge from the expert and deciding how to represent it effectively. After the development team implements and tests the system, it requires much less effort to reimplement it in another language as long as the system has stabilized and does not require continual refinement and expansion.

IX.   *Pitfall* • The tool chosen to build the expert system is found to contain programming errors that prevent the use of many of the tool's features. As a result, the development team must spend a large portion of its time tracking down and correcting errors.

How to Avoid It • Choose an expert-system-building tool that has an established track record, one that has been used successfully in other application areas. Avoid new tools that are still under development. On the other hand, don't choose a tool so old that it is no longer maintained or supported.

When choosing an expert-system-building tool, the development team should consider the status of the tool. Who developed it? How successfully has it been used in the past? How reliable is it?

18

Pitfalls in Dealing with the Domain Expert

Without a knowledgeable and cooperative domain expert, the system building effort is doomed to failure. In this chapter, we consider some of the problems that might arise in choosing the expert and in acquiring the expert's knowledge.

Choosing the Domain Expert

I.   *Pitfall* • The knowledge engineer has great difficulty extracting high-quality rules from the expert. Interactions with the expert are laborious and seem to provide a small payoff.

How to Avoid It • Be sure to pick an expert highly skilled in the target domain. Rely on the opinions of the expert's peers and other knowledgeable people. Be sure the expert is articulate, motivated, and aware of the usefulness of computers in scientific endeavors.

Competency in the relevant area is the most important criterion for selecting a domain expert. The expert should be exceptionally skillful at finding good solutions to difficult problems. The expert must also be open, articulate, and able to convey ideas easily to others. Finally, the expert must be aware of the advent of computer technology and appreciate the computer's potential and usefulness. The more the expert knows about computers and programming, the better.

II. *Pitfall* • The domain expert chosen for development work cannot find enough time for the project.

How to Avoid It • Get a commitment from the expert, *before* the project starts, to spend at least half-time on the project. Be sure the expert understands the importance of his or her contribution to this effort. Pick a nearby expert, preferably in the same city. Otherwise, consider relocating the expert for the duration of the project.

The knowledge engineer builds an expert system through a series of intensive interactions with a domain expert. This can only happen if the expert is both *available* and *accessible*. By available we mean the expert must be able to interact regularly with the knowledge engineer for extended periods of time. To make this easier (and less expensive), the expert should also be located near the development work.

Interacting with the Expert

III. *Pitfall* • Both the in-house experts and outside experts who interact with the prototype system during development have trouble correcting and modifying the system's rules. They just aren't sure what the rules mean.

How to Avoid It • Use the same terminology in the program that the experts use while solving problems in the domain. Define all terms used, even those that seem obvious, and build a mechanism into the program that allows the expert to access these definitions. If the program code is not readable, provide a means for translating the code into statements that the expert can understand.

Expert system development requires collaboration between the knowledge engineer and the expert; the expert supplies the knowledge for the system while the knowledge engineer organizes and maps the knowledge into a form usable by the computer. During this mapping process, the knowledge engineer must provide the system with a faithful translation of the expert's knowledge, but one it can process intelligently. Both the expert and the system must be able to understand the rules embodying the knowledge. Some expert system building languages make this easier than others. For example, experts understand rules written in ROSIE more easily than rules written in less English-oriented languages, such as LISP.

IV. *Pitfall* • The rules generated by the expert are so short and simple that they don't provide a high degree of accuracy when used in complex situations.

How to Avoid It • Monitor the expert as the expert solves realistic problems. Don't use toy problems or problems so abstracted that they differ qualitatively from actual problems in the domain. Include realistic data in the problem statements, such as letters, reports, laboratory tests, or other data taken from real problems.

To extract sufficiently rich information from the domain expert, the knowledge engineer must watch the expert solve problems, ask the expert probing questions, and develop a set of problems for the expert to solve that span the domain, covering all the types of problems that the expert would normally encounter. The knowledge engineer should systematically vary the data for each problem to explore the solution paths likely to be taken by the expert. Normally, the expert will help to define what constitutes a realistic problem and to identify the kinds of data that must be included. The knowledge engineer may then create the test problems or rely on other domain experts for assistance.

V.   *Pitfall* • The expert no longer seems excited about helping develop the expert system and finds the work somewhat uninteresting and routine. The time that the expert makes available for meeting with the knowledge engineer is steadily decreasing.

How to Avoid It • Be sure the knowledge engineer and expert meet frequently on a regular basis, such as two or three times a week. Involve the expert in the actual building and modification of the system—on line, so he or she can make changes and test their effects. Provide computer tools engineered to be helpful and friendly.

Maintaining the expert's interest in the development effort is critical to its success. Interview sessions should be scheduled at frequent and regular intervals and distributed evenly over the project's length. Long periods between sessions will reduce both the expert's interest and the project's momentum. Making the expert feel like an integral part of the system-building process will motivate him or her, as will showing the expert how the system will ultimately produce a useful tool.

Remember that the expert is not an expert in computer technology. Although he or she will learn something about AI methods and computer usage during normal system development, don't ask the expert to try things on the computer that are beyond his or her current abilities. An expert disillusioned with the system will be of little help.

VI. *Pitfall* • The expert is not familiar with computers and doubts that an approach using computers will be of any use.

How to Avoid It • Gradually increase the functionality of the expert system in the workplace.

A special problem may arise when trying to develop a system in a domain where the experts are blue-collar workers—for example, experts in oil-well log analysis. These experts tend to be skeptical of the academic approach to problem solving and even more skeptical about the value of using artificial intelligence and computers. To defuse this problem before it becomes serious, show the experts how the computer, initially at least, is a way of replacing paper. Then as they become familiar with the computer, show how they can use it to test the emerging system.

VII. *Pitfall* • So many different experts are being used that the knowledge engineer doesn't have time to explore the reasoning processes of one or two experts in great depth. The result is a shallow analysis of their problem-solving techniques.

How to Avoid It • At the beginning involve just one or two experts. Interact with these experts until their methods are understood and a working prototype has been built. Use additional experts for the final testing and revision of the system.

The knowledge engineer has only a limited amount of time to devote to interviews with experts. Spending short amounts of time with many experts leads to a superficial understanding of how an expert solves problems in the domain. Another reason for spending substantial amounts of time with very few experts is to build a strong working relationship with them. Part of the knowledge acquisition process is *education;* the knowledge engineer becomes somewhat of an expert in the problem domain, and the expert becomes more than just casually familiar with AI ideas and methods. For this educational process to be effective, a sense of mutual confidence and respect must be developed between the knowledge engineer and the expert. This takes time, patience, and exposure.

19

Pitfalls During the Development Process

A number of pitfalls await the novice development team during other aspects of the development process. We'll now turn our attention to these. In some cases, we address problems that less experienced knowledge engineers might face; in other cases, we focus on potential difficulties for management.

System Implementation

I.   *Pitfall* • During system development, the knowledge of the expert has become so entwined in the program that it's difficult to tell the expert's knowledge from general problem-solving knowledge and control or search strategies.

How to Avoid It • Carefully separate the domain-specific knowledge from the rest of the program and represent it in meaningful chunks at a useful level of detail. This may be easier to accomplish if a *rule-based* organization is used, where domain knowledge is represented as sets of IF-THEN rules.

A basic tenet of expert systems is to separate the knowledge of the expert from the other knowledge in the system and to make that expert knowledge clear and explicit. This organization simplifies the process of explanation, makes it easier to extend or augment the system, and, in simple cases, makes it possible to check for inconsistencies in the rules and data.

II.   *Pitfall* • After many months of interaction with the expert, the knowledge engineer has extracted hundreds of rules and has represented them in a high-level knowledge engineering language. However, in implementing the prototype expert system and starting to test it, the knowledge engineer finds that many fundamental concepts were omitted from the rules.

How to Avoid It • Test your ideas during all phases of development by implementing them on the computer. During each phase be prepared to revise previously formed ideas. For example, being in the implementation phase doesn't mean you won't need to revise your basic concepts or representations.

All large programming systems evolve to a certain extent. They go through a period of implementation, testing, correction, and retesting. The evolution of an expert system is something substantially more than this simple type of growth. It requires cycling back and forth between the various phases of development, revising and refining the ideas generated. In Chapter 12, we discussed five phases of expert system building. The experienced knowledge engineer jumps back and forth between these phases. This approach of implementing and testing new concepts and representations as early as possible saves time in the long run.

III.   *Pitfall* • The expert system is developed in a language that doesn't provide built-in explanation facilities. After the system performs well, the development team attempts to add mechanisms for allowing the system to explain and justify its operation. The team has difficulty doing this.

How to Avoid It • From the very beginning, design the system to facilitate self-examination. Either pick a tool that has built-in explanation facilities or handcraft simple explanation capabilities for the early prototypes. This will speed implementation. Be sure that the final system has a sophisticated explanation facility to assist the end-user.

Self-knowledge means that the expert system can analyze its own operation and thus understand and explain how and why it reaches particular conclusions. This feature has the most potential for innovative advances, but it is also the least understood and developed. Standard explanation techniques, such as displaying chains of rules used to reach a conclusion, are fairly well understood. More sophisticated techniques, such as justifying the use of particular rules or strategies, is a research problem currently being studied by AI researchers. Although current explanation facilities are quite primitive, they have proved crucial to system operation because 1) they speed system development by helping with debugging, testing, and refinement, and 2) they increase user acceptance by inspiring confidence in the system's performance and reasoning processes.

IV.   *Pitfall* • The expert system contains a very large number of highly specific rules. This slows system execution and makes the system complex and unwieldy.

How to Avoid It • Collapse sets of special-purpose rules into single, more general rules wherever possible. This will make the expert system more compact, efficient, and manageable.

The knowledge engineer extracts rules from the expert by watching the expert solve actual problems and asking appropriate questions about that problem-solving activity. However, this technique tends to produce overly specific or specialized rules. The knowledge engineer must investigate alternative solutions with the expert to gain an understanding of the general principles underlying the rules. Sometimes the knowledge engineer will find it useful to name high-level concepts that the expert uses in the rules but doesn't verbalize. Rules containing these high-level concepts can often replace many lower-level (i.e., more specific) rules.

System Testing and Evaluation

V.   *Pitfall* • When the expert system is tested and evaluated, the users find its performance disappointing in terms of both quality and utility of answers produced.

How to Avoid It • Start planning evaluation techniques during the identification phase of system building. This helps guide system design and assists the development team in assessing the progress being made. *During these early phases of development, be sure to specify the minimum acceptable performance that will allow the system to be considered a success.*

Evaluating an expert system is difficult because there may be no formal way to prove a given answer is correct or the best possible choice. The validity of the answer may depend on the persuasiveness of the argument given to support that answer. Nor will performance alone suffice: Accurate answers to questions that users consider unimportant will not be acceptable. To insure useful results, involve the system users in the system design from the very beginning.

VI. *Pitfall* • The users find it difficult to interact with the expert system. They don't understand the error messages when things go wrong, slow response times frustrate them, and they keep forgetting how to use the editing system to change or add new rules.

How to Avoid It • Use good "human-engineering" practices in the design of the expert system. Insulate the users from technical problems unrelated to the problem domain, such as standard (unfriendly) editing systems or operating systems. Be sure the user never has to wait more than a few seconds before receiving some kind of response from the system, even if it's only a message describing what the system is doing at the time. Make the input and output a clear, concise, stylized form of English, but not abbreviated to the point of being cryptic.

User acceptance can make or break an expert system. Users won't accept a system that performs poorly, but neither will they accept a high-quality performance system that is confusing, tedious, or frustrating. Design the system to be sensitive to the needs of different types of users, in particular, domain experts, end-users, and clerical staff. Slighting any one of these groups can lead to trouble.

VII. *Pitfall* • As the expert system begins to exceed a few hundred rules, corrections or additions to the rules tend to introduce as many as or more errors than they fix. Debugging seems like an endless chore.

How to Avoid It • Keep a record of the problems presented to the system and the answers they produce. Use this to create a set of standard problems for testing system consistency. Run this standard problem set each time you make major changes or additions to the rules, looking for errors caused by the modifications. Also keep track of which rules produce particular conclusions; unused rules indicate either erroneous rule premises or a faulty control scheme.

An expert system, like any complex program, becomes increasingly difficult to modify as it grows larger. Adding new code may inadvertently affect the results produced by already existing code. The use of a collection of standard problems to help debug the system can prove invaluable. This will be even more useful if combined with a mechanism for more or less automatically running the problem set after system changes are made.

Expert Systems in the Marketplace

The expert system area is a rapidly burgeoning field. Across the country, major universities, research institutions, and private corporations are working to bring the promise of expert systems to fulfillment. In this section, we survey the major institutional players in expert system development, speculate on future applications, and list sources of additional information.

20

Where Is Expert System Work Being Done?

We can divide the work on expert systems into efforts by three major groups—universities, research organizations, and businesses. We now briefly discuss the kinds of work being done by each of these groups.

Expert System Work at Universities

Many of the advances in AI technology were spurred by research efforts at universities, usually through doctoral dissertations. Although most large universities offer courses or full-scale graduate programs in AI and expert systems, just a few universities account for a majority of the work in this area. The centers of university-related AI activity in the United States are Stanford, Carnegie-Mellon, and MIT. Two of these universities, Stanford and Carnegie-Mellon, have pioneered the work in expert systems and knowledge engineering.

The research that spawned the development of knowledge-based systems and knowledge engineering grew from an interchange of ideas between Stanford University (SU) and Carnegie-Mellon University (CMU). In the 1960s, Allen Newell and Herbert Simon at CMU studied human problem solving, developing and applying information processing techniques to model human cognition and memory [NEW72]. Newell's key idea was to represent a person's long-term memory as a series of situation-action rules called *productions* and the short-term memory as a set of situations. Each rule would essentially say, "If I recognize some situation S in short-term memory, then I take some action A." Actions consisted of changing the content of short-term memory. Once the contents were changed, new situations would arise—evoking new rules. Newell used this process of rule-evocation and memory modification to model human problem solving and called the resulting system a *production system*.

Newell's idea of using rules to describe cognitive processes was then generalized by work at Stanford in the late 1960s. Here a program called *P* was developed to explore ways of representing an AI program's heuristics as a set of explicit and separate rules [WAT68, WAT70]. This technique of separating the performance knowledge in an AI program from the rest of the program influenced work on DENDRAL at Stanford in the early 1970s and led to the *knowledge-based system* concept. Heuristic knowledge in DENDRAL was encoded as separate rules, and DENDRAL's success influenced the design of MYCIN at Stanford in the mid-1970s. The success of DENDRAL, MYCIN, and other Stanford projects led to the realization that much of a program's intelligence and skill comes from the high-powered expertise built into it. Ed Feigenbaum at Stanford coined the term *knowledge engineering* to describe the process of building such a system, and the era of the expert system began.

Even today, Stanford and Carnegie-Mellon rank among the most prolific and productive of the university-based expert system research centers. Other universities, such as Rutgers, MIT, and the University of Illinois, have also developed interesting research agendas in the expert systems area. Research at Stanford began in chemistry and medicine but expanded to other areas such as electronics and engineering. Research at Carnegie-Mellon first focused on computer systems and manufacturing but expanded to include electronics and process control. Rutgers initially concentrated on expert systems for medicine but later branched to other areas such as electronics, computer systems, and engineering. At MIT and the University of Illinois, research has encompassed many areas, including medicine and mathematics. Table 20.1 summarizes the current and past expert systems research at these universities. See Chapters 25 and 28 for descriptions of the systems and tools mentioned in this table.

Expert System Work at Research Organizations

The research organizations engaged in expert system work come in a variety of types, ranging from experienced leaders in AI to bold newcomers. Some are large corporations with an AI division or group; others are small companies devoted almost exclusively to AI and expert system applications. Because of the large number of such organizations, we cannot mention them all here. However, we can describe the activi-

TABLE 20.1 Expert system work at selected universities.

University	*Location*	*Domains*	*Examples of Systems & Tools*
Stanford	Palo Alto, CA	Medicine Chemistry Computer systems Electronics Engineering Management science	BLUE BOX, CRYSALIS, DENDRAL, EMYCIN, FOLIO, GA1, HASP, MRS, MYCIN, NEO-MYCIN, ONCOCIN, PUFF, PALLADIO, RLL, ROGET, SACON, SPEX, TEIRESIAS, UNITS, VM
Carnegie- Mellon	Pittsburgh, PA	Computer systems Manufacturing Military Process control Electronics	CALLISTO, DAA, ISIS, KBS, MUD, OPS5, OPS83, PDS, PTRANS, SRL, TALIB, XCON, XSEL,
Rutgers	New Brunswick, NJ	Medicine Geology Electronics Law	AI/RHEUM, CASNET, ELAS, EXPERT, MI, REDESIGN, SEEK, SPE, TAXMAN
MIT	Cambridge, MA	Mathematics Medicine	ABEL, FRL, HODGKINS, MACSYMA, NETL, PIP
Univ. of Illinois	Urbana, IL	Agriculture Law Medicine	ADVISE, AL/X, BABY, PLANT/ds, TAXADVISOR

The heading "Expert System Work at Universities" spans the table.

ties of a representative sampling of these organizations: The Rand Corporation, Xerox Palo Alto Research Center, Advanced Information & Decision Systems, and the Ford Aerospace AI Laboratory. Chapter 30 provides a more complete list of such organizations.

The Rand Corporation, formed in 1948, is a large, private, nonprofit research institution that addresses problems affecting national security and public welfare. Rand entered the AI field at its inception in the mid-1950s with the seminal work of Newell, Shaw, and Simon on a program that discovers proofs to theorems in symbolic logic [NEW57a, NEW57b]. Currently, Rand's AI work focuses on expert system tools and applications. Much of this work is funded by government agencies such as DARPA, the Defense Advanced Research Projects Agency. Rand's AI research takes place within its Information Sciences Department and includes developing knowledge engineering languages, simulation languages, software support environments, and applications of expert systems. One thrust of the expert system work involves the development of ROSIE, an English-like knowledge engineering language. The goal of this effort is to extend and refine ROSIE and to create support facilities, such as explanation and tutoring for ROSIE-based expert systems. Another thrust concerns expert system building, including the development of systems for legal reasoning in the product liability area.

Advanced Information & Decision Systems contrasts sharply with the Rand Corporation. This small research and development company was founded in 1979 to provide services and products in AI, estimation and control, and decision theory. Much of the current work at AI&DS focuses on AI, and a number of expert system projects are under way. These include expert systems for analyzing radar signals, diagnosing faults in aircraft inertial navigation systems, and performing intelligent information retrieval. Many of these systems are written in efficient, low-level programming languages such as FORTRAN or C [KER78]. The company has also addressed the problem of building an expert system for identifying and correcting faults in an environmental-control, life-support system for a space station.

The Xerox Palo Alto Research Center (PARC) is a research laboratory set up by Xerox to explore the commercial potential of information systems. Founded in 1970, PARC's research efforts span many areas, including integrated circuit electronics, materials science, and cognitive science. Their expert system work has focused on languages and tools, such as LOOPS and SMALLTALK, and on some applications in VLSI circuit design. At PARC the Intelligent Systems Laboratory supports the knowledge engineering work as well as research in natural language theory and human-machine interaction.

The Artificial Intelligence Laboratory at Ford Aerospace typifies the move by large commercial organizations to acknowledge the value and importance of AI and expert systems in business. Formed in 1982, this very small AI group is conducting research in planning and scheduling, diagnostic expert systems, and smart display systems. A number of projects undertaken by this group involve diagnostic and scheduling systems for the space shuttle program.

Table 20.2 summarizes the work at the research organizations just discussed. Chapters 25 and 28 contain descriptions of the systems and tools mentioned in the table.

Expert System Work at Knowledge Engineering Companies

In the last few years, AI companies have been springing up at a rapid rate. These companies tend to specialize; they focus on various commer-

TABLE 20.2 Expert system work at selected research organizations.

			Expert System Work at Research Organizations		
Organization	*Location*	*Domains*	*Examples of Systems & Tools*
The Rand Corporation	Santa Monica, CA	Military Law Crisis management	LDS, SCENARIO AGENT, SPILLS, SWIRL, TATR, TWIRL, RITA, ROSIE, ROSS
Xerox Palo Alto Research Center (PARC)	Palo Alto, CA	Electronics Data base management	INTERLISP, KRL, LOOPS, PALLADIO, SMALLTALK-80
Advanced Information and Decision Systems (AI&DS)	Mountain View, CA	Military	AMUID, ASTA, RTC, RUBRIC
Ford Aerospace AI Laboratory	Houston, TX	Space program	RBMS, RICS, RPMS

cial aspects of AI ranging from natural language understanding to knowledge engineering. The financial services industry has shown particular interest in expert systems. Companies like APEX, Syntelligence, and CGI have been developing systems in this area. Both Teknowledge and Intellicorp have produced knowledge engineering languages as products, as have a number of other new AI companies. Some of the new companies also offer training courses or short tutorials in AI and knowledge engineering.

Table 20.3 summarizes the activities at some of the AI companies that specialize in knowledge engineering. We will now describe five of these companies in more detail: APEX, CGI, Intellicorp, Syntelligence, and Teknowledge.

APEX

Founded in 1983, Applied Expert Systems, Inc. develops AI-based integrated software products for the financial services industry. The products are not custom-made but may be adapted to a particular client's

TABLE 20.3 Selected knowledge engineering companies.

	Knowledge Engineering Companies		
Name	*Location*	*Founded*	*Activities and Products*
Applied Expert Systems (APEX)	Cambridge, MA	1983	AI-based integrated software products for the financial services industry
Carnegie Group, Inc. (CGI)	Pittsburgh, PA	1982	AI products for project management, process diagnosis, production management, and natural language interface systems; AI training courses; consulting; custom expert system development
Computer* Thought Corporation (C*T)	Plano, TX	1981	Custom expert system development; consulting; AI training courses; software engineering tools
Inference Corporation	Los Angeles, CA	1979	ART, an expert system building language; SMP, a program that performs mathematical symbolic manipulation; custom expert system development
Intellicorp	Menlo Park, CA	1980	KEE, a knowledge engineering language; BION, a minicomputer with software for genetic engineering; custom expert system development
Production System Technologies, Inc.	Pittsburgh, PA	1984	OPS83, an expert system building language
Smart Systems Technology (SST)	McLean, VA	1981	AI training courses; DUCK, a knowledge engineering language; consulting; custom expert system development
Software Architecture and Engineering, Inc. (Software A & E)	Arlington, VA	1978	KES, a knowledge engineering language; custom expert system development; AI training courses
Syntelligence	Sunnyvale, CA	1983	Custom expert system development for financial institutions
Teknowledge	Palo Alto, CA	1981	M.1 and S.1, knowledge engineering languages; expert systems tutorial package (videotapes, software); custom expert system development

needs. Although APEX develops only software products, it can supply its customers with an integrated hardware and software package that it maintains, services, and supports. APEX has produced a number of software products for large banks, brokerage firms, insurance companies, and big eight accounting firms. APEX's first product—a system for helping decision making and production planning in financial services—was developed for an IBM PC-XT and installed in June 1983 in sites around the country. A second related product was installed on the Xerox 1100 workstation and is now in commercial operation. Other products are now under development.

CGI

Carnegie Group, Inc. develops knowledge-based systems and software tools for industrial and manufacturing applications. CGI customizes its prototype and commercial expert systems to meet the needs of its clients and can provide the client with an integrated hardware and software system developed and supported by CGI. The company also provides training and tutorial courses in AI.

Since its founding in 1982 by AI researchers from Carnegie-Mellon University, CGI has developed a number of products that support expert system building, including SRL+, PLUME, and a knowledge engineering workstation. SRL+ is a frame-based knowledge engineering language that integrates logic-based, rule-based, and object-oriented representation paradigms. PLUME is a natural language interpreter that enables users to develop their own domain-specific language interfaces. These tools operate within the Carnegie Group workstation, a powerful minicomputer providing a Common LISP programming environment with high-resolution, bit-mapped raster graphics. The tools are also available on the DEC VAX/VMS family of computers and on the Symbolics 3600 series.

Intellicorp

Intellicorp designs, develops, and markets expert systems and system-building tools for biotechnology and other applications. Much of the company's revenues come from its genetic engineering software and its tools for building commercial and industrial expert systems. Intellicorp also provides custom expert system development on a contract basis.

Founded in 1980, Intellicorp offers both specialized and general-purpose software products. To assist molecular biologists, Intellicorp provides expert systems for simulation and design of recombinant DNA experiments, analysis of nucleic acid sequences, biological data base management, and other genetic engineering applications. The company has also developed the BION workstation for use with its software. This workstation is a graphics-oriented computer incorporating the M68010 microprocessor, and it uses UNIX as its operating system.

To assist knowledge engineers with expert system building, Intellicorp has developed a general-purpose knowledge engineering language called KEE. This object-oriented language integrates frame-based, rule-based, and procedure-oriented representation paradigms and includes an explanation facility that uses graphic displays to indicate the lines of reasoning followed by the KEE expert system. KEE can be used with the Xerox 1100 or Symbolics 3600 series computer systems.

Syntelligence

Like APEX, Syntelligence develops and markets expert systems for the financial services industry. The company works with financial institutions to jointly develop the initial prototype systems using standard core software that can be tailored to the customer's needs. It also provides time-shared versions of its expert systems that permit customers to evaluate them before purchase or to use them on a regular but limited basis. Typical customers of Syntelligence include insurance companies, banks, investment advisers, and brokers.

Since its founding in 1983, Syntelligence has developed a number of expert systems for the financial services industry. These include systems that 1) help insurance underwriters analyze and rate commercial risks, 2) assist lending officers with the evaluation of middle-market commercial loans, and 3) support the preparation of complex bids by engineering and construction firms. To facilitate expert system building, the company has developed a proprietary knowledge engineering language called SYNTEL/1. This tool, modeled after the KAS system, has been tailored to handle decision making common to most financial problems.

Teknowledge

Teknowledge is an international knowledge engineering company that offers products and services related to constructing expert systems. Their product line includes knowledge engineering languages for both personal computers and LISP-based workstations and a knowledge engineering tutorial package composed of videotapes and software. Teknowledge also offers custom expert system development on a contractual basis.

Since its founding in 1981 by a group of AI researchers from Stanford University, Teknowledge has developed several software tools, such as S.1 and M.1. Both tools are rule-based knowledge engineering languages, and both incorporate graphic-oriented debugging aids and facilities for explaining the system's reasoning process. S.1 operates on the Xerox 1100 series workstations while M.1 operates on the IBM Personal Computer. Teknowledge also markets T.1 (a tutorial package containing videotape lectures by leading AI researchers), software demonstration systems using the IBM Personal Computer, and AI reading materials.

Teknowledge has developed prototype expert systems in a variety of application areas. These include DRILLING ADVISOR, a system for Elf-Aquitaine that advises drilling rig supervisors on ways to avoid problems related to drilling and sticking, and for NCR a computer hardware order-entry and configuration system that is somewhat similar to XCON.

The most important terms discussed in this chapter are summarized in Table 20.4. For a more complete description of these concepts see the glossary of expert system terms at the end of the book.

TABLE 20.4 More expert system terminology.

Term	Meaning
Production	An IF-THEN statement used to represent knowledge in a human's long-term memory.
Production system	A type of rule-based system containing IF-THEN statements with conditions that may be satisfied in a data base and actions that change the data base.

21

How Are Expert Systems Faring in the Commercial Marketplace?

Most expert systems never get past the research prototype stage. This is because until recently most were developed in research rather than in commercial environments. In many research environments once the concept is demonstrated the work is finished. However, commercial expert systems now exist that perform useful work on a regular basis from both a research and a business vantage point. Table 21.1 summarizes a few of the more important expert systems in this category. The table does not include all of the current commercial expert systems or those under development that will soon become commercial systems.

High Performance Expert Systems Used in Research

The SYNCHEM2 expert system synthesizes complex organic molecules without assistance or guidance from a chemist. The system uses knowledge about chemical reactions to generate a plan for creating the target molecule from basic building block molecules. It then attempts to find an optimal synthesis route from the starting materials to the target compound by applying heuristics that limit the search to pathways satisfying the problem constraints. These constraints may include information about toxic reaction conditions and the quality and yield of the desired product. The SYNCHEM project, started in 1968, has amassed a large body of knowledge that comprises the SYNCHEM2 knowledge base.

TABLE 21.1 High performance research and business expert systems.

Type	Name	Application	Developer
RESEARCH	SYNCHEM2	Synthesizes complex organic molecules without help from a chemist	State University of New York at Stony Brook, NY
	DENDRAL	Identifies molecular structures from mass spectral data	Stanford University, Stanford, CA
	MACSYMA	Solves algebraic simplification and integration problems	MIT, Cambridge, MA
BUSINESS	ACE	Provides trouble-shooting reports and analyses for telephone cable maintenance	AT&T Bell Laboratories, Whippany, NJ
	DELTA	Helps diagnose and repair diesel electric locomotives	General Electric Company, Schenectady, NY
	SPE	Diagnoses inflammatory conditions by interpreting *scanning densitometer* data	Helena Labs, Beaumont, TX and Rutgers Univ., New Brunswick, NJ
	XCON	Configures VAX-11/780 computer systems	Digital Equipment Corporation, Hudson, MA and Carnegie-Mellon Univ., Pittsburgh, PA
	YES/MVS	Helps computer operators monitor the MVS operating system	IBM, Yorktown Heights, NY

This includes a library of nearly 1,000 chemical reactions and 5,000 chemical compounds. SYNCHEM2 can duplicate the more routine re-sults of competent synthetic organic chemists, which is no small feat. One of the goals of this ongoing research project is to develop the so-phisticated search heuristics necessary for extremely clever or novel syn-theses.

The DENDRAL expert system infers the molecular structure of unknown compounds from mass spectral and nuclear magnetic response data. The system uses an algorithm developed by J. Lederberg to systematically enumerate all possible molecular structures and applies special expertise to prune this list of possibilities to a manageable size. DENDRAL derives its expertise from a collection of handcrafted knowledge about chemistry, including fragmentation rules associated with particular molecular structures. Research chemists throughout the United States regularly use DENDRAL for testing and experimentation. The DENDRAL project, which began in 1965, was one of the first to represent expertise as sets of explicit rules. In fact, DENDRAL is notable for originating many of the ideas underlying the expert system approach to program construction.

The MACSYMA system performs symbolic manipulation of algebraic expressions, assisting the user with problems involving limit calculations, symbolic integration, solution of equations, canonical simplification, and pattern matching. The system uses mathematical expertise organized as modules or individual knowledge sources. These modules are chosen for a particular problem by sophisticated pattern-matching routines. MACSYMA achieves high quality and efficient performance on the mathematical problems within its scope and is used on a regular basis by mathematicians, engineers, and scientists throughout the United States. MACSYMA, like SYNCHEM2 and DENDRAL, is an early expert system originating in the mid-1960s. It's notable as one of the first expert systems to achieve high levels of competency. Both MACSYMA and DENDRAL required extremely long development times—more than 30 person-years of effort each [DAV82]. Today the development time for a commercial expert system seems to lie closer to 10 person-years of effort (see Chapter 16). This decline probably stems from a better understanding of how to apply AI methods to practical problems and from the availability of better tools for building expert systems.

High Performance Expert Systems Used in Business

YES/MVS, DELTA, and ACE are expert systems developed by businesses for commercial applications. Although all exhibit high performance, they are just beginning to be used commercially. YES/MVS, developed by IBM, helps the computer operator monitor and control the MVS (multiple virtual storage) operating system. YES/MVS runs in real time; it monitors the MVS operation, schedules large batch jobs, and alerts human operators to network link problems. This rule-based system is written in an extended version of OPS5. In Chapter 10 we further discuss YES/MVS and show a typical rule from the system (see Figure 10.9).

Delta was developed by the General Electric Company to help maintenance personnel diagnose and repair malfunctions in diesel electric locomotives. The system queries the user for symptoms and then uses them to select appropriate diagnostic strategies for locomotive repair. The system can lead the user through an entire repair procedure, giving specific repair instructions once the malfunction is identified. During this process the system will retrieve diagrams of parts and subsystems and display videodisc movies of repair sequences. DELTA is a rule-based expert system with relatively simple rules. A typical rule is shown below.

> **IF:** EQ [ENGINE SET IDLE] and
> EQ [FUEL PRESSURE BELOW NORMAL] and
> EQ [FUEL-PRESSURE-GAUGE USED IN TEST] and
> EQ [FUEL-PRESSURE-GAUGE STATUS OK],
> **THEN:** WRITE [FUEL SYSTEM FAULTY] 1.0.

This rule states that if the fuel pressure is below normal with the engine at idling speed and the readings were taken from an accurate locomotive fuel pressure gauge, then there is definitely (with certainty 1.0) a fault in the fuel system. Although the system was prototyped in LISP, it was later reimplemented in FORTH for installation on microprocessor-based systems.

ACE provides troubleshooting and diagnostic reports for telephone cable analysts. The system works by analyzing maintenance activity data and generating reports describing the physical location of the trouble and the characteristics of the network at that spot. ACE does not interact with the user; instead it interacts with CRAS, a data base management and report generation system that contains information about telephone network repairs. ACE autonomously retrieves high-level reports from CRAS on a daily basis, requesting more detailed information when needed. It then decides what areas of the telephone network may require replacement or rehabilitation and stores a summary of its conclusion in a special data base that cable analysts can access. For example, ACE might conclude, "the trouble is in a ready access aerial terminal located in a branch of cable 4 and was probably caused by telephone company employees working on previous problems in the area." ACE is a forward chaining, rule-based system implemented in OPS4 and Franz LISP. Below we show the English equivalent of an OPS4 rule from ACE.

> **IF:** A range of pairs within a cable have generated a large number
> of customer reports and
> a majority of the work on those pairs was done in the terminal
> block,
>
> **THEN:** Look for a common address for those repairs.

ACE can generate conclusions but cannot explain the reasoning behind them. Instead, ACE adds to its report a summary of the data that led to its conclusions, an explanation that seems to satisfy the system users. ACE was developed on a VAX-11/780 computer, field-tested, and then transferred to AT&T 3B-2 Model 300 supermicro computers that operate in the cable analysts' offices. The ACE developers, AT&T Bell Laboratories, plan to market the system in the near future.

SPE and XCON are expert systems that have been used commercially for a number of years. Both systems were developed by university researchers working with commercial organizations.

The SPE expert system, usually called the *serum protein electrophoresis diagnostic program* by its developers, distinguishes between various causes of inflammatory conditions in a patient (e.g., cirrhosis of the liver, myeloma—a form of cancer). The system interprets waveforms (serum protein electrophoresis patterns) from a device called a *scanning densitometer* by applying knowledge about how the instrument readings and patient data relate to disease categories. The system represents knowledge in the form of rules and was initially implemented in EXPERT. Below we show an example of a rule from the system, followed by its English translation [WEI84].

> F(AGEM, 0:4.99) & F(GAMMA, 0:.19) → H(DG,.9)
>
> **IF:** The patient is less than 5 months old,
> and the gamma quantity is less than 0.19 gm/dl,
>
> **THEN:** The patient does have decreased gamma globulin
> (with certainty 0.9).

The unique aspect of the SPE expert system is its incorporation directly into a laboratory instrument—CliniScan, Helena Laboratories' scanning densitometer. Researchers at Rutgers first developed SPE in the EXPERT language using a DEC-20 computer. During this phase, the program consisted of fewer than 100 EXPERT rules. After testing and refining the system, the developers translated it into the assembly language for the Motorola 6809 processor, an inexpensive and efficient microprocessor used within CliniScan. This translation was done automatically, using a set of programs written by the developers expressly for this task. Then Helena Laboratories took the system and incorporated it into a read-only memory in their instrument. CliniScan, incorporating the SPE expert system, was marketed by Helena Laboratories in 1982.

XCON: The Expert Configurer for Computer Systems

XCON has the distinction of being one of the most mature and widely used expert systems currently operating on a commercial basis. It was developed jointly by an AI group at Carnegie-Mellon University (CMU) and an intelligent systems group at Digital Equipment Corporation. In 1980, XCON could configure VAX-11/780 computer systems; today it configures all VAX family systems for Digital Equipment Corporation (DEC) in its United States and European plants [OCO84]. XCON takes over the job previously performed by technical editors, people who examine a customer's purchase order and determine what computer components need to be substituted or added to make the order consistent and complete.

XCON configures the systems at a very detailed level. For each order it determines necessary modifications, produces diagrams showing the spatial and logical relationships between the hundreds of components that comprise a complete system, defines cable lengths between system components, and handles other jobs usually relegated to skilled technicians. XCON performs at a level similar to that of an experienced technical editor, but it operates much faster. For example, although it takes the editor as long as 20 minutes to configure a system order, XCON can typically do it in less than a minute.

The early versions of XCON were implemented in OPS4, later versions in OPS5. Chapter 10 includes a description of the OPS5 language, and Chapter 5 contains an example of an OPS5 rule from XCON. In reviewing the literature on this computer system configurer, you will find that the system has two names: The DEC people call it XCON, while the CMU people prefer to call it R1. Both names refer to the same expert system.

Because XCON is a mature and widely used system, its development may hold some lessons for other expert-system building efforts. First, XCON's developers found that the level of effort required to develop and extend the system remained fairly constant over the life of the project. The effort stayed at about four person-years per year. This reflects the fact that knowledge required by the system grew at a relatively constant rate.

Second, the developers found they didn't have to wait until the system was complete before putting it to use [BAC84].

> To expect anything close to perfection during the first few years a
> system is being used (especially if the task is significantly more than toy)
> is probably a very serious mistake. We believe the data suggest that to
> keep an expert system from regular use until its knowledge is complete

would be a poor idea. It has taken 80,000 orders to uncover some of the inadequacies in R1's configuration knowledge, and the configuration task is continually redefined as new products are introduced.

XCON was providing significant assistance to technical editors well before it reached its performance goal, which was set by DEC as configuring orders perfectly 90 to 95 percent of the time. But the redundancy in the configuration process (no single person was given total responsibility for an order) allowed XCON to be useful even during its early stages, before it achieved high-level performance. Regardless of XCON's maturity, it will never have all the knowledge it needs and will thus make mistakes. The users and developers of the system now understand and accept this fact.

Finally, the developers of XCON found that building an expert configurer is a seemingly unending process, requiring incremental growth over long periods of time [BAC84].

> Though much of R1's knowledge was added to correct or complement existing knowledge, a significant part of the additions came as a result of R1 having to have the knowledge to perform new tasks. Some of these were the result of Digital introducing new computer system types and the rest resulted from the users' observations that things would be better if R1 could do one more thing. We believe all expert systems will be hounded to continue to grow for both of these reasons. Tasks that expert systems are good for are just those whose objects change significantly over time. Moreover, in such tasks no clear boundaries delimit what should and should not be within the province of the expert. Thus, whenever an expert system finds itself on a boundary, its public encourages it to extend the boundary.

DEC's experience provides a good argument for the use of expert systems. Without the flexibility and modular organization inherent in the rule-based expert systems approach, the developers would have been hard pressed to maintain the incremental growth needed to support DEC's changing product lines. Figure 21.1 shows the way in which XCON's growth has provided support for an increasing range of DEC products.

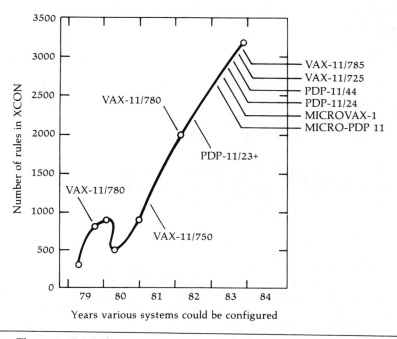

FIGURE 21.1 The growth of XCON (adapted from [BAC84]).

22

What's Next for Expert Systems?

The expert systems area is expanding rapidly. Both government and industry are beginning to invest in commercial expert systems, and within a few years a very large number of U.S. companies will be involved in AI or expert system research and development. Companies that ignore this high technology advance will certainly find themselves at a competitive disadvantage in the near future.

One of the most important by-products of this expert system development will be the codification of knowledge. As developers construct large, sophisticated knowledge bases, a market will develop for the knowledge itself, independent of any associated computer system. Tutoring facilities will be developed to help disseminate this information to students trying to learn about the application domain, and "knowledge decompilers" will be designed to translate the knowledge bases into coherent books or written reports. Since *metaknowledge*, knowledge about effective strategies and procedures for using the domain knowledge, will be used more extensively in future expert systems, it, too, will become an important commodity.

Advances in computer hardware have contributed significantly to the expansion of expert systems. Feigenbaum, one of the pioneers in the expert system field, comments about the effect of hardware advances on expert system development [FEI81]:

> The microelectronic revolution of the 1980s will put the average expert system into a relatively inexpensive and small hardware package. This is an unremarkable prediction based on the progress of VLSI toward million-gate and ten-million gate chips. The knowledge bases will be held in disk, bubble, or semiconduction memories of large sizes,

accessed as needed. We will see a spectrum of expert systems, from those of modest scope of knowledge that may be packaged in small, highly portable machines costing less than a thousand dollars, to powerful aids for professionals that will reside in workstations costing a few tens of thousands of dollars. Very large knowledge bases will be stored in central repositories, accessed by communication networks as needed.

The advent of small and inexpensive hardware for expert systems has made practical very small computers designed for and dedicated to particular expert systems. These tiny computer system/expert system packages can be embedded in equipment to help monitor or control it. We discuss the implications of this in the next section.

Expert system progress and expansion has also been helped by the success of a few highly visible expert systems (see Chapter 21). This trend should continue, with success in particular application areas spurring interest in other areas. We expect increased interest in new areas, such as law, financial planning, process control, business management, and crisis management. Potential applications for the legal area are described in some detail in the second section of this chapter.

Expert Systems Will Lead to Intelligent Systems

Computer hardware advances have made possible *integrated expert systems*, that is, expert systems embedded in microprocessor chips to form an integrated hardware/software package. One example of this is the EEG Analysis System, an expert system embedded in a Motorola MC6801 single-chip, eight-bit microcomputer and designed to interpret electroencephalograms recorded from renal patients. In an integrated expert system, there is no need to distinguish between the expert system proper, the language in which the expert system is written, and the computer that executes that language. For all practical purposes they are one unit. These integrated expert systems can be embedded in a piece of equipment, such as complex electronic gear, to form what we will call an *intelligent system*.

The intelligent system concept is actually a merging of ideas about fault-tolerant equipment and expert systems. Computer hardware size and price reductions have made it feasible for complex equipment to contain its own dedicated computer running an expert system that takes care of the equipment in some way. The integrated expert system could handle tasks like monitoring and controlling equipment operation, detecting and diagnosing equipment faults, assisting in correcting the faults, and planning ways to work around the faults until they are corrected. Figure 22.1 illustrates the idea of an intelligent system.

As the figure implies, the integrated expert system is "hardwired" into the equipment with direct connections to sensors and switches that allow the expert system to monitor and, in some cases, control the equipment. Together, the equipment and expert system form the intelligent system, which may help an operator to use the equipment. For applications where dangerous or unexpected situations are unlikely to arise, the operator could be taken out of the loop completely.

In some cases, the integrated expert system could be fine-tuned to the idiosyncrasies of a particular piece of equipment. This might not be particularly useful for electronic gear, but it could prove valuable for

FIGURE 22.1 The intelligent system may help monitor, control, diagnose, and repair the equipment.

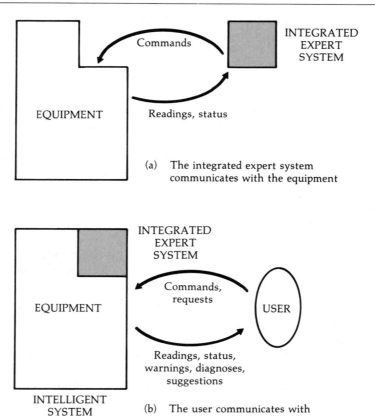

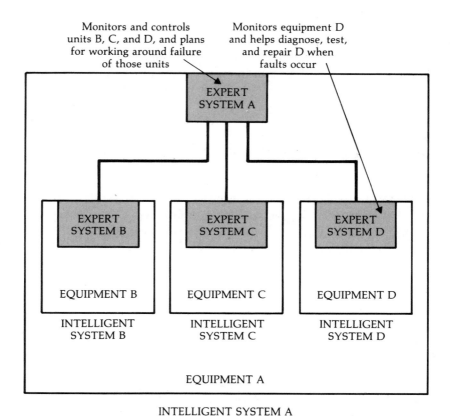

FIGURE 22.2 A hierarchical intelligent system.

large, expensive equipment, like a refinery distillation column, where a small improvement in efficiency could lead to a huge savings in cost.

The intelligent system configuration will be particularly useful when the equipment to be monitored forms a hierarchy of physical units arranged in some network structure, as shown in Figure 22.2. Each unit can then have an attached expert system that monitors its own operation and the operation of its component units and suggests how to work around lower-level system components when they are not operational.

It may even be possible to develop the expert system in conjunction with the design of the physical unit or equipment. In this case it could influence the design process and result in a more fault-tolerant design. Alternatively, the expert system could be developed to work with CAD (computer-aided design) systems to help the equipment designer develop a fault-tolerant design.

An intelligent system has already been developed and put into commercial use. The SPE expert system (see Chapter 21) runs on a microprocessor inside CliniScan, Helena Laboratories' scanning densitometer. This expert system interprets waveforms from the densitometer to determine which of several diseases a patient might have.

A New Application Area: Expert Systems for Law

Expert systems are beginning to be noticed by the legal profession. Although a relatively small number of expert systems exist for this area, the potential is great. Four important types of applications for expert systems in law are document generation, legal interpretation, monitoring, and case management. Table 22.1 describes these applications.

TABLE 22.1 Important application areas for expert systems in law.

Application Areas for Law	System Description
Document generation	Produces legal documents (e.g., wills, contracts, draft legislation) by selecting or composing appropriate pieces of text and organizing them into document form.
Interpretation and prediction	Interprets the law (e.g., statutes, regulations) in the context of a particular question or problem, anticipates the legal consequences of proposed actions, and predicts the effects of changes in legislation.
Scheduling and monitoring	Schedules attorneys' activities and periodically inspects legal data bases and knowledge bases for changes in the law that could affect clients and active cases.
Case management	Organizes case information, estimates case value, and suggests tactics and strategies for negotiation and case disposition.

Document Generation

Expert systems for document generation would help acquire, integrate, and organize the knowledge needed to produce the document. To produce a standard document such as a will or contract, the system would conduct an interview to determine the client's needs, produce a plan for addressing those needs, and then generate a document reflecting that plan. In some situations, such as a simple will, the system could select and arrange routine pieces of text used as the document's building blocks, guided by its knowledge of how the elements of the plan relate to those building blocks. In other more complex situations, such as business contracts or draft legislation, the system could help the user plan and organize the document and suggest contingencies that the user might otherwise overlook.

Interpretation and Prediction

Expert systems for interpretation and prediction would help the user interpret legal authority, anticipate the legal consequences of proposed actions, and predict the effect of changes to the law. These systems would contain legal statutes and regulations put into program form so that the user could determine their effect by executing the program. For example, the user could examine the effect of particular legal statutes on a given case by supplying the system with data describing the case and noting the role that the statutes play in determining case outcome. The user could similarly determine the legality of particular positions (e.g., tax status) and the legal consequences of particular acts (e.g., business mergers). To predict the effect of changes in legislation (or other legal environment changes), the user could modify the program to reflect the proposed changes and then execute it on a set of cases previously analyzed by the program. This could also help the user find inconsistencies between proposed law and existing legal authority.

Scheduling and Monitoring

Expert systems for scheduling and monitoring would handle a range of applications from calendar and scheduling activities to periodic inspection and review of legal data bases. These systems could monitor legal data bases for the purpose of identifying clients affected by law changes. For example, clients given legal help with estate planning, wills, or business contracts would want to be notified when laws were enacted that nullified key provisions in those documents. These systems would work by setting up links between particular documents and the pieces or types of legislation that could affect them and then notifying the attorneys when the linked legislation was changed.

Case Management

Expert systems for case management would organize case information, estimate case value, and help manage the case at different levels of involvement. For example, at the local level they could find and summarize arguments to be made for or against particular propositions. At a more global level they could suggest tactics and strategies for negotiation and case settlement.

This type of application holds even more promise for very complex cases. Managing large-scale litigation, such as antitrust lawsuits, is inordinately complex. Cases with large economic and business stakes are so complex that one person cannot be expected to recognize and understand all the legal and factual issues raised. Trial preparation often takes years; issues and evidence change or are forgotten. During this time the litigation staffs change, and key personnel with valuable knowledge may be lost. This complexity makes large-scale litigation extraordinarily expensive, uncertain, and difficult.

An expert system for managing complex, large-scale litigation would organize litigation documents, data, and evidence by specifying how they fit into the overall litigation plan. It would use the potential effects (both positive and negative) of this information to suggest litigation strategies and explain why such strategies could be useful. The system would contain a compilation of the staff's best analyses, and it would be used to build a common understanding of the case and a basis for consensus on trial issues. During the trial it would determine the likely impact of trial events and their effect on case value. After the trial it would be used to train new staff or to help the staff deal with similar litigation.

23

Sources of Additional Information about Expert Systems

We hope this book has whetted your appetite for more information about expert systems. In this chapter, we suggest the next steps for readers who want to learn more about this frontier of information technology. We have categorized the references in terms of the reader's technical background. We suggest that you read the material in the order listed within each category.

AI/Expert Systems Papers

I. There are a number of good nontechnical descriptions of various aspects of expert systems. The references listed here do not require any background in computers or in artificial intelligence.

Introduction to Expert Systems

1. Waterman, D. *A Guide to Expert Systems.* Addison-Wesley, 1985.
2. Austin, H. Market trends in artificial intelligence. in W. Reitman (ed.) *Artificial Intelligence Applications for Business,* Norwood, N.J.: Ablex, 1984.

3. O'Connor, D. Using expert systems to manage change and complexity in manufacturing. in W. Reitman (ed.) *Artificial Intelligence Applications for Business*, Norwood, N.J.: Ablex, 1984.

4. Kinnucan, P. Computers that think like experts. *High Technology*, pp. 30–42, January 1984.

Introduction to AI

5. Minsky, M. Why people think computers can't. *The AI Magazine*, pp. 3–15, Fall 1982.

6. Raphael, B. About computers. chapter 1, *The Thinking Computer*, W. H. Freeman, 1976.

7. Waltz, D. Artificial intelligence. *Scientific American*, vol. 247, pp. 118–133, October 1982.

8. Rich, E. What is artificial intelligence? chapter 1, *Artificial Intelligence*, McGraw-Hill, 1983.

Introduction to AI Tools

9. Sheil, B. Power tools for programmers. *Datamation*, pp. 131–144, February 1983.

10. Rich, E. Implementing AI systems: languages and machines. chapter 12, *Artificial Intelligence*, McGraw-Hill, 1983.

II. Readers committed to learning about AI will find the following detailed discussions useful. They do not assume any background in AI beyond the kind of general introduction provided by references in Category I.

Artificial Intelligence

11. Raphael, B. Representation. chapter 2, *The Thinking Computer*, W. H. Freeman, 1976.

12. Raphael, B. Search. chapter 3, *The Thinking Computer*, W. H. Freeman, 1976.

13. Raphael, B. Problem solving methods: background and formal approaches. chapter 4, *The Thinking Computer*, W. H Freeman, 1976.

14. Raphael, B. Problem solving methods: informal and combined approaches. chapter 5, *The Thinking Computer*, W. H. Freeman, 1976.

15. Rich, E. Basic problem-solving methods. chapter 3, *Artificial Intelligence*, McGraw-Hill, 1983.

16. Rich, E. Structured representations of knowledge. chapter 7, *Artificial Intelligence*, McGraw-Hill, 1983.

17. Ritchie, G. and Thompson, H. Natural language processing. in T. O'Shea and M. Eisenstadt (eds.) *Artificial Intelligence*, Harper & Row, 1984.

18. Rich, E. Natural language understanding. chapter 9, *Artificial Intelligence*, McGraw-Hill, 1983.

III. These more detailed descriptions of expert systems require some familiarity with the terms and concepts in AI.

Expert Systems

19. Hayes-Roth, F., Waterman, D., and Lenat, D. An overview of expert systems. in *Building Expert Systems*, Hayes-Roth, Waterman, and Lenat (eds.) Addison-Wesley, 1983.

20. Brachman, R., Amarel, S., Engelman, C., Engelmore, R., Feigenbaum, E., and Wilkins, D. What are expert systems? in F. Hayes-Roth, D. Waterman, and D. Lenat (eds.) *Building Expert Systems*, Addison-Wesley, 1983.

21. Stefik, M., Aikins, J., Balzar, R., Benoit, J., Birnbaum, L., Hayes-Roth, F., and Sacerdoti, E. Basic concepts for building expert systems. in F. Hayes-Roth, D. Waterman, and D. Lenat (eds.) *Building Expert Systems*, Addison-Wesley, 1983.

22. Davis, R. Expert systems: Where are we? And where do we go from here? *The AI Magazine*, pp. 3–22, Spring 1982.

IV. All of the references in the following section are designed for computer professionals or for those with extensive experience in both AI and expert systems.

Rule-based Systems

23. Davis, R. and King, J. The origin of rule-based systems in AI. in B. G. Buchanan and E. H. Shortliffe (eds.) *Rule-Based Expert Systems*, Addison-Wesley, 1984.

24. Waterman, D. and Hayes-Roth, F. An overview of pattern-directed inference systems. in *Pattern-Directed Inference Systems*, Waterman and Hayes-Roth (eds.) Academic Press, 1978.

Frame Systems

25. Minsky, M. A framework for representing knowledge. in P. Winston (ed.) *The Psychology of Computer Vision*, McGraw-Hill, 1975.

26. Goldstein, I. and Papert, S. Artificial intelligence, language, and the study of knowledge. *Cognitive Science,* vol 1., no. 1, January 1977.

27. Winston, P. Representing knowledge in frames. chapter 7, *Artificial Intelligence,* Addison-Wesley, 1977.

Semantic Nets

28. Nilsson, N. Structured object representations. chapter 9, *Principles of Artificial Intelligence,* Palo Alto: Tioga Publishing Company, 1980.

29. Brachman, R. On the epistemological status of semantic networks. in N. Findler (ed.) *Associative Networks: Representation and Use of Knowledge by Computers,* Academic Press, 1979.

Building the Expert System

30. Chandrasekaran, B. Expert systems: matching techniques to tasks. in W. Reitman (ed.) *Artificial Intelligence Applications for Business,* Norwood, N.J.: Ablex, 1984.

31. Buchanan, B., Bechtal, R., Bennett, J., Clancey, W., Kulikowski, C., Mitchell, T., and Waterman, D. Constructing an expert system. in F. Hayes-Roth, D. Waterman, and D. Lenat (eds.) *Building Expert Systems,* Addison-Wesley, 1983.

32. Stefik, M., Aikins, J., Balzar, R., Benoit, J., Birnbaum, L., Hayes-Roth, F., and Sacerdoti, E. The architecture of expert systems. in R. Hayes-Roth, D. Waterman, and D. Lenat (eds.) *Building Expert Systems,* Addison-Wesley, 1983.

Evaluating the Expert System

33. Chandrasekaran, B. On evaluating AI systems for medical diagnosis. *The AI Magazine,* vol. 4, no. 2, Summer 1983.

34. Gaschnig, J., Klahr, P., Pople, H., Shortliffe, E., and Terry, A. Evaluation of expert systems: issues and case studies. in F. Hayes-Roth, D. Waterman, and D. Lenat (eds.) *Building Expert Systems,* Addison-Wesley, 1983.

35. Lenat, D., Davis, R., Doyle, J., Genesereth, M., Goldstein, I., and Schrobe, H. Reasoning about reasoning. in F. Hayes-Roth, D. Waterman, and D. Lenat (eds.) *Building Expert Systems,* Addison-Wesley, 1983.

Tools for Expert Systems

36. Waterman, D. and Hayes-Roth, F. An investigation of tools for building expert systems. in *Building Expert Systems,* F. Hayes-Roth, D. Waterman, and D. Lenat (eds.) Addison-Wesley, 1983.

37. Barstow, D., Aiello, N., Duda, R., Erman, L., Forgy, C., Gorlin, D., Greiner, R., Lenat, D., London, P., McDermott, J., Nii, P., Politakis, P., Reboh, R., Rosenschein, S., Scott, C., van Melle, W., and Weiss, S. Languages and tools for knowledge engineering. in F. Hayes-Roth, D. Waterman, and D. Lenat (eds.) *Building Expert Systems,* Addison-Wesley, 1983.

V. These articles provide a low-level introduction to some common AI programming languages. They are intended for programmers.

Introduction to AI Programming Tools

38. Hasemer, T. An introduction to LISP. in T. O'Shea and M. Eisenstadt (eds.) *Artificial Intelligence,* Harper & Row, 1984.
39. Clocksin, W. F. An introduction to PROLOG. in T. O'Shea and M. Eisenstadt (eds.) *Artificial Intelligence,* Harper & Row, 1984.
40. Laubsch, J. Advanced LISP programming. in T. O'Shea and M. Eisenstadt (eds.) *Artificial Intelligence,* Harper & Row, 1984.

Survey of AI Languages and Machines

41. Boley, H. Artificial intelligence languages and machines. *Technology and Science of Informatics,* North Oxford Academic, vol. 2, no. 3, 1983.

AI/Expert Systems Books

Many of the articles listed in the categories above are drawn from the following books. Although they differ somewhat in terms of the detail with which they treat topics, none of these books assumes more than a very general familiarity with expert systems or AI. These are the first books to buy if you are just entering the AI/expert systems field.

Waterman, D. *A Guide to Expert Systems.* Addison-Wesley, 1985.

Reitman W. (ed.) *Artificial Intelligence Applications for Business.* Norwood, N.J.: Ablex, 1984.

Hayes-Roth, F., Waterman, D., and Lenat, D. (eds.) *Building Expert Systems.* Addison-Wesley, 1983.

Raphael, B. *The Thinking Computer.* W. H. Freeman, 1976.

Rich, E. *Artificial Intelligence.* McGraw-Hill, 1983.

Barr, A. and Feigenbaum, E. *The Handbook of Artificial Intelligence, Volume I.* William Kaufmann, Inc., 1981.

Many other books and publications are available on AI and expert systems. Some are listed here, but most of the ones shown assume a substantial background in artificial intelligence.

Alty, J. and Coombs, M. *Expert Systems, Concepts and Examples*. Manchester, England: NCC Publications, 1984.

Barr, A. and Feigenbaum, E. *The Handbook of Artificial Intelligence, Volume II*. William Kaufmann, Inc., 1982.

Buchanan, B. and Shortliffe, E. *Rule-Based Expert Systems*. B. Buchanan and E. Shortliffe (eds.) Addison-Wesley, 1984.

Clancey, W. and Shortliffe, E. *Readings in Medical Artificial Intelligence: The First Decade*. Addison-Wesley, 1984.

Cohen, C. and Feigenbaum, E. *The Handbook of Artificial Intelligence, Volume III*. William Kaufmann, Inc., 1982.

Coombs, M. *Developments in Expert Systems*. M. Coombs (ed.) Orlando, Fla.: Academic Press, 1984.

Feigenbaum, E. and McCorduck, P. *The Fifth Generation*. Addison-Wesley, 1983.

Gevarter, W. *Artificial Intelligence, Expert Systems, Computer Vision and Natural Language Processing*. Park Ridge, N.J.: Noyes Publications, 1984.

Hayes, J. and Michie, D. (eds.) *Intelligent Systems*. Chichester, England: Ellis Horwood Limited, 1983.

Negoita, C. *Expert Systems and Fuzzy Systems*. Menlo Park, Calif.: Benjamin/Cummings, 1985.

Michie, D. (ed.) *Introductory Readings in Expert Systems*. Gordon and Breach, Science Publishers, 1982.

Schank, R. and Childers, P. *The Cognitive Computer*. Addison-Wesley, 1984.

Weiss, S. and Kulikowski, C. *A Practical Guide to Designing Expert Systems*. New Jersey: Rowman & Allanheld, 1984.

Winston, P. and Prendergast, K. *The AI Business*. Cambridge, Mass.: The MIT Press, 1984.

AI/Expert Systems Magazines, Newsletters, and Journals

These two publications are probably the best for most purposes and most audiences because they are the least demanding technically.

The AI Magazine, American Association for Artificial Intelligence, 445 Burgess Drive, Menlo Park, CA 94025.

Expert Systems: The International Journal of Knowledge Engineering, Learned Information Ltd., Besselsleigh Road, Abingdon, Oxford, OX13 6LG, England.

Newsletters are a useful way to get the current news on research and new products. Those listed here would be appropriate for any audience. However, the journals in this category are very technical and are recommended for experienced AI researchers.

Newsletters

The Artificial Intelligence Report, Artificial Intelligence Publications, 95 First Street, Los Altos, CA 94022. (monthly newsletter)

Applied Artificial Intelligence Reporter, Intelligent Computer Systems Research Institute, P.O. Box 1308-EP, Fort Lee, NJ 07024. (monthly newsletter)

Machine Intelligence News, Oyez International Business Communications Ltd., 56 Holborn Viaduct, London, EC1A 2EX, England. (monthly newsletter)

Artificial Intelligence Markets, AIM Publications, P.O. Box 156, Natick, MA 01760. (monthly newsletter)

AISB Quarterly, Newsletter of the Society for the Study of Artificial Intelligence and Simulation of Behavior, Institute of Educational Technology, The Open University, Walton Hall, Milton Keynes, MK7 6AA, England. (quarterly newsletter)

SIGART Newsletter, ACM Special Interest Group in Artificial Intelligence, Association for Computing Machinery, 11 West 42nd Street, New York, NY 10036. (quarterly newsletter)

Canadian AI Newsletter, Canadian Artificial Intelligence Society, 243 College Street, Toronto, Canada M5T 2Y1.

Journals

Artificial Intelligence, Elsevier Science Publishers B.V., Journals Department, P.O. Box 211, 1000 AE Amsterdam, The Netherlands.

International Journal of Man-Machine Studies, Academic Press, 24-28 Oval Road, London, NW1 7DX, England.

Cognitive Science, Ablex Publishing Corporation, 355 Chestnut Street, Norwood, NJ 07648.

Conferences to Attend

Because the expert system area is changing so rapidly, anyone seriously interested in participating in it needs to find ways to keep up-to-date. Conferences are an ideal way to do this. They are an important meeting ground for people with common interests and goals, and they provide a forum for the display of new products. Some of the major conferences are listed here.

National Conference on Artificial Intelligence (AAAI). Proceedings published by William Kaufmann, Inc., 95 First Street, Los Altos, CA.

International Expert Systems Meeting. Organized by Learned Information Ltd., Besselsleigh Road, Abingdon, Oxford, OX13 6LG, England.

International Joint Conference on Artificial Intelligence (IJCAI). Proceedings published by Walter Kaufmann, Inc., 95 First Street, Los Altos, CA.

Conference on Artificial Intelligence Applications (CAIA), IEEE Computer Society, Proceedings published by IEEE Computer Society Press, 1109 Spring Street, Silver Spring, MD.

European Conference on Artificial Intelligence (ECAI).

AI/Expert Systems Formal Training

The following firms offer training in building and implementing expert systems. See Chapter 28 for information on the services they provide.

The Institute of Artificial Intelligence
1888 Century Park East, Suite 1207
Los Angeles, CA 90067

The Carnegie Group
5867 Douglas Street
Pittsburgh, PA 15217

Computer Thought Corporation
1721 Plano Parkway
Plano, TX 75074

Smart Systems Technology
Suite 421 North
7700 Leesburg Pike
Falls Church, VA 22043

Software Architecture and Engineering, Inc.
Artificial Intelligence Center
Suite 1220, 1401 Wilson Boulevard
Arlington, VA 22209

AI/Expert Systems Data Bases

The U.S. Naval Ocean Systems Center (NOSC) in San Diego has developed a robotics and artificial intelligence data base (RAID) to promote communication between groups involved in U.S. Department of Defense-sponsored research in robotics and AI. This data base contains over 500 descriptions of current defense department projects in this area, including information on who is performing the work, what kind of work is under way, and how much funding is involved.

The RAID data base may be accessed by personnel working on defense department projects in robotics and AI. This access can be made through the ARPAnet or MILnet communications networks and by conventional U.S. mail via the RAID support staff. For additional information on RAID contact:

The RAID Data Base Analyst
Computer Sciences Corporation
4045 Hancock Street
San Diego, CA 92110.

Expert Systems and Tools

Expert systems and tools for building them are being developed at a surprisingly rapid rate. We briefly describe some of the existing systems and tools to provide some idea of their scope and diversity. The section is divided into two chapters, a catalog of selected expert systems and one of parts, a catalog of selected expert systems and one of selected expert system tools. Each catalog is organized by categories, expert systems by problem domain and tools by representation methods. Each catalog has its own bibliography for readers interested in finding out more about expert systems and tools.

24

Index for Expert Systems

How to Use This Index

This index will help you locate any particular expert system described in Chapter 25, the catalog of expert systems. The systems in this index are arranged alphabetically by system name. Each has a category associated with it that describes the primary application area of the expert system. Look under this category in Chapter 25 for a brief summary of the system.

Expert Systems and Their Application Areas

ABEL:	medicine
ACE:	electronics
ACES:	military science
ADEPT:	military science
ADVISOR:	mathematics
AI/COAG:	medicine
AI/MM:	medicine
AI/RHEUM:	medicine
AIRID:	military science
AIRPLAN:	military science
AMUID:	military science
ANALYST:	military science
ANGY:	medicine

EXAMINER:	medicine
EXPERT NAVIGATOR:	military science
FAITH:	space technology
FALCON:	process control
FG502-TASP:	electronics
FOLIO:	information management
FOREST:	electronics
GALEN:	medicine
GAMMA:	physics
GA1:	chemistry
GCA:	information management
GUIDON:	medicine
HANNIBAL:	military science
HASP:	military science
HDDSS:	medicine
HEADMED:	medicine
HEART IMAGE INTERPRETER:	medicine
HEME:	medicine
HT-ATTENDING:	medicine
HYDRO:	geology
IDT:	computer systems
IMACS:	manufacturing
IN-ATE:	electronics
INTERNIST-I/CADUCEUS:	medicine
IRIS:	medicine
IR-NLI:	information management
ISA:	computer systems
ISIS:	manufacturing
I&W:	military science
JUDITH:	law
KNEECAP:	space technology
KNOBS:	military science
LDS:	law
LEGAL ANALYSIS SYSTEM:	law
LES:	space technology
LITHO:	geology
LRS:	law
MACSYMA:	mathematics
MATHLAB 68:	mathematics
MDX:	medicine
MECHO:	physics
MECS-AI:	medicine
MEDICO:	medicine
MED1:	medicine

R1-SOAR:	computer systems
SACON:	engineering
SADD:	electronics
SAL:	law
SARA:	law
SCENARIO AGENT:	military science
SECS:	chemistry
SEQ:	chemistry
SIAP:	military science
SOPHIE:	electronics
SPAM:	military science
SPE:	medicine
SPERIL-I:	engineering
SPERIL-II:	engineering
SPEX:	chemistry
STEAMER:	engineering
SWIRL:	military science
SYN:	electronics
SYNCHEM:	chemistry
SYNCHEM2:	chemistry
SYSTEM D:	medicine
TALIB:	electronics
TATR:	military science
TAXADVISOR:	law
TAXMAN:	law
THYROID MODEL:	medicine
TIMM/TUNER:	computer systems
TQMSTUNE:	chemistry
TRANSISTOR SIZING SYSTEM:	electronics
TWIRL:	military science
VM:	medicine
WHEEZE:	medicine
WILLARD:	meteorology
XCON:	computer systems
XSEL:	computer systems
YES/MVS:	computer systems

25

Catalog of
Expert Systems

This catalog contains summaries of selected expert systems from a number of different application areas. Chapter 24 will help you determine in which area a particular expert system belongs. Although many expert systems belong in more than one area, no attempt has been made to indicate all the areas in which these expert systems might belong. Only the major area is indicated here.

Chapter 26 contains a bibliography for the expert systems described here, arranged by application area. These papers describe the expert systems in detail and are written for people with an AI/expert systems background.

This catalog of expert systems is not complete: It contains only a small portion of the many expert systems that have been developed. The intent was to provide a broad enough selection for the reader to gain a feeling for the scope and nature of current expert system development efforts.[1]

Agriculture

PLANT/cd predicts the damage to corn due to the black cutworm. The system uses knowledge about the particular field being studied,

---

[1] If your expert system is not included in this catalog and you would like it included in the next edition of the book, please send a one-paragraph description of the system (using a format similar to that used in this chapter) plus research reports describing your work to the author.

such as moth trap counts, field weediness, larval age spectrum, soil condition, and corn variety to predict the degree of damage the cutworm will cause. The system uses a combination of rules and a set of black cutworm simulation programs to produce the predictions. Knowledge is represented as rules accessed by a backward chaining control mechanism. The system is implemented in ADVISE. It was developed at the University of Illinois and reached the stage of a research prototype. [BOU83]

PLANT/ds provides consultation on the diagnosis of soybean diseases using knowledge about disease symptoms and plant environment. The system uses information such as the month of occurrence, the temperature, plant height, and condition of leaves, stems, and seeds to decide which of 15 or so diseases is most likely. Knowledge is in the form of two types of rules: 1) rules representing the system's diagnostic expertise, and 2) rules obtained from an automated inductive inference program called AQ11. PLANT/ds is implemented in ADVISE. It was developed at the University of Illinois and reached the stage of a research prototype. [MIC80a, MIC80b, MIC82b, UHR82]

POMME helps farmers manage apple orchards by providing advice on how to improve the apple crop. The system contains expertise obtained from plant pathologists and entomologists on pest control and weather-damage recovery. This includes knowledge about fungicides, insecticides, and freeze, frost, and drought damage. POMME uses a combination of rule-based and frame-based representation methods. It is implemented in PROLOG and runs on a VAX 11/780 computer. The system was developed at Virginia Polytechnic Institute and State University and has reached the stage of a research prototype. (Pest and Orchard ManageMent Expert system) [ROA85]

Chemistry

CONGEN helps structural chemists determine a set of possible structures for an unknown compound. The chemist provides CONGEN with spectroscopic and chemical data and a set of required and forbidden constraints on the possible interconnections among the atoms in the compound. CONGEN finds all possible ways of assembling the atoms into molecular structures which satisfy the specified constraints, and it presents the chemist with a set of structural drawings describing this exhaustive list of candidate structures. The system generates candidate structures by using a variety of graph-theoretic algorithms. CONGEN is implemented in INTERLISP. It was developed at Stanford University as part of the DENDRAL project and serves as Heuristic DENDRAL's hypothesis generator. CONGEN reached the stage of a research prototype. (CONstrained GENerator) [BUC78, CAR79]

CRYSALIS infers the three-dimensional structure of a protein from an electron density map (EDM). The system interprets X-ray diffraction data composed of position and intensity of diffracted waves to infer this atomic structure. The system uses knowledge about protein composition and X-ray crystallography, and heuristics for analyzing EDMs to generate and to test hypotheses about plausible protein structure. CRYSALIS uses a blackboard architecture, containing independent knowledge sources that build and test a multilevel hypothesis structure. The system is implemented in LISP. It was developed at Stanford University and reached the stage of a research prototype. [ENG79b, TER83]

C-13 aids organic chemists in determining the structure of newly isolated, naturally occurring compounds. C-13 helps the chemist analyze carbon-13 nuclear magnetic resonance spectra by using a constraint refinement search to determine the arrangement of atoms and bonds of complex organic molecules. The system's knowledge base contains rules relating substructural (bonding) and spectral (resonance) features, derived automatically from data for known structures. C-13 was developed as part of the DENDRAL project and follows DENDRAL's plan-generate-test paradigm. The system is implemented in INTERLISP. It was developed at Stanford University and reached the stage of a demonstration prototype. (Carbon-13) [GRA84]

DENDRAL infers the molecular structure of unknown compounds from mass spectral and nuclear magnetic response data. The system uses a special algorithm developed by J. Lederberg to systematically enumerate all possible molecular structures; it uses chemical expertise to prune this list of possibilities to a manageable size. Knowledge in DENDRAL is represented as procedural code for the molecular structure generator and as rules for the data-driven component and evaluator. The system is implemented in INTERLISP and was developed at Stanford University. It has reached the stage of a production prototype. (DENDritic ALgorithm) [BUC78, LIN80b, ALT84a]

GA1 analyzes DNA structure from restriction enzyme segmentation data. The system accepts enzyme digest data, topology, tolerance, and other constraints. After repeatedly generating and discarding possible candidate structures, it finally determines plausible DNA structures. The expertise contained in GA1 is a textbook model of the mechanism involved in enzyme digestion analysis of DNA structures, augmented with knowledge of the nature of errors inherent in laboratory test environments. GA1 follows the generate-and-test paradigm used in DENDRAL: Hypotheses are proposed by a generator based on a procedure for enumerating all possible solutions. The system provides a user-adjustable contradiction tolerance level to compensate for small amounts of erroneous data. GA1 is written in INTERLISP. It was developed at Stanford University and reached the stage of a research prototype. (Geneticist's Assistant 1) [STE78]

META-DENDRAL helps chemists determine the dependence of mass spectrometric fragmentation on substructural features. It does this by discovering fragmentation rules for given classes of molecules. The system derives these rules from training instances consisting of sets of molecules with known three-dimensional structures and mass spectra. META-DENDRAL first generates a set of highly specific rules which account for a single fragmentation process in a particular molecule. Then it uses the training examples to generalize these rules. Finally, the system reexamines the rules to remove redundant or incorrect rules. META-DENDRAL is implemented in INTERLISP. It was developed at Stanford University and reached the stage of a research prototype. [BUC78, LIN80b, ALT84a]

MOLGEN assists the geneticist in planning gene-cloning experiments in molecular genetics. These experiments involve splicing a gene coding for a desired protein product into bacteria so that the bacteria will manufacture it. The system uses knowledge about genetics and the user's goal to create an abstract plan and then refines it to a set of specific laboratory steps. MOLGEN uses an object-oriented and frame-based representation and control scheme, and it is implemented in LISP and UNITS. It was developed at Stanford University. MOLGEN is primarily a vehicle for testing approaches for reasoning about design, rather than an operational expert system for molecular genetics. [STE81c, STE81d, ALT84d]

OCSS assists chemists in synthesizing complex organic molecules. The system analyzes target molecules devised by the chemist by recognizing functional groups, chains, rings and redundancy, or symmetry in the molecular skeleton, applying chemical transformations to them, and evaluating the resulting structure for correctness, uniqueness, and simplicity. The system was implemented on a DEC PDP-1 computer at Harvard University. It reached the stage of a research prototype. [COR69]

SECS assists chemists in synthesizing complex organic molecules. The chemist presents the structure of a target molecule, and the system generates a plan to create the target molecule from basic building block molecules. The plan is basically a series of chemical reactions applied to functional groups of atoms. The system, with the help of the chemist, systematically works backward from the target toward simpler molecules until a synthesis route is found from the target to the building blocks. SECS is implemented in FORTRAN. It was developed at the University of California, Santa Cruz, and reached the stage of a research prototype. (Simulation and Evaluation of Chemical Synthesis) [WIP78]

SEQ helps molecular biologists perform several types of nucleotide sequence analysis. The system can store, retrieve, and analyze nucleic acid sequences, and it can provide a statistical analysis of structural homologies and symmetries. SEQ's searching routines can be customized by manipulating a set of default parameters; for example, the biologist may vary the weights for penalties and size of gap results during a Needleman-Wunch alignment. SEQ is implemented in LISP. It was developed as part of the MOLGEN project at Stanford University and then further developed by Intellicorp. It reached the stage of a commercial system. (SEQuence analysis system) [CLA81b, INT84e]

SPEX assists scientists in planning complex laboratory experiments. The scientist describes the objects to be manipulated (i.e., the physical environment of the experiment and the structure of the experimental objects), and the system assists in developing a skeletal plan for achieving the experimental goal. The system then refines each abstract step in the plan, making them more specific by linking them to techniques and objects stored in the system's knowledge base. Although the system has been tested exclusively in the domain of molecular biology, it contains no built-in molecular biology mechanisms; thus it could be applied to other problem areas. SPEX is implemented in UNITS, a frame-based language for representation. The system was developed at Stanford and reached the stage of a research prototype. (Skeletal Planner of EXperiments) [IWA82a, IWA82b]

SYNCHEM synthesizes complex organic molecules without requiring user interaction. The system uses knowledge about chemical reactions to create a plan for developing the target molecule from a set of given starting molecules. The system works backward, beginning with the target molecule, and tries to determine which reactions could produce it and what materials (molecules) would be required. This continues until a synthesis route is found from the target to the starting materials. The system is implemented in PL/1. It is the predecessor of SYNCHEM2 and was developed at the State University of New York at Stony Brook. It reached the stage of a research prototype. [GEL77]

SYNCHEM2 synthesizes complex organic molecules without assistance or guidance from a chemist. It tries to discover a plausible sequence of organic synthetic reactions that will turn a set of available starting materials into the desired target molecule. SYNCHEM2 uses knowledge about chemical reactions to generate a plan for creating the target molecule from basic building block molecules. The system attempts to find an optimal synthesis route from the starting materials to the target compound by applying heuristics that limit the search to pathways satisfying the problem constraints. These constraints may include information about toxic reaction conditions and the quality and yield of the desired product. The system is implemented in PL/1. It is the successor to SYNCHEM and was developed at the State University of New York at Stony Brook. It has reached the stage of a field prototype. [GEL77, GEL84]

TQMSTUNE fine-tunes a triple quadrupole mass spectrometer (TQMS) by interpreting signal data from the TQMS, such as spectral peak ratios, widths, and shapes. The system uses knowledge about how varying the TQM's instrument control settings affects sensitivity and spectral configurations. Knowledge is represented using the frame-based features of KEE, the implementation language for TQMSTUNE. The system was developed by Intellicorp and reached the stage of a research prototype. (Triple-Quadrupole Mass Spectrometer TUNEr) [WON83, WON84]

Computer Systems

CRIB helps computer engineers and system maintainers locate computer hardware and software faults. The engineer gives the system a description of his or her observations in simple English-like terms. CRIB matches this against a data base of known faults. By successively matching larger and larger groups of symptoms with the incoming description, CRIB arrives at a subunit which is either repairable or replaceable. If a subunit is reached and the fault is not cured, the system backtracks automatically to the last decision point and tries to find another match. CRIB contains hardware and software fault diagnostic expertise as a collection of action-symptom pairs (called *symptom patterns*) where the action is designed to elicit the symptom from the machine. CRIB models the machine under diagnosis as a simple hierarchy of subunits in a semantic net. The system is written in CORAL 66. It was developed as a combined effort by International Computers Limited (ICL), the Research and Advanced Development Centre (RADC), and Brunel University. CRIB reached the stage of a research prototype. (Computer Retrieval Incidence Bank) [ADD80, HAR84c]

DART assists in diagnosing faults in computer hardware systems using information about the design of the device being diagnosed. The system works directly from information about the intended structure and expected behavior of the device to help find design flaws in newly created devices. The system has been applied to simple computer circuits and the teleprocessing facility of the IBM 4331. DART uses a device-independent inference procedure that is similar to a type of resolution theorem proving, where the system attempts to generate a proof related to the cause of the device's malfunction. The system is implemented in MRS and was developed at Stanford University. It reached the stage of a research prototype. (Diagnostic Assistance Reference Tool) [BEN81, GEN82, JOY83, GEN83c, GEN84a, GEN84d]

IDT helps a technician locate the field replaceable units that should be replaced to fix faults in PDP 11/03 computers. The system uses knowledge about the unit under test, such as the functions of its components and their relation to one another, to select and execute diagnostic tests and interpret the results. The system is rule-based using forward chaining and is implemented in FRANZ LISP and OPS5. IDT was developed by Digital Equipment Corporation and reached the stage of a research prototype. [SHU82]

ISA schedules customer computer system orders against the current and planned material allocations. ISA takes customer orders, including changes and cancellations, and produces a schedule date for each order. It displays additional information about a problematic order, including the schedule proposed, the problems uncovered, and alternative proposals for scheduling the order. ISA contains significant scheduling expertise, such as knowledge about order cancellation probabilities, material availability, and strategies for relaxing scheduling constraints. ISA is a forward chaining, rule-based system implemented in OPS5. It was developed by Digital Equipment Corporation and is in use at DEC's manufacturing plants. It reached the stage of a commercial system. (Intelligent Scheduling Assistant) [OCO84, ORC84]

MIXER helps programmers write microprograms for the Texas Instruments' TI990 VLSI chip. Given a microprogram description, the system generates optimized horizontal microcodes for the TI990.

MIXER contains knowledge about TI990 microprogramming taken from manuals and from an analysis of the microcode in the TI990 control ROM. This includes knowledge about how to map written descriptions into sets of intermediate operations, how to allocate appropriate registers to variables, and how to expand intermediate operations into sets of microoperations. MIXER uses this knowledge to determine which microoperations are best for implementing the microprogram. The system represents knowledge as rules and data, with inferencing controlled unification and dynamic backtracking. MIXER is implemented in PROLOG. It was developed at Tokyo University and reached the stage of a demonstration prototype. [SHI83]

R1: See XCON.

R1-SOAR performs a portion of the computer system configuration task. It uses some of the knowledge embedded in XCON (also called R1) related to configuring VAX 11/780 computer systems. Configuration involves looking at a customer's order and deciding what components must be added to produce a complete operational system, subject to the functional and spatial constraints of the components. R1-SOAR works by performing a search through a problem space of possible solutions, looking for an acceptable one. R1-SOAR was developed within the general problem-solving architecture SOAR with the goal of better understanding how to overcome the limitations of both expert systems and general problem solvers. It was developed at Carnegie-Mellon University as a demonstration prototype. [ROS84]

TIMM/TUNER assists in tuning VAX/VMS computer systems in order to reduce performance problems that arise in a constantly changing computer environment. It interacts with the system manager, asking a series of questions that lead to a recommended action, such as adjusting system parameters or user authorization values, redistributing or reducing user demand, changing user software design, or purchasing new hardware. The system uses a rule-based representation scheme created within TIMM, a commercial system for automated knowledge acquisition. TIMM/TUNER was developed by General Research Corporation and reached the stage of a commercial system. (The Intelligent Machine Model TUNER) [GRC83, KOR84a]

XCON configures VAX 11/780 computer systems. From a customer's order it decides what components must be added to produce a complete operational system and determines the spatial relationships among all of the components. XCON outputs a set of diagrams indicating these spatial relationships to technicians who then assemble the VAX system. XCON handles the configuration task by applying knowledge of the constraints on component relationships to standard procedures for configuring computers. The system is noninteractive, is rule-based, and uses a forward chaining control scheme. XCON is implemented in OPS5 and was developed through a collaboration between researchers at Carnegie-Mellon University and Digital Equipment Corporation (DEC) in Hudson, Massachusetts. This commercial expert system configures VAX computers on a daily basis for DEC and is the largest and most mature rule-based expert system in operation. (eXpert CONfigurer of VAX 11/780 computer systems) [MCD80b, MCD81, MCD82, MCD82a, BAC84, MCD84, OCO84, POL85]

XSEL helps a salesperson select components for a VAX 11/780 computer system and assists in designing a floor layout for them. XSEL selects a central processing unit, primary memory, software, and peripheral devices, such as terminals and disk drives, and then passes it to XCON to be expanded and configured. XSEL contains domain knowledge about the relations between components and the various applications a customer might have and knowledge about how to lead a user through a selection process. The system is interactive, is rule-based, and uses a forward chaining control scheme. XSEL is implemented in OPS5. It was developed through a collaboration between researchers at Carnegie-Mellon University and Digital Equipment Corporation (DEC) in Hudson, Massachusetts, and reached the stage of a field prototype. (eXpert SELling assistant) [MCD81a, MCD81b, MCD82a, MCD82b, MCD84]

YES/MVS helps computer operators monitor and control the MVS (multiple virtual storage) operating system, the most widely used operating system in large mainframe IBM computers. YES/MVS addresses six major categories of tasks: maintaining adequate JES (job entry system) queue space, handling network communications between computers on the same site, scheduling large batch jobs off prime shift, responding to hardware errors, monitoring subsoftware systems, and monitoring overall system performance. YES/MVS runs in real time, directly interpreting MVS messages and sending either commands to the operating system or recommendations to the console operator. YES/MVS is a rule-based expert system with a forward chaining control scheme. It is implemented in an extended version of OPS5 by an expert systems group at the IBM T.J. Watson Research Center in Yorktown Heights, New York. The developers plan to use the YES/MVS system on a regular commercial basis. (Yorktown Expert System for MVS operators) [GRI84, SCH84]

Electronics

ACE identifies trouble spots in telephone networks and recommends appropriate repair and rehabilitative maintenance. The system operates without human intervention, analyzing maintenance reports generated on a daily basis by CRAS, a cable repair administration computer program. Once ACE locates the faulty telephone cables, it decides whether they need preventive maintenance and selects the type of maintenance most likely to be effective. ACE then stores its recommendations in a special data base that users can access. The system makes decisions by applying knowledge about wire centers, CRAS maintenance reports, and network analysis strategies. It uses a rule-based knowledge representation scheme controlled by forward chaining. ACE is implemented in OPS4 and FRANZ LISP and runs on AT&T 3B-2 microcomputers located in the cable analysts' offices. It was developed by Bell Laboratories at Whippany, New Jersey. ACE has been field-tested and has reached the stage of a commercial expert system. (Automated Cable Expertise) [VES83, WRI84]

BDS helps locate faulty modules in a large signal-switching network, an electronic device called a *baseband distribution subsystem.* The system uses test equipment readings to isolate faulty printed circuit boards or other chassis-mounted parts which could have caused the failure. BDS bases its diagnosis on both the strategies of the expert diagnostician and knowledge about the structure, function, and causal relations of the components in the electronic device. BDS is implemented in the LES (Lockheed Expert System) language and uses a rule-based representation scheme with backward chaining. It was developed at the Lockheed Palo Alto Research Laboratory and reached the stage of a research prototype. (Baseband Distribution Subsystem) [LAF84b]

CADHELP simulates an expert demonstrating the operation of the graphical features of a computer-aided design (CAD) subsystem for designing digital logic circuits. It explains to the user how to use the CAD subsystem, tailoring its explanations to fit the needs and desires of the user. It provides explanations in English when the user makes an error or asks for help and generates the text of the explanation from its knowledge base in a dynamic way, relying on scripts associated with the different features of the CAD subsystem. As the user becomes more experienced, the explanations created by CADHELP become more terse. Knowledge in the system is organized as a set of cooperating subsystems or "experts" controlled by a higher-level task manager program. The system is implemented in FRANZ LISP and runs on a DEC VAX 11/780 under UNIX. CADHELP was developed at the University of Connecticut and reached the stage of a research prototype. (Computer-Aided Design HELP) [CUL82]

COMPASS analyzes telephone switching systems maintenance messages for GTE's No. 2 EAX Switch and suggests maintenance actions to perform. The system examines maintenance messages describing error situations that occurred during the telephone call-processing operation of the switch. It then identifies groups of messages likely caused by a common fault, determines the possible specific faults in the switch, and suggests maintenance actions to verify and remedy the faults. The system embodies the expertise of a top switch expert and integrates knowledge about individual switch structure, switch faults, maintenance messages, and possible maintenance actions. COMPASS is implemented in KEE and INTERLISP-D for use on Xerox 1108 workstations. It was developed by GTE Laboratories, Inc. and reached the stage of a field prototype. (Central Office Maintenance Printout Analysis and Suggestion System) [SHR85]

CRITTER helps circuit design engineers analyze the correctness, timing, robustness, and speed of VLSI circuit designs. The system accepts circuit schematics and I/O specifications from the engineer and builds a comprehensive model of the circuit's performance. CRITTER summarizes this information and presents it to the engineer with an assessment of the circuit's feasibility as well as diagnostic and repair information. The knowledge embedded in CRITTER includes information about circuit diagrams and circuit analysis techniques, such as subcircuit simulation and path delay analysis. Circuit diagrams are represented using frames, while other knowledge is in the form of algebraic formulas and predicate calculus. CRITTER is implemented in INTERLISP. It was developed at Rutgers University and reached the stage of a demonstration prototype. [KEL82, KEL84]

DAA assists VLSI designers by performing a hardware allocation from an algorithmic description of a VLSI system. The system takes a data flow description of a VLSI system and produces a list of technology-independent registers, operators, data paths, and control signals. The system's expertise consists of algorithms for hardware allocation collected from expert designers as well as knowledge found in the CMU/DA allocator (another VLSI design tool). DAA is a forward chaining, rule-based system implemented in OPS5. It was developed at Carnegie-Mellon University and reached the stage of a research prototype. (Design Automation Assistant) [KOW83, KOW84]

DFT helps VLSI designers check for DFT (design for testability) rule violations and transform the design to remove them. Once the system locates DFT-rule violations, it analyzes them and corrects the design using expertise based on a technique called the level sensitive scan design method. DFT also extracts control and observation information from the design structure and uses it for automatic test pattern generation. Knowledge in the system is represented within a logic-oriented framework. A digital design consists of a set of logic assertions that describe the VLSI node interconnects and the functions of the nodes. DFT is implemented in PROLOG. It was developed at Syracuse University and reached the stage of a demonstration prototype. (Design For Testability system) [HOR83]

EL performs a steady-state analysis of resistor-diode-transistor circuits. Given a description of a circuit schematic, the system analyzes the circuit and determines the values of various circuit parameters, such as voltage or current values at given points. EL's expertise includes general principles of electronics (e.g., Ohm's law) and circuit component characteristics (e.g., the functional properties of transistors). The system uses a rule-based knowledge representation scheme with forward chaining and an indexed data base of facts and assertions. A limited explanation facility exists, built upon the property that EL remembers the justifications for new assertions. EL is implemented in ARS. It was developed at MIT and reached the stage of a research prototype. [SUS75, STA79, DUD80]

EURISKO learns new heuristics and new domain-specific definitions of concepts in a problem domain. The system can learn by discovery in a number of different problem domains, including VLSI design. EURISKO has tackled the problem of inventing new kinds of three-dimensional microelectronic devices that can be fabricated using laser recrystallization techniques and has designed new and interesting microelectronic devices. EURISKO operates by generating a device configuration, computing its input/output behavior, assessing its functionality, and then evaluating it against other comparable devices. The system is implemented in INTERLISP for the Xerox 1100 series workstations. It was developed at Stanford University and is more an AI program for learning by discovery than an expert system. [LEN82a, LEN82b, LEN83a, STE83e]

FG502-TASP assists technicians in the diagnosis of malfunctioning Tektronix FG502 function generators. The system uses ad hoc rules about system behavior together with heuristics gathered from experienced technicians rather than a theoretical model of the FG502 operation which would require advanced electronics principles. In addition to querying the technician to direct the diagnosis, the system provides a graphical display of the parts layout on the relevant circuit board and a picture of what the waveform should look like when measured at a given point on the board. FG502-TASP is an object-oriented system implemented in SMALLTALK-80. It was developed by Tektronix and reached the stage of a research prototype. (FG502 function generator Troubleshooting Assistant System Prototype) [ALE84a, ALE84b]

FOREST isolates and diagnoses faults in electronic equipment. The system supplements the fault detection and isolation capabilities of current automatic test equipment (ATE) diagnostic software. FOREST's knowledge includes experiential rules of thumb from expert engineers (e.g., if all pulse period measurements fail, then look for a pulse amplitude problem), knowledge of the use of circuit diagrams (e.g., the generation of the main pulse triggers the system clock reset), and general electronic troubleshooting principles (e.g., insufficient amplitude of a signal may result from excessive resistance along the signal path). This knowledge is encoded using rules with PROSPECTOR-like certainty factors and a MYCIN-like explanation facility. FOREST is implemented in PROLOG. It was developed at the University of Pennsylvania in cooperation with RCA Corporation and reached the stage of a demonstration prototype. [FIN84]

IN-ATE helps a technician troubleshoot a Tektronix Model 465 oscilloscope by analyzing symptoms and producing a decision tree of test points to be checked by the technician. The system applies two types of rules: those supplied by an expert diagnostician, and those generated automatically from an internal model of the oscilloscope, which is a block diagram of the unit augmented with component failure rates. Knowledge is represented as rules incorporating probabilistic measures of belief about circuit malfunctions. As the rules are applied, the beliefs are updated through a procedure similar to minimaxing. The system is implemented in FRANZ LISP. It was developed at the Naval Research Laboratory and reached the stage of a research prototype. [CAN83]

MESSAGE TRACE ANALYZER helps debug real-time systems such as large telecommunication switching machines containing hundreds of processors. The system examines interprocess message traces, identifying illegal message sequences to localize the fault to within a process. The system considers the sender process ID, the receiver process ID, the message type, and the time stamp fields of messages in the trace. General debugging heuristics and facts about the specific system being debugged are represented as rules and applied using both forward and backward chaining. The system contains a limited explanation facility that allows it to answer questions about its reasoning. MESSAGE TRACE ANALYZER is written in PRO-LOG. It was developed at the University of Waterloo and reached the stage of a demonstration prototype. [GUP84]

NDS locates multiple faults in a nationwide communications network called COMNET by applying expert diagnostic strategies based on knowledge about the network's topology and composition. The system suggests diagnostic tests to perform, and the outcome of each test provides evidence for or against a fault existing in some set of components. The components under consideration include telecommunication processors, modems, telephone circuits, and computer terminals. NDS is a rule-based system implemented in ARBY. The system was developed by Smart Systems Technology in cooperation with Shell Development Company and reached the stage of a demonstration prototype. [WIL82, WIL83b]

PALLADIO assists circuit designers in the design and testing of new VLSI circuits. PALLADIO is a circuit design environment that includes interactive graphics editors that manipulate high-level electronic components, a rule editor that helps modify the behavioral specifications of circuit components, a simulator that uses the structural and behavioral specification of a circuit to simulate it, and mechanisms for refining and creating design specifications at different levels of abstraction. PALLADIO has been used to design a variety of nMOS circuits. The system is implemented in LOOPS, which provides object-oriented, rule-based, and logic-oriented representation mechanisms. PALLADIO was developed at Stanford University and reached the stage of a research prototype. (It is named after the Italian architect Andrea Palladio (1508–1580).) [STE82a, STE82b, TOM83, YAN83, BRO83b]

PEACE assists engineers in the design of electronic circuits. The system is a CAD tool that performs analysis and synthesis of passive and digital circuits by applying knowledge about circuit design. This knowledge includes the functional description of basic circuit components, connection rules for forming more complex circuits and networks, functional and topological circuit transformations, strategies for analysis and synthesis, and heuristics for anticipating failures. PEACE can synthesize passive circuits from their functional descriptions and digital circuits from the mathematical expression of their transfer functions. PEACE is a logic-oriented system implemented in PROLOG. It was developed at the University of Manchester, UK, and reached the stage of a demonstration prototype. [DIN80]

REDESIGN assists engineers in the redesign of digital circuits to meet altered functional specifications. Given the redesign goal, the system generates plausible local changes to make within the circuit, ranks the changes based on implementation difficulty and goal satisfaction, and checks for undesirable side effects associated with the changes. The system provides design assistance by combining causal reasoning, analyzing the cause-effect relations of circuit operation with functional reasoning, and analyzing the purposes or roles of the circuit components. Circuit knowledge in REDESIGN is represented as a network of modules and data paths. The system was developed at Rutgers University and reached the stage of a research prototype. [LAF82, MIT83]

SADD assists engineers in the design of digital circuits. From the engineer the system accepts a functional description of the proposed circuit in English and uses this to build an internal model of the circuit. The system uses knowledge about the model, component characteristics, and circuit behavior to design a plausible circuit, which it tests for correctness by simulating its operation. SADD uses a frame-based representation of knowledge about circuit components. The system is implemented in LISP. It was developed at the University of Maryland and reached the stage of a demonstration prototype. (Semi-Automatic Digital Designer) [GRI80]

SOPHIE teaches students how to troubleshoot electrical circuits. The system demonstrates how to locate a circuit fault by allowing the student to select a fault in a simulated circuit and then proceeding through the steps necessary to find the fault. At each step the system asks the student to predict the qualitative behavior of the test instrument. (For example, will the measured voltage be too high, too low, or about right?) When the student makes an error, the system shows the measurement and explains it. The system provides a printed history of the diagnosis session for the student's review. The circuit simulator in SOPHIE contains a mechanism for modeling and portraying causal fault propagation, i.e., how the failure of one component can cause other components to fail. SOPHIE is implemented in INTERLISP and FORTRAN, the latter being used for the circuit simulation package. The system was developed at Bolt, Beranek and Newman and has evolved through three versions. It reached the stage of a research prototype. (SOPHisticated Instructional Environment) [BRO75a, BRO75b, BRO75c, BRO82b]

SYN assists engineers in synthesizing electrical circuits. The engineer inputs partially specified circuit diagrams and constraints on particular circuit components, and the system combines this information with knowledge about constraints inherent in the circuit structure to specify the circuit completely (e.g., fill in the impedance of resistors and voltages of power sources). The system combines constraints by using symbolic algebraic manipulation of the formulas describing the circuit components. The system was developed at MIT and reached the stage of a research prototype. (circuit SYNthesis program) [DEK80]

TALIB automatically synthesizes integrated circuit layouts for nMOS cells. The system takes as input a description of the circuit components to be laid out on the silicon wafer, their interconnections, and the topological and geometric requirements around the outside boundary of the circuit. From these specifications the system produces correct and compact cell layouts. TALIB creates and refines plans for laying out the circuit and then applies the plans using knowledge about subcircuit interconnection characteristics and the propagation of constraints between subcircuits. TALIB is a forward chaining, rule-based system implemented in OPS5. It was developed at Carnegie-Mellon University and reached the stage of a research prototype. [KIM83]

TRANSISTOR SIZING SYSTEM helps circuit designers with the design of integrated circuits by performing part of the refinement from a schematic circuit diagram to an nMOS layout. The system determines the physical size of the transistors in the circuit by considering designer goals of speed and power consumption combined with knowledge of the relationship between speed and power for nMOS circuits. TRANSISTOR SIZING SYSTEM analyzes the circuit to determine critical paths with respect to delay and produces a trade-off curve based on simple delay models. The designer then selects a goal point on the curve, and the system resizes the transistors in accordance with that goal. TRANSISTOR SIZING SYSTEM uses a frame-base and object-oriented knowledge representation scheme. It is implemented in LOOPS and embedded in the PALLADIO environment. The system was developed at Stanford University and reached the stage of a research prototype. [FOY84]

Engineering

CONPHYDE helps chemical engineers select physical property estimation methods. The system handles the selection of vapor-liquid equilibrium coefficients for setting up a process simulation, given information about required accuracy and the expected concentrations, temperatures, and pressure ranges. Knowledge in CONPHYDE is represented in a combined rule-based and semantic net formalism, similar to PROSPECTOR. Its inferences are based on the use of certainty factors and Bayesian decision theory for propagating probabilities associated with the data. The system is implemented in KAS and uses the KAS explanation facility. CONPHYDE was developed at Carnegie-Mellon University and reached the stage of a demonstration prototype. (CONsultant for PHYsical property DEcisions) [BAN83]

DELTA helps maintenance personnel to identify and correct malfunctions in diesel electric locomotives by applying diagnostic strategies for locomotive maintenance. The system can lead the user through an entire repair procedure, presenting computer-aided drawings of parts and subsystems, repair sequences in the form of videodisc movies, and specific repair instructions once the malfunction is identified. DELTA is a rule-based system developed in a general-purpose representation language written in LISP. DELTA accesses its rules through both forward and backward chaining and uses certainty factors to handle uncertain rule premises. Although the system was prototyped in LISP, it was later reimplemented in FORTH for installation on microprocessor-based systems. The General Electric Company developed this system at their research and development center in Schenectady, New York. They are completing field-testing of DELTA as a prelude to its use on a commercial basis. (Diesel-Electric Locomotive Troubleshooting Aid) [MAR83, BON83b, DEL84]

NPPC helps nuclear power plant operators determine the cause of some abnormal event (e.g., greater than normal containment temperature) by applying rules in conjunction with a model of plant operation. The system uses a model of the primary coolant system, including pumps, reactor, steam generator, and emergency core cooling system to diagnose the cause of an abnormality or accident, and then suggests procedures for correcting the problem. The model consists of a *commonsense algorithm* network that accesses appropriate diagnostic rules. The system was developed at the Georgia Institute of Technology and reached the stage of a research prototype. (Nuclear Power Plant Consultant) [UND82, NEL84]

REACTOR assists reactor operators in the diagnosis and treatment of nuclear reactor accidents by monitoring instrument readings, such as feed-water flow and containment radiation level, looking for deviations from normal operating conditions. When the system detects a deviation, it evaluates the situation and recommends appropriate action, using knowledge about the reactor configuration and the functional relations of its components together with knowledge about the expected behavior of the reactor under known accident conditions. REACTOR is implemented in LISP as a rule-based system that uses both forward and backward chaining. It was developed by EG&G Idaho and reached the stage of a research prototype. [NEL82, NEL84]

SACON helps engineers determine analysis strategies for particular structural analysis problems. The engineers can then implement this strategy with MARC, a program that uses finite-element analysis methods to simulate the mechanical behavior of objects. SACON identifies the analysis class of the problem and recommends specific features of the MARC program to activate when performing the analysis. SACON uses knowledge about stresses and deflections of a structure under different loading conditions to determine the appropriate strategy. Structures that can be analyzed include aircraft wings, reactor pressure vessels, rocket motor casings, and bridges. SACON is a backward chaining, rule-based system implemented in EMYCIN. It was developed at Stanford University and reached the stage of a research prototype. [BEN78, FIS82, BEN84]

SPERIL-I performs structural damage assessment of existing structures which are subjected to earthquake excitation. Given accelerometer and visual inspection data, the system determines the damage state of the structures. SPERIL-I's expertise consists of knowledge collected from experienced civil engineers and includes relations between factors such as structural damping, stiffness, creep, and buckling. This knowledge is represented as rules accessed through a forward chaining inference procedure. The system uses certainty factors combined with Fuzzy Logic to calculate the damage class of a structure. SPERIL-I is written in the programming language C. It was developed at Purdue University's school of civil engineering and reached the stage of a demonstration prototype. [ISH81a, ISH81b, ISH81c]

SPERIL-II evaluates the general safety and damageability of an existing structure. The system analyzes inspection data and instrument records of structural responses during an earthquake, such as acceleration and displacement at certain locations in the structure. It then evaluates relevant safety characteristics (e.g., interstory drift, stiffness, and damping) and the damageability of the structure's elements. The system's knowledge comes from case studies and is represented as rules of predicate logic. SPERIL-II uses several reasoning methods including both forward and backward chaining. It also uses certainty factors which are combined using the Dempster-Shafer algorithm. The system is implemented in a dialect of PRO-LOG. SPERIL-II was developed at Purdue University and reached the stage of a demonstration prototype. [OGA84, OGA84a]

STEAMER instructs Navy propulsion engineering students in the operation of a steam propulsion plant for a 1078-class frigate. The system can monitor the student executing the boiler light-off procedure for the plant, acknowledging appropriate student actions and correcting inappropriate ones. The system works by tying a mathematical simulation of the propulsion plant to a sophisticated graphical interface program that displays animated color diagrams of plant subsystems. The student can manipulate simulated components, such as valves, switches, and pumps, and observe the effects on plant parameters, such as change in pressures, temperatures, and flows. STEAMER is implemented in ZETALISP and uses the object-oriented representation scheme supported by ZETALISP's FLAVORS package. The system was developed by the Naval Personal Research and Development Center in cooperation with Bolt, Beranek and Newman. It reached the stage of a field prototype. [WIL83a, HOL84]

Geology

DIPMETER ADVISOR infers subsurface geological structure by interpreting dipmeter logs, measurements of the conductivity of rock in and around a borehole as related to depth below the surface. The system uses knowledge about dipmeter patterns and geology to recognize features in the dipmeter data and relate them to underground geological structure. The system provides the user with a menu-driven graphical interface incorporating smooth scrolling of log data. The system uses a rule-based knowledge representation scheme controlled by forward chaining. It is implemented in INTERLISP-D and operates on the Xerox 1100 series workstations. The system was developed by Schlumberger-Doll Research and reached the stage of a research prototype. [DAV81, GER82, SMI83, AUS84, SMI84c, SMI84d]

DRILLING ADVISOR assists an oil-rig supervisor in resolving problems related to the drilling mechanism sticking within the borehole during drilling. The system diagnoses the most likely causes of the sticking (e.g., conical hole, debris plugging the drill pipe), and recommends a set of treatments to alleviate the problem and lessen its chance of reoccurrence (e.g., jarring the drill string up and/or down). The system bases its decisions on knowledge of the geological formations at the drill site and the relation between observed symptoms and suspected causes of problems. Knowledge is represented as rules handled by a backward chaining control scheme. The system was originally implemented in KS300 and reimplemented in S.1. It was developed by Teknowledge in cooperation with Societe Nationale Elf Aquitaine and reached the stage of a research prototype. [ELF83, HOL83, HAY84]

ELAS gives advice on how to control and interpret results from INLAN, a large-scale interactive program for well log analysis and display developed by Amoco. ELAS assists the user by recommending analysis methods, warning of inconsistencies or unpromising directions of analysis, and by summarizing and interpreting the results of the user-INLAN interaction. The user directs both the mathematical analysis of INLAN and the interpretive analysis of ELAS by changing parameters or invoking tasks through a sophisticated graphical display. The system is primarily rule-based and is implemented in EXPERT. It was developed at Rutgers University in cooperation with Amoco Production Research. ELAS reached the stage of a research prototype. (Expert Log-Analysis System) [APT82, WEI82, APT84a, APT84b]

HYDRO helps a hydrologist use HSPF, a computer program that simulates the physical processes by which precipitation is distributed throughout a watershed. The system assists in describing watershed characteristics to HSPF in the form of numerical parameters. The system estimates these parameters using knowledge about soil type, land use, vegetation, geology, and their affect on the specific parameter in question. The system is patterned after PROSPECTOR; it uses a combination rule-based and semantic net formalism to encode its knowledge and bases its inferences on the use of certainty factors and the propagation of probabilities associated with the data. The system is implemented in INTERLISP and was developed by SRI International. HYDRO reached the stage of a research prototype. [GAS81a, REB82]

LITHO assists geologists in interpreting data from oil-well logs. These data include curves reflecting measurements of rock density, resistivity, sound transmission, and radioactivity. The system uses the log data plus knowledge of the region's geological environment (e.g., geography, paleontology) to characterize the rock encountered in a well. This characterization includes porosity, permeability, composition, texture, and type of layering. LITHO uses a separate pattern recognition program to extract features directly from the log data. Knowledge is represented as rules and accessed through backward chaining. LITHO is implemented in EMYCIN. The system was developed by Schlumberger and reached the stage of a research prototype. (LITHOlog: a description of rocks encountered in a well) [BON83c]

MUD helps engineers maintain optimal drilling fluid properties. It does this by diagnosing the causes of problems with drilling fluids and suggesting treatments. Possible causes include contaminants, high temperatures or pressures, and inadequate use of chemical additives. MUD contains knowledge extracted from domain experts about drilling fluids and the diagnosis of drilling problems. It is a forward chaining, rule-based system and uses MYCIN-like certainty factors to represent the subjective determinations of experts. In addition, it can provide explanations about its recommended treatment plans. MUD is implemented in OPS5. It was developed at Carnegie-Mellon University in cooperation with NL Baroid and reached the stage of a field prototype. (Drilling fluids have a muddy appearance, hence MUD) [KAH84a, KAH84b, KAH84c, KAH84d]

PROSPECTOR acts as a consultant to aid exploration geologists in their search for ore deposits. Given field data about a geological region, it estimates the likelihood of finding particular types of mineral deposits there. The system can assess the potential for finding a variety of deposits, including massive sulfide, carbonate lead/zinc, porphyry copper, nickel sulfide, sandstone uranium, and porphyry molybdenum deposits. Its expertise is based on 1) geological rules which form models of ore deposits, and 2) a taxonomy of rocks and minerals. PROSPECTOR uses a combination rule-based and semantic net formalism to encode its knowledge and bases its inferences on the use of certainty factors and the progagation of probabilities associated with the data. The system was implemented in INTERLISP and developed by SRI International. PROSPECTOR reached the stage of a production prototype. [GAS81, CAM82, GAS82, GAS82a, DUD84, ALT84e]

Information Management

CARGuide helps drivers find routes and navigate in city streets. The system uses the starting and destination locations, together with its map information, to calculate an optimum route from starting point to destination. Optimum route finding is accomplished using a combination of a divide-and-conquer method, precomputed routes, and Dijkstra's shortest-path algorithm. Once found, the route is displayed and highlighted on a graphical display of a street map. During the trip the car's position along the route is updated and displayed. Before each intersection, the system pronounces a direction (straight, left, or right) and the name of the street to take. The street map data base contains information relating street names to intersections and intersections to routes. It also contains pictorial information for picture generation. CARGuide was developed at Carnegie-Mellon University and reached the stage of a demonstration prototype. (Computer for Automobile Route Guidance) [SUG84]

CODES helps a data base developer who wants to use the IDEF1 approach to defining the conceptual schema of a data base. While IDEF1 is useful as an approach, its intricate rules often hamper its application. The developer describes the features and relationships desired in the data base under the interactive guidance of CODES. The system then uses its knowledge of IDEF1 rules and heuristics to generate a conceptual schema of the data base. Knowledge in CODES is represented as rules that use a backward chaining control strategy. CODES is implemented in UCI LISP. It was developed at the University of Southern California and reached the stage of a demonstration prototype. (COnceptual DESign system) [RUO84]

EDAAS helps information specialists decide which information concerning the manufacture and distribution of toxic chemicals may be released to the public. The system uses knowledge specifying when information must be released (from the Toxic Substances Control Act) together with knowledge about when sensitive information cannot be released (because it is classified as confidential business information). EDAAS is implemented in FORTRAN, but it uses a rule-based knowledge representation scheme as well as a modified linear programming algorithm to reach a decision. The system was developed by Booz, Allen & Hamilton for use by the Environmental Protection Agency (EPA) which uses it on a regular basis. The system reached the stage of a production prototype. [FEI84, FEI85]

FOLIO helps portfolio managers determine client investment goals and select portfolios that best meet those goals. The system determines the client's needs during an interview and then recommends percentages of each fund that provide an optimum fit to the client's goals. FOLIO recognizes a small number of classes of securities (e.g., dividend-oriented, lower-risk stocks and commodity-sensitive, higher-risk stocks) and maintains aggregate knowledge about the properties (e.g., rate of return) of the securities in each class. The system uses a forward chaining, rule-based representation scheme to infer client goals and a linear programming scheme to maximize the fit between the goals and the portfolio. FOLIO is implemented in MRS. It was developed at Stanford University and reached the stage of a demonstration prototype. [COH83]

GCA helps graduate students plan their computer science curriculum. The system gathers information about a student's academic history and interests and then acts as a faculty adviser by suggesting a schedule of courses for the student. GCA's expertise includes departmental and university regulations regarding graduate degree programs, course descriptions, and sequences of courses frequently taken by computer science students. The knowledge in GCA is organized as four interacting subsystems under the direction of a manager program. These subsystems determine 1) the number of courses the student should take, 2) the courses the student is permitted to take, 3) the best courses to take, and 4) the best schedule for the student. GCA's knowledge is encoded as rules with associated certainty factors. The system is implemented in PROLOG using a MYCIN-like inference engine. It was developed at Duke University and reached the stage of a research prototype. (Graduate Course Advisor) [VAL84]

IR-NLI provides nontechnical users with a natural language interface to the information retrieval services offered by on-line data bases. The system acts as a front end to several available data bases and decides which will be the most appropriate for answering the user's requests. IR-NLI combines the expertise of a professional intermediary for on-line searching with the capability for understanding natural language and carrying out a dialogue with the user. Knowledge is encoded as rules which operate on two knowledge bases. One contains domain-specific (DS) knowledge and the other vocabulary (VOC) knowledge. The DS knowledge base uses a semantic net representation technique to define the data base concepts and indicate how they are related. The VOC knowledge base uses frames to define the lexicon of the application domain. IR-NLI is implemented in FRANZ LISP. It was developed at the University of Udine, Udine, Italy, and reached the stage of a demonstration prototype. (Information Retrieval-Natural Language Interface) [GUI83]

PROJCON helps a software development project manager diagnose the project's problems and their causes. The system consults with the project manager and builds a model of the specific project and its problems (e.g., schedule slippage). When possible causes of the problem have been determined, PROJCON displays its diagnosis and explains its reasoning processes. PROJCON's expertise comes from project management experts. This knowledge is encoded as rules applied by a goal-directed, backward chaining inference mechanism. PROJCON is implemented in EMYCIN. It was developed at Georgia Institute of Technology and reached the stage of a feasibility demonstration. (PROJect CONsultant) [UND81]

RABBIT helps users formulate data base queries. This intelligent data base assistant guides the formulation of queries for users who have only a vague idea of what they want or who have limited knowledge of the given data base. The system's retrieval expertise involves "retrieval by reformulation," where the user makes a query by incrementally constructing a partial description of the desired data base items. RABBIT is implemented in SMALLTALK and operates on a set of data bases represented in KL–ONE. The system was developed at Xerox Palo Alto Research Center and reached the stage of a demonstration prototype. [TOU82]

RESEDA helps a user retrieve biographical data from the field of medieval French history. The user initiates a query which is either satisfied by direct look up or results in a search of information implicit in the data base, making use of inference procedures. The data base of biographical data consists of frames built using a metalanguage based on case grammar. This data base includes all events in the public or private lives of the people of interest. The expertise required for retrieval of implicit information is embodied in rules which can perform simple inferences or automatically establish new causal links between frames in the knowledge base. RESEDA is implemented in the programming language VSAPL. It was developed at the Centre Inter-Regional de Calcul Electronique (CIRCE) in France and reached the stage of a demonstration prototype. [ZAR83, ZAR84a, ZAR84b]

Law

AUDITOR helps a professional auditor evaluate a client's potential for defaulting on a loan. The system uses information about the client's payment history, economic status, credit standing, and other knowledge to determine whether money should be held in reserve to cover a client's loan default. AUDITOR is a rule-based system implemented in AL/X, a derivative of KAS. It operates in a version of AL/X adapted for use in PASCAL systems on microcomputers. The system was developed at the University of Illinois, Champaign-Urbana, as a PhD dissertation and reached the stage of a research prototype. [DUN83]

DSCAS helps contractors analyze the legal aspects of differing site condition (DSC) claims. A DSC claim is a contractually granted remedy for additional expenses incurred by a contractor because physical conditions at the site differ materially from those indicated in the original contract. DSCAS provides a contracting officer (CO) on a construction job site with the legal expertise needed to handle the DSC claim. If DSCAS determines there is a reason for not including the requested additional expenses, the analysis stops and an explanation is given. DSCAS contains a model of the decision process used by lawyers for analyzing DSC claims. This knowledge is represented in the form of forward chaining rules. DSCAS is implemented in ROSIE. It was developed at the University of Colorado and reached the stage of a research prototype. (Differing Site Condition Analysis System) [KRU84]

JUDITH helps lawyers reason about civil law cases. The system queries the lawyer to establish the factual and legal premises of the cause of action. It then suggests additional premises for the lawyer's consideration, until all relevant premises for the case have been considered. JUDITH's knowledge base consists of premises and construction files indicating the relationships that exist between sets of premises. JUDITH is written in FORTRAN. It was developed at the Universities of Heidelberg and Darmstadt and is more an AI environment for exploring legal reasoning than an actual expert system. [POP75]

LDS assists legal experts in settling product liability cases. Given a description of a product liability case, it calculates defendant liability, case worth, and equitable settlement amount. Its expertise is based on both formal legal doctrine and informal principles and strategies of attorneys and claims adjustors. The system calculates the value of the case by analyzing the effect of *loss:* the special and general damages resulting from the injury; *liability:* the probability of establishing the defendant's liability; *responsibility:* the proportion of blame assigned to the plaintiff for the injury; *characteristics:* subjective considerations such as attorneys' skill and litigants' appearance; and *context:* considerations based on strategy, timing, and type of claim. LDS is a rule-based system implemented in ROSIE and was developed by the Rand Corporation. LDS reached the stage of a research prototype. (Legal Decisionmaking System) [WAT80, WAT81]

LEGAL ANALYSIS SYSTEM helps lawyers perform simple legal analyses about the intentional torts of assault and battery. The lawyer presents the system with a set of facts which the system attempts to relate to relevant legal doctrine. The system then presents its conclusions, including the logic behind them. It provides support for the conclusions by referencing judicial decisions and secondary legal authority. Legal expertise, doctrine, and case facts are represented in semantic net form. LEGAL ANALYSIS SYSTEM is implemented in PSL (preliminary study language). It was developed at MIT and reached the stage of a demonstration prototype. [MEL75]

LRS helps lawyers retrieve information about court decisions and legislation in the domain of negotiable instruments law, an area of commercial law that deals with checks and promissory notes. LRS contains subject descriptors that link each data item to the subject area concepts the item is about. A semantic net containing more than 200 legal concepts, built up from six primitive concepts (*party*, *legal instrument*, *liability*, *legal action*, *account*, and *amount of money*), forms the basis for this knowledge. The knowledge in LRS provides it with the ability to make inferences about the meanings of queries and to extend user queries to include terms that are implied but not mentioned by the user. LRS was developed at the University of Michigan and reached the stage of a research prototype. (Legal Research System) [HAF81]

SAL helps attorneys and claims adjustors evaluate claims related to asbestos exposure. The system currently handles one class of diseases, asbestosis, and one class of plaintiffs, insulators. SAL provides estimates of how much money should be paid to plaintiffs in active cases, helping to promote rapid settlement. The system uses knowledge about damages, defendant liability, plaintiff responsibility, and case characteristics such as the type of litigants and skill of the opposing attorneys. SAL is a forward chaining, rule-based system implemented in ROSIE. The system is being developed at the Rand Corporation and has reached the stage of a demonstration prototype. (System for Asbestos Litigation)

SARA helps lawyers analyze decisions governed by discretionary norms. Given the facts of a case and the decision reached, the lawyer identifies factors deemed relevant to the decision; for example, the rent paid for an apartment may be a relevant factor in granting social aid. The lawyer then indicates to SARA the factors (and their values) relevant to a particular decision. On the basis of examples like these, SARA assigns weights to each factor, adjusted to explain as many of the specified decisions as possible. Factors assigned high weights are deemed important with respect to the discretionary norm under consideration. Factors and decisions are represented as frames, and an iterative correlation method is employed for weight calculation. SARA was developed at the Norwegian Research Center for Computers and Law and reached the stage of a demonstration prototype. [BIN80]

TAXADVISOR assists an attorney with tax and estate planning for clients with large estates (greater than $175,000). The system collects client data and infers actions the clients need to take to settle their financial profile, including insurance purchases, retirement actions, transfer of wealth, and modifications to gift and will provisions. TAXADVISOR uses knowledge about estate planning based on attorneys' experiences and strategies as well as more generally accepted knowledge from textbooks. The system uses a rule-based knowledge representation scheme controlled by backward chaining. TAXADVISOR is implemented in EMYCIN. It was developed at the University of Illinois, Champaign-Urbana, as a PhD dissertation and reached the stage of a research prototype. [MIC82a, MIC83a, MIC84a]

TAXMAN assists in the investigation of legal reasoning and legal argumentation using the domain of corporate tax law. The system provides a framework for representing legal concepts and a transformation methodology for recognizing the relationships among those concepts. Transformations from the case under scrutiny to related cases create a basis for analyzing the legal reasoning and argumentation. The knowledge contained in TAXMAN is represented using frames and includes corporate tax cases, tax law, and transformation principles. TAXMAN I originally used a frame-like, logical template representational formalism. Later versions employ a prototype-plus-deformation model, describing concepts in terms of their differences from certain prototypical legal concepts. TAXMAN is implemented in AIMDS. It was developed at Rutgers University and reached the stage of a research prototype. [MCC82, KED84]

Manufacturing

IMACS assists managers in a computer systems manufacturing environment with paperwork management, capacity planning, inventory management, and other tasks related to managing the manufacturing process. IMACS takes a customer's order and generates a rough build plan from which it can estimate the resource requirements for order. Just before the computer system in the order is built, IMACS generates a detailed build plan and uses it to monitor the computer system's implementation. IMACS is a forward chaining, rule-based system organized as a set of cooperating knowledge-based subsystems. It is implemented in OPS5. IMACS was developed by Digital Equipment Corporation and reached the stage of a field prototype. (Intelligent Management Assistant for Computer System manufacturing) [OCO84]

ISIS constructs factory job shop schedules. The system selects a sequence of operations needed to complete an order, determines start and end times, and assigns resources to each operation. It can also act as an intelligent assistant, using its expertise to help plant schedulers maintain schedule consistency and identify decisions that result in unsatisfied constraints. Knowledge in the system includes organizational goals such as due dates and costs, physical constraints such as limitations of particular machines, and causal constraints such as the order in which operations must be performed. ISIS uses a frame-based knowledge representation scheme together with rules for resolving conflicting constraints. The system is implemented in SRL. It was developed at Carnegie-Mellon University and tested in the context of a Westinghouse Electric Corporation turbine component plant. ISIS reached the stage of a research prototype. (Intelligent Scheduling and Information System) [FOX82b, FOX82c, FOX83b, FOX84b]

PTRANS helps control the manufacture and distribution of Digital Equipment Corporation's computer systems. It uses customer order descriptions and information about plant activity to develop a plan for assembling and testing the ordered computer system, including when to build the system. PTRANS monitors the progress of the technicians implementing the plan, diagnoses problems, suggests solutions, and predicts possible impending shortages or surpluses of materials. PTRANS is designed to work with XSEL, a salesperson's assistant, so that once an order is made, the delivery date can be confirmed. PTRANS is a forward chaining, rule-based system implemented in OPS5. It was developed jointly by Digital Equipment Corporation and Carnegie-Mellon University and reached the stage of a research prototype. [HAL83, MCD84]

Mathematics

ADVISOR assists novice users of MACSYMA by diagnosing their misconceptions and providing advice tailored to each user's needs. The user gives ADVISOR a sequence of user-entered MACSYMA commands and a statement of the overall goal which was not met by the command sequence. The system infers the user's plan for achieving the goal, identifies the misconception, confirms it with the user, then generates advice. ADVISOR combines expertise about using MACSYMA with a model of novice user behavior that helps ADVISOR recognize users' plans and misconceptions. User plans and goals are represented as data-flow graphs and goal trees. ADVISOR was written in MACLISP at MIT and reached the stage of a demonstration prototype. [GEN79]

MACSYMA performs symbolic manipulation of algebraic expressions and handles problems involving limit calculations, symbolic integration, solution of equations, canonical simplification, and pattern matching. The system uses mathematical expertise organized as individual knowledge sources and chosen for a particular problem by sophisticated pattern-matching routines. MACSYMA achieves very high quality and efficient performance on the mathematical problems within its scope. The system was implemented in LISP and developed under Project MAC at MIT. MACSYMA has reached the stage of a commercial system and is used regularly by engineers and scientists throughout the United States. [MAR71]

MATHLAB 68 assists mathematicians, scientists, and engineers with the symbolic algebraic manipulation encountered in analysis problems. The system performs differentiation, polynomial factorization, indefinite integration, and direct and inverse Laplace transforms, and solves linear differential equations with constant symbolic coefficients. It contains mathematical expertise in individual modules each with a particular functional speciality. Users' data are classified into three categories: expressions, equations, and functions. Rules for the algebraic manipulation of the data vary with the categories. The system is implemented in LISP and formed the cornerstone for the development of MACSYMA. MATHLAB 68 was developed at MIT and reached the stage of a research prototype. [ENG71]

Medicine

ABEL assists the clinician in diagnosing acid-base and electrolyte disorders in patients by applying knowledge about the diseases and the symptoms they produce. The system uses a causal model of the patient's possible diseases to order queries to the clinician and guide the diagnostic reasoning process. This model contains data about the patient as well as knowledge about the relations between various disease states. The system checks for erroneous data by comparing query responses to expectations generated by the model. Knowledge is represented within a causal network, a type of semantic net specifying cause-effect relations between diseases and findings. The system was developed at MIT and reached the stage of a research prototype. (a program for Acid-Base and ElectroLyte disturbances) [PAT81b, PAT82c, PAT82d]

AI/COAG assists physicians in diagnosing diseases of hemostasis by analyzing and interpreting clinical blood coagulation laboratory tests. The system handles six types of coagulation screening tests, including those for platelet count and urea clot solubility. In addition, the system can evaluate a clinical hemostasis history of the patient to confirm the diagnosis suggested by the screening tests.

AI/COAG was developed at the University of Missouri School of Medicine and was implemented on a DEC LSI-11 microcomputer. It reached the stage of a research prototype. [LIN81, GAS83]

AI/MM analyzes behavior in the renal physiology domain and explains the rationale for its analyses. The system answers queries about the values of various parameters, such as the volume of body water, and interprets observations, such as abnormally high water intake. AI/MM's expertise includes the laws of physics and anatomy, fundamental principles of physiology, and empirical knowledge of physiological processes. This knowledge is represented as rules which comprise a detailed causal model. Each rule also contains a description of its underlying principle for use in explaining the system's operation. AI/MM is implemented in MRS. It was developed at Stanford University and reached the stage of a demonstration prototype. (Artificial Intelligence/Mathematical Modeling system) [KUN83]

AI/RHEUM assists physicians in diagnosing connective tissue diseases of clinical rheumatology by applying formal diagnostic criteria obtained from rheumatology experts. The system uses patient symptoms and laboratory findings to provide assistance with seven diseases, including rheumatoid arthritis, progressive systemic sclerosis, and Sjoegren's disease. AI/RHEUM is a rule-based system implemented in EXPERT and accesses its rule through forward chaining. It was developed at the University of Missouri School of Medicine and reached the stage of a research prototype. [LIN80a, LIN82]

ANGY assists physicians in diagnosing the narrowing of coronary vessels by identifying and isolating coronary vessels in angiograms. The system first processes digital angiograms of coronary vessels in order to extract initial line and region features. This information is then given to ANGY's knowledge-based expert subsystem, which addresses both low- and high-level stages of vision processing. The low-level image processing stage uses rules for segmentation, grouping, and shape analysis to develop the initial lines and regions into more meaningful objects. The high-level stage then uses knowledge of cardiac anatomy and physiology to interpret the result, recognize relevant structures (e.g., the aorta), and eliminate irrelevant structures or artifacts caused by noise. The low-level image processing routines are implemented in the C programming language and include the edge detector and region grower. The medical expertise is represented as rules implemented in OPS5 and LISP. ANGY was developed at the University of Pennsylvania and reached the stage of a demonstration prototype. [STA84]

ANNA assists physicians in administering digitalis to patients with heart problems, such as arrhythmia and congestive heart failure. The system uses patient symptoms and history to determine the appropriate dosage regimen, including the amount of digitalis to administer and the rate at which it should be taken. Once the system prescribes an initial dosage, it monitors the patient's response to the drug, adjusting the dosage appropriately when the demonstrated response fails to match the expected response. ANNA is implemented in LISP. It was developed at MIT and reached the stage of a research prototype. [SIL74]

ARAMIS helps physicians assess new patients with rheumatic diseases. The system retrieves data about previous rheumatic disease patients and performs statistical analyses on that data. Based on this activity, ARAMIS offers a prognostic analysis with respect to a variety of endpoints (e.g., death, pleurisy), recommends therapy, and generates a prose case analysis. ARAMIS' knowledge consists of a collection of statistical analysis methods plus a number of data bases containing detailed patient records. Patient data are stored in a tabular data base using TOD (Time-Oriented Databank System), a system able to follow relevant clinical parameters over time. ARAMIS is written in PL/X, a specialized form of PL/I. It was developed at Stanford University and reached the stage of a field prototype. (American Rheumatism Association Medical Information System) [FRI72, FRI76, FRI79, MCS79, SHO79]

ATTENDING instructs medical students in anesthesiology by critiquing students' plans for anesthetic management. The system presents the student with a hypothetical patient about to undergo surgery and analyzes the management plan devised by the student. The system bases its analysis on an assessment of the risks involved in the context of the patient's medical problems. The critique produced by the system has the form of commentary, typically four or five paragraphs of English text. ATTENDING was developed at the Yale University School of Medicine and reached the stage of a research prototype. [MIL83]

BABY aids clinicians by monitoring patients in a newborn intensive care unit (NICU). The system attempts to find clinically important patterns in the medical and demographic data about NICU patients. It monitors all on-line data in the NICU, keeps track of the clinical states of the patients, suggests further evaluation for important findings, and answers questions about the patients. BABY contains neonatology medical expertise for interpreting the clinical and demographic data. BABY is a forward chaining, rule-based system that uses rules embedded in a PROSPECTOR-like network. The system handles certainty by using a Bayesian probabilistic method similar to that used in PROSPECTOR. BABY is written in PASCAL and is situated within the ADVISE system, an integrated, rule-based software environment. It was developed at the University of Illinois, Champaign-Urbana, and reached the stage of a demonstration prototype. [ROD84]

BLUE BOX advises a physician on selection of appropriate therapy for a patient complaining of depression. The system uses knowledge about the patient's symptoms and information about the patient's medical, psychiatric, drug, and family histories to diagnose the type and extent of depression and to suggest a management plan for controlling it. This plan includes decisions about hospitalization and drug treatments. BLUE BOX is a rule-based system implemented in EMYCIN and was developed at Stanford University. The system was tested in the environment of the Palo Alto VA Mental Health Clinical Research Center and reached the stage of a research prototype. [MUL84]

CASNET/GLAUCOMA diagnoses disease states related to glaucoma and prescribes plans or therapies for treating them. The system bases its decisions on knowledge about the relations between patient symptoms, test results, internal abnormal conditions, disease states, and treatment plans. The system provides a narrative interpretation of the case and can retrieve literature references to support its conclusions. Knowledge is represented in a particular type of semantic net known as a causal-association network. The system is implemented in FORTRAN and was developed at Rutgers University. It reached the stage of a research prototype. (Causal-Association NETwork/GLAUCOMA [SZO78, WEI78, KUL80a, WEI81c, KUL82, ALT84b]

CENTAUR assists pulmonary physiologists in diagnostic interpretation of pulmonary function tests. The system uses measurements of the amount of gas in the lungs and the rates of flow of gases into and out of the lungs to determine the presence and severity of lung disease in the patient. The expertise contained in CENTAUR includes pulmonary physiology and prototypical lung test results for each pulmonary disease or subtype. Knowledge is represented as a combination of frames and rules, and certainty measures similar to EMYCIN's certainty factors are used to indicate how closely the actual data match the expected data values of the prototype. In addition, CENTAUR has an explanation capability that provides justifications from an underlying model of pulmonary physiology. CENTAUR is implemented in INTERLISP. It was developed at Stanford University and reached the stage of a research prototype. [AIK83a]

CLOT assists physicians with the evaluation of evidence for disorders of the blood coagulation system. The system diagnoses a bleeding defect by identifying which of the two coagulation subsystems, the platelet-vascular or the coagulative, might be defective. The primary motivation for implementing CLOT was to study knowledge acquisition tools and techniques; thus its medical expertise was not refined or fully tested. CLOT is a backward chaining, rule-based system implemented in EMYCIN, making use of EMYCIN's knowledge acquisition, explanation, and certainty factor mechanisms. The system was developed at Stanford University and reached the stage of a demonstration prototype. [BEN80, BEN84]

DIAGNOSER helps physicians identify congenital heart disease, specifically, the cardiac anomaly known as total anomalous pulmonary venous connection. The system was intended to help artificial intelligence researchers develop and test predictions about the nature of errors in diagnostic reasoning. Presented with auscultation and X-ray data, DIAGNOSER determines its diagnosis by hypothesizing diseases whose prototype fits the observations. DIAGNOSER contains knowledge about diagnostic reasoning, as well as knowledge about cardiac physiology, anatomy, and the pathophysiology of the causal structures underlying congenital heart diseases. The disease knowledge is represented using frames, the diagnostic reasoning knowledge using rules embedded in frames. DIAGNOSER is implemented in LISP 1.4. It was developed at the University of Minnesota and reached the stage of a research prototype. [JOH81]

DIALYSIS THERAPY ADVISOR helps physicians select an initial dialysis regimen for a patient about to begin maintenance hemodialysis treatment. The system is given the patient's sex, height, weight, BUN, urine volume, and urea nitrogen concentration and produces a list of acceptable therapies. Expertise in the system consists of rules corresponding to the reasoning of medical experts on how to specify initial hemodialysis prescriptions. The rules are accessed via forward and backward chaining. The system also incorporates equation solving, explanation handling, data base retrieval mechanisms, metarules for planning, and a communication facility for user interaction. The DIALYSIS THERAPY ADVISOR is implemented in FRANZ LISP. It was developed at Vanderbilt University and reached the stage of a research prototype. [SCA84c]

DIGITALIS ADVISOR aids physicians by recommending appropriate digitalis therapy for patients with congestive heart failure or conduction disturbances of the heart. The system questions the clinician about the patient's history, e.g., age, cardiac rhythm, serum potassium level, then produces a set of recommendations for initial therapy. After the patient has received an initial dose, the program analyzes the reaction of the patient, as given by the clinician's responses to another set of questions, and produces a new dosage regimen. Digitalis therapy expertise is represented as a hierarchy of concepts in a semantic net. An interpreter executes plans in the knowledge base (e.g., checking for digitalis sensitivity due to advanced age). The system contains an explanation facility that produces explanations directly from the executed code. DIGITALIS ADVISOR is implemented in OWL I. It was developed at MIT and reached the stage of a demonstration prototype. [SWA77]

DRUG INTERACTION CRITIC helps physicians decide how to administer drugs in the presence of other drugs. The system identifies both adverse and beneficial interactions, explains why the interactions occur, answers questions about the interactions, and suggests corrective action for adverse effects. The knowledge base of drug types is arranged as a hierarchy of frames that includes information related to specific drugs, such as the drug's affinities, storage sites, and interaction characteristics. Knowledge about the mechanism of drug interaction is organized by frames according to one of the four mechanism types: chemicophysical, pharmacodynamic, pharmacokinetic, and physiologic. The system provides a limited natural language interface, including a spelling corrector since drug names are commonly typed incorrectly. The system is implemented in PROLOG. It was developed at Virginia Polytechnic Institute & State University and reached the stage of a demonstration prototype. [ROA84]

EEG ANALYSIS SYSTEM analyzes electroencephalograms (EEGs) recorded from renal patients. The system analyzes EEGs fed to it directly from an EEG machine by using a fast Fourier transformation method. It then uses the resulting spectral features to classify the EEGs as either normal or abnormal. The system uses knowledge obtained from a professional electroencephalographer, represented in the form of rules with associated certainty factors. The system explains its results by simply displaying the outcomes of certain rules. A rule-editing program, written in C, helps system developers maintain and update the rules. The system is implemented in assembly language and the C programming language and embedded in a Motorola MC6801 single-chip microprocessor. The EEG ANALYSIS SYSTEM was developed at Vanderbilt University and reached the stage of a research prototype. [BAA84]

EMERGE assists physicians in the analysis of chest pain in an emergency-room environment. The system decides whether an emergency-room patient who is suffering with chest pain should be admitted to the hospital. It also provides advice on possible treatments, together with an indication of the severity of the condition. EMERGE contains expertise derived from existing medical outlines, known as *criteria maps,* which reflect a collection of knowledge gained over a period of years from consultations with experts. The system represents this knowledge as rules organized in a hierarchy to improve performance. It also handles certainty calculations and provides explanations showing the logical paths taken by rule searches. EMERGE is implemented in standard PASCAL and operates on mainframes, minicomputers, and microcomputers. The system was developed at UCLA and reached the stage of a field prototype. [HUD81, HUD84a, HUD84b, HUD84c]

EXAMINER analyzes physicians' diagnostic behavior on cases in internal medicine. The system presents a hypothetical case, and the physician identifies the disease most likely to cause the manifestations present and indicates other diseases or problems which could be present. The system performs this analysis using 1) heuristic knowledge about how to relate diseases to their manifestations, and 2) medical knowledge obtained directly from the INTERNIST data base. The system produces a text commentary that evaluates the physician's diagnosis, acknowledging correct assumptions and explaining why incorrect ones are wrong. Knowledge is in the form of procedures embodying principles of internal medicine. The system is implemented in LISP and was developed at the University of Pittsburgh. It reached the stage of a demonstration prototype. [OLE77]

GALEN diagnoses cases of congenital heart disease in children. The system uses data describing the patient's medical history, physical examinations, X-rays, and EKGs to identify the disease present. GALEN hypothesizes a small set of possible diseases and then prioritizes them based on the degree of fit between its expectations for each disease and the actual patient data values. GALEN's expertise is based on models of pediatric cardiology diseases. Knowledge is represented as a combination of rules and frames, with the rules describing the conditions under which a hypothesis should be considered, accepted, rejected, or modified. GALEN uses the frames to collect information relevant to a particular disease hypothesis. The system was developed at the University of Minnesota and reached the stage of a research prototype. [THO83]

GUIDON instructs students in the selection of antimicrobial therapy for hospital patients with bacterial infections. The system selects a case, solves it, presents it to the student to solve, and analyzes the student's responses and queries during the solution process. From this the system determines how closely the student's knowledge and reasoning match the diagnosis procedure it used to solve the case. The differences found are used to guide the system's tutoring and explanation mechanisms. GUIDON actually uses the MYCIN expert system to solve the cases; thus it teaches students the rules and procedures embedded in MYCIN. GUIDON is a rule-based system containing both rules and metarules (rules to decide how to use the rules). It is implemented in INTERLISP and was developed at Stanford University. The system reached the stage of a research prototype. [CLA79, CLA79a, CLA83a, CLA83d]

HDDSS helps physicians determine and select appropriate treatment for patients with Hodgkin's disease. The system applies Bayesian estimation techniques to produce a priori probabilities of the extent of tumor spread. It then uses these probabilities to help select a diagnostic procedure or treatment. After it chooses a diagnostic procedure, it uses Bayes' theorem to revise the probabilities and the process continues. HDDSS finally produces an optimal diagnostic plan and a set of near optimal plans for the physician to study. The system contains radiotherapy knowledge in a hierarchical taxonomy and patient data in a relational data base. HDDSS is implemented in MACLISP. It was developed at MIT and reached the stage of a research prototype. (Hodgkin's Disease Decision Support System) [SAF76]

HEADMED advises physicians on matters of clinical psychopharmacology by diagnosing a range of psychiatric disorders and recommending drug treatment. The system was designed for use as a tutorial and consulting aid. HEADMED uses approximately 120 clinical parameters to perform its diagnosis and treatment recommendations (e.g., drug dosage and therapy duration). HEADMED contains knowledge about the differential diagnosis of the major affective disorders, schizophrenia, and the general category of organic brain disorders. The knowledge base also includes the Minnesota Multiphasic Personality Inventory (MMPI) and skeletal knowledge about neuroses, behavior disorders, and substance abuse. HEADMED is written in EMYCIN and uses EMYCIN's certainty factors, explanation, knowledge acquisition, and other support facilities. It was developed at University of California, Irvine, and reached the stage of a research prototype. [HEI78]

HEART IMAGE INTERPRETER helps physicians perform a diagnostic interpretation of the motional behavior of the heart. The system analyzes two-dimensional intensity distribution images of the heart produced by injecting radionuclide substance Technetium 99-m into the patient's vein. A scintillation camera produces a sequence of 12 to 64 images for the system to analyze and interpret. Knowledge in the system includes the structural properties of the heart and left ventricle, the motional phases of a heart cycle, and rules for relating medical evidence to diagnoses. Image processing and medical diagnostic knowledge is encoded in a semantic net containing frames and associated rules that use certainty factors. HEART IMAGE INTERPRETER is implemented in RATFOR, a dialect of FORTRAN. It was developed at the University of Erlangen and reached the stage of a demonstration prototype. [NIE84]

HEME helps physicians diagnose hematologic diseases. The system uses patient findings entered by a physician and a version of Bayes' theorem to compute the probability that the patient has each of the diseases currently registered in the system. HEME then displays a listing of differential diagnoses together with their probability of occurrence. Knowledge in HEME includes estimates of the frequency of occurrence of a given disease, the probability that a patient with the disease has a given finding, and the probability that a patient without the disease has a given finding. These conditional probabilities represent the judgments of experienced hematology clinicians and include measures of how confident the clinicians are about their original probability estimates. HEME was developed at Cornell University and reached the stage of a field prototype. [ENG76]

HT-ATTENDING critiques a physician's approach to the pharmacologic management of essential hypertension. The system helps physicians manage hypertensive patients and provides information about new drugs and treatments. It extends the approach used in AT-TENDING to the domain of hypertension. HT-ATTENDING uses information about the patient (e.g., age, medical problems) together with information about the patient's present antihypertensive regimen and the proposed change to that regimen to critique the proposed change. The critique is generated as several paragraphs of English text. The system contains knowledge about antihypertensive agents used in outpatient treatment, treatment modalities, and conditions affecting hypertension management. It uses a frame-based knowledge representation scheme and is implemented in LISP. The system was developed at Yale University and reached the stage of a research prototype. (HyperTension-ATTENDING system) [MIL84]

INTERNIST-I/CADUCEOUS assists the physician in making multiple and complex diagnoses in general internal medicine given a patient's history, symptoms, or laboratory test results. The system bases it decisions on a set of disease profiles containing findings that occur in association with each disease. The system is one of the largest medical expert systems developed, containing profiles of more than 500 diseases described by more than 3500 manifestations of disease. Knowledge in the system is represented as a network of findings and diseases and is accessed based on the constraints of the disease taxonomy and causality relations. The system is implemented in LISP. The first version of the system was called INTERNIST-I; the second, CADUCEOUS. It was developed at the University of Pittsburgh and reached the stage of a field prototype. [MIL82, POP84]

IRIS helps physicians diagnose and treat diseases. The system collects information from the physician about the patient's symptoms, giving rise to a set of possible diagnoses. IRIS then chooses a diagnosis and treatment corresponding to the diagnosis. The medical diagnostic expertise is represented using a semantic net that defines the relationships among symptoms, diseases, and treatments. The inference process is controlled by decision tables associated with the nodes of the semantic net. IRIS propagates MYCIN-like certainty factors through the net to help it choose a diagnosis. IRIS was developed at Rutgers University and is more an environment for exploring medical decision making than an actual expert system. [TRI77]

MDX diagnoses the existence and cause of the liver syndrome known as *cholestasis*. The system bases its diagnosis on patient history, signs, symptoms, and clinical data. MDX functions as a community of cooperating expert diagnosticians, each with different specialities. These experts call upon one another to resolve problems requiring special knowledge and expertise. Communication is via a blackboard mechanism. MDX's expertise consists of diagnostic heuristics and a hierarchical, deep model of the conceptual structure of cholestasis. This knowledge is represented as rules and frames organized around the cholestasis model. PATREC and RADEX are members of the community of expert systems called upon by MDX. MDX is implemented in LISP. It was developed at Ohio State University and reached the stage of a research prototype. [CHA79, CHA81, GOM81 CHA83]

MECS-AI helps physicians make diagnoses and suggest treatments for cardiovascular and thyroid diseases. Although developed specifically for cardiovascular diseases, it was revised into a more general tool for developing medical consultation systems and was applied to thyroid diseases. MECS-AI uses knowledge of cardiovascular and thyroid disease diagnosis obtained from medical experts. It is a backward chaining, rule-based system and contains a knowledge-base editor to facilitate defining and modifying system expertise.

Two versions of MECS-AI exist, one implemented in INTERLISP and the other in EPICS-LISP. It was developed at the University of Tokyo Hospital and reached the stage of a research prototype. (MEdical Consultation System-by means of Artificial Intelligence) [KAI78, KAI82]

MEDICO gives ophthalmologists advice about the management of chorioretinal diseases. The system contains general clinical knowledge and a large data base of facts about previous patients and events. MEDICO is a forward chaining, rule-based system that handles certainty by associating likelihood estimates provided by domain experts with the rules. Interactive rule acquisition from domain experts is supported by a knowledge acquisition and maintenance module (KAMM). Another module, RAIN (Relational Algebraic INterpreter), supports the examination, update, and reorganization of the rules in the knowledge base. MEDICO is implemented in the programming language C. It was developed at the University of Illinois and reached the stage of a research prototype. [WAL76, WAL77]

MED1 helps physicians diagnose diseases associated with chest pain. The system uses findings such as heart beat frequency and blood pressure to help it determine the disease or diseases that best account for the findings. Disease hypotheses are suggested by forward chaining through rules that accumulate suggestive evidence. The top-ranking diagnosis is then subjected to further evaluation using backward chaining through MYCIN-like rules to either confirm the hypothesis or suggest alternatives. MED1 uses a modified version of MYCIN's certainty factor scheme in which the score of a disease diagnosis is transformed into one of seven probability classes from "excluded" to "confirmed." The system also provides knowledge acquisition and explanation facilities. MED1 is implemented in INTERLISP. It was developed at the University of Kaiserslautern and reached the stage of a research prototype. (Meta-Ebenen Diagnosesystem, *Meta-Level Diagnostics System*) [PUP83]

MI helps physicians diagnose myocardial infarction through analysis of enzyme activity. The system reaches its diagnosis of heart damage by checking for elevated levels of certain enzymes in the blood over a period of several days. MI's expertise includes knowledge about how to deal with the time-dependent nature of the medical findings, including techniques for automatically updating, revising, and interpreting a patient's record. MI is a forward chaining, rule-based system. It is implemented in a version of EXPERT modified to represent and manipulate time-dependent rules and data. MI was developed at Rutgers University and reached the stage of a demonstration prototype. (Myocardial Infarction system) [KAS83b]

MODIS helps physicians diagnose various forms of arterial hypertension. The system first collects patient information, such as complaints, symptoms, and laboratory test results. It then hypothesizes groups of illnesses having characteristics consistent with the collected information. If several possibilities exist, the system selects the group of illnesses ranked most likely by medical experts. The system can explain its rationale for asking questions, formulating diagnoses, and examining hypotheses. The diagnostic expertise embodied in MODIS comes from surgeons and therapeutic experts in the field. This knowledge is represented as a semantic net containing frames whose slots contain rules as well as data. The system is implemented in LISP. It was developed in Tbilisi, Georgian USSR and reached the stage of a demonstration prototype. (Machine-Oriented Diagnostic Interactive System) [BOK82]

MYCIN assists physicians in the selection of appropriate antimicrobial therapy for hospital patients with bacteremia, meningitis, and cystitis infections. The system diagnoses the cause of the infection (e.g., the identity of the infecting organism is pseudomonas) using knowledge relating infecting organisms with patient history, symptoms, and laboratory test results. The system recommends drug treatment (type and dosage) according to procedures followed by physicians experienced in infectious disease therapy. MYCIN is a rule-based system employing a backward chaining control scheme. It includes mechanisms for performing certainty calculations and providing explanations of the system's reasoning process. MYCIN is implemented in LISP. It was developed at Stanford University and reached the stage of a research prototype. [SHO73, SHO75, SHO75a, SHO76, BUC82, SHO82, DAV82a, CEN84, BUC84a, BUC84b, BUC84c, ALT84e]

NEOMYCIN helps physicians diagnose and treat patients with meningitis and similar diseases. The system incorporates expertise derived from MYCIN, represented in a way that facilitates explanation and teaching. The system's knowledge is in the form of rules organized by a disease hierarchy and controlled by forward chaining metarules that constitute the diagnostic procedure. The key difference between MYCIN and NEOMYCIN is the explicit separation of the diagnostic procedure from the disease knowledge. NEOMYCIN provides explanations of diagnostic strategy as well as those relating to a causal model of the domain. GUIDON2 uses the NEOMYCIN knowledge base and diagnostic metarules as its source of teaching materials. NEOMYCIN is implemented in INTERLISP-D. It was developed at Stanford University and reached the stage of a research prototype. [CLA81, CLA81a, HAS83a, CLA83b, HAS83b, CLA83c, CLA83d, CLA84a]

NEUREX helps physicians diagnose patients with diseases of the nervous system. The system uses the results of a neurological examination of unconscious patients to locate the nervous system damage and classify the patients according to the damage locale (e.g., subtentorial lesion, nonfocal). NEUREX is a rule-based system employing both forward and backward chaining and a MYCIN-like certainty factor mechanism. Rules containing neurological localization expertise are organized into an inference hierarchy in which successively higher levels in the hierarchy represent greater levels of abstraction of the information about the patient. NEUREX is implemented in Wisconsin LISP. It was developed at the University of Maryland and reached the stage of a demonstration prototype. [REG78a, REG78b]

NEUROLOGIST-I helps physicians diagnose neurological disorders by localizing lesions occurring within the central nervous system (CNS). The system analyzes patient data, including neurologic complaints and physical examination results, and then produces a summary of malfunctioning tracts by mapping symptoms to tract status. The system uses physiological knowledge encoded as an analogic/geometric model of the CNS in which nervous tract cross-sections are approximated by polygons represented as sets of vertices. NEUROLOGIST-I is implemented in FRANZ LISP. It was developed at the State University of New York at Buffalo and reached the stage of a demonstration prototype. [XIA84]

OCULAR HERPES MODEL assists a physician in diagnosing and treating patients with ocular herpes complex. The system associates patient clinical history and laboratory findings with disease categories and uses this knowledge to diagnose the disease (e.g., patient has a corneal epithelial lesion) and recommend treatment (e.g., administer vidarabine ointment five times daily). The system selects therapy based on drug effectiveness and the patient's drug resistance and allergic reaction. The system is a forward chaining, rule-based system implemented in EXPERT. It was developed at Rutgers University and reached the stage of a demonstration prototype. [KAS82]

ONCOCIN assists physicians in treating and managing cancer patients undergoing chemotherapy experiments called *protocols*. The system selects therapy by relating information about the patient's diagnosis, previous treatments, and laboratory tests to knowledge about protocols—past experiments aimed at measuring the therapeutic benefits and toxic side effects of alternative cancer treatments. The system contains knowledge about 34 Hodgkin's disease and lymphoma protocols. ONCOCIN is a rule-based system employing both forward and backward chaining. It is implemented in INTERLISP.

The system was developed at Stanford University and reached the stage of a research prototype. (Named after its domain of expertise: cancer therapy) [SHO81, TSU83, LAN83a, SHO84]

PATHFINDER helps pathologists interpret findings occurring from the microscopic examination of lymph node tissue. The system poses questions to the pathologist in a manner designed to reduce the uncertainty in the differential diagnosis, and it can provide a justification for the most recent question posed. The system bases its decisions on a set of disease profiles containing findings that are normally associated with each disease. This expertise in the diagnosis of lymph node pathology comes from expert hematopathologists. PATHFINDER's knowledge is encoded using frames. The system was developed at Stanford University and reached the stage of a demonstration prototype. [HOR84]

PATREC manages a data base of patient records, providing diagnostic physicians and the MDX expert system with sophisticated access to the records. It handles patient data in the context of diagnosing for the syndrome called *cholestasis*. PATREC accepts data from the user, stores it appropriately, provides a query language for question answering, prepares summary reports, and makes suggestions helpful in diagnosis. Knowledge in PATREC includes a conceptual model of medical data (e.g., the significance of a particular lab test and its expected values) and a patient model (e.g., individual patient histories and clinical episodes). Knowledge is represented as frames with attached rules to perform bookkeeping functions, data input, and automatic temporal inferencing. PATREC is implemented in LISP. It was developed at Ohio State University and reached the stage of a research prototype. (PATient RECords system) [MIT80]

PEC helps primary health workers diagnose and treat common and potentially blinding eye disorders. Its initial set of yes/no questions (such as, "Is the eye red?") leads to further sets of questions about the patient. When enough information has been gathered, the system outputs a summary of the case, followed by its diagnostic conclusions and management recommendations. PEC's knowledge comes from the World Health Organization guide to primary eye care, and it is represented as rules using a forward chaining inference scheme. The system was initially implemented in EXPERT, then translated automatically into BASIC for use on microcomputers. PEC was developed at Rutgers University and reached the stage of a research prototype. (Primary Eye Care system) [KAS84]

PIP assists physicians by taking the history of the present illness of a patient with edema. The system interweaves the processes of information gathering and diagnosis, alternating between asking questions to gain new information and integrating this new information into a developing picture of the patient. Knowledge contained in PIP includes prototypical findings such as signs, symptoms, laboratory data, the time course of the given illness, and rules for judging how closely a given patient matches a hypothesized disease or state. PIP's questions are controlled by a set of diagnostic hypotheses suggested by the patient's complaints. The ability of the hypotheses to account for the findings of the case is averaged with the measure of fit to arrive at a final certainty measure for ranking hypotheses. Knowledge in PIP is represented using frames. PIP is implemented in CONNIVER and was developed at MIT. It reached the stage of a research prototype. (Present Illness Program) [PAU76, KUL80a]

PUFF diagnoses the presence and severity of lung disease in a patient by interpreting measurements from respiratory tests administered in a pulmonary (lung) function laboratory. The data being interpreted include test results (e.g., total lung capacity, residual volume) and patient history. The system bases its decisions on knowledge about the kinds of tests results produced by different pulmonary disorders. PUFF is a backward chaining, rule-based system implemented in EMYCIN. It was developed at Stanford University and tested at the Pacific Medical Center in San Francisco. PUFF reached the stage of a production prototype. [HPP80a, AIK83b]

RADEX helps physicians and the MDX expert system diagnose the liver syndrome cholestasis. This radiology consultant takes summary descriptions of a patient's medical images and uses them as a basis for answering questions about the patient's anatomical or physiological abnormalities. The system's expertise consists of a conceptual model of relevant organs and organ abnormalities that can appear on various images. Knowledge is represented as frames containing the descriptions, default values, relationships, and attached procedures for four kinds of entities: the imaging procedures, such as liver scan and ultrasonogram; major organs, such as liver and gall bladder; parts of organs, such as lumen and lobe; and abnormalities and deformities in the organs, such as tumor and stricture. RADEX is implemented in LISP. It was developed at Ohio State University and reached the stage of a research prototype. (RADiology EXpert) [CHA80]

RX helps users perform studies on large nonrandomized, time-oriented, clinical data bases by automating the process of hypothesis generation and exploratory analysis. RX has been applied to the problem of finding causal relationships within the American Rheumatism Association Medical Information System (ARAMIS) data base. The system uses nonparametric correlations to generate lists of hypothe-

sized relationships. The hypotheses are tested using appropriate
statistical methods, and positive results are incorporated into the
data base. RX contains a tree-structured knowledge base representing a taxonomy of relevant aspects of medicine and statistics. The
medical expertise includes knowledge about systemic lupus ery-
thematosus and limited areas of general internal medicine. RX is
implemented in INTERLISP. It was developed at Stanford University and reached the stage of a demonstration prototype. [HEU80,
BLU82a, BLU82b, BLU82c, BLU83]

SPE distinguishes between various causes of inflammatory conditions in
a patient (e.g., cirrhosis of the liver, myeloma—a form of cancer) by
interpreting waveforms (serum protein electrophoresis patterns)
from a device called a scanning densitometer. The system makes
interpretations by applying knowledge about how the instrument
readings and patient data relate to disease categories. SPE is a forward chaining, rule-based system, first implemented in EXPERT
and then translated into the assembly language for the Motorola
6809 microprocessor. The system was developed at Rutgers University and has been incorporated into CliniScan, a scanning densitometer marketed by Helena Laboratories. SPE reached the stage of a
commercial system. (Serum Protein Electrophoresis diagnostic program) [KUL80b, WEI81b]

SYSTEM D helps physicians diagnose the probable cause of dizziness in
a patient. The system prompts the physician to enter findings (e.g.,
current medications) and manifestations (e.g., sensation of impending faint) and produces a diagnosis, including a ranking of compet-
ing alternatives. SYSTEM D handles situations where multiple
causes of dizziness may be present simultaneously. The knowledge
contained in SYSTEM D includes both case-specific information and
expertise concerning diagnosis of causes of dizziness. The diagnostic knowledge is distributed across multiple medical specialties corresponding to the numerous potential causes of dizziness. The system uses a frame-based knowledge representation scheme and a
sequential generate-and-test inference mechanism. SYSTEM D is
implemented in KMS. It was developed at the University of Maryland and reached the stage of a research prototype. (SYSTEM for
Diagnostic problem solving) [REG83]

THYROID MODEL helps physicians diagnose disorders of the thyroid,
such as hypothyroidism. The system accepts an initial set of patient
findings (e.g., demographic information, symptoms, laboratory test
results) and prompts for the additional data needed for a diagnosis.
The system's expertise consists of diagnostic reasoning rules and a
taxonomic structure of thyroid function and thyroid pathology.

THYROID MODEL is a forward chaining, rule-based system. It explains why hypotheses are confirmed by showing the decision rules applied and the associated certainty factors. THYROID MODEL is implemented in EXPERT. It was developed at Rutgers University and reached the stage of a demonstration prototype. [KUL82]

VM provides diagnostic and therapeutic suggestions about postsurgical patients in an intensive care unit (ICU). The system identifies possible alarm conditions, recognizes spurious data, characterizes the patient state, and suggests useful therapies. The system interprets quantitative measurements from an ICU monitoring system, such as heart rate, blood pressure, and data regarding a mechanical ventilator that provides the patient with breathing assistance by applying knowledge about patient history and expectations about the range of monitored measurements. VM is a rule-based system implemented in INTERLISP. It was developed at Stanford University and tested at the Pacific Medical Center and the Stanford University Medical Center. It reached the stage of a field prototype. (Ventilator Manager) [FAG78, OSB78, FAG79a, FAG79b, SHO82, FAG84]

WHEEZE diagnoses the presence and severity of lung disease by interpreting measurements of pulmonary function tests. The system bases its diagnosis on clinical laboratory test results (e.g., total lung capacity) and patient history (e.g., age, history of smoking). WHEEZE's expertise consists of a translation of the rules used by PUFF into a frame-based representation. The frames contain two types of certainty factors, one indicating the likelihood of an assertion when its manifestations are believed, and the other indicating the degree to which the assertion is believed to be true during a particular consultation. WHEEZE's control mechanism provides a kind of backward and forward chaining, implemented by using an agenda, with each suggested assertion placed on the agenda according to a specified priority. WHEEZE is implemented in RLL. It was developed at Stanford University and reached the stage of a research prototype. [SMI80, SMI84a]

Meteorology

WILLARD helps meteorologists forecast the likelihood of severe thunderstorms occurring in the central United States. The system queries a meteorologist about pertinent weather conditions for the forecast area and then produces a complete forecast with supporting justifications. The user may specify a particular geographical area for WIL-

LARD to consider. The system characterizes the certainty of severe thunderstorm occurrence as "none," "approaching," "slight," "moderate," or "high," and each is given a numerical probability range. WILLARD's expertise is represented as rules generated automatically from examples of expert forecasting. WILLARD was implemented using RULEMASTER, an inductive rule generator. It was developed at Radian Corporation and reached the stage of a demonstration prototype. [MIC84b]

Military Science

ACES performs the cartographer's job of map labeling. The system takes as input an unlabeled map plus data describing points where objects are located and the text string and symbol type to be displayed at each point. The system produces a map containing the desired symbols and labels, all positioned to aesthetically place the labels next to the symbols without overlap. The system chooses the symbol placement, type font, label size, and level of description that best fits the map in question. It uses an object-oriented knowledge representation scheme and is implemented in LOOPS for the Xerox Dolphin workstation. The system was developed by ESL and reached the stage of a research prototype. (AI Cartographic Expert System) [PFE84]

ADEPT aids battlefield situation assessment analysts by providing tactical interpretations of intelligence sensor reports. The system uses these reports to generate a display of combat locations on the battlefield. Military knowledge and expertise are encoded as rules concerning how and why enemy forces operate and the tactical significance of situation interpretations. The system is able to explain the reasoning behind its battlefield assessments. The expert reasoning component of ADEPT is implemented in ROSIE, and a Chromatics CGC 7900 color graphics system is used to display maps and military symbology. The system was developed at TRW and reached the stage of a research prototype. [TAY84]

AIRID identifies aircraft on the basis of visually observed characteristics. The user enters observed features and the conditions under which the observation occurred (e.g., bad weather) from which AIRID determines the identity of the target aircraft. AIRID's expertise includes physical characteristics of aircraft, extracted from *Jane's All the World's Aircraft 1982-83*. The relevant features include wing shape, engine configuration (number and mounting position), fuselage shape, and tail assembly shape. The system is implemented in KAS and uses a combined rule-based and semantic network representation technique. AIRID assumes it has a successful identification when the certainty level in its network reaches 98 percent confidence. The system was developed at Los Alamos National Laboratory and reached the stage of a demonstration prototype. (AIRcraft IDentifier) [ALD84]

AIRPLAN assists air operations officers with the launch and recovery of aircraft on a carrier. The system analyzes current information (e.g., the aircraft's fuel level, the weather conditions at a possible divert site) and alerts the air operations officer of possible impending problems. AIRPLAN assesses the seriousness of a situation and manages its use of time by attending first to the most significant aspects of a problem. If time permits, it extends the analysis based on its initial conclusions. AIRPLAN is a rule-based system implemented in OPS7. It interfaces with the ship's officers through ZOG, a rapid-response, large-network, menu-selection system for human-machine communication. The system was developed at Carnegie-Mellon University and tested aboard the Carl Vinson. It reached the stage of a field prototype. [MAS83]

AMUID assists military commanders with land battlefield analysis. The system integrates information from intelligence reports, infrared and visual imaging sensors, and MTI (moving target indicator) radar. AMUID classifies targets and organizes them into higher-level units (e.g., battalions and regiments). It provides real-time analysis and situation updating as data arrive continuously over time. AMUID's expertise is encoded as rules which operate on domain knowledge (e.g., types of military equipment, deployment patterns for military units, and tactics) maintained in a semantic net. Certainty factors are employed to handle the uncertainty typically involved in the analysis of sensor data. The control structure is event driven, where events are new sensor reports, major decisions made by the system itself, or user queries. AMUID was developed at Advanced Information & Decision Systems and reached the stage of a demonstration prototype. (Automated Multisensor Unit Identification system) [DRA83]

ANALYST assists field commanders with battlefield situation assessment. The system generates displays of enemy combat unit deployment and does so in real time from multisource sensor returns. ANALYST aggregates information from these multiple sensor sources to 1) locate and classify enemy battlefield units by echelon, general function, and relative location, and 2) detect force movement. The system contains expertise obtained from intelligence ana-

lyts, including how to interpret and integrate sensor data. ANA-
LYST is implemented in FRANZ LISP and represents knowledge
using a combination of frames and rules. It was developed at the
Mitre Corporation and reached the stage of a demonstration prototype. [BON83a, BON84]

ASTA helps an analyst identify the type of radar that generated an inter-
cepted signal. The system analyzes the radar signal in light of general knowledge it has about the physics of radar and specific knowledge it has about particular types of radar systems. ASTA also helps
the analyst by providing access to relevant data bases and explanations for the conclusions it reaches. Knowledge in ASTA is represented in the form of rules. The system was developed by Advanced
Information & Decision Systems and reached the stage of a research
prototype. (Assistant for Science and Technology Analysis) [WIL84]

ATR detects and classifies military targets from sensor images. The system integrates low-level image processing and high-level, domain-
specific rules for object detection and identification. ATR first ex-
ploits contextual information (e.g., temporal, structural) to form
hypotheses about the existence of certain objects in the image. It
then seeks the evidence required to satisfy those hypotheses. Further hypotheses are generated by model-driven processing which
redirects low-level image processing algorithms in order to gain new
information from the image. The system uses frames and certainty
factors together with an object-oriented control scheme to represent
and access its knowledge. ATR is implemented in ZETALISP. It was
developed at Hughes Aircraft Company and reached the stage of a
demonstration prototype. (Automatic Target Recognizer) [KIM84]

BATTLE provides weapon allocation recommendations to military commanders in combat situations. The system improves the performance of the U.S. Marine Corps' Marine Integrated Fire and Air
Support System by providing timely recommendations for the allocation of a set of weapons to a set of targets. To address the critical
time aspect of real battle situations, the system uses a best-first strategy during consultations, considering first those propositions (battle
conditions) likely to have the most cost-effective influence on
higher-level propositions. BATTLE represents knowledge as rules
with associated PROSPECTOR-like certainty values. BATTLE was
developed at the Naval Research Laboratory in Washington D.C.
and reached the stage of a demonstration prototype. [SLA83b]

DART helps Command, Control and Communications (C3) countermeasures analysts process intelligence information. The system
gives advice to the analyst on the identification of critical enemy C3
network nodes and assists in the processing of messages related to

battle situations. DART is implemented in PASCAL and C for the VAX 11/780 computer system. It was developed by Par Technology Corporation and reached the stage of a research prototype. (Duplex Army Radio/radar Targeting aid) [FIG83, BAR83a]

EPES assists F-16 pilots in handling in-flight emergency procedures, such as loss of canopy. The system uses knowledge about aircraft features (e.g., canopy, pilot) and mission goals (e.g., maintain the current state of the aircraft) to decide how to respond to emergencies. EPES' primary goal is to maintain the aircraft at a constant airspeed, heading, and altitude. When emergencies arise, violating this goal, the system first warns the pilot and then takes corrective action, sending requests for changes to a robot-pilot. Knowledge in EPES is represented in both rule-based and semantic net form. The rules decide when to set new goals and are linked via semantic net to all parts and goals that affect their activation. EPES is implemented in ZETALISP. The system was developed at Texas Instruments and reached the stage of a demonstration prototype. (Emergency Procedures Expert System) [ANC84]

EXPERT NAVIGATOR monitors navigation sensors on advanced tactical aircraft. The system manages and reconfigures the onboard navigation sensors (e.g., radio aids, inertial navigation systems, and digital terrain aids), monitors their ability to support the aircraft's primary mission, and suggests viable alternatives when the primary mission is threatened. Knowledge in the system is in the form of rules operating within a blackboard architecture. EXPERT NAVIGATOR is implemented in LISP for the Symbolics 3600 workstation. It was developed at the Analytic Sciences Corporation and reached the stage of a demonstration prototype. [PIS84]

HANNIBAL performs situation assessment in the area of communications intelligence. It identifies enemy organizational units and their communication order of battle by interpreting data from sensors that monitor radio communications. These data include information about the location and signal characteristics (e.g., frequency, modulation, channel class, etc.) of the detected communications. Knowledge in HANNIBAL is represented within a blackboard architecture using multiple specialists or knowledge sources. The system is implemented in AGE. It was developed by ESL and reached the stage of a research prototype. [BRO82a]

HASP: See SIAP.

I&W assists an intelligence analyst in predicting where and when an armed conflict will next occur. The system analyzes incoming intelligence reports, e.g., reports of troop location, activity and movements, using knowledge about common indicators of troop activity. Knowledge is represented within a blackboard architecture that uses both frames and forward chaining rules to organize the expertise. The system is implemented in INTERLISP-D for the Xerox 1100 series workstations. It was developed through a joint effort by ESL and Stanford University and reached the stage of a demonstration prototype. (Indications & Warning) [KIR83]

KNOBS helps a controller at a tactical air command and control center perform mission planning. The system uses knowledge about targets, resources, and planned missions to check the consistency of plan components, to rank possible plans, and to help generate new plans. Knowledge in KNOBS is in the form of frames and backward chaining rules, and it uses a natural language subsystem for data base queries and updates. In the KNOBS literature, early articles refer to KNOBS as the expert system for mission planning. Later articles use the term *KNOBS* to mean the KNOBS architecture rather than a specific expert system. The system is implemented in FRL and ZETALISP. It was developed by the MITRE Corporation and reached the stage of a research prototype. (KNOwledge Based System) [ENG79a, ENG83, SCA83, KAS83a, PAZ83a]

MES helps aircraft technicians diagnose aircraft problems. It is designed to overcome the shortage of technically qualified maintenance personnel by allowing less-qualified technicians to accurately assess problems with aircraft. MES contains knowledge taken from aircraft maintenance manuals, such as component weight and dimensions, ground operations, and troubleshooting and repair procedures. This knowledge is augmented by experiential knowledge from expert technicians. MES is a forward chaining, rule-based system. It is implemented in LISP on an Apple II+ microcomputer. It was developed at the Air Force Institute of Technology and reached the stage of a demonstration prototype. (Maintenance Expert System) [FER83]

OCEAN SURVEILLANCE helps naval personnel aboard a surveillance ship determine a remotely sensed vessel's destination and mission. The system uses information about the vessel's correlated tracks, history, location, and status to determine its likely destination, arrival time, and probable mission. The knowledge contained in the system includes: deployment histories of particular vessel types, ongoing US/allied naval activities in the area of interest, and the surveillance ship's own activities and movement. The system uses a rule-based knowledge representation scheme employing forward chaining and certainty factors, and it provides a simple explanation facility. OCEAN SURVEILLANCE is implemented in OPS5 and

FRANZ LISP. The system was developed at Science Applications, Inc. and reached the stage of a research prototype. [GRO84]

RTC classifies ships by interpreting radar images. The system extracts features from the images and matches them against the high-level models of the possible ship classes stored in the system's knowledge base. RTC stores only one three-dimensional (3-D) model for each ship, matching image features to the model by mapping the 3-D model into the 2-D view appropriate for the given features. RTC is a rule-based system implemented in FRANZ LISP. It was developed by Advanced Information & Decision Systems and reached the stage of a research prototype. (Radar Target Classification system) [MCC83a]

RUBRIC helps a user to access unformatted textual data bases. The system performs conceptual retrieval; e.g., when the user names a single topic, RUBRIC automatically retrieves all documents containing text related to that topic. In RUBRIC, the relationships between topics, subtopics, and low-level word phrases are defined in rule form. The rules also define alternative terms, phrases, and spellings for the same topic or concept. The user can formulate a query in the form of a rule that specifies retrieval criteria, e.g., a heuristic weight that specifies how strongly the rule's pattern indicates the presence of the rule's topic. During retrieval, RUBRIC presents the user with documents that lie in a cluster containing at least one document with a weight above a user-provided threshold. This prevents an arbitrary threshold from splitting closely ranked documents. RUBRIC is implemented in FRANZ LISP. It was developed at Advanced Information & Decision Systems and reached the stage of a research prototype. (RUle-Based Retrieval of Information by Computer) [MCC83a, MCC83b]

SCENARIO-AGENT assists war gamers by providing a model of nonsuperpower behavior in strategic conflict situations. SCENARIO-AGENT provides the user and the war gaming system with information on whether the nonsuperpowers will grant access rights to the superpowers (including the use of military bases) and whether they will contribute forces to the main conflict. This knowledge is encoded as rules describing the behavior of the nonsuperpowers in various conflict situations. The system uses a forward chaining, rule-based, and procedure-oriented inference mechanism. SCENARIO-AGENT is implemented in ROSIE. It was developed at the Rand Corporation and reached the stage of a demonstration prototype. [SCH82]

SIAP detects and identifies various types of ocean vessels using digitized acoustic data from hydrophone arrays. These data take the form of sonogram displays, which are analog histories of the spectrum of received sound energy. The system uses knowledge about the sound signature traits of different ship classes to perform the interpretation. SIAP attempts to identify the vessels and to organize them into higher-level units, such as fleets. It provides real-time analysis and situation updating for continuously arriving data. Knowledge is represented as rules within a blackboard architecture using a hierarchically organized control scheme. HASP (also known as SU/X) was an initial investigation phase and formed the foundation for SIAP. The system is implemented in INTERLISP and was developed through a joint effort by Stanford University and Systems Control Technology. It reached the stage of a research prototype. (Surveillance Integration Automation Project) [NII82, DRA83, HAY83c]

SPAM interprets high resolution airport scenes where the image segmentation has been performed in advance. The system labels individual regions in the image (e.g., runways and hangars) and interprets the collection of those regions as major functional areas of an airport model. SPAM has three major system components: 1) an image/map data base (called MAPS) that stores facts about feature existence and location, 2) a set of image processing tools that include an interactive segmentation system and a linear feature extraction and 3-D junction analysis program, and 3) a rule-based inference system that guides scene interpretation by providing the image processing system with the best next task to perform. Knowledge of spatial constraints comes from a body of literature on airport planning. SPAM is implemented in OPS5. It was developed at Carnegie-Mellon University and reached the stage of a research prototype. (System for Photo interpretation of Airports using MAPS) [MCK84]

SWIRL aids military strategists by providing interactive simulations of air battles and an environment in which to develop and to debug military strategies and tactics. The system embodies an air penetration simulation of offensive forces attacking a defensive area. Here penetrators enter an airspace with a preplanned route and bombing mission, and the defensive forces must eliminate them before they reach their targets. As SWIRL executes, it displays animated simulations on a color graphics output device. SWIRL's expertise consists of simulation analysis abilities and offensive and defensive battle strategies and tactics. The system uses an object-oriented knowledge representation scheme, where objects, such as offensive penetrators, defensive radars, and SAMs, communicate via the transmission of messages. SWIRL is implemented in ROSS. It was developed at the Rand Corporation and reached the stage of a research prototype. (Simulating Warfare In the ROSS Language) [KLA82]

TATR helps an air force tactical air targeteer develop a plan for attacking enemy airfields. The system, under the interactive guidance of the targeteer, produces a preferential ordering of enemy airfields, determines the target elements to attack on those airfields, and identifies the weapons systems that would be most effective against those target elements. The system projects the effects of implementing the plan over a period of days so the targeteer can revise the plan if it fails to meet the attack objectives. TATR is a forward chaining, rule-based system implemented in ROSIE. It was developed at the Rand Corporation and reached the stage of a research prototype. (Tactical Air Target Recommender) [CAL84]

TWIRL aids military tacticians by providing interactive simulations of ground combat engagements between two opposing military forces and an environment in which to develop and debug military tactics. The system uses a hasty river-crossing simulation as a test for exploring issues in command, control, communications countermeasures, electronic warfare, and electronic combat. Its expertise includes simulation control and offensive and defensive battle tactics. TWIRL uses an object-oriented knowledge representation scheme with rules defining the behaviors of objects. The system includes a color graphics facility that produces an animated display of the simulation. TWIRL is implemented in ROSS. It was developed at the Rand Corporation and reached the stage of a research prototype. (Tactical Warfare In the ROSS Language) [KLA84]

Physics

GAMMA helps nuclear physicists identify the composition of unknown substances by interpreting gamma-ray activation spectra produced when the substance is bombarded with neutrons. The system performs the identification by using knowledge about characteristic radiation energies and intensities emitted by different substances. Knowledge in the system is processed via the generate-and-test paradigm. The system was developed by Schlumberger-Doll Research and reached the stage of a research prototype. [BAR79]

MECHO solves problems in mechanics, such as pulley systems, moment-of-inertia, and distance-rate-time problems. Given a problem in the form of English text, MECHO builds a knowledge base of facts, inferences, and default values derived from the problem statement. It uses a means-end search strategy base similar to that used by GPS (General Problem Solver) to produce sets of simultaneous equations and inequalities. It passes them to an algebra module which solves them and produces a final answer. MECHO uses a rule-based formalism for representing its knowledge. The system is implemented in PROLOG. MECHO was developed at the University of Edinburgh and reached the stage of a research prototype. [BUN79, LUG81]

Process Control

FALCON identifies probable causes of process disturbances in a chemical process plant by interpreting data consisting of numerical values from gauges and the status of alarms and switches. The system interprets the data by using knowledge of the effects induced by a fault in a given component and how disturbances in the input of a component will lead to disturbances in the output. Knowledge is represented in two ways—as a set of rules controlled by forward chaining and as a causal model in network form. The system is implemented in LISP and was developed at the University of Delaware. It reached the stage of a demonstration prototype. [CHE84]

PDS diagnoses malfunctions in machine processes by interpreting information from sensors attached to the process. The system uses diagnosis methods that relate sensor readings to component malfunctions. PDS uses a forward chaining, rule-based representation scheme implemented in SRL, a frame-based knowledge engineering language. The result is an inference net representation paradigm similar to that found in PROSPECTOR. The system was developed at Carnegie-Mellon University in cooperation with Westinghouse Electric Corporation. This system is actually closer to an architecture or tool for building expert sensor-based diagnosis systems than an expert system. (Portable Diagnostic System) [FOX83a]

Space Technology

ECESIS provides autonomous control of an environmental control/life support subsystem (EC/LSS) for use aboard a manned space station. The system decides how to shift the modes of the various EC/LSS subsystems during the transition from shadow to sun. It also monitors the EC/LSS, triggering actions in response to various events.

Although ECESIS is intended to operate autonomously, it has a simple explanation capability to facilitate system demonstration. ECESIS has a hybrid architecture involving both rule-based and semantic net formalisms, and it uses the Bayesian scoring model developed for PROSPECTOR to handle uncertainty. The system is implemented in YAPS. It was developed at Boeing Aerospace Company and reached the stage of a demonstration prototype. (Environmental Control Expert System In Space) [DIC84]

FAITH is a general-purpose diagnostician whose initial application is the troubleshooting of spacecraft by monitoring the telemetry stream transmitted to earth. This stream contains test measurements from a wide variety of subsystems. FAITH uses its knowledge of the system under scrutiny to evaluate the data and to discover the most likely causes of the symptoms. FAITH represents declarative knowledge as frames which are expanded into logical assertions as required. Procedural knowledge is represented as production rules. FAITH's reasoning engine employs predicate logic and alternates between backward and forward chaining. FAITH was developed at the Jet Propulsion Laboratory and reached the stage of a demonstration prototype. [FRI83, FRI84]

KNEECAP aids in the planning of crew activity on board the space shuttle orbiter. As the user plans the entire flight mission, the system checks for inconsistencies in the schedule. KNEECAP uses knowledge about orbiter vehicles, launch and landing sites, astronauts' skill qualifications, current payloads, shuttle activities, and crew roles to make its decisions. This knowledge is encoded as frames using a knowledge representation method similar to the FRL language. KNEECAP is implemented in INTERLISP within a framework taken from the KNOBS expert system. It was developed by the MITRE Corporation and reached the stage of a demonstration prototype. [SCA84a]

LES monitors the loading of liquid oxygen (LOX) for the space shuttle orbiter at Kennedy Space Center. The input to LES is a sequence of time-tagged measurements from the launch processing system (LPS), a real-time process controller that controls liquid oxygen loading. LES monitors measurements, such as temperature, pressure, flow rate, and valve position, and determines whether or not the LPS is receiving valid sensor data. When LES detects an anomaly, it notifies monitoring personnel and activates troubleshooting algorithms. If LES cannot identify the problem, it offers a list of suspect components and instructions for performing tests to isolate the faulty component. LES contains knowledge about the LOX loading process, including information about components, measurement values, and the relations between components. The system encodes its knowledge as frames using a knowledge representation method similar to that used in the FRL language. LES is implemented in ZETALISP within a framework taken from the KNOBS expert system. It was developed by the Mitre Corporation in cooperation with Kennedy Space Center and reached the stage of a research prototype. (Liquid oxygen Expert System) [SCA84a, SCA84b]

NAVEX monitors radar station data that estimate the velocity and position of the space shuttle, looks for errors, and warns the mission control center console operators when errors are detected or predicted. When it detects errors, the system recommends actions to take, such as excluding data from a particular radar station or restarting the analysis of the current data. NAVEX is rule-based and frame-oriented and runs in real time, making recommendations based on actual radar data. It is implemented in ART. NAVEX was developed by Inference Corporation in cooperation with NASA at the Johnson Space Center. It has reached the stage of a research prototype. (NAVigation EXpert) [MAR84a, MAR84b]

RBMS uses a flight manifest to schedule the use of Johnson Space Center FCRs (flight control rooms) over a period of months. The system replaces the STAP computer program that uses a statistical approach to the problem. The input to RBMS is the flight manifest containing flight numbers, launch dates, type of flight, duration, whether it is a space laboratory mission, and other data. RBMS produces as output a schedule indicating the daily FCR usage (activities scheduled, number of hours required) and the average hours per day used by each FCR per month. The system is written in LISP and OPS5 and runs on the DEC VAX computers. RBMS was developed by Ford Aerospace for NASA and reached the stage of a demonstration prototype. (Rule-Based Modeling System) [MAR84c]

RPMS assists the user with general planning and scheduling tasks, such as defining a schedule and minimizing resources like time, manpower, and materials. The schedule is represented graphically as a network containing tasks with bars indicating their durations and arrows pointing to successor and predecessor tasks. The user can define formal constraints between tasks, such as Task A must occur before Task B by moving tasks (nodes) in the network. The system also contains rules that allow it to reconfigure the network itself, attempting to level out the use of resources. The system is implemented in ZETALISP and OPS5 and makes heavy use of the FLAVORS object-oriented features of ZETALISP. RPMS was developed by Ford Aerospace and is being applied to the space shuttle reconfiguration process for the Johnson Space Center. It is closer to a tool for expert system design than an expert system. (Resource Planning and Management System) [KIN83]

26

Bibliography of Expert Systems

This bibliography contains references to the expert systems described in Chapter 25.

Agriculture

References

[BOU83] Boulanger, A. G. The expert system PLANT/CD: A case study in applying the general purpose inference system ADVISE to predicting black cutworm damage in corn, M.S. thesis, Computer Science Dept., University of Illinois at Champaign-Urbana, July 1983. (PLANT/CD)

[MIC80a] Michalski, R. S. and Chilausky, R. L. Learning by being told and learning from examples: an experimental comparison of two methods of knowledge acquisition in the context of developing an expert system for soybean disease diagnosis. A Special Issue on Knowledge Acquisition and Induction, *Policy Analysis and Information Systems*, no. 2, 1980. (PLANT/DS)

[MIC80b] Michalski, R. S. and Chilausky, R. L. Knowledge acquisition by encoding expert rules versus computer induction from examples:

a case study involving soybean pathology. *International Journal of Man-Machine Studies,* vol. 12, pp. 63–87, 1980. (PLANT/DS)

[MIC82b] Michalski, R. S., Davis, J. H., Bisht, V. S., and Sinclair, J. B. PLANT/ds: an expert consulting system for the diagnosis of soybean diseases. *Proceedings of the Fifth European Conference on Artificial Intelligence,* Orsay, France, July 1982. (PLANT/DS)

[ROA85] Roach, J. W. and Virkar, R. S. POMME: A computer-based consultation system for apple orchard management using PRO-LOG. Technical Report, Department of Computer Science and Applications, Virginia Polytechnic Institute and State University, 1985. (POMME)

[UHR82] Uhrik, C. T. PLANT/ds revisited: non-homogeneous evaluation schema in expert systems. *Proceedings AAAI-82,* pp. 217–220, 1982. (PLANT/DS)

Chemistry

References

[ALT84a] Alty, J. L. and Coombs, M. J. Reducing large search spaces through factoring—heuristic DENDRAL and Meta-DENDRAL. *Expert Systems, Concepts and Examples.* Manchester, England: NCC Publications, 1984. (DENDRAL) (META-DENDRAL)

[ALT84d] Alty, J. L. and Coombs, M. J. Handling large search spaces through the use of abstraction -R1 and MOLGEN. *Expert Systems, Concepts and Examples.* Manchester, England: NCC Publications, 1984. (R1) (MOLGEN)

[BUC78] Buchanan, B. G. and Feigenbaum, E. A. DENDRAL and Meta-DENDRAL: their applications dimension. *Artificial Intelligence,* vol. 11, 1978. (DENDRAL) (META-DENTRAL) (CONGEN)

[CAR79] Carhart, Raymond E. CONGEN: An expert system aiding the structural chemist. In D. Michie (ed.), *Expert Systems in the Micro-Electronic Age.* Edinburgh: Edinburgh University Press, 1979. (CONGEN)

[CLA81b] Clayton, J., Friedland, P., Kedes, L., and Brutlag, D. SEQ-sequence analysis system. Report HPP-81-3, Computer Science Dept., Stanford University and Departments of Medicine and Biochemistry, Stanford University School of Medicine, Stanford, Calif., 1981. (SEQ)

[COR69] Corey, E. J. and Wipke, W. T. Computer assisted design of complex organic synthesis. *Science,* vol. 166, pp. 178–192, 1969. (OCSS)

[ENG79b] Engelmore, R. and Allan, T. Structure and function of the crysalis system. *Proceedings IJCAI-79,* 1979. (CRYSALIS)

[GEL77] Gelernter, H. L., Sanders, A. F., Larsen, D. L., Agarwal, K. K., Boivie, R. H., Spritzer, G. A., and Searleman, J. E. Empirical explorations of SYNCHEM. *Science,* vol. 197, no. 4308, pp. 1041–1049, 1977. (SYNCHEM) (SYNCHEM2)

[GEL84] Gelernter, H., Miller, G. A., Larsen, D. L., and Berndt, D. J. Realization of a large expert problem-solving system, SYNCHEM2: a case study. *Proceedings of the First Conference on Artificial Intelligence Applications,* IEEE Computer Society, December 1984. (SYNCHEM2)

[GRA84] Gray, Neil A. B. Applications of artificial intelligence for organic chemistry: Analysis of C-13 spectra. *Artificial Intelligence,* vol. 22, 1984. (C-13)

[INT84e] Intellicorp. Nucleic acid sequence analysis. Intellicorp brochure, 1984. (SEQ)

[IWA82a] Iwasaki, Y. and Friedland, P. SPEX: a second-generation experiment design system. *Proceedings AAAI-82,* 1982. (SPEX)

[IWA82b] Iwasaki, Yumi. SPEX: skeletal planner for experiments. Report HPP-82-22, Computer Science Dept., Stanford University, Stanford, Calif. September 1982. (SPEX)

[LIN80b] Lindsay, Robert K., Buchanan, B. G., Feigenbaum, E. A., and Lederberg, J. Applications of artificial intelligence for organic chemistry. *The DENDRAL Project,* McGraw-Hill, 1980. (DENDRAL) (META-DENDRAL)

[STE78] Stefik, M. Inferring DNA structures from segmentation data. *Artificial Intelligence,* vol. 11, pp. 85–114, 1978. (GA1)

[STE81c] Stefik, M. J. Planning with constraints, MOLGEN: Part 1. *Artificial Intelligence,* vol. 16, 1981. (MOLGEN)

[STE81d] Stefik, M. J. Planning and meta-planning, MOLGEN: Part 2. *Artificial Intelligence,* vol. 16, 1981. (MOLGEN)

[TER83] Terry, Allan, The CRYSALIS project: hierarchical control of production systems. Memo HPP-83-19, Computer Science Dept., Stanford University, Stanford, Calif., May 1983. (CRYSALIS)

[WIP78] Wipke, W. Todd, Ouchi, Glen I., and Krishnan, S. Simulation and evaluation of chemical synthesis—SECS: an application of artificial intelligence techniques. *Artificial Intelligence,* vol. 11, 1978. (SECS)

[WON83] Wong, C. M., Crawford, R. W., Kunz, J. C., and Kehler, T. P.

Application of artificial intelligence to triple quadrupole mass spectrometry (TQMS). Proceedings of the Nuclear Science Symposium, Institute of Electrical and Electronics Engineers, San Francisco, Calif., 1983. (TQMSTUNE)

[WON84] Wong, C. M. and Lanning, S. Artificial intelligence in chemical analysis. *Energy and Technology Review,* Lawrence Livermore National Laboratory, February 1984. (TQMSTUNE)

Additional Reading

[BAC84a] Bach, R., Iwasaki, Y., and Friedland, P. Intelligent computational assistance for experiment design. Report HPP 84-33, Computer Science Dept., Stanford University, Stanford, Calif., January 1984.

[BAN82] Banares-Alcantara, R. Development of a Consultant for Physical Property Predictions. Master's thesis, Chemical Engineering Dept., Carnegie-Mellon University, May 1982.

[CHI79] Chisholm, I. H. and Sleeman, D. H. An aide for theory formation. In D. Michie (ed.), *Expert Systems in the Micro-Electronic Age.* Edinburgh: Edinburgh University Press, 1979.

[GOT84] Gottinger, H. W. HAZARD: an expert system for screening environmental chemicals on carcinogenicity. *Expert Systems,* vol. 1, no. 2, 1984.

[WIP79] Wipke, W. T., Dyott, T. M., Still, C., and Friedland, P. ALCHEM: a language for describing chemical reactions. Report, Chemistry Department, University of California, Santa Cruz, Calif., 1979.

Computer Systems

References

[ADD80] Addis, T. R. Expert systems: an evolution in information retrieval. *International Computers Limited (ICL) Technical Journal,* May 1980. (CRIB)

[BAC84] Bachant, J. and McDermott, J. R1 revisited: four years in the trenches. *AI Magazine,* vol. 5, no. 3, Fall 1984. (XCON/R1)

[BEN81] Bennett, J. S. and Hollander, C. R. DART: an expert system for computer fault diagnosis. *Proceedings IJCAI-81,* pp. 843–845, 1981. (DART/EMYCIN)

[GEN82] Genesereth, M. R. Diagnosis using hierarchical design models. Proceedings AAAI-82, pp. 278–283, 1982. (DART/MRS)

[GEN83c] Genesereth, M. R. The DART project. *The AI Magazine*, p. 85, Fall 1983. (DART/MRS)

[GEN84a] Genesereth, M. R. The use of design descriptions in automated diagnosis. *Artificial Intelligence*, vol. 24, pp. 411–436, 1984. (DART)

[GEN84d] Genesereth, M. R. The use of design descriptions in automated diagnosis. Memo HPP-81-20, Computer Science Dept., Stanford University, Stanford, Calif., January 1984. (DART/MRS)

[GRC83] GRC, TIMM/Tuner. General Research Corporation, P.O. Box 6770, Santa Barbara, CA 93160, 1983. (TIMM/TUNER)

[GRI84] Griesmer, J. H., Hong, S. J., Karnaugh, M., Kastner, J. K., Schor, M. I., Ennis, R. L., Klein, D. A., Milliken, K. R., and Van Woerkom, H. M. YES/MVS: A continuous real time expert system. *Proceedings AAAI-84*, 1984. (YES/MVS)

[HAR84c] Hartley, R. T. CRIB: computer fault-finding through knowledge engineering. *Computer*, vol. 17, no. 3, March 1984. (CRIB)

[JOY83] Joyce, R. Reasoning about time-dependent behavior in a system for diagnosing digital hardware faults. Memo HPP-83-37, Computer Science Dept., Stanford University, August 1983. (DART/MRS)

[KOR84a] Kornell, Jim. A VAX tuning expert built using automated knowledge acquisition. *Proceedings of the First Conference on Artificial Intelligence Applications*, IEEE Computer Society, December 1984. (TIMM/Tuner)

[MCD80b] McDermott, J. R1: an expert in the computer systems domain. Proceedings AAAI-80, 1980. (XCON/R1)

[MCD81] McDermott, J. R1's formative years. *AI Magazine*, vol. 2, no. 2, 1981. (XCON/R1)

[MCD81a] McDermott, J. Domain Knowledge and the design process. *ACM/IEEE 13th Design Automation Conference Proceedings*, 1981, (R1) (XSEL)

[MCD81b] McDermott, J. and Steele, B. Extending a knowledge-based system to deal with ad hoc constraints. *Proceedings IJCAI-81*, pp. 824–828, 1981. (XSEL)

[MCD82] McDermott, J. RI: a rule-based configurer of computer systems. *Artificial Intelligence*, vol. 19, no. 1, September 1982. (XCON/R1)

[MCD82a] McDermott, John. Domain knowledge and the design process. *Design Studies*, vol. 3, no. 1, January 1982. (XCON) (XSEL)

[MCD82b] McDermott, J. XSEL: a computer sales person's assistant. In J. E. Hayes, D. Michie, and Y. H. Pao (eds.) *Machine Intelligence, 10,* Chichester, England: Horwood, pp. 325–337, 1982. (XSEL)

[MCD84] McDermott, J. Building expert systems. In W. Reitman (ed.) *Artificial Intelligence Applications for Business,* Norwood, N.J.: Ablex, 1984. (XCON) (PTRANS) (XSEL)

[OCO84] O'Connor, D. E. Using expert systems to manage change and complexity in manufacturing. In W. Reitman (ed.) *Artificial Intelligence Applications for Business,* Norwood, N.J.: Ablex, 1984. (XCON) (IMACS) (ISA)

[ORC84] Orciuch, E. and Frost, J. ISA: an intelligent scheduling assistant. *Proceedings of the First Conference on Artificial Intelligence Applications,* IEEE Computer Society, December 1984. (ISA)

[POL85] Polit, Stephen. R1 and beyond: AI technology transfer at DEC. *The AI Magazine,* Winter 1985. (XCON)

[ROS84] Rosenbloom, P. S., Laird, J. E., McDermott, J., Newell, A., and Orciuch, E. R1-SOAR, an experiment in knowledge-intensive programming in a problem-solving architecture. *Proceedings of the IEEE Workshop on Principles of Knowledge-Based Systems,* IEEE Computer Society, IEEE Computer Society Press, 1109 Spring Street, Silver Spring, Md., 1984. (R1-SOAR)

[SCH84] Schor, M. I. Using declarative knowledge representation techniques: implementing truth maintenance in OPS5. *Proceedings of the First Conference on Artificial Intelligence Applications,* IEEE Computer Society, December 1984. (YES/MVS)

[SHI83] Shimizu, T. and Sakamura, K. MIXER: an expert system for microprogramming. Proceedings of the Sixteenth Annual Microprogramming Workshop, ACM, pp. 168–175, October 1983. (MIXER)

[SHU82] Shubin, H. and Ulrich, J. W. IDT: an intelligent diagnostic tool. *Proceedings AAAI-82,* pp. 290–295, 1982. (IDT)

Additional Reading

[GRI82b] Grinberg, M. R. SHAM—a hierarchical simulation environment. HPP Report, Computer Science Dept., Stanford University, Stanford, Calif., 1982.

[KEE84] Keen, M. J. R. DRAGON: the development of an expert sizing system. *Database and Network Journal,* vol. 14, no. 1, Great Britain, 1984.

Electronics

References

[ALE84a] Alexander, J. H. and Freiling M. J. Building an expert system in SMALLTALK-80. Technical Report No. CR-85-06, Artificial Intelligence Dept., Computer Research Laboratory, Tektronix, Inc., November 1984. (FG502-TASP)

[ALE84b] Alexander, J. H. and Freiling M. J. Troubleshooting with the help of an expert system. Technical Report No. CR-85-05, Artificial Intelligence Dept., Computer Research Laboratory, Tektronix, Inc., August 1984. (FG502-TASP)

[BRO75a] Brown, J. S. and Bobrow, R. J. Applications of artificial intelligence techniques in maintenance training. New Concepts in Maintenance Trainers and Performance Aids, Report NAVTRAEQUIP-CEN IH-255, October 1975. (SOPHIE)

[BRO75b] Brown, J. S. and Burton, R. R. Multiple representations of knowledge for tutorial reasoning. In D. Bobrow and A. Collins (eds.), *Representation and Understanding: Studies in Cognitive Science*, Academic Press, pp. 311–349, 1975. (SOPHIE)

[BRO75c] Brown, J. S., Burton, R. R., and Bell, A. G. SOPHIE: a step toward creating a reactive learning environment. *International Journal of Man-Machine Studies*, vol. 7, pp. 675–696, 1975. (SOPHIE)

[BRO82b] Brown, J. S., Burton, R. R., and DeKleer, J. Pedagogical, natural language and knowledge engineering techniques in SOPHIE I, II and III. In D. Sleeman and J. S. Brown (eds.) *Intelligent Tutoring Systems*, New York: Academic Press, pp. 227–282, 1982. (SOPHIE)

[BRO83b] Brown, H., Tong, C., and Foyster, G. PALLADIO: an exploratory environment for circuit design. *IEEE Computer*, pp. 41–55, December 1983. (PALLADIO)

[CAN83] Cantone, R. R., Pipitone, F. J., Lander, W. B., and Marrone, M. P. Model-based probabilistic reasoning for electronics troubleshooting. *Proceedings IJCAI-83*, Karlsruhe, West Germany, August 1983. (IN-ATE)

[CUL82] Cullingford, R. E., Krueger, M. W., Selfridge, M., and Bienkowski, M. A. Automated explanations as a component of a computer-aided design system. *IEEE Transactions on Systems, Man, and Cybernetics*, vol. SMC-12, no. 2, pp. 168–181, April 1982. (CAD-HELP)

[DEK80] DeKleer, J. and Sussman, G. J. Propagation of constraints applied to circuit synthesis. *Circuit Theory and Applications,* vol. 8, John Wiley & Sons, Ltd., pp. 127–144, 1980. (SYN)

[DIN80] Dincbas, M. A knowledge-based expert system for automatic analysis and synthesis in CAD. *Information Processing 80, IFIPS Proceedings,* pp. 705–710, 1980. (PEACE)

[FIN84] Finin, Tim, McAdams, J., and Kleinosky, P. FOREST: an expert system for automatic test equipment. *Proceedings of the First Conference on Artificial Intelligence Applications,* IEEE Computer Society, December 1984. (FOREST)

[FOY84] Foyster, G. A knowledge-based approach to transistor sizing. Report HPP-84-3, Computer Science Dept., Stanford University, March 1984. (TRANSISTOR SIZING SYSTEM)

[GRI80] Grinberg, Milton R. A knowledge based design system for digital electronics. *Proceedings AAAI-80,* pp. 283–285, 1980. (SADD)

[GUP84] Gupta, N. K. and Seviora, R. E. An expert system approach to real time system debugging. *Proceedings of the First Conference on Artificial Intelligence Applications,* IEEE Computer Society, December 1984. (MESSAGE TRACE ANALYZER)

[HOR83] Horstmann, P. W. Design for testability using logic programming. *Proceedings of the 1983 International Test Conference,* IEEE Computer Society Press, Silver Spring, Md., 1983. (DFT)

[KEL82] Kelly, V. E. and Steinberg, L. I. The CRITTER system: analyzing digital circuits by propagating behaviors and specifications. *Proceedings AAAI-82,* pp. 284–289, 1982. (CRITTER)

[KEL84] Kelly, Van E. The CRITTER system: automated critiquing of digital circuit designs. Report LCSR-TR-55, Laboratory for Computer Science Research, Rutgers University, May 1984. (CRITTER)

[KIM83] Kim, J. and McDermott, J. TALIB: an IC layout design assistant. *Proceedings AAAI-83,* 1983. (TALIB)

[KOW83] Kowalski, Ted and Thomas, D. The VLSI design automation assistant: prototype system. *Proceedings of the Twentieth Design Automation Conference,* ACM and IEEE, June 1983. (DAA)

[KOW84] Kowalski, T. J. and Thomas, D. E. The VLSI design automation assistant: an IBM system/370 design. *IEEE Design & Test,* vol. 1, no. 1, February 1984. (DAA)

[LAF82] Lafue, G. M. E. and Mitchell, T. M. Data base management systems and expert systems for CAD. Technical Report LCSR-TR-28, Laboratory for Computer Science Research, Rutgers University, New Brunswick, N.J., May 1982. (REDESIGN)

[LAF84b] Laffey, T. J., Perkins, W. A., and Firschein, O. LES: a model-based expert system for electronic maintenance. *Proceedings of the Joint Services Workshop on AI in maintenance*, October 4–6, 1984, pp. 1-17. (BDS) (LES)

[LEN82a] Lenat, D. B. HEURETICS: theoretical and experimental study of heuristic rules. *Proceedings AAAI-82*, pp. 159–163, 1982. (EURISKO)

[LEN82b] Lenat, D., Sutherland, W., and Gibbons, J. Heuristic search for new micro-circuit structures: an application of artificial intelligence. *AI Magazine*, vol. 3, no. 3, pp. 17–33, Summer 1982. (EURISKO)

[LEN83a] Lenat, D. B. EURISKO: a program that learns new heuristics and domain concepts. *Artificial Intelligence*, vol. 21, pp. 61–98, 1983. (EURISKO)

[MIT83] Mitchell, T. M., Steinberg, L. I., Kedar-Cabelli, S., Kelly, V. E., Shulman, J., and Weinrich, T. An intelligent aid for circuit redesign. *Proceedings AAAI-83*, pp. 274–278, 1983. (REDESIGN]

[SHR85] Goyal, S. K., Prerau, D. S., Lemmon, A. V., Gunderson, A. S., and Geinke, R. E. COMPASS: An expert system for telephone cable maintenance. Report, Computer Science Laboratory, GTE Laboratories, Inc., Waltham, Mass., 1985. (COMPASS)

[STA79] Stallman, R. M. and Sussman, G. J. Problem solving about electrical circuits. In P. Winston and R. Brown (eds.) *Artificial Intelligence: An MIT Perspective, vol. 1*, MIT Press, pp. 30–91, 1979. (EL)

[STE82a] Stefik, M., Bobrow, D., Bell, A., Brown, H., Conway, L, and Tong, C. The partitioning of concerns in digital system design. Proceedings of the Conference on Advanced Research in VLSI, MIT, 1982. (PALLADIO)

[STE82b] Stefik, M. J. and Conway, L. Towards the principled engineering of knowledge. *The AI Magazine*, pp. 4–16, Summer 1982. (PALLADIO)

[STE83e] Stefik, M. J. and de Kleer, J. Prospects for expert systems in CAD. *Computer Design*, pp. 65–76, April 21, 1983. (EURISKO)

[SUS75] Sussman, G. J. and Stallman, R. M. Heuristic techniques in computer-aided circuit analysis. *IEEE Transactions on Circuits and Systems*, vol. CAS-22, no. 11, pp. 857–865, November 1975. (EL)

[TON83] Tong, C. A framework for circuit design. Report HPP-83-45, Computer Science Dept., Stanford University, Stanford, Calif., December 1983. (PALLADIO)

[VES83] Vesonder, Gregg, T., Stolfo, Salvatore J., Zielinski, John E., Miller, Frederick D., and Copp, David H. ACE: an expert system for telephone cable maintenance. *Proceedings IJCAI-83*, pp. 116–121, 1983. (ACE)

[WIL82] Williams, T. L. Isolating multiple faults in NDS, Technical Report 010, Smart Systems Technology, 7700 Leesburg Pike, Falls Church, Va., 1982. (NDS)

[WIL83b] Williams, T. L., Orgren, P. J., and Smith, C. L. Diagnosis of multiple faults in a nationwide communcations network. *Proceedings IJCAI-83*, pp. 179–181, 1983. (NDS)

[WRI84] Wright, J. R., Miller, F. D., Otto, G. U. E., Siegfried, E. M., Vesonder, G. T., and Zielinski, J. E. ACE: going from prototype to product with an expert system. *ACM Conference Proceedings*, October 1984. (ACE)

[YAN83] Yan, J., Foyster, G., and Brown, H. An expert system for assigning mask levels to interconnect in integrated circuits. Report HPP-83-39, Computer Science Dept., Stanford University, Stanford, Calif., July 1983. (PALLADIO)

Additional Reading

[ALE85] Alexander, J. H., Freiling, M. J., Messick, S. L., and Rehfuss, S. Efficient expert system development through domain-specific tools. Technical Report No. CR-85-11, Artificial Intelligence Dept., Computer Research Laboratory, Tektronix, Inc., February 1985.

[DAV83b] Davis, Randall. Reasoning from first principles in electronic troubleshooting. *International Journal of Man-Machine Studies*, vol. 19, 1983.

[KNA83b] Knapp, D., Granacki, J., and Parker, A. An expert synthesis system. *Proceedings of the ICCAD 1983 Conference*, September 1983.

[SCH84] Schindler, M. Artificial intelligence begins to pay off with expert systems for engineering. *Electronic Design*, vol. 32, no. 16, August 9, 1984.

[SIN82] Singh, N. SHAM: a hierarchical simulator for digital circuits. Computer Science Dept., Stanford University, Stanford, Calif., 1982.

[SUS80] Sussman, G. J., Holloway, J., and Knight, T. Computer aided evolutionary design for digital integrated systems. *Proceedings of the 1980 AISB Conference*, 1980.

Engineering

References

[BAN83] Banares-Alcantara, R., Westerberg, A. W., and Rychener, M. D. Development of an expert system for physical property predictions. Report, Design Research Center & Robotics Institute, Carnegie-Mellon University, Pittsburgh, Pa., 1983. (CONPHYDE)

[BEN78] Bennett, J., Creary, L., Engelmore, R., and Melosh, R. A knowledge-based consultant for structural analysis, Computer Science Dept., Stanford University, Stanford, Calif., September 1978. (SACON)

[BEN84] Bennett, James S. and Engelmore, Robert S. Experience using EMYCIN. In B. Buchanan & E. Shortliffe (eds.) *Rule-Based Expert Systems*, Reading, Mass.: Addison-Wesley, pp. 314–328, 1984. (SACON) (CLOT)

[BON83b] Bonissone, P. P. and Johnson, H. E. Expert system for diesel electric locomotive repair. *Knowledge-based Systems Report*, General Electric Co., Schenectady, N.Y., 1983. (DELTA)

[DEL84] DELTA/CATS-1. *The Artificial Intelligence Report*, vol. 1, no. 1, January 1984. (DELTA)

[HOL84] Hollan, J. D., Hutchins, E. L., and Weitzman, L. STEAMER: an interactive inspectable simulation-based training system. *The AI Magazine*, vol. 5, no. 2, 1984. (STEAMER)

[ISH81a] Ishizuka, M., Fu, K. S., and Yao, J. T. P. SPERIL I: computer based structural damage assessment system. Report CE-STR-81-36, School of Civil Engineering, Purdue University, 1981. (SPERIL-I)

[ISH81b] Ishizuka, M., Fu, K. S., and Yao, J. T. P. Inexact Inference for Rule-Based Damage Assessment of Existing Structures. *Seventh International Joint Conference on Artificial Intelligence*, Vancouver, August 1981.

[ISH81c] Ishizuka, M., Fu, K. S., and Yao, J. T. P. Inference Procedure with Uncertainty for Problem Reduction Method. Purdue University Structural Engineering Report, CE-STR-81-24, August 1981.

[MAR83] Marcus, Steven J. Computer systems applying expertise. *The New York Times*, August 29, 1983. (DELTA)

[NEL82] Nelson, W. R. REACTOR: an expert system for diagnosis and treatment of nuclear reactor accidents. *Proceedings AAAI-82*, pp. 296–301, 1982. (REACTOR)

[NEL84] Nelson, William R. Response trees and expert systems for nuclear reactor operations. Report NUREG/CR-3631, Idaho National Engineering Laboratory, EG&G Idaho, Inc., Idaho Falls, Idaho, February 1984. (DICON) (LPIS) (NPPC) (REACTOR)

[OGA84] Ogawa, H., Fu, K. S., and Yao, J. T. P. An expert system for damage assessment of existing structures. *Proceedings of the First Conference on Artificial Intelligence Applications*, IEEE Computer Society, December 1984. (SPERIL-II)

[OGA84a] Ogawa, H., Fu, K. S., and Yao, J. T. P. Knowledge representation, and inference control of SPERIL-II. *ACM Conference Proceedings,* November 1984. (SPERIL-II)

[SCA84a] Scarl, E. Applications of a non-rule knowledge-based system to NASA scheduling and monitoring problems. *IECEC Proceedings,* San Francisco, August 1984. (KNOBS) (KNEECAP) (LES)

[SCA84b] Scarl, E., Jamieson, J., and Delaune, C. Knowledge-based fault monitoring and diagnosis in space shuttle propellant loading. *Proceedings of the National Aeronautics and Electronics Conference,* Dayton, Ohio, 1984. (LES)

[UND82] Underwood, W. E. A CSA model-based nuclear power plant consultant. Proceedings AAAI-82, pp. 302–305. (NPPC)

[WIL83a] Williams, M. D., Hollan, J. D., and Stevens, A. L. Human reasoning about a simple physical system. In D. Genter and A. Stevens (eds.) *Mental Models,* Hillsdale, N.J.: Erlbaum, 1983, pp. 131–153. (STEAMER)

Additional Reading

[FEN83] Fenves, S., Bielak, J., Rehak, D., Rychener, M., Sriram, D., and Maher, M. L. An expert system for diagnosis and repair of an automated transportation system. Technical Report, Robotics Institute, Carnegie-Mellon University, January 1983.

[GRI82a] Grimes, L. E., Rychener, M. D., and Westerberg, A. W. The synthesis and evolution of networks of heat exchange that feature the minimum number of units. *Chemical Engineering Communications,* vol. 14, 1982.

[KNA83b] Knapp, D. and Parker, A. A data structure for VLSI synthesis and verification, Digital Integrated Systems Center. Report DISC-83-6, Electrical Engineering Systems Dept., University of Southern California, Los Angeles, Calif., 1983.

[LEH83b] Lehner, P. E. and Donnell, M. L. Maintainability design expert system. PAR Technology Corporation Report, Seneca Plaza, Rt. 5, New Hartford, NY 13413, 1983.

[SIM84] Simmons, M. K. Artificial intelligence for engineering design. *Computer Aided Engineering,* (GB) vol. 1, no. 3, 75–83, April 1984.

[SRI82] Sriram, D., Maher, M. L., Bielak, J., and Fenves, S. J. Expert systems for civil engineering—a survey. Technical Report R-82-137, Civil Engineering Dept., Carnegie-Mellon University, Pittsburgh, Pa., July 1982.

[SRI84] Sriram, D. A bibliography on knowledge-based expert systems in engineering. *SIGART Newsletter,* pp. 32–40, July 1984.

Geology

References

[ALT84e] Alty, J. L. and Coombs, M. J. The handling of uncertain evidence—MYCIN and PROSPECTOR. *Expert Systems, Concepts and Examples,* Manchester, M1 7ED, England: NCC Publications, 1984. (MYCIN) (PROSPECTOR)

[APT82] Apte, Chidanand. Expert knowledge management for multilevel modeling with an application to well-log analysis. Report LCSR-TR-41, Laboratory for Computer Science Research, Rutgers University, New Brunswick, N.J., December 1982. (ELAS)

[APT84a] Apte, C. V. and Weiss, S. M. A framework for expert control of interactive software systems. Report CBM-TR-144, Laboratory for Computer Science Research, Rutgers University, New Brunswick, N.J., October 1984. (ELAS)

[APT84b] Apte, C. V. and Weiss, S. M. A knowledge representation framework for expert control of interactive software systems. Report CBM-TR-143, Laboratory for Computer Science Research, Rutgers University, New Brunswick, N.J., October 1984. (ELAS)

[AUS84] Austin, H. Market trends in artificial intelligence. In W. Reitman (ed.) *Artificial Intelligence Applications for Business,* Norwood, N.J.: Ablex, 1984. (DIPMETER ADVISOR)

[BON83c] Bonnet, A. and Dahan, C. Oil-well data interpretation using expert system and Pattern Recognition Technique. *Proceedings IJCAI-83,* pp. 185–189, 1983. (LITHO)

[CAM82] Campbell, A. N., Hollister, V. F., Duda, R. O., and Hart, P. E. Recognition of a hidden mineral deposit by an artificial intelligence program. *Science,* vol. 217, pp. 927–929, September 3, 1982. (PROSPECTOR)

[DAV81] Davis, R., Austin, H., Carlbom, I., Frawley, B., Pruchnik, P., Sneiderman, R., and Gilreath, J. A. The dipmeter advisor: interpretation of geologic signals. *Proceedings IJCAI-81,* pp. 846–849, 1981. (DIPMETER ADVISOR)

[DUD84] Duda, R. O. and Reboh, R. AI and decision making: the PROSPECTOR experience. In W. Reitman (ed.) *Artificial Intelligence Applications for Business,* Norwood, N.J.: Ablex, 1984. (PROSPECTOR)

[ELF83] Elf-Aquitane and Teknowledge. The drilling advisor. Fundamentals of Knowledge Engineering, Teknowledge Report, 1983. (DRILLING ADVISOR)

[GAS81] Gaschnig, J. PROSPECTOR: an expert system for mineral exploration. In Machine Intelligence, Infotech State of the Art Report 9, no. 3, 1981. (PROSPECTOR)

[GAS81a] Gaschnig, J., Reboh, R., and Reiter, J. Development of a knowledge-based expert system for water resource problems. Report SRI 1619, AI Center, SRI International, Menlo Park, Calif., August 1981. (HYDRO)

[GAS82] Gaschnig, J. Application of the PROSPECTOR system to geological exploration problems. In J. E. Hayes, D. Michie, and Y. H. Pao (eds.) *Machine Intelligence* 10, Chichester, England: Horwood, 1982. (PROSPECTOR)

[GAS82a] Gaschnig, J. PROSPECTOR: an expert system for mineral exploration. In D. Michie (ed.) *Introductory Readings in Expert Systems*, Gordon and Breach, Science Publishers, 1982. (PROSPECTOR)

[GER82] Gershman, A. Building a geological expert system for dipmeter interpretation. *Proceedings of the European Conference on Artificial Intelligence*, pp. 139–140, 1982. (DIPMETER ADVISOR)

[HAY84] Hayes-Roth, F. The industrialization of knowledge engineering. In W. Reitman (ed.) *Artificial Intelligence Applications for Business*, Norwood, N.J.: Ablex, 1984. (DRILLING ADVISOR)

[HOL83] Hollander, C. R. and Iwasaki, Y. The drilling advisor: an expert system application. In Fundamentals of Knowledge Engineering, Teknowledge Report, 1983. (DRILLING ADVISOR)

[KAH84a] Kahn, G. On when diagnostic systems want to do without causal knowledge. *Proceedings of Advances in Artificial Intelligence, ECAI-84*, 1984. (MUD)

[KAH84b] Kahn, G. and McDermott, J. MUD, a drilling fluids consultant. Technical Report, Department of Computer Science, Carnegie-Mellon University, Pittsburgh, Pa., 1984. (MUD)

[KAH84c] Kahn, G. and McDermott, J. The MUD system. *Proceedings of the First Conference on Artificial Intelligence Applications*, IEEE Computer Society, December 1984. (MUD)

[KAH84d] Kahn, G., Nowlan, S., and McDermott, J. A foundation for knowledge acquisition. *Proceedings of the IEEE Workshop on Principles of Knowledge-Based Systems*, IEEE Computer Society, IEEE Computer Society Press, 1109 Spring Street, Silver Spring, Md., 1984. (MUD)

[REB82] Reboh, R., Reiter, J., and Gaschnig, J. Development of a knowledge-based interface to a hydrological simulation program. SRI Technical Report 3477, SRI International, Menlo Park, Calif., May 1982. (HYDRO)

[SMI83] Smith, R. G. and Baker, J. D. The DIPMETER advisor system. *Proceedings IJCAI-83*, pp. 122–129, 1983. (DIPMETER ADVISOR)

[SMI84c] Smith, R. G. On the development of commercial expert systems. *The AI Magazine*, vol. 5, no. 3, Fall 1984. (DIPMETER ADVISOR)

[SMI84d] Smith, R. G. and Young R. L. The design of the DIPMETER ADVISOR system. ACM Conference Proceedings, November 1984. (DIPMETER ADVISOR)

[WEI82] Weiss, S., Kulikowski, C., Apte, C., Uschold, M., Patchett, J., Brigham, R., and Spitzer, B. Building expert systems for controlling complex programs. *Proceedings AAAI-82*, pp. 322–326, 1982. (ELAS)

Additional Reading

[DUD77] Duda, R., Hart, P. E., Nilsson, N. J., Reboh, R., Slocum, J., and Sutherland, G. Development of a computer-based consultant for mineral exploration. SRI Report, Stanford Research Institute, 333 Ravenswood Avenue, Menlo Park, Calif., October 1977.

[DUD78] Duda, R., Hart, P. E., Nilsson, N. J., Barrett, P., Gaschnig, J. G., Konolige, K., Reboh, R., and Slocum, J. Development of the PROSPECTOR consultation system for mineral exploration. SRI Report, Stanford Research Institute, 333 Ravenswood Avenue, Menlo Park, Calif., October 1978.

[OLS82] Olson, J. P. and Ellis, S. P. PROBWELL—an expert advisor for determining problems with producing wells. *Proceedings of the IBM Scientific/Engineering Conference*, pp. 95–101, 1982.

Information Management

References

[COH83] Cohen, P. and Lieberman, M.D. A report on FOLIO: An expert assistant for portfolio managers. *Proceedings IJCAI-83*, pp. 212–214, 1983. (FOLIO)

[FEI84] Feinstein, J.L. A knowledge-based expert system used to prevent the disclosure of the sensitive information at the United States Environmental Protection Agency. *Proceedings of the Law and Technology Conference*, Houston, Tex., 1984. (EDAAS)

[FEI85] Feinstein, J.L. and Siems, F. EDASS: An expert system at the U.S. Environmental Protection Agency for avoiding disclosure of confidential business information. *Expert Systems*, vol. 2, no. 2, 1985. (EDAAS)

[GUI83] Guida, Giovanni and Tasso, C. An expert intermediary system for interactive document retrieval. *Automatica*, vol. 19, no. 6, pp. 759–766, November 1983. (IR-NLI)

[RUO84] Ruoff, Karen. CODES: a database design expert system prototype. *Proceedings of the First Conference on Artificial Intelligence Applications*, IEEE Computer Society, December 1984. (CODES) (IDEF1)

[SUG84] Sugie, M., Menzilcioglu, O., and Kung, H.T. CARGuide—onboard computer for automobile route guidance. *Proceedings of the National Computer Conference*, 1984. (CARGuide)

[TOU82] Tou, F.N., Williams, M.D., Fikes, R., Henderson, A., and Malone, T. RABBIT: an intelligent database assistant. *Proceedings AAAI-82*, pp. 314–318, 1982. (RABBIT)

[UND81] Underwood, W.E. and Summerville, J.P. PROJCON: a prototype project management consultant. *Proceedings of the International Conference on Cybernetics and Society*, IEEE, pp. 149–155, October 1981. (PROJCON)

[VAL84] Valtorta, M.G., Smith, B.T., and Loveland, D.W. The graduate course advisor: a multi-phase rule-based expert system. *Proceedings of the IEEE Workshop on Principles of Knowledge-Based Systems*, IEEE Computer Society, IEEE Computer Society Press, 1109 Spring Street, Silver Spring, Md., 1984. (GCA)

[ZAR83] Zarri, G.P. An outline of the representation and use of temporal data in the RESEDA system. *Information Technology: Research and Development*, vol. 2, 1983. (RESEDA)

[ZAR84a] Zarri, G.P. Expert systems and information retrieval: an experiment in the domain of biographical data management. *International Journal of Man-Machine Studies*, vol. 20, 1984. (RESEDA)

[ZAR84b] Zarri, G.P. Inference techniques for intelligent information retrieval. *Proceedings of the Law and Technology Conference*, Houston, Tex., 1984. (RESEDA)

Additional Reading

[CAR83] Carbonell, J.G., Boggs, W.M., Mauldin, M.L., and Anick, P.G. XCALIBUR project report 1, first steps toward an integrated natural language interface. Report CMU-CS-83-143, Computer Science Dept., Carnegie-Mellon University, July 1983.

[HAR84b] Harris, L.R. "Experience with INTELLECT: artificial intelligence technology transfer." *The AI Magazine*, Summer 1984.

[SAG84] Sage, A.P. and White, C.C. "Ariadne: a knowledge-based interactive system for planning and decision support." *IEEE Transactions on Systems, Man, and Cybernetics*, vol. 14, no. 1, pp. 35–47, January/February 1984.

Law

References

[BIN80] Bing, Jon. Legal norms, discretionary rules and computer programs. In B. Niblett (ed.) *Computer Science and Law*, Cambridge, England: Cambridge University Press, 1980, pp. 119–146. (SARA)

[DUN83] Dungan, C. A model of an audit judgment in the form of an expert system, PhD Dissertation, University of Illinois, Champaign-Urbana, 1983. (AUDITOR)

[HAF81] Hafner, Carole D. Representation of knowledge in a legal information retrieval system. In R. Oddy, S. Robertson, C. van Rijsbergen, and P. Williams (eds.) *Information Retrieval Research*, London: Butterworths & Co., 1981. (LRS)

[KED84] Kedar-Cabelli, Smadar. Analogy with purpose in legal reasoning from precedents. Report LRP-TR-17, Laboratory for Computer Science Research, Rutgers University, July 1984. (TAXMAN)

[KRU84] Kruppenbacher, T.A. The application of artificial intelligence to contract management, vol. 1. Master's thesis, Dept. of Civil, Environmental and Architectural Engineering, University of Colorado, Boulder, Colo., 1984. (DSCAS)

[MCC82] McCarty, L.T. and Sridharan, N.S. A computational theory of legal argument. Report LRP-TR-13, Laboratory for Computer Science Research, New Brunswick, N.J., January 1982. (TAXMAN)

[MEL75] Meldman, J.A. A preliminary study in computer-aided legal analysis. PhD thesis, Departments of Electrical Engineering and Computer Science, MIT, August 1975. (LEGAL ANALYSIS SYSTEM)

[MIC82a] Michaelsen, R. A knowledge-based system for individual income and transfer tax planning, PhD thesis, University of Illinois, Accounting Dept., Champaign-Urbana, 1982. (TAXADVISOR)

[MIC83a] Michaelsen, R. and Michie, D. Expert systems in business. *Datamation*, pp. 240–246, November 1983. (TAXADVISOR)

[MIC84a] Michaelsen, R. An expert system for federal tax planning. Report, University of Nebraska, 1984. (TAXADVISOR)

[POP75] Popp, W.G. and Schlink, B. Judith, a computer program to advise lawyers in reasoning a case. *Jurimetrics Journal*, vol. 15, no. 4, pp. 303–314, Summer 1975. (JUDITH)

[WAT80] Waterman, D.A. and Peterson, M. Rule-based models of legal expertise. *Proceedings of the First Annual National Conference on Artificial Intelligence*, 1980. (LDS)

[WAT81] Waterman, D.A. and Peterson, M.A. Models of legal decision-making. Report R-2717-ICJ, Rand Corporation, 1981. (LDS)

Additional Reading

[COO81] Cooke, S., Hafner, C., McCarty, T., Meldman, M., Peterson, M., Sprowl, J., Sridharan, N., and Waterman, D.A. The applications of artificial intelligence to law: a survey of six current projects. *AFIPS Conference Proceedings*, vol. 50, 1981.

[DAV80] Davis, E. and Strobel, C. Estate planning by computer: what are the choices available to practitioners? *The Journal of Taxation*, vol. 53, no. 6, pp. 378–384, December 1980.

[HAF78] Hafner, C.D. An information retrieval system based on a computer model of legal knowledge. PhD thesis, University of Michigan, Ann Arbor, 1978.

[HAN83] Hansen, J.V. and Messier, W.F. A knowledge-based expert system for auditing advanced computer systems. ARC Working Paper 83-5, University of Florida, September 1983.

[LEH83a] Lehmann, H. A knowledge acquisition and query system. Heidelberg Science Center Report, Heidelberg, Germany, 1983.

[MES83] Messier, W.F. and Hansen, J.V. Expert systems in accounting and auditing: a framework and review. *Proceedings of the University of Oklahoma Behavioral Research Conference*, August 1983.

Manufacturing

References

[FOX82b] Fox, M.S., Allen, B., and Strohm, G. Job-shop scheduling: an investigation in constraint-directed reasoning. *Proceedings AAAI-82*, pp. 155–158, 1982. (ISIS)

[FOX82c] Fox, M.S., Allen, B., and Strohm, G. Job-shop scheduling: an investigation in constraint-directed reasoning. *Proceedings AAAI-82*, pp. 155–158, 1982. (ISIS)

[FOX83b] Fox, M.S., Smith, S.F., Allen, B.P., Strohm, G.A., and Wimberly, F.C. ISIS: a constraint-directed reasoning approach to job shop scheduling. *Proceedings of the IEEE Conference on Trends and Applications*, May 1983. (ISIS)

[FOX84b] Fox, M.S. and Smith, S.F. ISIS: a knowledge-based system for factory scheduling. *Expert Systems*, vol. 1, no. 1, 1984. (ISIS)

[HAL83] Haley, P., Kowalski, J., McDermott, J., and McWhorter, R. PTRANS: A rule-based management assistant. Technical Report, Computer Science Dept., Carnegie-Mellon University, Pittsburgh, Pa., January 1983. (PTRANS)

[MCD84] McDermott, J. Building expert systems. In W. Reitman (ed.) *Artificial Intelligence Applications for Business*, Norwood, N.J.: Ablex, 1984. (XCON) (PTRANS) (XSEL)

[OCO84] O'Connor, D.E. Using expert systems to manage change and complexity in manufacturing. In W. Reitman (ed.) *Artificial Intelligence Applications for Business*, Norwood, N.J.: Ablex, 1984. (XCON) (IMACS) (ISA)

Additional Reading

[FOX84a] Fox, M.S., Greenberg, M., and Sathi, A. Issues in knowledge representation for project management. Report, Robotics Institute, Carnegie-Mellon University, Pittsburgh, Pa., July 1984.

[FOX84c] Fox, Mark, Sathi, A., and Greenberg, M. Issues in knowledge representation for project management. *Proceedings of the IEEE Workshop on Principles of Knowledge-Based Systems*, IEEE Computer Society, IEEE Computer Society Press, Silver Spring, Md., 1984.

Mathematics

References

[ENG71] Engelman, C. The legacy of MATHLAB 68. *Proceedings of the Second Symposium on Symbolic and Algebraic Manipulation*, pp. 29–41, 1971. (MATHLAB)

[GEN79] Genesereth, M.R. The role of plans in automated consultation. *Proceedings IJCAI-79*, pp. 311–319, 1979. (ADVISOR)

[MAR71] Martin, W.A. and Fateman, R.J. The MACSYMA system. *Proceedings of the Second Symposium on Symbolic and Algebraic Manipulation*, pp. 59–75, March 1971. (MACSYMA)

Medicine

References

[AIK83a] Aikins, J.S. Prototypical knowledge for expert systems. *Artificial Intelligence*, vol. 20, pp. 163–210, 1983. (CENTAUR)

[AIK83b] Aikins, J.S., Kunz, J.C., and Shortliffe, E.H. PUFF: an expert system for interpretation of pulmonary function data. *Computers and Biomedical Research*, vol. 16, pp. 199–208, 1983. (PUFF)

[ALT84b] Alty, J.L. and Coombs, M.J. Associative and causal approaches to diagnosis—INTERNIST and CASNET. *Expert Systems, Concepts and Examples*, Manchester, England: NCC Publications, 1984. (INTERNIST) (CASNET/GLAUCOMA)

[BAA84] Baas, L. and Bourne, J.R. A rule-based microcomputer system for electroencephalogram evaluation. *IEEE Transactions on Biomedical Engineering*, vol. BME-31, no. 10, October 1984. (EEG ANALYSIS SYSTEM)

[BEN80] Bennett, J.S. and Goldman, D. CLOT: a knowledge-based consultant for diagnosis of bleeding disorders. Report HPP-80-7, Computer Science Dept., Stanford University, Stanford, Calif. 1980. (CLOT)

[BEN84] Bennett, James S. and Engelmore, Robert S. Experience using EMYCIN. In B. Buchanan & E. Shortliffe (eds.) *Rule-Based Expert Systems*, Reading, Mass.: Addison-Wesley, pp. 314–328, 1984. (SACON and CLOT)

[BLU82a] Blum, R.L. Discovery, confirmation and incorporation of causal relationships from a large time-oriented clinical database: the RX project. *Computers and Biomedical Research*, vol. 15, pp. 164–187, 1982. (RX)

[BLU82b] Blum, R.L. Induction of causal relationships from a time-oriented clinical database: an overview of the RX project. *Proceedings AAAI-82*, 1982, pp. 355–357. (RX)

[BLU82c] Blum, R.L. Discovery and representation of causal relationships from a large time-oriented clinical database: The RX Project. In D. Lindberg and P. Reichertz (eds.) *Medical Informatics Series*, (monograph) New York: Springer-Verlag, 1982. (RX)

[BLU83] Blum, R.L. Representation of empirically derived causal relationships. *Proceedings IJCAI-83*, pp. 268–271, 1983. (RX)

[BOK82] Bokhua, N.K., Gelovani, V.A., Kovrigin, O.V., and Smol'yaninov, N.D. An expert for diagnostics of various forms of arterial hypertension. *Tekh. Kibern.* [engineering cybernetics], vol. 20, no. 6, pp. 106–111, November/December 1982. (MODIS)

[BUC82] Buchanan, B.G. New research on expert systems. In J.E. Hayes, D. Michie, and Y.H. Pao (eds.) *Machine Intelligence 10*, Chichester, England: Horwood, pp. 269–299, 1982. (MYCIN) (EMYCIN)

[BUC84a] Buchanan, B. and Shortliffe, E. The problem of evaluation. In Buchanan and Shortliffe (eds.) *Rule-Based Expert Systems*, Reading, Mass.: Addison-Wesley, pp. 571–596, 1984. (MYCIN)

[BUC84b] Buchanan, B. and Shortliffe, E. Uncertainty and evidential support. In Buchanan and Shortliffe (eds.) *Rule-Based Expert Systems*, Reading, Mass: Addison-Wesley, pp. 209–232, 1984. (MYCIN & EMYCIN)

[BUC84c] Buchanan, B. and Shortliffe, E. Use of MYCIN inference engine. In Buchanan and Shortliffe (eds.) *Rule-Based Expert Systems*, Reading, Mass.: Addison-Wesley, pp. 295–301, 1984. (MYCIN)

[CEN84] Cendrowska, J. and Bramer, M. A. A rational reconstruction of the MYCIN consultation system. *International Journal of Man-Machine Studies.* vol. 20, pp. 229–317, 1984. (MYCIN)

[CHA79] Chandrasekaran, B., Gomez, F., Mittal, S., and Smith, J. An approach to medical diagnosis based on conceptual structures. *Proceedings IJCAI-79*, pp. 134–142, 1979. (MDX)

[CHA80] Chandrasekaran, B., Mittal, S., and Smith, J.W. RADEX— towards a computer-based radiology consultant. In E.S. Gelsema and L.N. Kanal (eds.) *Pattern-Recognition in Practice*, pp. 463–477, North-Holland Publishing Co., 1980. (RADEX)

[CHA81] Chandrasekaran, B., Mittal, S., and Smith, J.W. MDX and related medical decision-making systems. *Proceedings IJCAI-81*, p. 1055, 1981. (MDX)

[CHA83] Chandrasekaran, B. and Mittal, Sanjay. Deep versus compiled knowledge approaches to diagnostic problem-solving. *International Journal of Man-Machine Studies*, vol. 19, pp. 425–436, 1983. (MDX)

[CLA79] Clancey, W.J. Tutoring rules for guiding a case method dialogue. *International Journal of Man-Machine Studies.* vol. 11, pp. 25–49, 1979. (GUIDON)

[CLA79a] Clancey, W.J. Dialogue management for rule-based tutorials. *Proceedings IJCAI-79*, pp. 155–161, 1979. (GUIDON)

[CLA81] Clancey, W.J. Methodology for building an intelligent tutoring system. Report STAN-CS-81-894, Computer Science Dept., Stanford University, Stanford, Calif., October 1981. (NEOMYCIN)

[CLA81a] Clancey, W.J. and Letsinger, R. NEOMYCIN: reconfiguring a rule-based expert system for application to teaching. Proceedings IJCAI-81, pp. 829–836, 1981. (NEOMYCIN)

[CLA83a] Clancey, W.J. GUIDON. *Journal of Computer-Based Instruction,* vol. 10, nos. 1 and 2, pp. 8–15, Summer 1983. (GUIDON)

[CLA83b] Clancey, W.J. The advantages of abstract control knowledge in expert system design. *Proceedings AAAI-83,* pp. 74–78, 1983. (NEOMYCIN)

[CLA83c] Clancey, W.J. and Bock, C. MRS/NEOMYCIN: representing metacontrol in predicate calculus. Report No. HPP-82-31, Computer Science Dept., Stanford University, Stanford, Calif., January 1983. (NEOMYCIN)

[CLA83d] Clancey, W.J., Warner, D., Wilkins, D., Sleeman, D., and Buchanan, B. The NEOMYCIN/GUIDON2 project. *The AI Magazine,* p. 86, Fall 1983. (GUIDON) (NEOMYCIN)

[CLA84a] Clancey, W.J. Acquiring, representing, and evaluating a competence model of diagnostic strategy. Report HPP-84-2, Computer Science Dept., Stanford University, Stanford, Calif., February 1984. (NEOMYCIN)

[DAV82a] Davis, R. Consultation, knowledge acquisition, and instruction: a case study. In P. Szolovits (ed.) *Artificial Intelligence in Medicine,* Boulder, Colo.: Westview Press, pp. 57–78, 1982. (MYCIN)

[ENG76] Engle, R.L., Flehinger, B.J., Allen, S., Friedman, R., Lipkin, M., Davis, B.J., and Leveridge, L.L. HEME: a computer aid to diagnosis of hematologic disease. *Bulletin of N.Y. Academy of Medicine,* vol. 52, no. 5, pp. 584–600, June 1976. (HEME)

[FAG78] Fagan, L. Ventilator manager: a program to provide on-line consultative advice in the intensive care unit. Report HPP-78-16, Computer Science Dept., Stanford University, Stanford, Calif., September 1978. (VM)

[FAG79a] Fagan, L.M., Kunz, J.C., and Feigenbaum, E.A. Representation of dynamic clinical knowledge: measurement interpretation in the intensive care unit. *Proceedings IJCAI-79,* pp. 260–262, 1979. (VM)

[FAG79b] Fagan, L.M., Kunz, J.C., Feigenbaum, E.A., and Osborn, J.J. A symbolic processing approach to measurement interpretation in the intensive care unit. *Proceedings of the Third Annual Symposium on Computer Applications in Medical Care,* New York: IEEE, pp. 30–33, 1979. (VM)

[FAG84] Fagan, Lawrence M., Kunz, John C., Feigenbaum, Edward A., and Osborn, John J. Extensions to the rule-based formalism for a monitoring task. In B. Buchanan and E. Shortliffe (eds.) *Rule-Based Expert Systems*, Reading, Mass.: Addison-Wesley, pp. 397–423, 1984. (VM)

[FRI72] Fries, J.F. Time-oriented patient records and a computer data-bank. *J. Amer. Med. Assoc.*, vol. 222, no. 12, pp. 1536–1542, 1972. (ARAMIS)

[FRI76] Fries, J.F. A data bank for a clinician? *New England Journal of Medicine*, vol. 294, no. 25, pp. 1400–1402, June 1976. (ARAMIS)

[FRI79] Fries, J.F. and McShane, D. ARAMIS: a national chronic disease data bank system. *Proceedings of the Third Annual Symposium on Computer Applications in Medical Care*, IEEE, pp. 798–801, 1979. (ARAMIS)

[GAS83] Gaston, L.W., Lindberg, D.A.B., Vanker, A.D., and Kingsland, L. AI/COAG, A knowledge-based surrogate for the human hemostasis expert. *Missouri Medicine*, vol. 80, no. 4, pp. 185–188, April 1983. (AI/COAG)

[GOM81] Gomez, F. and Chandrasekaran, B. Knowledge organization and distribution for medical diagnosis. *IEEE Transactions on Systems, Man & Cybernetics*, vol. SMC-11, no. 1, pp. 34–42, 1981. (MDX)

[HAS83a] Hasling, D.W., Clancey, W.J., and Rennels, G. Strategic explanations for a diagnostic consultation system. Report STAN-CS-83-996, Computer Science Dept., Stanford University, Stanford, Calif., November 1983. (NEOMYCIN)

[HAS83b] Hasling, D.W. Abstract explanations of strategy in a diagnostic consultation system. Report HPP-83-18, Computer Science Dept., Stanford University, Stanford, Calif., October 1983. (NEOMYCIN)

[HEI78] Heiser, J.F., Brooks, R.E., and Ballard, J.P. Progress report: a computerized psychopharmacology advisor. *Proceedings of the Eleventh Colloqium Internationale Neuro-Psychopharmacologicum*, Vienna, Austria, 1978. (HEADMED)

[HEU80] Heuristic Programming Project 1980. Computer Science Dept., Stanford University, Stanford, Calif., 1980. (RX)

[HOR84] Horvitz, E.J., Heckerman, D.E., Nathwani, B.N., and Fagan, L.M. Diagnostic strategies in the hypothesis-directed PATHFINDER system. *Proceedings of the First Conference on Artificial Intelligence Applications*, IEEE Computer Society, December 1984. (PATHFINDER)

[HPP80a] HPP staff. The Stanford heuristic programming project: goals and activities. *AI Magazine*, vol. 1, no. 1, pp. 25–30, Spring 1980. (DENDRAL) (META-DENDRAL) (CRYSALIS) (MOLGEN) (VM) (RX) (PUFF) (SACON) (ONCOCIN) (GUIDON)

[HUD81] Hudson, D.L. Rule-based computerization of emergency room procedures derived from criteria mapping. PhD thesis, Computer Science Dept., University of California at Los Angeles, 1981. (EMERGE)

[HUD84a] Hudson, D.L. and Cohen, M.E. EMERGE, a rule-based clinical decision making aid. *Proceedings of the First Conference on Artificial Intelligence Applications*, IEEE Computer Society, December 1984. (EMERGE)

[HUD84b] Hudson, D.L. and Estrin, T. Derivation of rule-based knowledge from established medical outlines. *Computers in Biology and Medicine*, Pergamon Press Ltd., vol. 14, no. 1, pp. 3–13, 1984. (EMERGE)

[HUD84c] Hudson, D.L. and Estrin, T. EMERGE, a data-driven medical decision making aid. *IEEE Transactions on Pattern Analysis and Machine Intelligence*, vol. PAMI-6, no. 1, January 1984. (EMERGE)

[JOH81] Johnson, P.E., Duran, A.S., Hassebrock, F., Moller, J., and Prietula, M. Expertise and error in diagnostic reasoning. *Cognitive Science*, vol. 5, pp. 235–283, 1981. (DIAGNOSER)

[KAI78] Kaihara, S., Koyama, T., Minamikawa, T., and Yasaka, T. A rule-based physicians' consultation system for cardiovascular diseases. *Proceedings of the International Conference on Cybernetics and Society*, IEEE, pp. 85–88, November 1978. (MECS-AI)

[KAI82] Kaihara, S. and Koyama, T. Medical consultation system with practical requirements—development of MECS-AI. *Computer Science and Technologies, Japan Annual Review in Electronics, Computers and Telecommunications*, vol. 4, Amsterdam: North-Holland, 1982. (MECS-AI)

[KAS82] Kastner, J.K., Weiss, S.M., and Kulikowski, C.A. Treatment selection and explanation in expert medical consultation: application to a model of ocular herpes simplex. *Proceedings MEDCOMP 1982—IEEE Conference on Medical Computer Science/Computational Medicine*, pp. 420–427, September 1982. (OCULAR HERPES MODEL)

[KAS83b] Kastner, J.K., Weiss, S.M., and Kulikowski, C.A. An efficient scheme for time-dependent consultation systems. Proceedings MEDINFO-83 Fourth World Conference on Medical Informatics, North-Holland, pp. 619–622, 1983. (MI)

[KAS84] Kastner, J.K., Chandler, R.D., Weiss, S.M., Kern, K., and Kulikowski, C.A. An expert consultation system for frontline health workers in primary eye care. *Journal of Medical Systems*, vol. 8, no. 5, 1984. (PEC)

[KUL80a] Kulikowski, C.A. Artificial intelligence methods and systems for medical consultation. *IEEE Transactions on Pattern Analysis and Machine Intelligence*, vol. PAMI-2, no. 5, pp. 464–476, September 1980. (CASNET) (MYCIN) (INTERNIST) (PIP)

[KUL80b] Kulikowski, C.A., Weiss, S.M., and Galen, R.S. On the diagnostic frontier. *Diagnostic Medicine,* November/December 1980. (SPE)

[KUL82] Kulikowski, C.A. and Weiss, S.M. Representation of expert knowledge for consultation: the CASNET and EXPERT projects. In P. Szolovits (ed.) *Artificial Intelligence in Medicine*, Boulder, Colo.: Westview Press, pp. 21–55, 1982. (THYROID MODEL) (CASNET/ GLAUCOMA) (EXPERT)

[KUN83] Kunz, J.C. Analysis of physiological behavior using a causal model based on first principles. *Proceedings AAAI-83,* pp. 225–228, 1983. (AI/MM)

[LAN83a] Langlotz, C.P. and Shortliffe, E.H. Adapting a consultation system to critique user plans. *International Journal of Man-Machine Studies*, vol. 19, pp. 479–496, 1983. (ONCOCIN)

[LIN80a] Lindberg, D.A.B., Sharp, G.C., Kingsland, L.C., Weiss, S.M., Hayes, S.P., Ueno, H., and Hazelwood, S.E. Computer based rheumatology consultant. *Proceedings of the Third World Conference on Medical Informatics*, pp. 1311–1315, 1980. (AI/RHEUM)

[LIN81] Lindberg, D.A.B., Gaston, L.W., Kingsland, L.C., and Vanker, A.D. AI/COAG, a knowledge-based system for consultation about human hemostasis disorders: progress report. *Proceedings of the Fifth Annual Symposium on Computer Applications in Medical Care*, pp. 253–257, 1981. (AI/COAG)

[LIN82]Lindberg, D.A.B., Kingsland, L.C., Roeseler, G.C., Kay, D.R., and Sharp G.C. A new knowledge representation for diagnosis in rheumatology. *Proceedings of AMIA Congress 82*, New York: Masson Publishing Co., pp. 299–303, 1982. (AI/RHEUM)

[MCS79] McShane, D.J., Harlow, A., Kraines, R.G., and Fries, J.F. TOD: a software system for the ARAMIS data bank. *IEEE Computer*, vol. 12, pp. 34–40, November 1979. (ARAMIS)

[MIL82] Miller, R.A., Pople, Jr., H.E., and Myers, J.D. INTERNIST-I, an experimental computer-based diagnostic consultant for general internal medicine. *New England Journal of Medicine*, vol. 307, no. 8, pp. 468–476, August 1982. (INTERNIST)

[MIL83] Miller, P.L. Medical plan-analysis: the ATTENDING system. *Proceedings IJCAI-83,* pp. 239–241, 1983. (ATTENDING)

[MIL84] Miller, P.L. and Black, H.R. Medical plan-analysis by computer: critiquing the pharmacologic management of essential hypertension. *Computers and Biomedical Research*, vol. 17, pp. 38–54, 1984. (HT-ATTENDING)

[MIT80] Mittal, S. and Chandrasekaran, B. Conceptual representation of patient databases. *Journal of Medical Systems*, vol. 4, no. 2, pp. 169–185, 1980. (PATREC)

[MUL84] Mulsant, B. and Servan-Schreiber, D. Knowledge engineering: a daily activity on a hospital ward. *Computers and Biomedical Research*, vol. 17, pp. 71–91, 1984. (BLUE BOX)

[NIE84] Niemann, H., Bunke, H., Hofmann, I., and Sagerer, G. Diagnostic inferences from image sequences—a knowledge based approach. *Proceedings of the First Conference on Artificial Intelligence Applications*, IEEE Computer Society, December 1984. (HEART IMAGE INTERPRETER)

[OLE77] Oleson, C.E. EXAMINER: a system using contextual knowledge for analysis of diagnostic behavior. *Proceedings IJCAI-77*, pp. 814–818, 1977. (EXAMINER)

[OSB78] Osborn, J.J., Kunz, J.C., and Fagan, L.M. PUFF/VM: interpretation of physiological measurements in the pulmonary function laboratory and the intensive care unit. *Proceedings of the Fourth Annual AIM Workshop*, pp. 67–68, June 1978. (VM)

[PAT81b] Patil, Ramesh S., Szolovits, Peter, and Schwartz, William B. Causal understanding of patient illness in medical diagnosis. *Proceedings IJCAI-81*, pp. 893–899, 1981. (ABEL)

[PAT82c] Patil, Ramesh S., Szolovits, Peter, and Schwartz, William B. Information acquisition in diagnosis. *Proceedings AAAI-82*, pp. 345–348, 1982. (ABEL)

[PAT82d] Patil, Ramesh S., Szolovits, Peter, and Schwartz, William B. Modeling knowledge of the patient in acid-base and electrolyte disorders. In P. Szolovits (ed.) *Artificial Intelligence in Medicine*, AAAS Symposium Series, Boulder, Colo.: Westview Press, pp. 191–226, 1982. (ABEL)

[PAU76] Pauker, S.G., Gorry, G.A., Kassirer, J.P., and Schwartz, W.B. Towards the simulation of clinical cognition: taking a present illness by computer. *American Journal of Medicine*, vol. 60, pp. 981–996, June 1976. (PIP)

[POP84] Pople, Jr., H.E. Knowledge-based expert systems: the buy or build decision. In W. Reitman (ed.) *Artificial Intelligence Applications for Business*, Norwood, N.J.: Ablex, 1984. (INTERNIST-I/CADUCEUS)

[PUP83] Puppe, Frank and Puppe, Bernhard. Overview on MED1: a heuristic diagnosis system with an efficient control structure. Report

SEKI-83-02, Fachbereich Informatik, Universitat Kaiserslautern, West Germany, 1983. (MED1)

[REG78a] Reggia, J.A. Representing and using medical knowledge for the neurological localization problem. Report TR-693, Computer Science Dept., University of Maryland, September 1978. (NEUREX)

[REG78b] Reggia, J.A. A production rule system for neurological localization. *Proceedings of the Second Annual Symposium on Computer Applications in Medical Care*, IEEE, November 1978. (NEUREX)

[REG83] Reggia, J.A., Nau, D.S., and Wang, P.Y. Diagnostic expert systems based on a set covering model. *International Journal of Man-Machine Studies*, vol. 19, pp. 437–460, 1983. (SYSTEM D)

[ROA84] Roach, J., Lee. S., Wilcke, J., and Ehrich, M. An expert system that criticizes decisions in combination drug therapy. *Proceedings of the First Conference on Artificial Intelligence Applications*, IEEE Computer Society, December 1984. (DRUG INTERACTION CRITIC)

[ROD84] Rodewald, L.E. BABY: an expert system for patient monitoring in a newborn intensive care unit. M.S. thesis, Computer Science Dept., University of Illinois, Champaign-Urbana, 1984. (BABY)

[SAF76] Safran, C., Desforges, J.F., and Tsichlis, P.N. Diagnostic planning and career management. MIT Technical Report TR-169, Laboratory for Computer Science, MIT, September 1976. (HDDSS)

[SCH84c] Schaffer, J.D., Teschan, J., Caviedes, J., and Bourne, J.R. A computer-based dialysis therapy advisor. *IEEE Transactions on Biomedical Engineering*, vol. BME-31, no. 2, February 1984. (DIALYSIS THERAPY ADVISOR)

[SHO73] Shortliffe, E.H., Axline, S.G., Buchanan, B.G., Merigan, T.C., and Cohen, S.N. An artificial intelligence program to advise physicians regarding antimicrobial therapy. *Computers and Biomedical Research*, vol. 6, pp. 544–560, 1973. (MYCIN)

[SHO75] Shortliffe, E.H. and Buchanan, B.G. A model of inexact reasoning in medicine. *Mathematical Biosciences*, vol. 23, 1975. (MYCIN)

[SHO75a] Shortliffe, E.H., Davis, R., Axline, S.G., Buchanan, B.G., Green, C.C., and Cohen, S.N. Computer-based consultations in clinical therapeutics: explanation and rule acquisition capabilities of the MYCIN system. *Computers and Biomedical Research*, vol. 8, pp. 303–320, 1975. (MYCIN)

[SHO76] Shortliffe, E.H. *Computer-based medical consultations: MYCIN.* New York: Elsevier, 1976.

[SHO79] Shortliffe, E.H., Buchanan, B.G., and Feigenbaum, E.A.

Knowledge engineering for medical decisionmaking: a review of computer-based clinical decision aids. *Proceedings of the IEEE*, vol. 67, no. 9, pp. 1207–1224, September 1979. (ARAMIS)

[SHO81] Shortliffe, E.H., Scott, A.C., Bischoff, M.B., Campbell, A.B., van Melle, W., and Jacobs, C.D. ONCOCIN: an expert system for oncology protocol management. *Proceedings IJCAI-81*, pp. 876–881, 1981. (ONCOCIN)

[SHO82] Shortliffe, E.H. and Fagan, L.M. Expert systems research: modeling the medical decision making process. Technical Memo HPP-82-3, Computer Science Dept., Stanford University, Stanford, Calif., 1982. (VM) (MYCIN)

[SHO84] Shortliffe, Edward H., Scott, A. Carlisle, Bischoff, Miriam B., Campbell, A. Bruce, van Melle, William, and Jacobs, Charlotte D. In B. Buchanan and E. Shortliffe (eds.) An expert system for oncology protocol management. *Rule-Based Expert Systems*, Reading, Mass.: Addison-Wesley, 1984. (ONCOCIN)

[SIL74] Silverman, H. A digitalis therapy advisor. MIT Technical Report TR-143, December 1974. (ANNA)

[SMI80] Smith, D.E. and Clayton, J.E. A frame-based production system architecture. *Proceedings AAAI-80*, pp. 154–156, 1980. (WHEEZE)

[SMI84a] Smith, David E. and Clayton, Jan E. Another look at frames. In B. Buchanan and E. Shortliffe (eds.) *Rule-Based Expert Systems*, pp. 441–452, Reading, Mass.: Addison-Wesley, 1984. (WHEEZE)

[STA84] Stansfield, S.A. ANGY: a rule-based expert system for identifying and isolating coronary vessels in digital angiograms. *Proceedings of the First Conference on Artificial Intelligence Applications*, IEEE Computer Society, December 1984. (ANGY)

[SWA77] Swartout, W.R. A digitalis therapy advisor with explanations. MIT Technical Report TR-176, February 1977. (DIGITALIS THERAPY ADVISOR)

[SZO78] Szolovits, P. and Pauker, S.G. Categorical and probabilistic reasoning in medical diagnosis. *Artificial Intelligence*, vol. 11, pp. 115–144, 1978. (CASNET/GLAUCOMA)

[THO83] Thompson, W.B., Johnson, P.E., and Moen, J.B. Recognition-based diagnostic reasoning. *Proceedings IJCAI-83*, pp. 236–238, 1983. (GALEN)

[TRI77] Trigoboff, M. and Kulikowski, C.A. IRIS: a system for the propagation of inferences in a semantic net. *Proceedings IJCAI-77*, pp. 274–280, 1977. (IRIS)

[TSU83] Tsuji, Shoko and Shortliffe, E.H. Graphical access to the knowledge base of a medical consultation system. Memo HPP-83-6, Computer Science Dept., Stanford University, Stanford, Calif., February 1983. (ONCOCIN)

[WAL76] Walser, R.L. and McCormick, B.H. Organization of clinical knowledge in MEDICO. *Proceedings of the Third Illinois Conference on Medical Information Systems,* University of Illinois, Champaign-Urbana, November 1976. (MEDICO)

[WAL77] Walser, R.L. and McCormick, B.H. A system for priming a clinical knowledge base. *Proceedings of the AFIPS National Computer Conference,* pp. 301–307, 1977. (MEDICO) (KAMM)

[WEI78] Weiss, S.M., Kulikowski, C.A., Amarel, Saul, and Safir, Aran. A model-based method for computer-aided medical decision-making. *Artificial Intelligence,* vol. 11, pp. 145–172, 1978. (CASNET/GLAUCOMA)

[WEI81b] Weiss, S.M. and Kulikowski, C.A. Developing microprocessor based expert models for instrument interpretation. *Proceedings IJCAI-81,* pp. 853–855, 1981. (SPE)

[WEI81c] Weiss, S.M. and Kulikowski, C.A. Expert consultation systems: the EXPERT and CASNET projects. In A.H. Bond (ed.) *Machine Intelligence,* Infotech State of the Art Report, Series 9, no. 3, Pergamon Infotech Limited, pp. 339–353, 1981. (CASNET/GLAUCOMA) (EXPERT)

[XIA84] Xiang, Z., Srihari, S.N., Shapiro, S.C., and Chutkow, J.G. Analogical and propositional representations of structure in neurological diagnosis. *Proceedings of the First Conference on Artificial Intelligence Applications,* IEEE Computer Society, December 1984. (NEUROLOGIST-I)

Additional Reading

[FOX80] Fox, J., Barber, D., and Bardhan, K.D. Alternatives to Bayes? A quantitative comparison with rule-based diagnostic inference. *Methods of Information in Medicine,* vol. 19, no. 4, pp. 210–215, 1980.

[JAG81] Jagannathan, V. An artificial intelligence approach to computerized electroencephalogram analysis. PhD thesis, Vanderbilt University, Nashville, Tenn., December 1981.

[JAG82] Jagannathan, V., Bourne, J.R., Jansen, B.H., and Ward, J.W. Artificial intelligence methods in quantitative electroencephalogram analysis. *Computer Programs Biomedical,* vol. 15, pp. 249–258, 1982.

[JOH83] Johannes, J.D. Representation and use of judgmental knowledge. *Proceedings of COMPSAC 83,* IEEE Computer Society, IEEE Computer Society Press, Silver Spring, Md., November 1983.

[JOH83a] Johnson, P.E. What kind of expert should a system be? *Journal of Medicine and Philosophy,* vol. 8, pp. 77–97, 1983.

[LAN83b] Langlotz, Curtis P. and Shortliffe, Edward. Adapting a consultation system to critique user plans. *International Journal of Man-Machine Studies,* vol. 19, no. 5, pp. 479–496, November 1983.

[MAR84] Marcovitz, Sorana and Miresco E.T. MUPPET: a program combining interactive data analysis and time-oriented database for clinical investigation of patients with pituitary tumors. *Computers in Biology and Medicine,* vol. 14, no. 2, pp. 225–235, 1984.

[MEL81] van Melle, W., Shortliffe, E.H., and Buchanan, B.G. EMYCIN: a domain-independent system that aids in constructing knowledge-based consultation programs, In A.H. Bond (ed.) *Machine Intelligence,* Infotech State of the Art Report, series 9, no. 3, Pergamon Infotech Limited, 1981.

[POP82] Pople, Jr., H.E. Heuristic methods for imposing structure on ill-structured problems: the structuring of medical diagnostics. In P. Szolovits (ed.) *Artificial Intelligence in Medicine,* AAAS Symposium Series, Boulder, Colo.: Westview Press, 1982.

[REG80] Reggia, J. et al. Towards an intelligent textbook of neurology. *Proceedings of the Fourth Symposium on Computer Applications in Medical Care,* 1980.

[RYA83] Ryan, S.A. Applications of a nursing knowledge based system for nursing practice: inservice, continuing education, and standards of care. *Proceedings of the Seventh Annual Symposium on Computer Applications in Medical Care,* Washington, D.C., October 1983.

Meteorology

References

[MIC84b] Michie, D., Muggleton, S., Riese, C., and Zubrick, S. RULEMASTER: a second-generation knowledge-engineering facility. *Proceedings of the First Conference on Artificial Intelligence Applications,* IEEE Computer Society, December 1984. (RULEMASTER) (WILLARD)

Military Science

References

[ALD84] Aldridge, Jack, P. AIRID—an application of the KAS/prospector expert system builder to airplane identification. *Proceedings of SPIE,* The International Society for Optical Engineering, Bellingham, Wash., vol. 485, Applications of Artificial Intelligence, 1984. (AIRID)

[ANC84] Anderson, B.M., Cramer, N.L., Lineberry, M., Lystad, G.S., and Stern, R.C. Intelligent automation of emergency procedures in advanced fighter aircraft. *Proceedings of the First Conference on Artificial Intelligence Applications,* IEEE Computer Society, December 1984. (EPES)

[BAR83a] Barth, S.W., Coyle, H., and Sobik, D. User guide for the duplex army radio/radar targeting aid (DART). Report, Par Technology Corporation, New Hartford, N.Y., 1983. (DART)

[BON83a] Bonasso, R.P. Expert systems for intelligence fusion. Proceedings of the Army Conference on Applications of AI to Battlefield Information Management, Report AD-A139 685 Battelle Columbus Laboratories, Washington, D.C., April 1983. (ANALYST)

[BON84] Bonasso, Jr., R.P. ANALYST, an expert system for processing sensor returns. Report MTP-83W00002, MITRE Corporation, 1820 Dolly Madison Blvd., McLean, Va., February 1984. (ANALYST)

[BRO82a] Brown, H., Buckman, J., Engelmore, R., Harrison, D., and Pfefferkorn, C. Communication intelligence task—HANNIBAL demonstration. Report, ESL, Inc., Sunnyvale, Calif., 1982. (HANNIBAL)

[CAL84] Callero, M., Waterman, D.A., and Kipps, J.R. TATR: a prototype expert system for tactical air targeting. Report R-3096-ARPA, Rand Corporation, June 1984. (TATR)

[DRA83] Drazovich, R.J. Sensor fusion in tactical warfare. AIAA Computers in Aerospace IV Conference, October 1983. (AMUID) (SIAP)

[DUD80] Duda, R.O. and Garvey, T.D. A study of knowledge-based systems for photo interpretation. Final report, SRI International, Menlo Park, Calif., p. 12, June 1980. (OIL) (EL)

[ENG79a] Engelman, C., Berg, C.H., and Bischoff, M. KNOBS: an experimental knowledge based tactical air mission planning system and a rule based aircraft identification simulation facility. *Proceedings IJCAI-79,* pp. 247–249, 1979. (KNOBS)

[ENG83] Engelman, C., Millen, J.K., and Scarl, E.A. KNOBS: an integrated AI interactive planning architecture. Report, MITRE Corporation, Burlington Road, Bedford, MA 01730, 1983. (KNOBS)

[FER83] Ferguson, G.R. Aircraft maintenance expert systems. Master's thesis, Air Force Institute of Technology, Wright-Patterson AFB, Ohio, November 1983. (MES)

[FIG83] Figgins, T.L., Barth, S.W., and Gates, K. Functional Description for the Duplex Army Radio/Radar Targeting Aid (DART), Report 83-117, Par Technology Corp., New Hartford, N.Y., August 1983. (DART)

[GRO84] Groundwater, E.H. A demonstration of an ocean surveillance information fusion expert system. Proceedings of SPIE, The International Society for Optical Engineering, Bellingham, Wash., vol. 485, Applications of Artificial Intelligence, 1984. (OCEAN SURVEILLANCE)

[HAY83c] Hayes-Roth, F. A blackboard model of control. Report HPP-83-38, Computer Science Dept., Stanford University, Stanford, Calif., June 1983. (SIAP)

[KAS83a] Kashner, F. Artificial intelligence aids military planners. *Electronic Business*, pp. 155–156, December 1983. (KNOBS)

[KIM84] Kim, J.H., Payton, D.W., Olin, K.E., and Tseng, D.Y. A context dependent automatic target recognition system. *Proceedings of SPIE, The International Society for Optical Engineering*, Bellingham, Wash., vol. 485, Applications of Artificial Intelligence, 1984. (ATR)

[KIR83] Kiremidjian G., Clarkson, A., and Lenat, D. Expert system for tactical indications and warning (I&W) analysis. *Proceedings of the Army Conference on the Application of AI to Battlefield Information Management*, Report AD-A139 685, Battelle Columbus Laboratories, Washington, D.C., 1983. (I&W)

[KLA82] Klahr, P., McArthur, D., Narain, S., and Best, E. SWIRL: simulating warfare in the ROSS language. Report N-1885-AF, Rand Corporation, September 1982. (SWIRL)

[KLA84] Klahr, P., Ellis, J., Giarla, W., Narain, S., Cesar, E., and Turner, S. TWIRL: tactical warfare in the ROSS language. Report R-3518-AF, Rand Corporation, Santa Monica, Calif., October 1984. (TWIRL)

[MAS83] Masui, S., McDermott, J., and Sobel, A. Decision-making in time-critical situations. *Proceedings IJCAI-83*, pp. 233–235, 1983. (AIRPLAN)

[MCC83a] McCune, B.P. and Drazovich, R.J. Radar with sight and knowledge. *Defense Electronics*, August 1983. (RTC) (RUBRIC)

[MCC83b] McCune, B.P., Tong, R.M., Dean, J.S., and Shapiro, D.G. RUBRIC: a system for rule-based information retrieval. *Proceedings of the Seventh International Computer Software and Applications Conference (COMPSAC 83)*, IEEE Computer Society, pp. 166–172, November 1983. (RUBRIC)

[MCK84]McKeown, D.M., Harvey, W.A., and McDermott, J. Rule based interpretation of aerial imagery. *Proceedings of the IEEE Workshop on Principles of Knowledge-Based Systems*, IEEE Computer Society, IEEE Computer Society Press, 1109 Spring Street, Silver Spring, Md., 1984. (SPAM)

[NII82] Nii, H.P., Feigenbaum, E.A., Anton, J.J., and Rockmore, A.J. Signal-to-symbol transformation: HASP/SIAP case study. *The AI Magazine*, pp. 23–35, Spring 1982. (SIAP)

[PAZ83a] Pazzani, M.J. Interactive script instantiation. *Proceedings of AAAI*, pp. 320–326, 1983. (KNOBS)

[PFE84] Pfefferkorn, C. ESL, Inc., private communication. 1984.

[PIS84] Pisano, A.D. and Jones, H.L. An expert systems approach to adaptive tactical navigation. *Proceedings of the First Conference on Artificial Intelligence Applications*, IEEE Computer Society, December 1984. (EXPERT NAVIGATOR)

[SCA83] Scarl, E.A., Engelman, C., Pazzani, M.J., and Millen, J. The KNOBS system. MITRE Report, MITRE Corporation, 1983. (KNOBS)

[SCH82] Schwabe, W. and Jamison, L.M. A rule-based policy-level model of nonsuperpower behavior in strategic conflicts. Report R-2962-DNA, Rand Corporation, December 1982. (SCENARIO-AGENT)

[SLA83b] Slagle, J. and Gaynor, M. Expert system consultation control strategy. *Proceedings AAAI-83*, pp. 369–372, 1983. (BATTLE)

[TAY84] Taylor, E.C., Beebe, H.M., Goodman, H.S., and Newell, D.H. Man and machines—a synergy of tactical intelligence. *Defense Electronics*, June 1984. (ADEPT)

[WIL84] Wilson, G., Cromarty, A., Adams, T., Grinberg, M., Tollander, C., and Cunningham, J. AI assists analysts in identifying Soviet radar systems. *Defense Systems Review*, pp. 23–26, January 1984. (ASTA)

Additional Reading

[BEC79] Bechtel, R.J. and Morris, P.H. STAMMER: system for tactical assessment of multisource messages, even radar. NOSC Technical Document 252, Naval Ocean Systems Center, San Diego, Calif., May 1979.

[LEN83b] Lenat, D.B., Clarkson, A., and Kiremidjian, G. An expert system for indications and warning analysis. *Proceedings IJCAI-83*, pp. 259–262, 1983.

[MCC79] McCall, D.C., Morris, P.H., Kibler, D.F., and Bechtel, R.J. STAMMER2 production system for tactical situation assessment. vol. 1, NOSC Technical Document 298, Naval Ocean Systems Center, San Diego, Calif., 1979.

Physics

References

[BAR79] Barstow, D.R. Knowledge engineering in nuclear physics. Proceedings IJCAI-79, vol. 1, pp. 34–36, 1979. (GAMMA)

[BUN79] Bundy, A., Byrd, L., Luger, G., Mellish, C., and Palmer, M. Solving mechanics problems using meta-level inference. In D. Michie (ed.) *Expert Systems in the Micro Electronic Age*, Edinburgh: Edinburgh University Press, 1979. (MECHO)

[LUG81] Luger, G.F. Mathematical model building in the solution of mechanics problems: human protocols and the MECHO trace. *Cognitive Science*, vol. 5, pp. 55–77, 1981. (MECHO)

Process Control

References

[CHE84] Chester, D., Lamb, D., and Dhurjati, P. Rule-based computer alarm analysis in chemical process plants. *Proceedings of the Seventh Annual Conference on Computer Technology*, MICRO-DELCON 84, IEEE, pp. 22–29, March 1984. (FALCON)

[FOX83a] Fox, M.S. Techniques for sensor-based diagnosis. Proceedings IJCAI-83, pp. 158–163, 1983. (PDS)

Additional Reading

[EVE84] Evers, D.C., Smith, D.M., and Staros, C.J. Interfacing an intelligent decision-maker to a real-time control system. Proceedings of SPIE, The International Society for Optical Engineering, Bellingham, Wash., vol. 485, Applications of Artificial Intelligence, 1984.

[MAM82] Mamdani, E.H. Rule-based methods for designing industrial process controllers. Proceedings of the Colloquium on Application of Knowledge Based or Expert Systems, London, 1982.

Space Technology

References

[DIC84] Dickey, F.J. and Toussaint, A.L. ECESIS: an application of expert systems to manned space stations. *Proceedings of the First Conference on Artificial Intelligence Applications*, IEEE Computer Society, December 1984. (ECESIS)

[FRI83] Friedman, L. Research at jet propulsion laboratory (JPL). *The AI Magazine*, pp. 58–59, Winter 1983. (DEVISOR) (FAITH)

[FRI84] Friedman, L. Controlling production firing: the FCL language. Report, Jet Propulsion Laboratory, California Institute of Technology, Pasadena, Calif., 1984. (FAITH)

[KIN83] King, Jr., F. Artificial intelligence. Report, Ford Aerospace & Communications Corporation, Houston, Tex., 1983. (RPMS)

[MAR84a] Marsh, A.K. Pace of artificial intelligence research shows acceleration *Aviation Week & Space Technology*, December 10, 1984. (NAVEX)

[MAR84b] Marsh, A.K. NASA to demonstrate artificial intelligence in flight operations. *Aviation Week & Space Technology*, September 17, 1984. (NAVEX)

[MAR84c] Marsh, C. AI Laboratory, Ford Aerospace & Communications Corporation, Houston, Texas, private communication, 1984. (RBMS)

[SCA84a] Scarl, E. Applications of a non-rule knowledge-based system to NASA scheduling and monitoring problems. *IECEC Proceedings*, San Francisco, August 1984. (KNOBS) (KNEECAP) (LES)

[SCA84b] Scarl, E., Jamieson, J., and Delaune, C. Knowledge-based fault monitoring and diagnosis in space shuttle propellant loading. *Proceedings of the National Aeronautics and Electronics Conference*, Dayton, Ohio, 1984. (LES)

General Surveys

[ANO82] An overview of expert systems. National Technical Information Service, PB83-217562, NBSIR-82-2505, October 1982.

[BAR81] Barr, A. and Feigenbaum, E.A. (eds.) *The Handbook of Artificial Intelligence*, Vol. 1. William Kaufmann, 1981.

[BRA83] Brachman, R., Amarel, S., Engelman, C., Engelmore, R., Feigenbaum, E., and Wilkins, D. What are expert systems? In F. Hayes-Roth, D.A. Waterman, and D. Lenat (eds.) *Building Expert Systems*, Reading, Mass.: Addison-Wesley, 1983.

[COH82] Cohen, P.R. and Feigenbaum, E.A. *The Handbook of Artificial Intelligence, Volume 3*. William Kaufmann, 1982.

[DAV82] Davis, R. Expert systems: Where are we? And where do we go from here? *The AI Magazine*, pp. 3–22, Spring 1982.

[DUD81] Duda, R.O. and Gaschnig, J. Knowledge-based systems come of age. *BYTE*, vol. 6, pp. 238–281, 1981.

[DUD83] Duda, R.O. and Shortliffe, E.H. Expert systems research. *Science*, vol. 220, no. 4594, April 1983.

[FEI81] Feigenbaum, E.A. Expert systems in the 1980s. In A.H. Bond, (ed.) *Machine Intelligence*, Infotech State of the Art Report, series 9, no 3., Pergamon Infotech Limited, 1981.

[GOL77a] Goldstein, I. and Papert, S. Artificial intelligence, language and the study of knowledge. *Cognitive Science*, vol. 1, no. 1, 1977.

[HAY83a] Hayes-Roth, F., Waterman, D.A., and Lenat, D. (eds.) *Building Expert Systems*, Reading, Mass.: Addison-Wesley, 1983.

[HAY83b] Hayes-Roth, F., Waterman, D.A., and Lenat, D. An overview of expert systems. In Hayes-Roth, Waterman, and Lenat (eds.) *Building Expert Systems*, Reading, Mass.: Addison-Wesley, 1983.

[WAT83] Waterman, D.A. and Hayes-Roth, F. An investigation of tools for building expert systems. In F. Hayes-Roth, D.A. Waterman, and D. Lenat (eds.) *Building Expert Systems*, Reading, Mass.: Addison-Wesley, 1983.

27

Index for Expert System Tools

How to Use This Index

This index will help you locate any particular expert system tool described in Chapter 28, the catalog of expert system tools. The tools in this index are arranged alphabetically by system name. The system-building aids are all grouped under the category *aid*, while the languages are grouped according to the primary knowledge representation method used by the language. To locate a tool in Chapter 28, first determine the appropriate category as indicated by this index; then look for the tool under that category.

Expert System Tools and Their Representation Methods

ACLS:	aid
ADVISE:	aid
AGE:	aid
AIMDS:	frame
ALICE:	logic
AL/X:	rule
AMORD:	rule
APES:	logic
APLICOT:	logic
ARBY:	rule
ARS:	rule

ART:	rule
C:	procedure
COMMON LISP:	procedure
CONCHE:	aid
CSRL:	frame
DETEKTR:	aid
DPL:	frame
DUCK:	logic
EMYCIN:	rule
ERS:	rule
ETS:	aid
EXPERT:	rule
EXPERT-EASE:	aid
EXPERT-2:	rule
EXPRS:	rule
FIT:	logic
FLAVORS:	object
FOL:	logic
FRL:	frame
GEN-X:	rule
GETREE:	aid
GLIB:	rule
GPSI:	rule
GUESS/1:	rule
HCPRVR:	logic
HEARSAY-III:	rule
HPRL:	frame
HSRL:	logic
IMPULSE:	aid
IN-ATE/KE:	aid
INTERLISP:	procedure
INTERLISP-D:	procedure
KANDOR:	frame
KAS:	rule
KBS:	object
KEE:	frame
KES:	rule
KL-ONE:	frame
KMS:	frame
KRL:	frame
KRT:	aid
KRYPTON:	frame
LES:	rule
LISP:	procedure

28

Catalog of Expert System Tools

This catalog contains summaries of selected expert system tools. See Chapter 27 to determine how the tools are categorized. Although most of the tools belong in more than one category, no attempt has been made to indicate all the categories to which the tools actually belong; they are listed under the major category only.

Chapter 29 contains a bibliography for the tools described here. The papers referenced in the bibliography are highly technical, and most are written for people with an AI/expert systems background.

This catalog of expert system tools is not complete; it represents only a small portion of the tools actually available for expert system applications. The intent was to provide the reader with a broad enough selection to understand the variety and nature of current tools for building expert systems.[1]

Aids to System Building

ACLS is a system-building aid that induces rules for an expert system from examples of decisions provided by a domain expert. The user specifies the problem in terms of the set of attributes relevant to the decision and the possible decision classes. The user then gives

---

[1] If your expert system tool is not included in this catalog and you would like it included in the next edition of the book, please send a one-paragraph description of the tool (using a format similar to that used in this chapter) plus research reports describing your work to the author.

ACLS examples of situation-decision pairs, from which it creates general rules that classify the examples in terms of their attributes. The user can supply examples and counterexamples interactively, thereby dynamically correcting or refining the rules. ACLS can output a rule either as a decision tree or as a PASCAL program. The rule induction is based on Ross Quinlan's ID3 inductive learning algorithm. ACLS is implemented in UCSD-PASCAL and operates on APPLE II+ and IBM PC microcomputers. ACLS was developed at the University of Edinburgh and is available from Intelligent Terminals Limited as a commercial system. (Analog Concept Learning System) [PAT82a]

ADVISE is a general-purpose, system-building aid consisting of an integrated set of development tools. The tools include support for multiple forms of knowledge representation (rules, semantic nets, and relational data bases), support for several certainty propagation schemes (probabilistic, approximate Bayesian, min/max logic, and weighting evidence), support for various control strategies (utility optimization, probabilistic network traversal, and forward and backward rule chaining), and the incorporation of inductive learning programs (GEM and CLUSTER) for inductively deriving decision rules and control information from examples. GEM generalizes examples of different concepts and creates formal logic rules for recognizing them. CLUSTER automatically constructs a classification of given entities using a conceptual clustering approach. In explanation mode, ADVISE paraphrases decision rules, allows simple interrogation of the knowledge base, and displays its reasoning steps. ADVISE is implemented in PASCAL and operates on DEC VAX computers under the UNIX operating system. ADVISE was developed at the University of Illinois as a research system. [MIC83b]

AGE is a system-building design aid that helps the builder select a framework, design a rule language, and assemble the pieces into a complete expert system. AGE consists of a set of *building blocks* in the form of INTERLISP functions that support various expert system architectures. These include inference engines for forward and backward chaining and structures for representing a *blackboard architecture*, a framework where independent groups of rules called *knowledge sources* communicate through a central data base called a *blackboard*. AGE is implemented in INTERLISP and is designed for use by experienced INTERLISP programmers. It was developed at Stanford University as a research system. (Attempt to GEneralize) [AIE81a, 81b, NII79]

CONCHE is a system-building aid that helps check the completeness and consistency of domain knowledge and theory formation in the context of organic reaction mechanisms. Using examples presented during an interactive dialogue with a chemist, CONCHE derives a set of rules related to the relative strengths of organic acids. The essential domain theory is represented as MYCIN-like rules with additional domain knowledge encoded as facts in a semantic net. CONCHE uses a standard backward-chaining inference mechanism with MYCIN-like certainty factors. Explanations are presented in terms of rule chaining, facts accessed, and unsatisfied/unsatisfiable conditions. CONCHE is implemented in a combination of LISP and FUZZY. It was developed at the University of Leeds and reached the stage of an experimental system. (CONsistency CHEcker) [CHI79]

DETEKTR is a system-building aid that helps domain experts construct expert troubleshooting systems. DETEKTER contains a diagram manager, a communications manager, a rule processor, and a rule acquisition subsystem built upon GLIB. The expert communicates with the system by pointing: An object is referred to by pointing at its representation in a diagram displayed on the screen. DETEKTR supports multiple diagrams relating to the task at hand, manages the pointing relations between them, and handles other display requirements, such as waveform pictures, English rule text, and question-answering dialogues. DETEKTR is written in SMALLTALK-80 and operates on the Tektronix 4404 Artificial Intelligence System. It was developed by Tektronix, Inc. as a research system. (Development Environment for TEKtronix TRoubleshooters) [FRE84a]

ETS is a system-building aid that helps a domain expert construct and analyze OPS5 knowledge bases. ETS interviews a domain expert, helps the expert analyze an initial set of heuristics and parameters for the problem, and automatically produces a set of rules. ETS helps the expert express the problem in terms of a rating grid, using elicitation techniques based on George Kelly's personal construct theory work in psychotherapy. ETS generates rules with certainty factors which may be reviewed and modified by the expert. ETS is written in INTERLISP-D and operates on Xerox 1100 series workstations. It was developed by Boeing Computer Services as a research system. (Expertise Transfer System) [BOO84]

EXPERT-EASE is a system-building aid that helps a domain expert construct an expert system. The expert defines the problem in terms of features or factors that lead to particular results, and the system queries the expert for examples describing conditions leading to each result. From the examples, the system learns a procedure for solving the problem and generates a decision tree representing that procedure. EXPERT-EASE is implemented in PASCAL and operates on an IBM PC or XT with 128K of memory. It was developed by

Intelligent Terminals Ltd. of Great Britain as a commercial system. [PER83, WHI84]

GETREE is a system-building aid for managing a knowledge base organized as a network that forms an AND/OR graph representation of rules. The AND/OR graph provides the mechanism for direct graphic documentation of the rules, for answering *how, how not, why,* and *why not* questions about conclusions and facts, for displaying execution traces of forward or backward chaining inferences, for modifying inference strategies, and for teaching the rules to a user. The support environment includes an interactive graphical interface that uses a VT100 alphanumeric terminal with graphics character set and spoken output via a speech synthesizer. GETREE operates on DEC VAX computers under the VMS operating system. It was developed by General Electric Company as a research system. [LEW83b]

GPSI is a system-building aid for the construction of rule-based systems. It consists of an integrated collection of tools that include: a monitor for supervising the interaction between different units in the system, a knowledge acquisition unit, an inference engine, a rule compiler, and a user interface. The knowledge acquisition unit provides both text and graphical editing facilities to help users construct rules. It also handles bookkeeping and answers user queries about the system's rules. GPSI contains mechanisms for certainty handling and automatic user querying. It can also execute the expert system by applying the inference engine to the compiled rules. GPSI was developed at the University of Illinois as an experimental system. (General Purpose System for Inferencing) [HAR83, 84a]

IMPULSE is a system-building aid that provides editing facilities for the STROBE knowledge engineering language. This display-oriented knowledge base editor provides four levels of editing: a top-level knowledge base manager, a knowledge base editor, an object/slot editor, and a facet editor. Each level has an editor window and associated command menus. IMPULSE also provides a graphical display of tree and graph hierarchies. Objects for editing may be selected from menus and from nodes in graphically displayed trees. IMPULSE is implemented in INTERLISP-D and operates on the Xerox 1100 series workstations. It was developed by Schlumberger-Doll Research as a research system. [SCH83b]

IN-ATE/KE is a system-building aid for constructing fault diagnosis expert systems. Knowledge is represented as a high-level block diagram of the unit under test and includes information about component/test point connectivity. IN-ATE/KE supports a PROS-PECTOR-like, rule-based semantic network and a data base containing component failure rates, accessible test points, test and setup costs, and component replacement costs. Semantic constraints on testing order are specified through rule preconditions. IN-ATE/KE generates an expert system in the IN-ATE framework and produces a testability report that includes a binary fault diagnosis decision tree. IN-ATE/KE (previously called IN-ATE/2) was developed at Automated Reasoning Corporation as a commercial system. (INtelligent-Automatic Test Equipment/Knowledge Engineering) [CAN84]

KRL is a knowledge engineering language for frame-based representation, but it also supports procedural representation methods. Its principal characteristics include procedural attachment such as associating procedures with the slots in a frame, inheritance of procedural as well as declarative properties of an object, and multiple perspectives such as permitting descriptors corresponding to different viewpoints to be attached to a single object. The KRL system is implemented in INTERLISP. It was developed by the Xerox Palo Alto Research Center as a research system. (Knowledge Representation Language) [BOB77, BRA79]

KRT is a system-building aid that helps members of a large engineering development effort record, communicate, and integrate their designs with other members of the team. With the KRT system, team members can describe what a particular engineering system (e.g., guidance analysis, navigation) does, how it functions, how it is organized, and how its parts are related. This includes a data flow diagram to provide a system overview, process specifications to show how input data are transformed into output data, and a data dictionary that provides a hierarchical description of data. The KRT system is implemented in ZETALISP and FLAVORS for the Symbolics 3600. It was developed by McDonnell Douglas as an experimental system. [MYE85]

MORE is a system-building aid that generates diagnostic rules through its interviews with domain experts. As the expert enters symptoms and findings, MORE asks for additional information that could provide a stronger diagnostic assessment. From this and other information, MORE develops a model of the domain and uses it to generate the diagnostic rules. As the rules are accumulated, MORE looks for weaknesses and suggests types of knowledge that would allow more powerful diagnostic rules to be generated. It also checks for inconsistencies in the way the expert has assigned certainty factors to the rules. MORE was developed at Carnegie-Mellon University as a research system. [KAH84e]

PICON is a system-building aid for developing process control expert systems. It supports object-oriented, frame-based, and rule-based representation methods and combines both forward and backward chaining control schemes. Knowledge acquisition from a domain expert is accomplished through a graphics-oriented interface which helps transfer structural information, process descriptions, and heuristics into the knowledge base. PICON also provides an explanation facility and the ability to dynamically update the expertise contained in the system. PICON is implemented in ZETALISP and the C programming language and operates on LMI's Lambda/Plus workstations. It was developed by Lisp Machines Inc. (LMI) as a commercial system. (Process Intelligent CONtrol system) [MOO84, MOR84]

PIE is a system-building aid that extends the capabilities of SMALL-TALK-76 by facilitating the representation and manipulation of designs. SMALLTALK-76 is an object-oriented programming language. PIE's principal characteristic is the use of multiple perspectives. This mechanism provides a way to specify independent specialized behaviors for an object. The support environment consists of all of the features and support facilities of SMALLTALK. PIE was developed by the Xerox Palo Alto Research Center as an experimental system. (Personal Information Environment) [GOL80]

PLUME is a system-building aid for developing natural language interfaces to expert systems. It is based on the DYPAR-II natural language interpreter developed at Carnegie-Mellon University. Adapting PLUME to a new application domain involves extending the lexicon and writing case frames and grammatical rules for the words and phrases commonly used within the domain application. PLUME can handle ellipsis, ambiguous input, and pronoun resolution. The support environment includes grammar rule and case frame editing tools and trace and debugging facilities. PLUME is implemented in COMMON LISP and operates on the Carnegie Group workstations, the DEC VAX/VMS systems, and the Symbolics 3600 series workstations. It was developed by Carnegie Group Inc. as a commercial system. [CAR84a]

ROGET is a system-building aid that helps a domain expert design a knowledge base for a diagnosis-type expert system. It interacts with the expert, asking pertinent questions that identify types of subproblems the expert system must solve, the results or solutions the system must produce, the evidence or data required to solve the problem, and the relationships between the data or facts of a case and its solution (e.g., what factors support the determination of the solution or indicate other factors). The system has been tested in the medical domain. ROGET is implemented in an extended version of EMYCIN that permits forward chaining rules and calls to subroutines called *task blocks*. It was developed at Stanford University as an experimental system. (It is named for Peter Mark Roget (1779-1869) of Roget's Thesaurus fame.) [BEN83]

RULEMASTER is a system-building aid for developing rule-based expert systems. It consists of an integrated set of tools including RADIAL, an extensible language for expressing rules, and a rule induction system that creates rules from sets of examples. Its principal characteristics include the induction of rules from examples, hierarchical structuring of generated rules, the capability to access external data and processes via programs written in any Unix supported language, automatic generation of explanations as complete English sentences, and user-definable data types and operators. RULE-MASTER is implemented in the C programming language and operates on minicomputers and microcomputers, such as VAXs and Sun workstations, under the Unix operating system. It was developed by Radian Corporation as a commercial system. [MIC84b, RIE85]

RULE WRITER is a system-building aid that helps knowledge engineers formulate rules in the EXPERT language. RULE WRITER uses knowledge about training cases, a taxonomy of plausible associations in the domain, and causal mechanisms to produce a model that correctly classifies the training cases on the basis of their stored findings. Its associational and causal knowledge guides a rule induction process performed on the example training cases. The classification rules learned from training cases are expressed directly in EXPERT. RULE WRITER is implemented in LISP. It was developed at Rutgers University as a research system. [DRA84]

SEEK is a system-building aid that gives advice about rule refinement during the development of a diagnostic-type expert system. It helps refine rules represented in the EXPERT language but expressed in a tabular format. SEEK suggests possible ways to generalize or specialize rules by looking for regularities in the rules' performance on a body of stored cases with known conclusions. The system is interactive; it suggests the type of change (generalization or specialization) and what components to change, but it lets the user decide exactly how to generalize or specialize those components. This refinement method works best when the expert's knowledge is fairly accurate, and small changes in the knowledge base may lead to significant improvement in the performance of the expert system. SEEK is implemented in FORTRAN and was originally designed to operate on a DEC-20 system. It was developed at Rutgers University as a research system. [POL84]

TEIRESIAS is a system-building aid that facilitates the interactive transfer of knowledge from a domain expert to a knowledge base. The system interacts with the user in a restricted subset of English to acquire new rules about the problem domain. TEIRESIAS also assists with knowledge base debugging, using mechanisms for explanation and simple consistency checking. TEIRESIAS is implemented in INTERLISP. It was developed at Stanford University as a research system. (Named for the blind seer Teiresias in the Greek tragedy *Oedipus the King*.) [DAV76, 78, 79]

TIMM is a system-building aid that helps a domain expert construct an expert system. The expert provides a list of all possible decisions that can be made and the names and values of factors to consider in arriving at a decision. The system then asks for examples of factors and their values that lead to each of the decisions and uses these examples to infer a set of IF-THEN rules for reaching the same decisions. TIMM supports the use of certainty values to represent probabilistic information. It was developed in FORTRAN and operates on the VAX 11/780 and other computers. TIMM was developed by General Research Corporation as a commercial system. (The Intelligent Machine Model) [KIS83, KOR84b, PAR84b]

T.1 is a system-building aid in the form of a tutorial package that provides an introduction to knowledge engineering for technical professionals and managers. It includes videotape lectures, laboratory exercises, demonstration software systems, and reading materials. The software systems used to demonstrate basic knowledge engineering concepts use a modified version of Teknowledge's M.1 language and operate on the IBM PC running the PC DOS 2.0 operating system. T.1 was developed by Teknowledge as a commercial system (or package). [TEK84c]

Frame-based Languages

AIMDS is a knowledge engineering language for frame-based representation, but it also supports procedure-oriented representation methods. Its principal characteristics include deductive and nondeductive reasoning, multiple inheritance, maintenance of belief contexts, automatic detection of knowledge-base inconsistencies, reasoning about hypothetical worlds, procedural attachment, and the use of expectations to guide actions and perform analogical inference. AIMDS is implemented in FUZZY, which is itself implemented in UCI-LISP, and provides access to all of the features and support tools of the LISP and FUZZY environments. AIMDS was developed at Rutgers University as a research system. [SRI78a]

CSRL is a knowledge engineering language for frame-based representation. It supports the representation of concepts in a diagnostic hierarchy as a collection of specialists. It also supports an establish-refine approach to diagnosis, implemented within CSRL via message passing among concepts. The support environment includes a syntax checker, commands for invoking any concept with any message, and a simple trace facility. CSRL is implemented in ELISP, uses a version of FRL, and operates on a DEC 20/60 computer system. It was developed at Ohio State University as a research system. (Conceptual Structures Representation Language) [BYL83, SMI84b]

DPL is a knowledge engineering language for creating and manipulating frame-based representations of LSI designs. Its principal characteristic is the ability to represent both design and structure information in a single set of data structures. This uniform representation scheme can be used as a data base for answering questions about such things as the connectivity of the device and also can be used to simulate the device's behavior. The support environment includes an interactive graphics editor for creating LSI designs in the form of DPL procedures. DPL is implemented in ZETALISP and operates on Symbolics 3600 Lisp Machines. It was developed at MIT as a research system. (Design Procedure Language) [BAT80, DAV82b, DAV83a]

FRL is a knowledge engineering language for frame-based representation. Its principal characteristics include support for multiple inheritance, defaults, constraints such as requirements and preferences, abstraction, indirection, and procedural attachment which includes IF-ADDED, IF-NEEDED, and IF-REMOVED methods. FRL was developed at MIT as an experimental system. (Frame Representation Language) [GOL77b, GOL79]

HPRL is a knowledge engineering language for frame-based representation. It integrates a frame representation scheme with a rule-based representation. A core set of LISP functions perform rule execution under the supervision of a frame-based rule interpreter. HPRL supports forward and backward chaining control schemes and metarules that enable users to construct arbitrarily complex reasoning strategies. HPRL is an extension of FRL; it is implemented in PSL (a portable dialect of LISP) and operates on DEC VAX and HP-9836 computer systems. HPRL was developed by the computer research laboratory of Hewlett-Packard as a research system. (Heuristic Programming and Representation Language) [ROS83, LAN84]

KANDOR is a knowledge engineering language for frame-based representation. Its expressive power is purposely limited to provide computational tractability in the form of ease of use and enhanced performance. The internal structure of KANDOR is intentionally hidden from the user, who is presented instead with a well-defined simple interface to frames, slots, restrictions, and slot fillers. KANDOR is implemented LISP. It was developed at the Fairchild Laboratory for Artificial Intelligence Research as a research system. [PAT84]

KEE is a knowledge engineering language for frame-based representation. It also supports rule-based, procedure-oriented, and object-oriented representation methods. Its principal characteristics include multiple knowledge bases to facilitate modular system design and forward and backward chaining for its rule interpreter. Its support environment includes a graphics-oriented debugging package and an explanation facility that uses graphic displays to indicate inference chains. KEE is written in INTERLISP and operates on the Xerox 1100 and Symbolics 3600 computer systems. It was developed by Intellicorp for applications in molecular genetics, but it is now available as a general-purpose commercial system. (Knowledge Engineering Environment) [KEH84, KUN84]

KL-ONE is a knowledge engineering language for frame-based representation. Its principal characteristics include automatic inheritance, support for semantic nets using subsumption and other relations, and an automatic classifier. The support environment contains an interactive graphics-oriented knowledge base editor and display tools. KL-ONE is implemented in INTERLISP-D and operates on Xerox 1100 LISP machines and DEC VAX computer systems. It was developed at Bolt, Beranek and Newman as a research system. [SCH81, SCH83a, WOO83]

KMS is a knowledge engineering language for frame-based representation, but it also supports rule-based representation methods. KMS consists of a collection of subsystems, each with it own knowledge representation and inference methods. Its principal characteristics include rule-based deduction, statistical pattern classification using Bayes' theorem, linear discriminant and other scoring functions, and frame-based inference generation. KMS is implemented in LISP and operates on a Univac 1100/40. It was developed at the University of Maryland as a research system. (Knowledge Management System) [REG81]

KRYPTON is a knowledge engineering language for frame-based representation, but it also supports logic-based representation methods. Its principal characteristics include a terminological component that helps define frames and networks of frames and an assertional component that uses a nonclausal connection graph resolution theorem prover for maintaining a data base of logical assertions about items defined using frames. KRYPTON is implemented in INTERLISP-D.

It was developed at Fairchild Laboratory for Artificial Intelligence Research as a research system. [BRA83a, PIG84]

NETL is a knowledge engineering language for frame-based representation of semantic networks. Its principal characteristic is the ability to create and manipulate virtual copies of arbitrarily large and complex portions of the semantic network. These copies inherit the entire structure of the descriptions that are copied, including all parts, subparts, and internal relationships. NETL is implemented in MAC-LISP. It was developed at MIT as a research system. [FAH79]

OWL is a knowledge engineering language for frame-based representation. Its principal characteristics include a semantic net framework that supports a conceptual taxonomy with concept specialization and a flexible inheritance mechanism. All knowledge is maintained in a single, large, unified knowledge base augmented by a small set of embedded LISP and machine language programs and their associated data structures. OWL is implemented in LISP. It was developed at MIT as a research system. [HAW75]

RLL is a knowledge engineering language for frame-based representation. Its flexibility allows the user to specify a domain-specific representation language by expressing a particular set of representations, inheritance strategies, and control schemes. RLL also allows procedural attachment and general LISP structures to be incorporated as slots of frames. The support environment includes a sophisticated editor capable of checking both syntax and semantics. RLL is implemented in INTERLISP. It was developed at Stanford University as a research system. (Representation Language Language) [GRE80, BAR83, WAT83]

SRL is a knowledge engineering language for frame-based representation. Its principal characteristics include automatic and user-definable inheritance relationships and multiple contexts. SRL provides a set of primitives for defining relations and their inheritance semantics including search specification parameters to modify the inheritance search procedure. Each frame or *schema* in SRL may have *metalevel knowledge* associated with it, that is, knowledge about how SRL uses its domain knowledge. Multiple contexts are provided to support revision management of models and for reasoning in alternative worlds. A dialect of SRL called SRL/1.5 is implemented in FRANZ LISP and operates on a DEC VAX running UNIX. It was developed at the Robotics Institute of Carnegie-Mellon University as a research system. (Schema Representation Language) [WRI83]

SRL+ is a knowledge engineering language for frame-based representation. It also supports logic-based, rule-based, and object-oriented representation methods. Its principal characteristics include user-definable inheritance relations, procedural attachment, an agenda mechanism, a discrete simulation language, and a user-definable error handling facility. The support environment includes an embedded data base management system, support for producing 2-D and business graphics, and an interface based on the PLUME natural language parser. SRL+ is implemented in COMMON LISP and FRANZ LISP and operates on Carnegie Group workstations, DEC VAXs under VMS, and Symbolics 3600 workstations. It was developed by the Carnegie Group Inc. as a commercial system. (Schema Representation Language +)

UNIT PACKAGE is a knowledge engineering language for frame-based representation. Its principal characteristic is the organization of frames into a partitioned semantic network. A built-in generalization relationship supports hierarchical structures with several modes of property inheritance. UNIT PACKAGE also provides pattern matchers and an attached procedure mechanism. UNIT PACKAGE is implemented in INTERLISP and operates under the TENEX and TOPS20 operating systems. It was developed at Stanford University as a research system. [STE79]

Logic-based Languages

ALICE is a knowledge engineering language for logic-based representation. Its principal characteristics include an extensive vocabulary for describing combinatorial problems in operations research and a process for achieving goals that involves finding any feasible solution, repeatedly building up better solutions, and giving the proof of the optimality of the solution. ALICE was developed at the Institut de Programmation, Paris, as an experimental system. (A Language for Intelligent Combinatorial Exploration) [LAU78]

APES is a knowledge engineering language for logic-based representation. It provides a user interface for writing expert systems in the Micro-PROLOG logic programming language. Its principal characteristics include handling of uncertain information, an explanation facility, and extensions to PROLOG that provide interactive facilities for user interfaces. Rules and facts in the knowledge base are expressed as PROLOG clauses. APES supports MYCIN-style, Bayesian-style, and user-defined certainty handling modules. It is implemented in Micro-PROLOG and operates on a wide range of microcomputers including North Star Horizons and IBM PCs. APES was developed at Imperial College, London, and is available as a commercial system. (A Prolog Expert system Shell) [HAM82, 83]

APLICOT is a knowledge engineering language for logic-based representation. Its principal characteristics include a flexible control scheme utilizing both forward and backward chaining, certainty factor handling, and an explanation mode. The support environment consists of PROLOG utility packages such as an interactive clause/rule editor. APLICOT is implemented in DEC-10 PROLOG and operates on an ICOT DEC-2060 computer system. It was developed at the University of Tokyo as an experimental system. [MIZ83]

DUCK is a knowledge engineering language for logic-based representation. Its principal characteristic is the combination of four AI paradigms: logic programming, rule-based systems, nonmonotonic reasoning, and deductive search. DUCK uses a notation based on first-order predicate calculus, where the conditions and actions of rules are logical predicates. DUCK achieves nonmonotonic reasoning through dependency directed backtracking that uses a truth maintenance system and data pools. DUCK supports forward and backward chaining control schemes. It is implemented in NISP, a portable dialect of LISP, and operates on DEC VAX's running UNIX or VMS and the Symbolics 3600 and Apollo workstations. It was developed by Smart Systems Technology as a commercial system. [APP84]

FIT is a programming language for logic-based representation. It can be viewed as an integration of some of PROLOG's relational features with functional LISP features. FIT consists of a kernel and an interactive user interface. Its principal characteristics include breadth-oriented, nonchronological parallelism, and the ability to define algorithms as functions or relations and then dynamically use the functions as relations or the relations as functions. FIT retains the nonsequenced meaning of logical conjunction by using simultaneous evaluation (AND parallelism). FIT is implemented in a purely functional subset of UCI-LISP and operates on DEC-10 computer systems. It was developed at the University of Hamburg as a research system. [BOL83]

HCPRVR is a logic-based programming language and interpreter. An HCPRVR program is an ordered list of axioms, each of which is either an atomic formula or an implication. An atomic formula is an arbitrary LISP expression beginning with a LISP atom which is referred to as its predicate name. HCPRVR allows the use of LISP functions in place of predicate names, in which case the function is called instead of having the HCPRVR interpreter prove the formula. The interpreter is a Horn clause-based theorem prover. HCPRVR is implemented in LISP and was originally designed to operate on DEC PDP-10 computer systems. It was developed at the University of Texas at Austin as a research system. (Horn Clause theorem PRoVeR) [CHE80]

HSRL is a knowledge engineering language that provides logic programming capabilities. HSRL is embedded in SRL and effectively combines frame-based and logic-based representations. Logic programs are expressed as SRL frames. Atomic formulas can refer to information embedded in the frames; thus rules about properties of frames may use information from both the SRL knowledge base and the axioms in a logic-program schema. The support environment includes an interactive facility for creating, editing, and executing HSRL programs. The HSRL interpreter is a modified version of the HCPRVR logic program interpreter. HSRL is implemented in FRANZ LISP as an extension to SRL and operates under UNIX. It was developed at the Robotics Institute of Carnegie-Mellon University as a research system. [WRI83]

PROLOG is a programming language for logic-based representation. Programs in PROLOG consist of rules (inference relations) for proving relations among objects. The PROLOG interpreter attempts to find proofs of the truth of specified relations through backward chaining, using unification and backtracking as needed. Many versions and implementations of PROLOG exist, a number of which embed PROLOG within a LISP environment for additional flexibility. PROLOG is available commercially from various vendors to run on a large number of computer systems. For example, Quintus Computer Systems is marketing a version of PROLOG that operates on DEC 10 and DEC 20 computers. [ALT84c, BOW82, CLA82a, CLA82b, CLO81, CLO84, KOW79a, KOW79b, MCD80a, ROB82, VER84, WAR77]

Object-oriented Languages

FLAVORS is a programming language for object-oriented representation within ZETALISP. It augments the ZETALISP environment, allowing it to support structured objects (much as STROBE provides object-oriented support for INTERLISP). Its principal characteristics include simple definition of abstract types, message passing, and generalization hierarchies. FLAVORS also allows property lists to be associated with objects. FLAVORS is implemented in ZETALISP and operates on the Symbolics 3600 series workstations. It was developed by Symbolics as a commercial system. [WEI81a]

KBS is a knowledge engineering language for object-oriented representation involving simulation models. It also supports frame-based representation methods. KBS's principal characteristic is its use of object-oriented modeling for simulation. The support environment contains interactive model construction and modification tools that are supported by generic schemata from model libraries of objects and relations. It also contains model consistency and completeness checking facilities. KBS is implemented in SRL which runs under the VAX FRANZ LISP system. It was developed at the Robotics Institute of Carnegie-Mellon University as an experimental system. (Knowledge-Based Simulation system) [RED82]

LOOPS is a knowledge engineering language for object-oriented representation. It also supports rule-based, access-oriented, and procedure-oriented representation methods. Its principal characteristic is the integration of its four programming schemes to allow the paradigms to be used together in system building. For example, rules and rule sets are considered LOOPS objects, and procedures can be LISP functions or rule sets. The support system contains display-oriented debugging tools, such as break packages and editors. LOOPS is implemented in INTERLISP-D and operates on Xerox 1100 series workstations. It was developed at the Xerox Palo Alto Research Center as a research system. [BOB83, STE83b, STE83d]

ROSS is a programming language for object-oriented respresentation and simulation. It supports inheritance of attributes and behaviors from multiple parents and permits the free mixing of ROSS commands and LISP function calls. The support environment consists of a display editor for objects and an abbreviation package to facilitate program readability. ROSS is implemented in FRANZ LISP and operates on DEC VAX systems under UNIX. It was developed by the Rand Corporation as a research system. (Rule-Oriented System for Simulation) [MCA82, MCA84]

SMALLTALK is a programming language for object-oriented representation. Objects are organized hierarchically into classes with each subclass inheriting the instance storage requirements and message protocols of its superclass. Subclasses may also add new information of their own and may override inherited behaviors. The SMALLTALK environment consists of a graphical, highly interactive user interface that makes use of a high-resolution graphics display screen and a mouse or other pointing device. SMALLTALK was developed by the Xerox Palo Alto Research Center throughout the 1970s and early 1980s as a research system and operates on Xerox 1100 workstations.

Tektronix offers the latest version of the language, SMALLTALK-8(as a commercial system that operates on the TEK 4404 workstatior [BOR82, GOL80, GOL83]

STROBE is a programming language for object-oriented representatior within INTERLISP. It augments the INTERLISP environment, giv ing it the ability to support structured objects (much as FLAVOR$ provides object-oriented support for ZETALISP). Its principal char acteristics include multiple resident knowledge bases, support foi generalization hierarchies, a flexible property inheritance mecha nism, procedural attachment, and indirect procedure invocation STROBE also allows nonobject nodes in its knowledge base, such a$ S-expressions, LISP functions, bit maps, and arrays. STROBE i$ implemented in INTERLISP. It was developed by Schlumberger Doll Research as a research system. [SMI83]

Procedure-oriented Languages

C is a programming language for procedure-oriented representation. A relatively low-level and efficient language, it is often used for writ ing operating systems and has been called a *system programming* lan guage. The UNIX operating system itself is written almost entirely in C. C deals directly with characters, numbers, and addresses rather than with character strings, sets, lists, or arrays, as a higher level language might. It offers straightforward tests, loops, and sub programs but not more exotic control, such as parallel operations or coroutines. C was designed for use with UNIX operating systems and operates on a wide variety of computers (e.g., DEC VAXs). It was developed by Bell Laboratories and is available as a commercial system. [KER78]

COMMON LISP is a programming language for procedural representa tion. This new LISP dialect is designed to provide a standard LISP that is compatible with a wide range of computers. It incorporates an extensive and complex set of data types and control structures into a portable system. It was developed at Carnegie-Mellon Univer sity. COMMON LISP is available as a commercial system from a number of companies, e.g., from Gold Hill Computers as GCLISP, and from Digital Equipment Corporation as VAX LISP. [STE81b, STE84]

INTERLISP is a programming language designed for procedure-oriented representation. This dialect of LISP has all the standard LISP fea tures plus an elaborate support environment that includes sophisticated debugging facilities with tracing and conditional breakpoints, a LISP-oriented editor, and a "do what I mean" facility that corrects many kinds of errors on the spot. The environment also allows users to modify normally fixed aspects of the system, such as interrupt characters and garbage collection allocation. INTERLISP operates on a variety of Xerox machines (see INTERLISP-D). It was developed by Xerox Corporaton as a commercial system. [TEI75, TEI81]

INTERLISP-D is a programming language designed for procedure-oriented representation. This version of INTERLISP operates on Xerox 1100 computer systems. It provides all the standard INTER-LISP features plus a sophisticated support environment tied to a graphical monitor. INTERLISP-D was developed by Xerox as a commercial system. [SHE83]

LISP is a programming language for procedure-oriented representation. This very flexible language provides a small set of primitive functions from which the user can construct higher-level functions tailored to the needs of the application. LISP has mechanisms for manipulating symbols in the form of list structures; such structures are useful building blocks for representing complex concepts. LISP provides automatic memory management and the uniform treatment of code and data, which allows a LISP program to modify its own code. Many dialects of LISP are available, e.g., INTERLISP, MACLISP, FRANZ LISP, COMMON LISP, and ZETALISP, just to mention a few. LISP was developed at MIT in the late 1950s and has become the most widely used programming language for AI applications. (LISt Processing language) [SIK76, ALL78, WIN81, VER84]

MUMPS is a procedure-oriented programming language. Like LISP, MUMPS is an interpreted, typeless language that supports atomic and composite variables. It differs from LISP principally in its support for multidimensional arrays as multiway trees with descendents ordered by the values of the array indexes. The implicit ordering of data inserted into the tree structures provides automatic sorting by insertion key. MUMPS supports recursion and provides a set of functions for tree traversal. It has no provision for parameterized procedures or local environments; thus all variables are global in scope. MUMPS was originally developed for use in medical computing. It is available for a wide variety of computer systems, and an ANSI standard definition of the language exists. [CUR84]

PSL is a procedure-oriented programming language. This portable dialect of LISP is designed to run on a wide variety of computer systems, providing all of the features of Standard LISP and additional language and interface extensions. The support environment includes an integrated compiler, a debugging facility, and a multiwindow, full-screen editor that permits the execution of expressions and display of output in windows. The PSL interpreter is written entirely in PSL itself and operates on a number of computer systems, including the DECSystem-20, DEC VAXs, and Apollo workstations. PSL was developed by the University of Utah as a research system. (Portable Standard LISP) [GRI82c]

SAIL is a programming language for procedure-oriented representation. It is a derivative of the block-structured programming language ALGOL 60, augmented with an associative memory capability and a large set of low-level input-output and data manipulation functions. Additional extensions include flexible linking to hand-coded assembly language procedures, a primitive multiprocessing facility, a compile-time macro system, and record, set, and list data types. The support environment consists of a high-level debugger and user-modifiable error handling, backtracking, and interrupt facilities. SAIL was originally designed to operate on PDP-10 computers under the TOPS-10 and TENEX operating systems. It was developed by the Stanford University artificial intelligence laboratory as a research system. [REI76, SMI76]

ZETALISP is a programming language for procedure-oriented representation. This dialect of LISP is based on MIT's MACLISP, but it is substantially extended and improved. It provides all of the standard LISP features, a large number of extensions (e.g. FLAVORS), and a sophisticated support environment. The support environment includes a high-resolution, bit-map graphics display, a window system, an integrated program/text editor, and a display-oriented debugger. ZETALISP operates on Symbolics' LM-2 and 3600 computer systems and on LMI's Lambda and Lambda/Plus machines. It was developed at MIT as a research system and is available from Symbolics, Inc. and Lisp Machines Incorporated (LMI) as a commercial system. [SYM81]

Rule-based Languages

AL/X is a knowledge engineering language for rule-based representation, but it also supports frame-based representation methods. Its principal characteristics include a combination backward and forward chaining control scheme, a semantic net that links rule components, certainty handling mechanisms, and automatic user querying. The support environment contains facilities for explaining the system's reasoning. AL/X closely resembles the KAS system, that is, PROSPECTOR stripped of its knowledge about geology. AL/X is implemented in PASCAL and operates on a PDP-11/34 running UNIX. It was developed by Intelligent Terminals, Ltd. as a research system. (Advice Language X) [PAT81a, REI80, REI81]

AMORD is a knowledge engineering language for rule-based representation. Its principal characteristics include discrimination networks for assertions and rules, a forward chaining control scheme, and a truth maintenance system (TMS) for maintaining justifications and program beliefs. Each AMORD fact or rule has an associated TMS node. The TMS uses a nonmonotonic dependency system for maintaining the logical grounds for belief in assertions. An explanation facility provides both justification and complete proof of belief in specific facts. AMORD is implemented in MACLISP and was developed at MIT as a research system. (A Miracle Of Rare Device, a name taken from S. T. Coleridge's poem *Kubla Khan*) [DEK78, WEI79a]

ARBY is a knowledge engineering language for rule-based representation. Its principal characteristics include the use of predicate calculus notation for expressing rules, a backward chaining facility (HYPO) for hypothesis generation, and a human interface subsystem (IFM) that manages a set of interaction frames (IFs). IFs are invoked when the HYPO component needs to retrieve information that is not yet in the data base but which could be obtained by asking the user. The support environment contains facilities for rule and IF editing, for explaining why a question is being asked, and for explaining why a given fact is currently believed. ARBY is implemented in FRANZ LISP and uses the DUCK general-purpose retriever. It was developed at Yale University as a research system. [MCD82c]

ARS is a knowledge engineering language for rule-based representation. Its principal characteristics include the representation of problem-solving rules as demons with pattern-directed invocation, an associative data base for maintaining assertions, and forward chaining with dependency-directed backtracking. ARS maintains complete records of all deductions it makes and uses the records for explanation and for processing contradictions during backtracking. ARS is implemented in MACLISP and operates under the MULTICS, TOPS-10, and ITS computer operating systems. ARS was developed at MIT as a research system. (Antecedent Reasoning System) [STA76]

ART is a knowledge engineering language for rule-based representation. Besides rules, it also supports frame-based and procedure-oriented representation methods. Its principal characteristics in-

clude forward and backward chaining control schemes, certainty handling mechanisms, and *hypothetical worlds*—a way to structure the
data base by defining the contexts in which facts and rules apply.
The support environment includes standard debugging aids, such
as trace facilities and break packages, that work in conjunction with
a graphical monitor. ART is written in LISP and operates on CADR
machines and the Symbolics 3600. It was developed by Inference
Corporation as a commercial system. (Advanced Reasoning Tool)
[CLA84b, WIL84a]

EMYCIN is a skeletal knowledge engineering language for rule-based
representation. Its principal characteristics include a restrictive backward chaining control scheme suitable for diagnosis and consulta-
tion-type problems, certainty handling mechanisms, and automatic
user querying facilities. The support environment contains sophisticated interface facilities for explaining the system's reasoning and
for acquiring new knowledge. The system is implemented in
INTERLISP and was originally designed to operate on a DEC PDP-
10 under TENEX or TOPS20. EMYCIN was developed at Stanford
University as a research system and is essentially MYCIN stripped
of its domain knowledge. (Essential MYCIN) [VAN79, VAN83,
VAN84]

ERS is a knowledge engineering language for rule-based representation.
Its principal characteristics include a PROSPECTOR-like semantic
network that links rule components, certainty handling mechanisms
including Bayesian and Fuzzy logic techniques, automatic user
querying, and the ability to call upon a set of application-specific
primitive functions for the evaluation of evidence nodes. The primitive functions can consult various data bases for factual information.
The support environment includes facilities for graphical display of
the results of analysis and for explaining the system's reasoning.
ERS is implemented in PASCAL and operates on an IBM PC-XT and
a DEC VAX 11/780. It was developed by PAR Technology Corporation as a research system. (Embedded Rule-based System) [BAR83b,
LEH84]

EXPERT is a skeletal knowledge engineering language for rule-based
representation. Its principal characteristics include a forward chaining control scheme designed for diagnosis or classification-type
problems, mechanisms for handling certainty, and efficient and
transportable code. The support environment contains sophisticated user interface facilities including those for explanation, acquisition, and consistency checking. EXPERT is implemented in FOR-
TRAN and operates on both DEC and IBM equipment. It is one of

the most widely used knowledge engineering languages for medical applications. EXPERT was developed at Rutgers University as a research system. [WEI80, WEI81c, WEI84]

EXPERT-2 is a knowledge engineering language for rule-based representation. Its principal characteristics include a backward chaining rule interpreter and support for analytic subroutines that allow full access to the underlying FORTH system. These include routines for interfacing with the user or specialized data processing. EXPERT-2 is implemented in FORTH and operates on the Apple II microcomputer system. It was developed by Helion Inc. as an experimental system. [PAR84a]

EXPRS is a knowledge engineering language for rule-based representation. Its principal characteristics include an English-like rule format, an attribute-object-value knowledge representation scheme, and a forward and backward chaining inference mechanism. The English-like nature of the rules facilitates the addition of complex rules and enables EXPRS to automatically generate answers to questions about why and how a rule fired. EXPRS has an automatic bookkeeping system that supports the explanation facility. PROLOG code can also be accessed directly using a rule clause form. EXPRS is implemented in PROLOG and operates on DEC-10 computer systems. It was developed by the Lockheed Palo Alto Research Laboratory as a research system. (EXpert PRolog System) [PEC84]

GEN-X is a knowledge engineering language for rule-based representations, but it also supports frame-based and decision table representation methods. The GEN-X system consists of a knowledge manager that provides an interactive graphics facility for knowledge base creation and editing, interpreters for the various representations that drive consultation sessions, and code generators that translate the knowledge base and appropriate interpreters into programs written in C, ADA, PASCAL, and FORTRAN. GEN-X is implemented in the C programming language and operates on the IBM PC and a variety of minicomputers. It was developed at General Electric's Research and Development Center as a research system. (GENeric-eXpert system) [LEW83a, LEW83c]

GLIB is a knowledge engineering language for rule-based representation. It is used to acquire troubleshooting rules for electronic instruments. GLIB provides a vocabulary and syntax for expressing rules, specifications, and observations about the behavior of general analog devices. Menu-based rule acquisition is supported through the use of expectation tables that provide the alternative choices for each word in the rule as it is being constructed. GLIB is implemented in SMALLTALK-80 and operates on the Tektronix 4404 Artificial Intelligence System. It was developed by Tektronix, Inc. as a research system. (General Language for Instrument Behavior) [FRE84a]

GUESS/1 is a knowledge engineering language for rule-based represen tation. It also supports relational tables, hierarchical trees, semanti nets, and frames. Control knowledge is encoded in frames and rule which allow both backward and forward chaining. Frames can trig ger rules and rules can invoke frames. Multiple knowledge source: communicate via a blackboard mechanism. A multilevel security mechanism allows each table, tree, network, or frame to be labeled to control access on the basis of a user's security clearance. GUESS 1's support environment includes an explanation facility and a natu ral language and menu facility. GUESS/1 is implemented in PRO LOG and runs under the VMS operating system on a DEC VA> 11/780. It was developed at the computer science department of Vir ginia Polytechnic Institute and State University as a research sys tem. (General pUrpose Expert Systems Shell) [LEE85]

HEARSAY-III is a knowledge engineering language for rule-based repre sentation. It integrates rules with a blackboard architecture consist ing of knowledge sources that communicate via a central blackboard or data base. Each knowledge source is a collection of rules tha execute by matching data and knowledge in the blackboard. In HEARSAY-III the blackboard has two parts: a domain blackboard for reasoning about the problem domain, and a scheduling blackboard for reasoning about when and how to apply the domain knowledge. HEARSAY-III supports the design of systems requiring asynchro nous processing of information and the design of control structure: for handling multiple goals. HEARSAY-III is implemented in LISP. It was developed by the Information Sciences Institute as a research system. [ERM80, BAL80, BAR83]

KAS is a skeletal knowledge engineering language for rule-based repre sentation. It is basically PROSPECTOR with the knowledge of geol ogy removed. KAS uses inference rules with associated certainty factors together with a partitioned semantic network to encode its knowledge. Inferences are based on forward and backward chaining and the propagation of probabilities through the semantic net. KAS's support environment includes facilities for explanation and knowledge acquisition and provides for synonym recognition, an swer revision, summarization, and tracing. The system is imple mented in INTERLISP. It was developed by SRI International as a research system. (Knowledge Acquisition System) [DUD78, REB81, DUD84]

KES is a knowledge engineering language for rule-based and frame-based representation. Its principal characteristics include a backward chaining control scheme, certainty handling mechanisms, and a statistical pattern classification subsystem based on Bayes' theorem. The support environment contains interface facilities for explaining the system's reasoning and for acquiring new knowledge. KES is implemented in FRANZ LISP and operates on Univac or DEC VAX systems. It was developed by Software Architecture and Engineering, Inc. as a commercial system. (Knowledge Engineering System) [NAG83, SOF83]

LES is a knowledge engineering language for rule-based representation, but it also supports frame-based representation. Rules are supported through the use of a case grammar frame format. LES's principal characteristics include forward and backward chaining control schemes, an agenda of relevant goals and subgoals manipulated by demons, and natural language and explanation facilities. LES is implemented in PL/1. It was developed by the Lockheed Palo Alto Research Laboratory as a research system. (Lockheed Expert System) [LAF84a, PER84]

MARS is a knowledge engineering language for rule-based representation of hierarchical, discrete, event-driven simulators. Its principal characteristics include hierarchical specification of the structure and behavior of a design, forward and backward chaining control schemes, and symbolic simulation. The support environment contains a compiler that compiles general, rule-based specifications into special procedures for simulation. It also contains a mixed-mode simulator that allows different parts of a design to be simulated at different abstraction levels. An explanation capability is also provided. MARS is implemented in MRS. It was developed at Stanford University as an experimental system. (Multiple Abstraction Rule-based System) [SIN83]

MELD is a knowledge engineering language for rule-based representation, but it also supports frame-based representation methods. Its principal characteristic is the separation of object-level and metalevel heuristic and causal rules. The metalevel rules contain all the knowledge required to select and apply the object-level (task-specific) rules. MELD supports forward and backward chaining, demons, certainty handling, and complex control schemes, and it uses the OPS5 conflict resolution strategy to select metalevel rules. MELD is implemented in OPS5. It was developed by the Westinghouse Research and Development Center as a research system. (MEta-Level Diagnosis) [THO84]

MRS is a knowledge engineering language for rule-based and logic-based representation. Its principal characteristics include a flexible control scheme utilizing forward chaining, backward chaining and resolution theorem proving, and the ability to represent *metalevel knowledge,* knowledge about the MRS system itself. The MRS programmer can write statements about MRS subroutines just as easily as statements about geology or medicine. The support environment contains interactive graphics-oriented debugging tools. MRS is implemented in INTERLISP. It was developed at Stanford University as a research system. (Metalevel Representation System) [CLA82c, GEN83a, GEN83b, GEN84c]

M.1 is a knowledge engineering language for rule-based representation. Its principal characteristics include a backward chaining control scheme and an English-like language syntax. The support environment contains graphics-oriented interactive debugging tools for tracing system operation, facilities for explaining the system's reasoning process, and mechanisms for automatically querying the user when the data base lacks the required information. M.1 is implemented in PROLOG and operates on the IBM Personal Computer running the PC DOS 2.0 operating system. It was developed by Teknowledge as a commercial system. [EXP84c, TEK84a]

OPS5 is a knowledge engineering language for rule-based representation. Its principal characteristics include a design that supports generality in both data representation and control structures, a powerful pattern-matching capability, and an efficient forward chaining interpreter for matching rules against the data. The support environment contains editing and debugging packages, including a mechanism to help determine why a rule didn't fire when the programmer thought it should. OPS5 has been implemented in BLISS, MACLISP, and FRANZ LISP. It is one of the most widely used knowledge engineering languages. OPS5 was developed at Carnegie-Mellon University as part of the OPS family of languages for AI and cognitive psychology applications. It is available as a commercial system from Verac Corporation (OPS5e) and from DEC (OPS5). [BAR83, FOR81b, FOR82, GUP83, VER83]

OPS83 is a knowledge engineering language for rule-based and procedure-oriented representation. Its principal characteristic is the integration of the forward chaining, rule-based programming paradigm and the procedural programming paradigm. OPS83 is essentially a PASCAL-like language augmented with the OPS5 constructs of working memory elements and rules. OPS83 also provides facilities for user-defined data types and permits the user to define conflict resolution procedures, control regimes, and tracing routines. OPS83 operates on DEC VAX 11/750 and 11/780 computer systems. It was developed at Carnegie-Mellon University as a research system and is available as a commercial system from Production Systems Technologies, Inc. [FOR83, FOR84a, FOR84b]

PERSONAL CONSULTANT is a knowledge engineering language for rule-based representation, but it also supports frame-based representation methods. Its principal characteristics include backward and forward chaining control schemes, certainty handling mechanisms, class hierarchies with inheritance, and the ability to access user-defined LISP functions. The user interface includes a window-oriented device that utilizes a color display and an explanation facility. The support environment contains a knowledge base editor, a trace facility, and a regression testing facility. PERSONAL CONSULTANT is written in IQLISP (a dialect of LISP) and operates on the TI Professional computer, the TI Explorer computer, and other MS-DOS compatible microcomputers. It was developed by Texas Instruments Inc. as a commercial system. [ART84b]

PRISM is a knowledge engineering language for rule-based representation. Its principal characteristics include forward and backward chaining control schemes, certainty handling mechanisms, and the ability to organize the knowledge base into hierarchical structures, each with its own inference engine and control strategy. The support environment consists of an integrated editor program for creating and maintaining the knowledge base in the form of English-like rules. PRISM is implemented in PASCAL and operates on IBM System 370 computers under the VM/CMS operating system. It was developed by the IBM Palo Alto Scientific Center as a research system. (PRototype Inference SysteM) [HIR84, MUR84]

PSYCO is a knowledge engineering language for rule-based representation, but it also supports frame-based representation methods. PSYCO was initially designed for building models of cognitive processes in human decision making but has evolved to a more general-purpose language. Its principal characteristics include a forward chaining control scheme, conflict resolution based upon the importance of data, and the organization of rules and data into a network of frames. PSYCO was developed by the Imperial Cancer Research Fund and Queen's Medical Centre as a research system. (Production SYstem COmpiler) [FOX82a]

RADIAL is a knowledge engineering language for rule-based and procedural representation. It is the underlying environment used by the RULEMASTER system-building aid and has its formal basis in finite automata theory. A RADIAL program consists of a set of modules, each containing a transition network of states, where each state contains a single rule in the form of a decision tree. RADIAL is a block-structured language with scoped variables, argument passing between modules, recursive module invocation, and conditional branching. It can explain its reasoning and has certainty handling mechanisms for dealing with Fuzzy logic. RADIAL is implemented in the C programming language and operates on minicomputers and microcomputers, such as VAXs and Sun workstations, under the Unix operating system. It was developed by the Radian Corporation as a commercial system. [MIC84b]

RITA is a knowledge engineering language for rule-based representation. Its principal characteristics include forward and backward chaining control schemes, and support for developing user agents, which are front ends to remote computing systems and networks. The support environment consists of tracing, debugging, and explanation facilities, a front end for the interactive creation and development of rule sets, and a mechanism for accessing the UNIX operating system support environment. RITA is implemented in the C programming language and operates under UNIX on PDP-11/45 and PDP-11/70 computer systems. It was developed by the Rand Corporation as a research system. (Rand Intelligent Terminal Agent) [AND76, AND77]

ROSIE is a knowledge engineering language for rule-based representation, but it also supports procedure-oriented representation methods. Its principal characteristics include an English-like syntax, a procedure-oriented structure that permits nested and recursive subroutines, powerful pattern-matching facilities, and an interface to the local operating system that gives ROSIE control over remote jobs. The support environment includes editing and debugging tools. ROSIE is implemented in INTERLISP and is being converted to run in the C programming language. ROSIE was developed at the Rand Corporation as a research system. (Rule-Oriented System for Implementing Expertise) [FAI81, FAI82, HAY81, BAR83]

SAVOIR is a knowledge engineering language for rule-based representation. Its principal characteristics include backward and forward chaining control schemes, a knowledge base compiler, support for Fuzzy logic, built-in certainty factor handling mechanisms, and demon control structures. The support environment contains an on-line help facility, a menu interface, and an explanation facility. SAVOIR operates on a wide range of computers and operating systems including DEC VAX systems and IBM PCs. It was developed by a British company called ISI (a joint venture between Isis Systems Ltd. and ICI Ltd.) as a commercial system. [EXP84b]

SOAR is a general problem-solving architecture for rule-based representation of heuristic search-oriented problem solving. The system provides a means for viewing a problem as a search through a *problem space*, a set of states representing solutions and a set of operators that transform one state into another. The principal characteristics of SOAR include the automatic creation of a hierarchy of subgoals and problem spaces and a parallel rule interpreter. Although SOAR is designed for generality, it has been applied to a knowledge-intensive expert system task (see R1-SOAR). SOAR was originally implemented in XAPS2 (a parallel production system architecture) and was reimplemented in a modified version of OPS5 with extensions for parallel execution. SOAR was developed at Carnegie-Mellon University as a research system. [LAI83, LAI84, ROS84]

S.1 is a knowledge engineering language for rule-based representation, but it also supports frame-based and procedure-oriented representation methods. Its principal characteristics include a backward chaining control scheme, built-in certainty handling mechanisms, and *control blocks* that support procedure-oriented representation and programming methods. The support environment contains an explanation facility and graphics-oriented debugging tools for tracing and breaking during consultations. S.1 is written in INTERLISP and operates on Xerox 1100 and 1108 workstations. It was developed by Teknowledge as a commercial system. (System.1) [ERM84, EXP84c, TEK84b]

29

Bibliography of Expert System Tools

This bibliography contains references to the expert system tools described in Chapter 28.

[AIE81a] Aiello, N. and Nii, H. P. AGEPUFF: a simple event-driven program. Report HPP-81-25, Computer Science Dept., Stanford University, June 1981. (AGE)

[AIE81b] Aiello, N., Bock, C., Nii, H. P., and White, W. C. Joy of AGE-ing: an introduction to the AGE-1 system. Report HPP-81–23, Computer Science Dept., Stanford University, 1981. (AGE)

[ALL78] Allen, J. R. *The Anatomy of LISP.* New York: McGraw-Hill, 1978. (LISP)

[ALT84c] Alty, J. L. and Coombs, M. J. Further developments in expert systems. *Expert Systems, Concepts and Examples,* Manchester, England: NCC Publications, 1984. (PROLOG)

[AND76] Anderson, R. H. and Gillogly, J. J. Rand Intelligent Terminal Agent (RITA): design philosophy. Report R-1809-ARPA, Rand Corporation, Santa Monica, Calif., 1976. (RITA)

[AND77] Anderson, R. H., Gallegos, M., Gillogly, J. J., Greenberg, R., and Villanueva, R. RITA reference manual. Rand Corporation, R-1808-ARPA, September 1977. (RITA)

[APP84] *Applied Artificial Intelligence Reporter,* DUCK builds intelligent systems. vol. 2, no. 2, November 1984. (DUCK)

[ART84b] Artificial Intelligence Publications, the personal consultant. *The AI Report,* vol. 1, no. 12, 1984. (PERSONAL CONSULTANT)

[BAL80] Balzer, R., Erman, L. D., London, P., and Williams, C. HEAR-

SAY-III: a domain-independent framework for expert systems. *Proceedings of the First Annual National Conference on Artificial Intelligence*, 1980. (HEARSAY-III)

[BAR83] Barstow, D. R., Aiello, N., Duda, R. O., Erman, L. D., Forgy, C., Gorlin, D., Greiner, R. D., Lenat, D. B., London, P. E., McDermott, J., Nii, H. P., Politakis, P., Reboh, R., Rosenschein, S., Scott, A. C., van Melle, W., and Weiss, S. M. Languages and tools for knowledge engineering. In F. Hayes-Roth, D. A. Waterman, and D. B. Lenat (eds.) *Building Expert Systems*, Reading, Mass.: Addison-Wesley, 1983. (HEARSAY-III) (RLL) (OPS5) (ROSIE)

[BAR83b] Barth, S. W. ERS user manual. Report, PAR Technology Corporation, New Hartford, N.Y., 1983. (ERS)

[BAT80] Batali, J. and Hartheimer, A. The design procedure language manual. Report AIM-598, AI Laboratory, MIT, Cambridge, Mass., September 1980. (DPL)

[BEN83] Bennett, J. S. ROGET: a knowledge-based consultant for acquiring the conceptual structure of an expert system. Report HPP-83-24, Computer Science Dept., Stanford University, Stanford, Calif., October 1983. (ROGET)

[BOB77] Bobrow, D. G. and Winograd, T. An overview of KRL, a knowledge representation language. *Cognitive Science*, vol. 1, no. 1, pp. 3–46, January 1977. (KRL)

[BOB83] Bobrow, D. G. and Stefik, M. *The LOOPS manual*. Xerox Corporation, December 1983. (LOOPS)

[BOL83] Boley, H. FIT-PROLOG: a functional/relational language comparison. Report SEKI-83-14, Fachbereich Informatik, Universitat Kaiserslautern, Postfach 3049, D-6750 Kaiserslautern 1, West Germany, December 1983. (FIT)

[BOO84] Boose, J. H. Personal construct theory and the transfer of human expertise. *Proceedings AAAI-84*, pp. 27–33, 1984. (ETS)

[BOR82] Borning, A. H. and Ingalls, D. H. H. Multiple inheritance in SMALLTALK-80. *Proceedings AAAI-82*, pp. 234–237, 1982. (SMALLTALK)

[BOW82] Bowen, K. A. Programming with full first-order logic. In J. E. Hayes, D. Michie, and Y. H. Pao (eds.) *Machine Intelligence* 10, Chichester, England: Horwood, pp. 421–470, 1982. (PROLOG)

[BRA79] Brachman, R. On the epistemological status of semantic networks. In N. Findler (ed.) *Associative Networks, Representation and Use of Knowledge by Computer*, Academic Press, 1979. (KRL)

[BRA83a] Brachman, R. J., Fikes, R. E., and Levesque, H. J. KRYPTON: a functional approach to knowledge representation. *IEEE Computer*, special issue on knowledge representation, September 1983. (KRYP-TON)

[BYL83] Bylander, T., Mittal, S., and Chandrasekaran, B. CSRL: a language for expert systems for diagnosis. *Proceedings IJCAI-83*, pp. 218–221, 1983. (CSRL) (MDX)

[CAN84] Cantone, R., Lander, W. B., Marrone, M., and Gaynor, M. IN-ATE/2: interpreting high-level fault modes. *Proceedings of the First Conference on Artificial Intelligence Applications*, IEEE Computer Society, December 1984. (IN-ATE/2)

[CAR84a] Carnegie Group, Inc., PLUME: A tool for developing natural language interfaces. Commerce Court, Pittsburgh, PA 15219, 1984.

[CHE80] Chester, D. HCPRVR: an interpreter for logic programs. *Proceedings AAAI-80*, pp. 93–95, 1980. (HCPRVR)

[CHI79] Chisholm, I. H. and Sleeman, D. H. An aide for theory formation. In D. Michie (ed.) *Expert Systems in the Micro Electronic Age*, Edinburgh: Edinburgh University Press, 1979. (CONCHE)

[CLA82a] Clark, K. L. An introduction to logic programming. In D. Michie (ed.) *Introductory Readings in Expert Systems*, Gordon and Breach, Science Publishers, 1982. (PROLOG)

[CLA82b] Clark, K. L. and McCabe, F. G. PROLOG: a language for implementing expert systems. In J. E. Hayes, D. Michie, and Y. H. Pao (eds.) *Machine Intelligence* 10, Chichester, England: Horwood, pp. 455–470, 1982. (PROLOG)

[CLA82c] Clayton, J. Welcome to the MRS tutor!!! Report HPP-82-33, Computer Science Dept., Stanford University, Stanford, Calif., November 1982. (MRS)

[CLA84b] Clayton, B. D. ART programming primer. Report, Inference Corporation, Los Angeles, Calif., 1984. (ART)

[CLO81] Clocksin, W. F. and Mellish, C. S. *Programming in PROLOG*. Heidelberg: Springer-Verlag, 1981. (PROLOG)

[CLO84] Clocksin, W. F. An introduction to PROLOG. In T. O'Shea and M. Eisenstadt (eds.) *Artificial Intelligence: Tools, Techniques and Applications*, New York: Harper & Row, 1984.

[CUR84] Curtis, Clayton A. A comparison of LISP and MUMPS as implementation languages for knowledge-based systems. *Proceedings of the Seventeenth Annual Hawaii International Conference on System Sciences*, 1984. (LISP) (MUMPS)

[DAV76] Davis, R. Applications of meta level knowledge to the construction, maintenance and use of large knowledge bases. Report STAN-CS-76-552, Stanford AI Laboratory, Stanford University, Stanford, Calif., July 1976. (TEIRESIAS)

[DAV78] Davis, R. Representation as a basis for system construction and maintenance. In D. A. Waterman and F. Hayes-Roth (eds.) *Pattern-Directed Inference Systems*, Academic Press, 1978. (TEIRESIAS)

[DAV79] Davis, R. Interactive transfer of expertise: acquisition of new inference rules. *Artificial Intelligence*, vol. 12, pp. 121–157, 1979. (TEIRESIAS)

[DAV82b] Davis, R., Shrobe, H., Hamscher, W., Wieckert, K., Shirley, M., and Polit, S. Diagnosis based on description of structure and function. *Proceedings AAAI-82*, 1982, pp. 137–142. (DPL)

[DAV83a] Davis, R. and Shrobe, H. Representing structure and behavior of digital hardware. Proceedings IEEE Computer, September 1983. (DPL)

[DEK78] DeKleer, J., Doyle, J., Rich, C., Steele, Jr., G. L., and Sussman, G. J. AMORD: a deductive procedure system. Report AIM-435, AI Laboratory, MIT, Cambridge, Mass., 1978. (AMORD)

[DRA84] Drastal, G. A. Experiments with RULE WRITER, a tool for building expert systems. *Proceedings of the Seventeenth Hawaii International Conference·on System Sciences*, 1984. (RULE WRITER)

[DUD78] Duda, R., Hart, P. E., Nilsson, N. J., Barrett, P., Gaschnig, J. G., Konolige, K., Reboh, R., and Slocum, J. Development of the PROSPECTOR consultation system for mineral exploration. SRI Report, Stanford Research Institute, 333 Ravenswood Avenue, Menlo Park, Calif., October 1978. (PROSPECTOR)

[DUD84] Duda, R. O. and Reboh, R. AI and decision making: the PROSPECTOR experience. In W. Reitman (ed.) *Artificial Intelligence Applications for Business*, Norwood, N.J.: Ablex, 1984. (PROSPECTOR)

[ERM80] Erman, L. D. The HEARSAY-II speech-understanding system: integrating knowledge to resolve uncertainties. *Computing Surveys*, vol. 12, no. 2, pp. 213–253, June 1980. (HEARSAY-II)

[ERM84] Erman, L., Scott, A. C., and London, P. Separating and integrating control in a rule-based tool. *Proceedings of the IEEE Workshop on Principles of Knowledge-Based Systems*, IEEE Computer Society, IEEE Computer Society Press, Silver Spring, Md., 1984. (S.1)

[EXP84b] SAVOIR: expert systems meet the videotex mass-market. *Expert Systems*, vol. 1., no. 2, pp. 105–106, 1984. (SAVOIR)

[EXP84c] Teknowledge/Framentec launch M1 and S1: shell systems from PCs to VAXs. *Expert Systems*, vol. 1, no. 2, 1984. (M.1) (S.1)

[FAH79] Fahlman, S. E. *NETL: a system for representing and using real world knowledge*. Cambridge, Mass.: MIT Press, 1979. (NETL)

[FAI81] Fain, J., Gorlin, D., Hayes-Roth, F., Rosenschein, S., Sowizral,

H., and Waterman, D. A. The ROSIE language reference manual. N-1647-ARPA, 1981. (ROSIE)

[FAI82] Fain, J., Hayes-Roth, F., Sowizral, H., and Waterman, D. Programming in ROSIE: an introduction by means of examples. Report N-1646-ARPA, Rand Corporation, February 1982. (ROSIE)

[FOR81b] Forgy, C. L. OPS5 user's manual. Report CMU-CS-81-135, Computer Science Dept., Carnegie-Mellon University, Pittsburgh, Pa., July 1981. (OPS5)

[FOR82] Forgy, C. L. Rete: a fast algorithm for the many pattern/many object pattern match problem. *Artificial Intelligence*, vol. 19, pp. 17–37, 1982. (OPS-5)

[FOR83] Forgy, C.L. Overview of OPS83. Computer Science Dept. report. Carnegie-Mellon University, Pittsburgh, Pa., June 1983. (OPS83)

[FOR84a] Forgy, C. L. A design for integrating procedural and rule-based programming paradigms. Technical report, Computer Science Dept., Carnegie-Mellon University, Pittsburgh, Pa., August 1984. (OPS83)

[FOR84b] Forgy, C. L. The OPS83 report: system version 2. Technical report, Production Systems Technologies, Inc., 642 Gettysburg Street, Pittsburgh, Pa., July, 1984. (OPS83)

[FOX82a] Fox, J. and Rector, A. Expert systems for primary medical care? *Automedica*, vol. 4, pp. 123–130, 1982. (PSYCO) (PSYCO/dyspepsia)

[FRE84a] Freiling, M. and Alexander, J. Diagrams and grammars: tools for mass-producing expert systems. *Proceedings of the First Conference on Artificial Intelligence Applications*, IEEE Computer Society, December 1984. (DETEKTR) (GLIB)

[GEN83a] Genesereth, M. R. An overview of meta-level architecture. Proceedings AAAI-83, pp. 119–124, 1983. (MRS)

[GEN83b] Genesereth, M. R. The MRS project. *The AI Magazine*, p. 89, Fall 1983. (MRS)

[GEN84c] Genesereth, M. R. An overview of MRS for AI experts. Memo HPP-82-27, Stanford University, Stanford, Calif., January 1984. (MRS)

[GOL77b] Goldstein, I. P. and Roberts, R. B. NUDGE, a knowledge-based scheduling program. *Proceedings IJCAI-77*, pp. 257–263, 1977. (FRL)

[GOL79] Goldstein, I. P. and Roberts, R. B. Using frames in scheduling. In P. Winston and R. Brown (eds.) *Artificial Intelligence: An MIT Perspective*, vol. 1, MIT Press, pp. 253–284, 1979. (FRL)

[GOL80] Goldstein, I. P. and Bobrow, D. G. Extending object-oriented programming in SMALLTALK. *Proceedings of the 1980 LISP Conference*, Stanford University, Stanford, Calif., 1980. (SMALLTALK) (PIE)

[GOL83] Goldberg, A. and Robson, D. *SMALLTALK-80: The language and its implementation*. Reading, Mass.: Addison-Wesley, 1983. (SMALLTALK)

[GRE80] Greiner, R. and Lenat, D. B. Details of RLL-1. Report HPP-80-23. Stanford University, Stanford, Calif., October 1980. (RLL)

[GRI82c] Griss, M. L., Benson, E., and Maguire, G. Q. PSL: a portable LISP system. *Proceedings of the ACM Symposium on LISP and Functional Programming*, Pittsburgh, Pa., 1982. (PSL)

[GUP83] Gupta, Anoop and Forgy, C. L. Measurements on production systems. Report CMU-CS-83-167, Computer Science Dept., Carnegie-Mellon University, Pittsburgh, Pa., December 1983. (OPS5)

[HAM82] Hammond, P. APES: a detailed description. Report 82/10, Computing Dept., Imperial College of Science and Technology, University of London, 180 Queens Gate, London, SW7 2BZ, UK, 1982. (APES)

[HAM83] Hammond, P. APES: a user manual. Report 82/9, Computing and Control Dept., Imperial College of Science and Technology, 180 Queen's Gate, London, SW7 2BZ, UK, May 1983. (APES)

[HAR83] Harandi, Mehdi T. A general purpose system for inferencing. *Proceedings of the IBM University Study Conference*, Raleigh, N.C., pp. 131–139, 1983. (GPSI)

[HAR84a] Harandi, Mehdi T. A tree based knowledge representation scheme for diagnostics expert systems. *Proceedings of 1984 Conference on Intelligent Systems and Machines*, Rochester, Minn., 1984. (GPSI)

[HAW75] Hawkinson, L. The representation of concepts in OWL. *Proceedings IJCAI-75*, pp. 107–114, 1975. (OWL)

[HAY81] Hayes-Roth, F., Gorlin, D., Rosenschein, S., Sowizral, H., and Waterman, D. A. Rationale and motivation for ROSIE. N-1648-ARPA, 1981. (ROSIE)

[HIR84] Hirsch, P., Meier, M., Snyder, S., Stillman, D., and Tucker, B. Prototype inference system (PRISM). Report G320-3470, IBM Palo Alto Scientific Center, 1530 Page Mill Road, Palo Alto, Calif., November 1984. (PRISM)

[KAH84e] Kahn, G., Nowlan, S., and McDermott, J. A foundation for knowledge acquisition. *Proceedings of the IEEE Workshop on Principles of Knowledge-Based Systems*, IEEE Computer Society, IEEE Computer Society Press, 1109 Spring Street, Silver Spring, Md., 1984. (MUD) (MORE) (geology)

[KEH84] Kehler, T. P. and Clemenson, G. D. An application development system for expert systems. *Systems and Software*, vol. 3, no. 1, January 1984. (KEE) (POL-I) (TQMSTUNE) (CORP) (SIMULAB)

[KER78] Kernighan, B. W. and Ritchie, D. M. *The C programming language*. Prentice-Hall, 1978. (C)

[KIS83] Kiselewich, S. TIMM—the intelligent machine model. General Research Corporation Report, 5383 Hollister Ave., Santa Barbara, Calif., September 1983. (TIMM)

[KOR84b] Kornell, Jim. Embedded knowledge acquisition to simplify expert systems development. *Applied Artificial Intelligence Reporter*, pp. 28–30, August-September 1984. (TIMM)

[KOW79a] Kowalski, R. *Logic for problem solving*. New York: American Elsevier, 1979. (PROLOG)

[KOW79b] Kowalski, R. Algorithm = logic + control. *Communications of the ACM*, vol. 22, no. 7, pp. 424–436, July 1979. (PROLOG)

[KUN84] Kunz, J. C., Kehler, T. P., and Williams, M. D. Applications development using a hybrid AI development system. *The AI Magazine*, vol. 5, no. 3, Fall 1984. (KEE)

[LAF84a] Laffey, T. J., Perkins, W. A., and Nguyen, T. A. Reasoning about fault diagnosis with LES. *Proceedings of the First Conference on Artificial Intelligence Applications*, IEEE Computer Society, December 1984. (LES)

[LAI83] Laird, J. E. and Newell, A. A universal weak method: summary of results. *Proceedings IJCAI-83*, 1983. (SOAR)

[LAI84] Laird, J. E., Rosenbloom, P. S., and Newell, A. Towards chunking as a general learning mechanism. *Proceedings AAAI-84*, 1984. (SOAR)

[LAN84] Lanam, D., Letsinger, R., Rosenberg, S., Huyn, P., and Lemon, M. Guide to the heuristic programming and representation language—Part 1: frames. Report AT-MEMO-83-3, Computer Research Center, Hewlett-Packard Company, 1501 Page Mill Road, Palo Alto, Calif., June 1984. (HPRL)

[LAU78] Lauriere, Jean-Louis. A language and a program for stating and solving combinatorial problems. *Artificial Intelligence*, vol. 10, pp. 29–127, 1978. (ALICE)

[LEE85] Lee, N. S. and Roach, J. W. GUESS/1: A general purpose expert systems shell. Technical Report TR-85-3, Computer Science Dept., Virginia Polytechnic Institute and State University, 1985.

[LEH84] Lehner, P. E. and Barth, S. W. Expert systems on microcomputers. PAR Technology Corporation Report, Seneca Plaza, Rt. 5, New Hartford, NY 13413, 1984. (ERS)

[LEW83a] Lewis, J. W. An effective graphics user interface to rules and inference mechanisms. *Proceedings of Computer and Human Interface 1983,* ACM, December 1983. (GEN-X)

[LEW83b] Lewis, J. W. and Lynch, F. S. GETREE: a knowledge management tool. *Proceedings of the Trends and Applications Conference on Automating Intelligent Behavior,* IEEE Press, May 1983. (GETREE)

[LEW83c] Lewis, J. W., Plevin, R. J., Wheeler, D. B. GEN-X: Generic Expert System. Information Science Laboratory Report, General Electric Co., Schenectady, N.Y. 1983. (GEN-X)

[MCA82] McArthur, D. and Klahr, P. The ROSS language manual. Report N-1854-AF, Rand Corporation, September 1982. (ROSS)

[MCA84] McArthur, D., Klahr, P., and Narain, S. ROSS: An object-oriented language for constructing simulations. Report R-3160-A, Rand Corporation, Santa Monica, Calif., 1984.

[MCD80a] McDermott, D. The PROLOG phonomenon. *SIGART Newsletter,* no. 72, pp. 16–20, July 1980. (PROLOG)

[MCD82c] McDermott, D. and Brooks, R. ARBY: diagnosis with shallow causal models. Proceedings AAAI-82, pp. 370–372, 1982. (ARBY)

[MIC83b] Michalski, R. S. and Baskin, A. B. Integrating multiple knowledge representations and learning capabilities in an expert system: the ADVISE system. *Proceedings IJCAI-38,* pp. 256–258, 1983. (ADVISE)

[MIC84b] Michie, D., Muggleton, S., Riese, C., and Zubrick, S. RULEMASTER: a second-generation knowledge-engineering facility. *Proceedings of the First Conference on Artificial Intelligence Applications,* IEEE Computer Society, December 1984. (RULEMASTER) (WILLARD) (RADIAL)

[MIZ83] Mizoguchi, F. PROLOG based expert system. *New generation computing,* Japan: Ohmsha, Ltd. and Springer-Verlag, vol. 1, 1983. (APLICOT)

[MOO84] Moore, R. L., Hawkinson, L. B., Knickerbocker, C. G., and Churchman, L. M. A real-time expert system for process control. *Proceedings of the First Conference on Artificial Intelligence Applications,* IEEE Computer Society, December 1984. (PICON) (tool)

[MOR84] Morris, David. LISP shows first process-control expert system. *Electronic Engineering Times,* August 13, 1984. (PICON)

[MUR84] Murphy, T. Artificial intelligence topics at IBM. *IBM Research Highlights,* no. 2, 1984. (PRISM)

[MYE85] Myers, R. M. private communication. (KRT)

[NAG83] Nagy, T. J., DiSciullo, Jr., J., and Crosslin, R. Reducing costs and improving services in unemployment insurance nonmonetary determinations using expert systems. *UI Research Exchange,* Fall 1983. (KES)

[NII79] Nii, H. Penny and Aiello, N. AGE (Attempt to Generalize): a knowledge-based program for building knowledge-based programs. *Proceedings IJCAI-79,* pp. 209–219, 1979. (AGE)

[PAR84a] Park, J. Expert systems and the weather. *Dr. Dobb's Journal,* vol. 9, no. 4, April 1984. (EXPERT-2)

[PAR84b] Parker, R. E. and Kiselewich, S. J. The modeling of human cognitive decision processes in the intelligent machine model (TIMM). Report, Artificial Intelligence Laboratory, General Research Corporation, Santa Barbara, Calif., 1984. (TIMM)

[PAT81a] Paterson, A. AL/X user manual. Intelligent Terminals Ltd., 15 Canal Street, Oxford, UK OX2 68H, 1981. (AL/X)

[PAT82a] Paterson, A. and Niblett, T. ACLS user manual. Report, Intelligent Terminals, Ltd., 15 Canal Street Oxford, UK OS2 6BH, 1982. (ACLS)

[PAT84] Patel-Schneider, P. Small can be beautiful in knowledge representation. *Proceedings of the IEEE Workshop on Principles of Knowledge-Based Systems,* IEEE Computer Society, IEEE Computer Society Press, Silver Spring, Md., 1984. (KANDOR)

[PEC84] Pecora, Jr., V. J. EXPRS—a prototype expert system using prolog for data fusion. *The AI Magazine,* Summer 1984. (EXPRS)

[PER83] Perrone, J. Expert systems get personal: modeling expertise with the IBM PC. Report, Jeffery Perrone & Associates, Inc., 3685 17th Street, San Francisco, Calif., 1983. (EXPERT-EASE)

[PER84] Perkins, W. A. and Laffey, T. J. LES: a general expert system and its applications. *Proceedings of SPIE,* The International Society for Optical Engineering, Bellingham, Wash., vol. 485, Applications of Artificial Intelligence, 1984. (LES)

[PIG84] Pigman, V. The interaction between assertional and terminological knowledge in KRYPTON. *Proceedings of the IEEE Workshop on Principles of Knowledge-Based Systems,* IEEE Computer Society, IEEE Computer Society Press, 1109 Spring Street, Silver Spring, Md., 1984. (KRYPTON)

[POL84] Politakis, P. and Weiss, S. M. Using empirical analysis to refine expert system knowledge bases. *Artificial Intelligence,* vol. 22, pp. 23–48, 1984. (SEEK)

[REB81] Reboh, René. Knowledge engineering techniques and tools in the PROSPECTOR environment. SRI technical note 243, Stanford

Research Institute, 333 Ravenswood Avenue, Menlo Park, Calif., June 1981. (KAS)

[RED82] Reddy, Y. V. and Fox, M. S. KBS: an artificial intelligence approach to flexible simulation. Report CMU-RI-TR-82-1, The Robotics Institute, Carnegie-Mellon University, Pittsburgh, Pa., 1982. (KBS)

[REG81] Reggia, J. A. Knowledge-based decision support systems: development through KMS. Ph D dissertation, Report TR-1121, Computer Science Dept., University of Maryland, College Park, Md., 1981. (KMS)

[REI76] Reiser, J. F. SAIL. Report AIM-289, Stanford Artificial Intelligence Laboratory, Stanford University, Stanford, Calif. August 1976. (SAIL)

[REI80] Reiter, J. AL/X: an expert system using plausible inference. Intelligent Terminals Ltd. Report, Machine Intelligence Research Unit, University of Edinburgh, 1980. (AL/X)

[REI81] Reiter, J. E. AL/X: an inference system for probabilistic reasoning. M. S. thesis, Computer Science Dept., University of Illinois, Champaign-Urbana, 1981. (AL/X)

[RIE85] Riese, C. Control strategies in RULEMASTER. Report R1-RS-00296, Radian Corporation, 8501 Mo-Pac Blvd. Austin, Tex., January 1985. (RULEMASTER)

[ROB82] Robinson, J. A. and Sibert, E. E. LOGLISP: an alternative to PROLOG. In J. E. Hayes, D. Michie, and Y. H. Pao (eds.) *Machine Intelligence* 10, Chichester, England: Horwood, pp. 399–419, 1982. (PROLOG)

[ROS83] Rosenberg, S. HPRL: a language for building expert systems. *Proceedings IJCAI-83*, pp. 215–217, 1983. (HPRL)

[ROS84] Rosenbloom, P. S., Laird, J. E., McDermott, J., Newell, A., and Orciuch, E. R1-SOAR, an experiment in knowledge-intensive programming in a problem-solving architecture. *Proceedings of the IEEE Workshop on Principles of Knowledge-Based Systems*, IEEE Computer Society, IEEE Computer Society Press, 1109 Spring Street, Silver Spring, Md., 1984. (R1-SOAR)

[SCH81] Schmolze, J. G. and Brachman, R. J. (eds.) *Proceedings of the 1981 KL-ONE Workshop*, Fairchild Laboratory for Artificial Intelligence Research, Palo Alto, Calif., May 1982. (KL-ONE)

[SCH83a] Schmolze, J. G. and Lipkis, T. A. Classification in the KL-ONE knowledge representation system. *Proceedings IJCAI-83*, pp. 330–332, 1983. (KL-ONE)

[SCH83b] Schoen, E., and Smith, R. G. IMPULSE: a display oriented editor for STROBE. AAAI Proceedings, 1983. (IMPULSE)

[SHE83] Sheil, B. A. and Masinter, L. M. (eds.) Papers on INTERLISP-D. Report CIS-5 Xerox Corporation, Palo Alto Research Center, January 1983. (INTERLISP) (INTERLISP-D)

[SIK76] Siklossy, L. Let's Talk LISP, Englewood Cliffs, N.J.: Prentice Hall, 1976. (LISP)

[SIN83] Singh, N. MARS: A multiple abstraction rule-based simulator. Report HPP-83-43, Stanford University, Stanford, Calif., December 1983. (MARS)

[SMI76] Smith, N. W. SAIL tutorial. Report STAN-CS-76-575, Computer Science Dept., Stanford University, October 1976. (SAIL)

[SMI83a] Smith, R. G. STROBE: support for structured object knowledge representation. *Proceedings IJCAI-83*, pp. 855–858, 1983. (STROBE)

[SMI84b] Smith, J. W., Speicher, C., and Chandrasekaran, B. Expert systems as aids for interpretive reporting. *Proceedings of the Seventeenth Hawaii International Conference on System Sciences*, 1984. (CSRL)

[SOF83] Software Architecture and Engineering, Inc., Knowledge engineering systems. Artificial Intelligence Center, Suite 1220, 1401 Wilson Blvd., Arlington, VA 22209, November 1983. (KES)

[SRI78a] Sridharan, N. S. AIMDS user manual, version 2. Technical report CBM-TR-89, Computer Science Dept., Rutgers University, New Brunswick, N.J., June 1978. (AIMDS)

[STA76] Stallman, R. M. and Sussman, G. J. Forward reasoning and dependency-directed backtracking in a system for computer-aided circuit analysis. Report no. 380, Artificial Intelligence Laboratory, MIT, September 1976. (ARS)

[STE79] Stefik, M. An examination of a frame-structured representation system. *Proceedings IJCAI-79*, pp. 845–852, 1979. (UNIT PACKAGE)

[STE81b] Steele, G. I. and Fahlman, S. F. Common LISP manual. SPICE project, Carnegie-Mellon Univ., Pittsburgh, Pa., September 1981. (COMMON LISP)

[STE83b] Stefik, M., Bobrow, D. G., Mittal, S., and Conway, L. "Knowledge programming in LOOPS: Report on an experimental course" *The AI Magazine*, pp. 3–13, Fall 1983. (LOOPS)

[STE83d] Stefik, M., Bell, A., and Bobrow, D. G. Rule-oriented programming in LOOPS. XEROX Palo Alto Research Center Memo, January 1983. (LOOPS)

[STE84] Steele, Jr., G. L. *Common LISP: the language.* Billerica, Mass.: Digital Press, 1984. (COMMON LISP)

[SYM81] Symbolics software. Report, Symbolics, Inc., 21150 Califa Street, Woodland Hills, Calif. 1981. (ZETALISP)

[TEI75] Teitelman, W. The INTERLISP reference manual. Xerox Palo Alto Research Center, Palo Alto, Calif., 1975. (INTERLISP)

[TEI81] Teitelman, W. and Masinter, L. The INTERLISP programming environment. *IEEE Computer*, vol. 14, no. 4, pp. 25–33, April 1981. (INTERLISP)

[TEK84a] Teknowledge, M.1 product description. Tecknowledge, 525 University Ave., Palo Alto, Calif., 1984. (M.1)

[TEK84b] Teknowledge, S.1 product description. Teknowledge, 525 University Ave., Palo Alto, Calif., 1984.

[TEK84c] Teknowledge. T.1 product description. Teknowledge, 525 University Ave., Palo Alto, Calif., 1984. (T.1)

[THO84] Thompson, T. F. and Wojcik, R. M. MELD: an implementation of a meta-level architecture for process diagnosis. *Proceedings of the First Conference on Artificial Intelligence Applications*, IEEE Computer Society, December 1984. (MELD)

[VAN79] van Melle, W. A domain-independent production-rule system for consultation programs. *Proceedings IJCAI-79*, pp. 923–925, 1979. (EMYCIN) (HEADMED)

[VAN81] van Melle, W., Shortliffe, E. H., and Buchanan, B. G. EMYCIN: a domain-independent system that aids in constructing knowledge-based consultation programs. *Machine Intelligence*, Infotech State of the Art report 9, no. 3, pp. 249–263, 1981. (EMYCIN)

[VAN84] van Melle, William, Shortliffe, Edward H., and Buchanan, Bruce G. EMYCIN: a knowledge engineer's tool for constructing rule-based expert systems. In B. Buchanan and E. Shortliffe (eds.) *Rule-based Expert Systems*, New York: Addison-Wesley, pp. 302–328, 1984. (EMYCIN)

[VER83] Verac Incorporated, OPS5e user's manual. P.O. Box 26669, San Diego, Calif., 1983. (OPS5e)

[VER84] Verity, J. W., PROLOG vs LISP. *DATAMATION*, pp. 50–76, January 1984. (PROLOG)

[WAR77] Warren, D. H. D., Pereira, L. M., and Pereira, F. PROLOG— the language and its implementation compared with LISP. *Proceedings of the Symposium on Artificial Intelligence and Programming Languages*, SIGPLAN Notices vol. 12, no. 8, and *SIGART Newsletters* 64, pp. 109–115, 1977. (PROLOG)

[WAT83] Waterman, D. A. and Hayes-Roth, F. An investigation of tools for building expert systems. In F. Hayes-Roth, D. A. Waterman, and D. Lenat (eds.) *Building Expert Systems*, Reading, Mass.: Addison-Wesley, 1983. (RLL)

[WEI79a] Weiner, J. L. The structure of natural explanations: theory and application. Report SP-4028, System Development Corp., Santa Monica, Calif., pp. 86–92, October 1979. (AMORD)

[WEI80] Weiss, S. M., Kern, K. B., and Kulikowski, C. A. A guide to the use of the EXPERT consultation system. Technical report CBM-TR-94, Computer Science Dept., Rutgers University, New Brunswick, N.J., January 1980. (EXPERT)

[WEI81a] Weinreb, D. and Moon, D. Objects, message passing, and flavors. *LISP machine manual*, Symbolics, Inc., pp. 279–313, July 1981. (FLAVORS)

[WEI81c] Weiss, S. M. and Kulikowski, C. A. Expert consultation systems: the EXPERT and CASNET projects. In A. H. Bond (ed.) *Machine Intelligence*, Infotech State of the Art Report, series 9, no. 3, Pergamon Infotech Limited, pp. 339–353, 1981. (CASNET) (EXPERT)

[WEI84] Weiss, S. M. and Kulikowski, C. A. *A practical guide to designing expert systems*. New Jersey: Rowman and Allanheld, 1984. (EXPERT) (SPE)

[WHI84] *Which Computer?* EXPERT-EASE. April 1984, pp. 68–71.

[WIL84a] Williams, C. ART: the advanced reasoning tool. Inference Corp. Report, Inference Corp., 5300 W. Century Blvd., Los Angeles, Calif., 1984. (ART)

[WIN81] Winston, P. H. and Horn, B. K. *LISP*. Reading, Mass.: Addison-Wesley, 1981.

[WOO83] Woods, W. A. What's important about knowledge representation? *IEEE Computer*, pp. 22–27, October 1983. (KL-ONE)

[WRI83] Wright, J. M. and Fox, M. S. SRL/1.5 user manual. Robotics Institute, Carnegie-Mellon University, Pittsburgh, Pa., December 1983. (SRL) (HSRL)

Additional Reading

[FEH84] Fehling, M. R. and Suppes, P. Shared responsibility and instructable systems. *International Journal of Man-Machine Studies*, 1984. (SCHEMER) (tool)

[FOD80] Foderaro, J. K. The FRANZ LISP manual. University of California, Berkeley, 1980. (FRANZ LISP)

[FRE83a] Freeman, M., Hirschman, L., and McKay, D. KNET—a logic based associative network framework for expert systems. Technical memo LBS 12, System Development Corp., Santa Monica, Calif., September 1983.

[HEW72] Hewitt, C. Description and theoretical analysis (using schemata) of PLANNER: A language for proving theorems and manipulating models in a robot. PhD thesis, Mathematics Dept., MIT, April 1972. (PLANNER)

[HEW77] Hewitt, C. Viewing control structures as patterns of passing messages. *Artificial Intelligence*, vol. 8, 1977. (ACTOR)

[MIN75] Minsky, M. A framework for representing knowledge. In P. Winston (ed.) *The psychology of computer vision*, New York: McGraw-Hill, 1975. (FRAMES)

[MIT84a] Mitchell, T. M., Steinberg, L. I., and Shulman, J. S. A knowledge-based approach to design. *Proceedings of the IEEE Workshop on Principles of Knowledge-Based Systems*, IEEE Computer Society, IEEE Computer Society Press, Silver Spring, Md., 1984. (VEXED)

[MIT84b] Mitchell, T. M., Steinberg, L. I., and Shulman, J. S. VEXED: a knowledge-based VLSI design consultant. Report LCSR-TR-57, Laboratory for Computer Science Research, Rutgers University, July 1984. (VEXED)

[MOU84] Mountain View Press, MVP-fourth. Mountain View Press brochure, P.O. Box 4656, Mountain View, Calif., 1984. (MVP-FORTH)

[WEY80] Weyhrauch, R. W. Prolegomena to a theory of mechanized formal reasoning. *Artificial Intelligence*, vol. 13, pp. 133–170, 1980. (FOL)

30

Companies Engaged in Expert System Work

These companies are all exploring the potential of expert systems, some from a research vantage point, others from a commercial one. This list is not meant to be complete—it is a collection of selected companies working in this area.

Company	Activities	Systems & Tools
Advanced Information & Decision Systems 201 San Antonio Circle Suite 286 Mountain View, CA 94040	AI and expert systems for military applications, estimation, and control theory work	AMUID, ASTA, RTC, RUBRIC
Amoco Production Company Research Center 4502 East 41st Street P.O. Box 591 Tulsa, OK 74102	Expert systems for well log data analysis	ELAS
Analytic Sciences Corp. Reading, MA 01867	AI and expert systems for military applications	EXPERT NAVIGATOR
Applied Expert Systems Five Cambridge Center Cambridge, MA 02142	AI-based, integrated software products for the financial services industry	

continued

Company	Activities	Systems & Tools
Arthur D. Little, Inc. 25 Acorn Park Cambridge, MA 02140	Expert systems, vision systems, robotics systems, and analyst workstations	
Artificial Intelligence Corp. 100 Fifth Ave Waltham, MA 02254	Natural language interfaces to software products	INTELLECT
Automated Reasoning Corp. 290 W. 12th Street Suite 1-D New York, NY 10014	Expert systems for fault diagnosis (e.g., electronic equipment)	IN-ATE/KE
Bell Laboratories Murray Hill, NJ 07974	Basic research in natural language processing, speech recognition and synthesis; expert systems for design	DAA
Bell Laboratories Whippany, NJ 07981	Expert systems for telephone cable maintenance	ACE
Boeing Computer Services Artificial Intelligence Center Bellevue, WA	Research and development in knowledge-based systems, cooperating expert systems, natural language processing, and robotics	ETS
Bolt, Beranek and Newman, Inc. Computer Science Division 50 Moulton Street Cambridge, MA 02238	Research and development in AI and expert systems	SOPHIE, STEAMER, KL-ONE
Booz, Allen & Hamilton, Inc. 4330 East West Highway Bethesda, MD 20814	Expert systems, including applications for the EPA	EDASS
Brattle Research Corp. 215 First Street Cambridge, MA 02142	Commercial knowledge-based systems for finance, information management, and electronic publishing; consulting and contract research	

continued

Company	Activities	Systems & Tools
The Carnegie Group Commerce Court at Station Square Pittsburgh, PA 15219	AI products for expert system development, consulting and contract research, AI training courses	PLUME, SRL +
Cognitive Systems Inc. Church Street New Haven, CT 06511	Knowledge-based systems for natural language processing and data retrieval	
Computer Thought Corporation 1721 Plano Parkway Suite 125 Plano, TX 75075	Custom expert system development, software engineering tools, consulting, AI training courses	
Digital Equipment Corporation 77 Reed Road Hudson, MA 01749	Expert systems computer configuration, sales, and manufacturing; AI software products	IDT, ISA, XCON, XSEL, IMACS, PTRANS, OPS5
EG&G Idaho, Inc. P.O. Box 1625 Idaho Falls, ID 83415	Expert systems for the Nuclear Regulatory Commission Operations Center.	REACTOR
ESL Inc 495 Java Drive P.O. Box 3510 Sunnyvale, CA 94088	Expert systems for military situation assessment, mission planning, signal understanding, and cartography	ACES, I&W, HANNIBAL
Expert-Knowledge Systems, Inc. 6313 Old Chesterbrook Road McLean, VA 22101	Training in knowledge acquisition and expert system development	

Fairchild Laboratory
  for Artificial Intelligence
  Research (FLAIR)
Fairchild Advanced Research
  and Development
4001 Miranda Avenue
Palo Alto, CA 94304
	AI research in machine perception (speech, images), expert system architectures, knowledge representation, and computer-aided design	KANDOR, KRYPTON

continued

Company	Activities	Systems & Tools
Ford Aerospace & Communications Corp. Artificial Intelligence Lab. P.O. Box 58487 1150 Gemini Avenue Houston, TX 77258	AI systems for planning and scheduling, expert systems for fault diagnosis and real-time control	RBMS, RPMS
General Electric Company Research & Development Center 1 River Road Schenectady, NY 12345	Expert system building tools and expert systems for fault diagnosis	DELTA, GEN-X, GETREE
General Research Corporation 5383 Hollister Avenue Santa Barbara, CA 93111	Expert system building tools and expert systems for fault diagnosis	TIMM/TUNER, TIMM
GTE Laboratories Sylvan Road Waltham, MA 02254	Knowledge-based front ends for data base access and expert systems for fault diagnosis	COMPASS
Hewlett-Packard Computer Research Center Applied Technology Laboratory 1501 Page Mill Road Palo Alto, CA 94304	Expert system tools and applications	HPRL
Hughes Aircraft Company Artificial Intelligence Center 23901 Calabasas Road Calabasas, CA 91302	AI research in knowledge acquisition, vision, planning, natural language understanding, and signal understanding	ATR
Inference Corporation 5300 W. Century Blvd. 5th Floor Los Angeles, CA 90045	Expert system tools and applications	NAVEX, ART
Information Sciences Institute 4676 Admiralty Way Marina del Rey, CA 90292	AI research and development, explanation techniques for expert systems	HEARSAY-III
Intellicorp 124 University Ave. Palo Alto, CA 94301	Expert system tools and applications for genetic engineering, general-purpose knowledge engineering tools	SEQ, TQMSTUNE, KEE

continued

Company	Activities	Systems & Tools
IBM Palo Alto Scientific Center 1530 Page Mill Road Palo Alto, CA 94303	Expert systems for fault diagnosis, tools for building expert systems	PRISM
International Business Machines Corp. Thomas J. Watson Research Center P.O. Box 218 Yorktown Heights, NY 10598	Expert systems for fault diagnosis, natural language query systems	YES/MVS
Jet Propulsion Laboratory California Institute of Technology 4800 Oak Grove Drive Pasadena, CA 91109	Expert system tools and applications, research in planning and scheduling systems	FAITH
Kestrel Institute Research Laboratory 1801 Page Mill Road Palo Alto, CA 94304	Research in very high-level languages, program design and synthesis, and knowledge-based programming environments	
LISP Machine Inc. (LMI) Suite 900 6033 W. Century Blvd. Los Angeles, CA 90045	LISP workstations, expert system tools for process control	PICON
Lockheed Missiles and Space Company, Inc. Lockheed Palo Alto Research Laboratory 3251 Hanover Street Palo Alto, CA 94304	Expert system tools, expert systems for fault diagnosis and design	LES, BDS, EXPRS
Los Alamos National Laboratory Group NSP/AWT MS F668 Los Alamos, NM 87545	Expert systems for military applications	AIRID
McDonnell Douglas 16441 Space Center Blvd. Houston, TX	AI systems for planning and information management	KRT
Microelectronics and Computer Technology Corp. 9430 Research Boulevard Echelon Building 1, Suite 200 Austin, TX 78759	AI and expert systems research and development	

continued

Company	Activities	Systems & Tools
The MITRE Corporation Burlington Road Bedford, MA 01730	Expert systems for military applications, tools for expert system development	ANALYST, KNOBS, KNEE-CAP, LES
Naval Personnel Research and Development Center San Diego, CA 92152	Research and development of AI tools for training and instruction	STEAMER
Navy Center for Applied Research in Artificial Intelligence (NCARAI) Naval Research Laboratory 4555 Overlook Ave, S.W. Washington, D.C. 20375	Expert systems for military applications, fault diagnosis expert systems	IN-ATE, BATTLE
PAR Technology Corporation Seneca Plaza, Rt. 5 New Hartford, NY 13413	AI applications in vision, military systems for intelligence analysis and planning	DART, ERS
Production System Technologies, Inc. 642 Gettysburg Street Pittsburgh, PA 15206	Expert system tools	OPS83
Radian Corporation 8501 Mo-Pac Blvd./P.O. Box 9948 Austin, TX 78766	Expert system tools, applications in automatic knowledge acquisition	WILLARD, RADIAL, RULE-MASTER
The Rand Corporation 1700 Main Street Santa Monica, CA 90406	AI and expert system research and development, expert system tools, expert systems for military and legal applications	LDS, SAL, TATR, SCENARIO-AGENT, SWIRL, TWIRL, ROSS, RITA, ROSIE
Schlumberger-Doll Research P.O. Box 307 Ridgefield, CT 06877	Expert system tools; expert log interpretation systems; research in natural language, problem solving, signal processing and learning	DIPMETER ADVISOR, LITHO, GAMMA, IMPULSE, STROBE

continued

Company	Activities	Systems & Tools
Science Applications International Corp. 1710 Goodridge Drive P.O. Box 1303 McLean, VA 22102	Expert consulting systems; research in natural language processing, theorem proving, robotics, and intelligent data base retrieval	OCEAN SURVEILLANCE
Smart Systems Technology Suite 421 North 7700 Leesburg Pike Falls Church, VA 22043	Custom expert system development, expert system tools, AI training courses	NDS, DUCK
Software Architecture and Engineering, Inc. Artificial Intelligence Center Suite 1220, 1401 Wilson Blvd. Arlington, VA. 22209	Custom expert system development, expert system tools, AI training courses	KES
Southwest Research Institute 6220 Culebra Road San Antonio, TX 78284	Research in robotics, vision, diagnostic reasoning, and natural language processing.	
SRI International 333 Ravenswood Avenue Menlo Park, CA 94025	Expert system applications; research in natural language processing, image processing, robotics.	HYDRO, KAS, PROSPECTOR
Symbolics, Inc. Research and Development Four Cambridge Center Cambridge, MA 02142	LISP workstations and associated software.	FLAVORS
Syntelligence 1000 Hamlin Court P.O. Box 3620 Sunnyvale, CA 94088	Custom expert system development for financial institutions.	
Systems Control Technology, Inc. 1801 Page Mill Road Palo Alto, CA 94303	Military application of AI and expert systems.	SIAP
Teknowledge 525 University Avenue Palo Alto, CA 94301	Expert system tools; custom expert system development; tutorial systems (videotapes, software)	DRILLING ADVISOR, M.1, S.1, T.1

continued

Company	Activities	Systems & Tools
Tektronix, Inc. Computer Research Laboratory Knowledge-based Systems Group P.O. Box 500 Beaverton, OR 97077	AI workstations; expert system tools; fault diagnosis systems	FG502-TASP, DETEKTR, GLIB
Texas Instruments Computer Science Laboratory P.O. Box 226015, MS 238 Dallas, TX 75266	Natural language interface systems; expert systems; automated computer system maintenance	PERSONAL CONSULTANT, EPES
TRW Defense Systems One Space Park Redondo Beach, CA 90278	Expert system applications for the military	ADEPT
Westinghouse Research and Development Center 1310 Beulah Road Pittsburgh, PA 15235	AI research and development in scheduling and planning, learning systems, expert systems and tools for process control	ISIS, PDS, MELD
Xerox Palo Alto Research Center Intelligent Systems Laboratory 3333 Coyote Hill Road Palo Alto, CA 94304	Knowledge engineering software and hardware; research in natural language processing	RABBIT, KRL, PIE, LOOPS, SMALL-TALK, INTERLISP

Glossary of Expert System Terms

Access-oriented methods. Programming methods based on the use of probes that trigger new computations when data are changed or read.

Active value. A procedure invoked when program data are changed or read, often used to drive graphical displays of gauges that show the values of the program variables.

AI. Artificial intelligence.

Algorithm. A formal procedure guaranteed to produce correct or optimal solutions.

Artificial intelligence. The subfield of computer science concerned with developing intelligent computer programs. This includes programs that can solve problems, learn from experience, understand language, interpret visual scenes, and, in general, behave in a way that would be considered intelligent if observed in a human.

Backward chaining. An inference method where the system starts with what it wants to prove, e.g., Z-, and tries to establish the facts it needs to prove Z. The facts needed to prove a conjecture (Z) are typically given in rule form; e.g., IF A & B, THEN Z. If A and B aren't known (aren't available as data), the system will try to prove A and B by establishing any additional facts (as specified by other rules) needed to prove them. The additional facts are established the same way A and B were established, and the process continues until all needed facts are established or the system gives up in defeat.

Blackboard. A data base accessible to independent knowledge sources and used by them to communicate with one another. The information they provide each other consists primarily of intermediate results of problem solving.

Blackboard architecture. A way of representing and controlling knowledge based on using independent groups of rules called *knowledge sources* that communicate through a central data base called a *blackboard*.

Break package. A mechanism in a programming or knowledge engineering language for telling the program where to stop so the programmer can examine the values of variables at that point.

C. A low-level, efficient, general-purpose programming language associated with the UNIX operating system. C is normally used for system programming.

CAD. Computer-aided design; the use of computer technology to assist in the design process, e.g., the design of integrated circuits.

CAI. Computer-assisted instruction; the application of computers to education. The computer monitors and controls the student's learning, adjusting its presentation based on the responses of the student.

Certainty factor. A number that measures the certainty or confidence one has that a fact or rule is valid.

Conflict resolution. The technique of resolving the problem of multiple matches in a rule-based system. When more than one rule's antecedent matches the data base, a conflict arises since (1) every matched rule could appropriately be executed next, and (2) only one rule can actually be executed next. A common conflict resolution method is *priority ordering,* where each rule has an assigned priority and the highest priority rule that currently matches the data base is executed next.

Cooperating knowledge sources. Specialized modules in an expert system that independently analyze the data and communicate via a central, structured data base called a *blackboard*.

Data base. The set of facts, assertions, and conclusions used to match against the IF-parts of rules in a rule-based system.

Demon. A procedure activated by the changing or accessing of values in a data base.

Dependency-directed backtracking. A programming technique that allows a system to remove the effects of incorrect assumptions during its search for a solution to a problem. As the system infers new information, it keeps dependency records of all its deductions and assumptions, showing how they were derived. When the system finds that an assumption was incorrect, it backtracks through the chains of inferences, removing conclusions based on the faulty assumption.

Domain expert.   A person who, through years of training and experience, has become extremely proficient at problem solving in a particular domain.

Domain knowledge.   Knowledge about the problem domain, e.g., knowledge about geology in an expert system for finding mineral deposits.

End-user.   The person who uses the finished expert system; the person for whom the system was developed.

ES.   Expert system.

Evaluation function.   A procedure used to determine the value or worth of proposed intermediate steps during a hunt through a search space for a solution to a problem.

Exhaustive search.   A problem-solving technique in which the problem solver systematically tries all possible solutions in some "brute force" manner until it finds an acceptable one.

Expert system.   A computer program that uses expert knowledge to attain high levels of performance in a narrow problem area. These programs typically represent knowledge symbolically, examine and explain their reasoning processes, and address problem areas that require years of special training and education for humans to master.

Expert-system-building tool.   The programming language and support package used to build the expert system.

Explanation facility.   That part of an expert system that explains how solutions were reached and justifies the steps used to reach them.

Forward chaining.   An inference method where the IF-portion of rules are matched against facts to establish new facts.

Frame.   A knowledge representation method that associates features with nodes representing concepts or objects. The features are described in terms of attributes (called *slots*) and their values. The nodes form a network connected by relations and organized into a hierarchy. Each node's slots can be filled with values to help describe the concept that the node represents. The process of adding or removing values from the slots can activate procedures (self-contained pieces of code) attached to the slots. These procedures may then modify values in other slots, continuing the process until the desired goal is achieved.

Frame-based methods.   Programming methods using frame hierarchies for inheritance and procedural attachment.

Fuzzy logic. An approach to approximate reasoning in which truth values and quantifiers are defined as possibility distributions that carry linguistic labels, such as *true, very true, not very true, many, not very many, few,* and *several.* The rules of inference are approximate, rather than exact, in order to better manipulate information that is incomplete, imprecise, or unreliable.

General-purpose knowledge engineering language. A computer language designed for building expert systems and incorporating features that make it applicable to different problem areas and types.

Generate and test. A problem-solving technique involving a generator that produces possible solutions and an evaluator that tests the acceptability of those solutions.

Granularity. The level of detail in a chunk of information, e.g., a rule or frame.

Heuristic. A rule of thumb or simplification that limits the search for solutions in domains that are difficult and poorly understood.

Heuristic rule. See *heuristic.*

Hypothetical worlds. A way of structuring knowledge in a knowledge-based system that defines the contexts (hypothetical worlds) in which facts and rules apply.

ICAI. Intelligent computer-assisted instruction; the application of AI methods to the CAI problem.

Image understanding. The use of AI methods to process and interpret visual images, e.g., analyzing the signals produced by a TV camera to recognize and classify the types of objects in the picture.

Inference chain. The sequence of steps or rule applications used by a rule-based system to reach a conclusion.

Inference engine. That part of a knowledge-based system or expert system that contains the general problem-solving knowledge. The inference engine processes the domain knowledge (located in the knowledge base) to reach new conclusions.

Inference method. The technique used by the inference engine to access and apply the domain knowledge, e.g., forward chaining and backward chaining.

Inference net. All possible inference chains that can be generated from the rules in a rule-based system.

Inheritance hierarchy. A structure in a semantic net or frame system that permits items lower in the net to inherit properties from items higher up in the net.

Interpreter. In an expert system, that part of the inference engine that decides how to apply the domain knowledge. In a programming system, that part of the system that analyzes the code to decide what actions to take next.

I/O. Input/output; the communication between a computer program and its user.

KE. Knowledge engineer.

Knowledge. The information a computer program must have to behave intelligently.

Knowledge acquisition. The process of extracting, structuring, and organizing knowledge from some source, usually human experts, so it can be used in a program.

Knowledge base. The portion of a knowledge-based system or expert system that contains the domain knowledge.

Knowledge-based system. A program in which the domain knowledge is explicit and separate from the program's other knowledge.

Knowledge engineer. The person who designs and builds the expert system. This person is usually a computer scientist experienced in applied artificial intelligence methods.

Knowledge engineering. The process of building expert systems.

Knowledge representation. The process of structuring knowledge about a problem in a way that makes the problem easier to solve.

LCD. Liquid crystal display.

List structure. A collection of items enclosed by parentheses, where each item can be either a symbol or another list, e.g., (ENGINE FUEL (Y5 BILL) 23 (CLAY 7)).

Logic-based methods. Programming methods that use predicate calculus to structure the program and guide execution.

LSI. Large scale integration. See VLSI.

Metaknowledge. Knowledge in an expert system about how the system operates or reasons, such as knowledge about the use and control of domain knowledge. More generally, knowledge about knowledge.

Metalevel knowledge. See *metaknowledge*.

Metarule. A rule that describes how other rules should be used or modified.

Multiple lines of reasoning. A problem-solving technique in which a limited number of possibly independent approaches to solving the problem are developed in parallel.

Natural language. The standard method of exchanging information between people, such as English (contrasted with artificial languages, such as programming languages).

Nonmonotonic reasoning. A reasoning technique that supports multiple lines of reasoning (multiple ways to reach the same conclusion) and the retraction of facts or conclusions, given new information. It is useful for processing unreliable knowledge and data.

Object-oriented methods. Programming methods based on the use of items called *objects* that communicate with one another via messages in the form of global broadcasts.

Predicate calculus. A formal language of classical logic that uses functions and predicates to describe relations between individual entities.

Probability propagation. The adjusting of probabilities at the nodes in an inference net to account for the effect of new information about the probability at a particular node.

Problem-oriented language. A computer language designed for a particular class of problems, e.g., FORTRAN designed for efficiently performing algebraic computations and COBOL with features for business record keeping.

Problem reformulation. Converting a problem stated in some arbitrary way to a form that lends itself to a fast, efficient solution.

Problem space. See *search space.*

Procedure-oriented methods. Programming methods using nested subroutines to organize and control program execution.

Production. An IF-THEN statement or rule used to represent knowledge in a human's long-term memory.

Production rule. The type of rule used in a production system, usually expressed as IF *condition* THEN *action.*

Production system. A type of rule-based system containing IF-THEN statements with conditions that may be satisfied in a data base and actions that may change the data base.

Pruning. Reducing or narrowing the alternatives, normally used in the context of reducing possibilities in a branching *tree structure,* such as the search through a problem space.

Real-world problem. A complex, practical problem which has a solution that is useful in some cost-effective way.

Representation. The process of formulating or viewing a problem so it will be easy to solve.

Resolution theorem proving. A particular use of deductive logic for proving theorems in the first-order predicate calculus. The method makes use of the following resolution principle: (A v B) and (-A v C) implies (B v C).

Robustness. That quality of a problem solver that permits a gradual degradation in performance when it is pushed to the limits of its scope of expertise or is given errorful, inconsistent, or incomplete data or rules.

Rule. A formal way of specifying a recommendation, directive, or strategy, expressed as IF *premise* THEN *conclusion* or IF *condition* THEN *action*.

Rule-based methods. Programming methods using IF-THEN rules to perform forward or backward chaining.

Rule-based system. A program organized as a set of rules. See *rules*

Scaling problem. The difficulty associated with trying to apply problem-solving techniques developed for a simplified version of a problem to the actual problem itself.

Scene anaylsis. See *image analysis*.

Scheduler. The part of the inference engine that decides when and in what order to apply different pieces of domain knowledge.

Schema. A frame-like representation formalism in a knowledge engineering language (e.g., SRL).

Search. The process of looking through the set of possible solutions to a problem in order to find an acceptable solution.

Search space. The set of all possible solutions to a problem.

Semantic net. A knowledge representation method consisting of a network of nodes, standing for concepts or objects, connected by arcs describing the relations between the nodes.

Skeletal knowledge engineering language. A computer language designed for building expert systems and derived by removing all domain-specific knowledge from an existing expert system.

Skeletal system. See *skeletal knowledge engineering language*.

Skill. The efficient and effective application of knowledge to produce solutions in some problem domain.

Slot. An attribute associated with a node in a frame system. The node may stand for an object, concept, or event; e.g., a node representing the object *employee* might have a slot for the attribute *name* and one for the attribute *address*. These slots would then be filled with the employee's actual name and address.

Speech understanding. The use of AI methods to process and interpret audio signals representing human speech.

Support environment. Facilities associated with an expert-system-building tool that help the user interact with the expert system. These may include sophisticated debugging aids, friendly editing programs, and advanced graphic devices.

Support facilities. See *support environment*.

Symbol. A string of characters that stands for some real-world concept.

Symbol-manipulation language. A computer language designed expressly for representing and manipulating complex concepts, e.g., LISP and PROLOG.

Symbolic reasoning. Problem solving based on the application of strategies and heuristics to manipulate symbols standing for problem concepts.

Tool. A shorthand notation for expert-system-building tool.

Tool builder. The person who designs and builds the expert-system-building tool.

Tools for knowledge engineering. Programming systems that simplify expert system development. They include languages, programs, and facilities that assist the knowledge engineer.

Toy problem. An artificial problem, such as a game, or an unrealistic adaptation of a complex problem.

Tracing facility. A mechanism in a programming or knowledge engineering language that can display the rules or subroutines executed, including the values of variables used.

Tree structure. A way of organizing information as a connected graph where each node can branch into other nodes deeper in the structure.

Units. A frame-like representation formalism employing slots with values and procedures attached to them.

User. A person who uses an expert system, such as an end-user, a domain expert, a knowledge engineer, a tool builder, or a clerical staff member.

VLSI. Very large scale integration; the development of complex and powerful circuits on small chips.

References

[BAC84] Bachant, J. and McDermott, J. R1 revisited: four years in the trenches. The AI Magazine, Vol. 5, No. 3, Fall, 1984.

[BAR81] Barr, A. and Feigenbaum, E. A. (eds.) The Handbook of Artificial Intelligence, vol 1., William Kaufmann, 1981.

[BAR83] Barstow, D. R., Aiello, N., Duda, R. O., Erman, L. D., Forgy, C., Gorlin, D., Greiner, R. D., Lenat, D. B., London, P. E., McDermott, J., Nii, H. P., Politakis, P., Reboh, R., Rosenschein, S., Scott, A. C., van Melle, W., and Weiss, S. M. Languages and tools for knowledge engineering. In Building Expert Systems, F. Hayes-Roth, D. A. Waterman, and D. B. Lenat (eds.), Addison-Wesley Publishing Co., Reading, MA, 1983.

[BEN83] Bennett, J. S. ROGET: A Knowledge-based Consultant for Acquiring the Conceptual Structure of an Expert System, Memo HPP-83-24, Computer Science Dept., Stanford University, October 1983.

[BOU83] Boulanger, A. G., The Expert System PLANT/cd: A Case Study in Applying the General Purpose Inference System ADVISE to Predicting Black Cutworm Damage in Corn, M. S. Thesis, Department of Computer Science, University of Illinois, Urbana, IL., 1983.

[BRA79] Brachman, R. J., On the epistemological status of semantic networks. In Associative Networks: Representation and Use of Knowledge by Computers, N. V. Findler (ed.), Academic Press, 1979.

[BRA83] Brachman, R., Amarel, S., Engelman, C., Engelmore, R., Feigenbaum, E., and Wilkins, D., What are expert systems? In F. Hayes-Roth, D. A. Waterman, and D. Lenat (eds.) Building Expert Systems, Addison-Wesley, 1983.

[BUC83] Buchanan, B., Bechtal, R., Bennett J., Clancey, W., Kulikowski, C., Mitchell, T., and Waterman, D. A., Constructing an Expert System. In Building Expert Systems, Hayes-Roth, Waterman, and Lenat (eds.), Addison-Wesley, 1983.

[CAL84] Callero, M., Waterman, D. A., and Kipps, J., TATR: A Prototype Expert System for Tactical Air Targeting, Rand Report R-3096-ARPA, The Rand Corporation, Santa Monica, CA, 1984.

[CAM82] Campbell, A. N., Hollister, V. F., Duda, R. O., and Hart, P. E. Recognition of a hidden mineral deposit by an artificial intelligence program. Science, Vol. 217, pp. 927–929, September 3, 1982.

[CHA84] Chandrasekaran, B., Expert systems: matching techniques to tasks. In W. Reitman (ed.) Artificial Intelligence Applications for Business, Norwood, NJ: Ablex, 1984.

[CLA79] Clancey, W. J., "Tutoring rules for guiding a case method dialogue," International Journal of Man-Machine Studies, Vol. 11, pp. 25–49, 1979.

[CLA81] Clancey, W. J., Methodology for Building an Intelligent Tutoring System, Report STAN-CS-81-894, Department of Computer Science, Stanford University, Stanford, CA, October, 1981.

[COH82] Cohen, P. R., and Feigenbaum, E. A., The Handbook of Artificial Intelligence, Volume 3. William Kaufmann, Inc., 1982.

[COO81] Cooke, S., Hafner, C., McCarty, T., Meldman, M., Peterson, M., Sprowl, J., Sridharan, N., and Waterman, D. A., The applications of artificial intelligence to law: a survey of six current projects. AFIPS Conference Proceedings, vol. 50, 1981.

[DAV76] Davis, R., Applications of Meta Level Knowledge to the Construction, Maintenance and Use of Large Knowledge Bases, Report STAN-CS-76-552, Stanford Artificial Intelligence Laboratory, Stanford University, July 1976.

[DAV82] Davis, R., Expert systems: Where are we? And where do we go from here? The AI Magazine, pp. 3–22, Spring 1982.

[DUD77] Duda, R., Hart, P. E., Nilsson, N. J., Reboh, R., Slocum, J., and Sutherland, G., Development of a Computer-based Consultant for Mineral Exploration. SRI Report, Stanford Research Institute, 333 Ravenswood Avenue, Menlo Park, CA, October, 1977.

[DUD78] Duda, R., Hart, P. E., Nilsson, N. J., Barrett, P., Gaschnig, J. G., Konolige, K., Reboh, R., and Slocum, J., Development of the PROSPECTOR consultation system for mineral exploration. SRI Report, Stanford Research Institute, 333 Ravenswood Avenue, Menlo Park, CA, October, 1978.

[FEI81] Feigenbaum, E. A., Expert systems in the 1980's. In Machine Intelligence, Infotech State of the Art Report, Series 9, No. 3., A. Bond (ed.), Pergamon Infotech Limited, 1981.

[GAS81] Gaschnig, J. PROSPECTOR: An expert system for mineral exploration. In Machine Intelligence, Infotech State of the Art Report Series 9, No. 3, 1981.

[GAS82] Gaschnig, J. Application of the PROSPECTOR system to geological exploration problems. In Machine Intelligence 10, J. E. Hayes, D. Michie, and Y. H. Pao (eds.), Chichester, England, Horwood, 1982.

[HAY83a] Hayes-Roth, F., Waterman, D. A., and Lenat, D. (eds.) Building Expert Systems, Addison-Wesley, 1983.

[HAY83b] Hayes-Roth, F., Waterman, D. A., and Lenat, D., An overview of expert systems. In Building Expert Systems, Hayes-Roth Waterman and Lenat (eds.), Addison-Wesley, 1983.

[JOH83a] Johnson, P. E. What kind of expert should a system be? The Journal of Medicine and Philosophy, Vol. 8, 1983, pp. 77–97.

[JOH83b] Johnson, P. The expert mind: a new challenge for the information scientist. In Beyond Productivity. Bemelmans Th. M. A. (ed.) North Holland Publishing Company, The Netherlands, 1983.

[KAP84] Kaplan, S. J., The industrialization of artificial intelligence from by-line to bottom line. The AI Magazine, Vol. 5, No. 2, Summer, 1984.

[KER78] Kernighan, B. W., and Ritchie, D. M. The C Programming Language, Prentice-Hall, 1978.

[KON79] Konolige, K. Bayesian methods for updating probabilities. In Duda, R., Hart, P., Konolige, K. and Reboh, R., A Computer-based Consultant for Mineral Exploration, Artificial Intelligence Center, SRI International, Menlo Park, CA. 1979.

[KOW79a] Kowalski, R. Logic for Problem Solving. New York: American Elsevier, 1979.

[KOW79b] Kowalski, R., Algorithm = logic + control. ACM Communications, Vol. 22, No. 7, July, 1979.

[LAR80] Larkin, J., McDermott, J., Simon, D. P. and Simon, H. Expert and novice peformance in solving physics problems. Science, Vol. 208, June 1980.

[LEN83] Lenat, D., Davis, R., Doyle, J., Genesereth, M., Goldstein, I., and Schrobe, H., Reasoning about reasoning. In F. Hayes-Roth, D. A. Waterman, and D. Lenat (eds.) Building Expert Systems, Addison-Wesley, 1983.

[MAR76] MARC User Information Manual, Available from MARC Analysis Research Corporation, Palo Alto, CA., September, 1976.

[MCD81] McDermott, J., R1's formative years. AI Magazine, Vol. 2, No. 2, 1981.

[MCD82] McDermott, J., R1: A rule-based configurer of computer systems. Artificial Intelligence, Vol. 19, pp. 39–88, 1982.

[MEL81] van Melle, W., Shortliffe, E. H., and Buchanan, B. G., EMYCIN: a domain-independent system that aids in constructing knowledge-based consultation programs. In Machine Intelligence, Infotech State of the Art Report, Series 9, No. 3., A. Bond, (ed.), Pergamon Infotech Limited, 1981.

[MIN75] Minsky, Marvin, A framework for representing knowledge. In The Psychology of Computer Vision, P. Winston (ed.), McGraw-Hill, 1975.

[MUL84] Mulsant, B. and Servan-Schreiber, D. Knowledge engineering: A daily activity on a hospital ward. Computers and Biomedical Research, Vol. 17, pp. 71–91, 1984.

[NEL82] Nelson, W. R., REACTOR: An expert system for diagnosis and treatment of nuclear reactor accidents. AAAI Proceedings, 1982.

[NEW57a] Newell, A., Shaw, J. C., and Simon, H. A., Empirical explorations of the logic theory machine. Proceedings of the Western Joint Computer Conference, pp. 218–239, 1957.

[NEW57b] Newell, A., Shaw, J. C., and Simon, H. A., Programming the logic theory machine. Proceedings of the Western Joint Computer Conference, pp. 230–240, 1957.

[NEW72] Newell, A. and Simon, H. A., Human Problem Solving. Englewood Cliffs, NJ: Prentice-Hall, 1972.

[NOR75] Norman, D. A., and Rumelhart, D. E., (eds.), Explorations in Cognition, San Francisco: W. H. Freeman and Company, 1975.

[OCO84] O'Conner, D., Using expert systems to manage change and complexity in manufacturing. In W. Reitman, (ed.) Artificial Intelligence Applications for Business, Norwood, N.J.: Ablex, 1984.

[POL84] Politakis, P. and Weiss, S. M., Using empirical analysis to refine expert system knowledge bases. Artificial Intelligence, Vol. 22, pp. 23–48, 1984.

[REB81] Reboh, Rene', Knowledge Engineering Techniques and Tools in the PROSPECTOR Environment. SRI Technical Note 243, Stanford Research Institute, 333 Ravenswood Avenue, Menlo Park, CA, June, 1981.

[REI80] Reiter, J. AL/X: An Expert System Using Plausible Inference, Intelligent Terminals Ltd. Report, Machine Intelligence Research Unit, University of Edinburgh, 1980.

[SHO75] Shortliffe, E. H., and Buchanan, B. G., A model of inexact reasoning in medicine. Mathematical Biosciences, Vol. 23, 1975.

[SHO76] Shortliffe, E. H., Computer-Based Medical Consultations: MYCIN. Elsevier, New York, 1976.

[SHO82] Shortliffe, E. H., and Fagan, L. M., Expert systems research: modeling the medical decisionmaking process. Heuristic Programming Project Report HPP-82-3, Departments of Medicine and Computer Science, Stanford University, Stanford, CA., March, 1982.

[SIK76] Siklossy, L., Let's Talk Lisp, Prentice Hall, Inc., Englewood Cliffs, N.J., 1976.

[SMI83] Smith, R. G. and Baker, J. D. The DIPMETER advisor system. IJCAI Proceedings, pp. 122–129, 1983.

[STE83a] Stefik, M., Aikins, J., Balzer, R., Benoit, J., Birnbaum, L., Hayes-Roth, F., and Sacerdoti, E., Basic concepts for building expert systems. In F. Hayes-Roth, D. A. Waterman, and D. Lenat (eds.) Building Expert Systems, Addison-Wesley, 1983.

[STE83b] Stefik, M., Bobrow, D. G., Mittal, S. and Conway, L. Knowledge programming in LOOPS: Report on an experimental course. The AI Magazine, pp. 3–13, Fall 1983.

[STE83c] Stefik, M., Aikins, J., Balzer, R., Benoit, J., Birnbaum, L., Hayes-Roth, F., and Sacerdoti, E., The architecture of expert systems. In F. Hayes-Roth, D. A. Waterman, and D. Lenat (eds.) Building Expert Systems, Addison-Wesley, 1983.

[TSU83] Tsuji, S. and Shortliffe, E. H., Graphical access to the knowledge base of a medical consultation system. Heuristic Programming Project Report HPP-83-6, Departments of Medicine and Computer Science, Stanford University, Stanford, CA., February, 1983.

[WAT68] Waterman, D. A., Machine Learning of Heuristics, PhD Dissertation, Computer Science Department, Stanford University, 1968.

[WAT70] Waterman, D. A., Generalization Learning Techniques for Automating the Learning of Heuristics. Artificial Intelligence, Vols. 1 and 2, pp. 121–170, 1970.

[WAT71] Waterman, D. A., and Newell, A., Protocol analysis as a task for artificial intelligence. Artificial Intelligence, Vol. 2, pp. 285–318, 1971.

[WAT78a] Waterman, D. A., and Hayes-Roth, F. (eds.), Pattern-directed inference systems. Academic Press, New York, 1978.

[WAT78b] Waterman, D. A., and Hayes-Roth, F., An overview of pattern-directed inference systems. In Pattern-Directed Inference Systems, D. A. Waterman and F. Hayes-Roth, (eds.). Academic Press, New York, 1978.

[WAT79] Waterman, D. A., and Jenkins, B. Heuristic modeling using rule-based computer systems. In Terrorism: Threat, Reality, Response, (R. H. Kupperman and D. M. Trent, eds.), Hoover Press, 1979.

[WAT80] Waterman, D. A., and Peterson, M., Rule-based models of legal expertise. Proceedings of the First Annual National Conference on Artificial Intelligence, 1980.

[WAT81] Waterman, D. A., and Peterson, M., Models of Legal Decision-making. Rand Report R-2717-ICJ, 1981.

[WAT83] Waterman, D. A., and Hayes-Roth, F., An investigation of tools for building expert systems. In F. Hayes-Roth, D. A. Waterman, and D. Lenat (eds.) Building Expert Systems, Addison-Wesley, 1983.

[WEI84] Weiss, S. M. and Kulikowski, C. A., A Practical Guide to Designing Expert Systems. New Jersey: Rowman & Allanheld, 1984.

[WON83] Wong, C. M., Crawford, R. W., Kunz, J. C., and Kehler, T. P., Application of artificial intelligence to triple quadrupole mass spectrometry. Proceedings of the IEEE Nuclear Science Symposium, San Francisco, CA, October, 1983.

Index